THE IMPACT OF THE REFORMATION

The Impact
of the
Reformation

Essays by

Heiko A. Oberman

WILLIAM B. EERDMANS PUBLISHING COMPANY
GRAND RAPIDS, MICHIGAN

Copyright © 1994 by Wm. B. Eerdmans Publishing Co.
255 Jefferson Ave. S.E., Grand Rapids, Michigan 49503

Printed in the United States of America

Library of Congress Cataloging-in-Publication Data

Oberman, Heiko Augustinus.
The impact of the Reformation : essays / by Heiko A. Oberman.
p.   cm.
Includes bibliographical references and index.
ISBN 0-8028-0732-1 (pbk.)
1. Reformation. 2. Christianity and antisemitism.
3. Religious thought—16th century. I. Title.
BR309.O22 1994
270.6—dc20   93-42559
                                         CIP

Contents

III. The Growth of Antisemitism

IV. Problems and Perspectives

Preface: The Past in Perspective

One of the first lessons children learn when initiated to the wonderful world of mazes is that in order to trace the escape route out of a labyrinth they are well advised to start at the exit and from there chart the path backward to the point of departure. Asked to describe my road as a historian, leading up to the articles collected here and written during the Arizona years 1984-1994, I resort to the child's old tried and tested trick. What may appear in this account as a clear, goal-oriented program of investigation is actually a winding path on which I have been repeatedly stopped in my tracks by dead ends and unforeseen curves. Perhaps the fact that I hail from the Low Countries has prepared me early on to withstand — and at times even exploit — the buffeting winds of confessions, Protestant and Catholic, of departmental tensions between History and Theology, and of the intense European cultural competition between the French, English, and German-speaking worlds. Indeed, this simile of stormy winds is probably a more honest and revealing explanation for my journey than the far more flattering highroad of exploration which — like a carefully plotted path — leads out of the labyrinth to the point where I find myself today.

To start at the beginning. In my first monograph, written at Oxford and defended as a doctoral dissertation at the University of Utrecht (1957), I stumbled over a theme that was to preoccupy me for well over a decade. In my effort to reconstruct the world of thought of Thomas Bradwardine (†1349) — philosopher and theologian, army chaplain in France and archbishop of Canterbury — I had to deal with the opponents whom this fourteenth-century Augustinian characterized as modern

Pelagians, the *pelagiani moderni*. It was clear that in his main work, *De causa Dei*, Bradwardine targeted William of Ockham and a group of less well-known contemporaries. What became increasingly clear to me was that these *moderni*, the late medieval nominalists, had not fared well at the hands of modern medievalists who almost without exception took pride in tracing their own pedigree to the *via antiqua* — the "Old Way" of Albert, Thomas, and Scotus — from which the nominalistic *via moderna* had programmatically distanced itself. Hence, such caricatures as "skepticism" and "fideism" continued to dominate the best of scholarship — personified at that time by the imposing historian of philosophy, Etienne Gilson, who characterized the later Middle Ages as a period of disintegration and "the End of the Journey."

This recovery of historical "nominalism" set my sights and determined the perimeters of research during my first American period: the Harvard years 1958 through 1966. There I wrote *The Harvest of Medieval Theology* (1963) in which the "Last of the Scholastics" and dedicated Ockham disciple, Gabriel Biel (†1495), held center stage but was consistently placed within the wider context of the medieval tradition. Biel tapped this tradition to develop a comprehensive system, thus providing late medieval Christianity with a truly catholic *Summa* on the eve of the Reformation. A second book completed while at Harvard, *Forerunners of the Reformation* (1966), included a variety of documents illustrating the richness and breadth of the late medieval period. Above all, it reclaimed the term "Forerunners" from its confessional Protestant usage as precursors or "road-runners" speeding toward Luther by showing that in the fourteenth and fifteenth centuries multiform efforts at reform were underway, initiating what is still widely called the Counter Reformation, but which, in the light of these findings, is more appropriately referred to as the Catholic Reformation.[1]

When I left Harvard for Tübingen — for what would become a period of eighteen years (1966-84) — I was exposed to that painful and creative shock of language and culture that Paul Tillich, when crossing the Atlantic in the opposite direction, experienced as liberating. While up to this time I had studied late medieval nominalism primarily as a chapter in the history of thought, in an effort to repossess that no-man's-land between the "Catholic" Middle Ages and the "Protestant" Reformation, I now became a nominalist historian myself by discovering the relevancy of its most critical edge: its acute sense of the singularity of

---

1. The major articles written in these years are accessible in the earlier collection *The Dawn of the Reformation* (Edinburgh, rev. ed. 1992 [1986]).

events, persons, and constellations. The history of ideas, in Germany revered as *Geistesgeschichte,* will, I trust, continue to fascinate me. In this volume, the first article on early Reformation thought as well as a critical analysis of the growth of Mariology represents this line of investigation. And indeed, it is both a privilege and a delight to be allowed to sit at the feet of the great minds of the past and to experience the thrills created by the risky experiment of bringing past masters to an imaginary symposium, invited to dialogue at a round table not of their own making.

This very description, however, reveals the artificial dimension of this procedure: it tends to transform people of flesh and blood, sweat and aspirations, to the ephemeral realm of ideas, and does not sufficiently recognize their distinctive location in time and space. Hence, I prefaced my *Werden und Wertung der Reformation* (1977)[2] with a self-critical manifesto calling for the redirection of intellectual history toward a social history of ideas that reflects two insights: the uniqueness and singularity of the matrix from which new ideas first emerge; and the fermentation phase when audiences become active recipients and develop their own networks of discourse. Accordingly, a well-advanced traditional *textual* analysis of Luther's thought could only be transformed into a profile of the historical *contextual* Luther after I had come to apply my nominalist lesson: reaching out for the person of flesh and blood, with sweat and aspirations, in his unique time and place without any effort to force him into the preconceived universals of our own making such as "the Middle Ages" or "Modern Times."[3]

Returning from Tübingen to the United States in 1984, the dangers of reductionist tendencies in the field of social history became equally apparent. Here the realm of thought, of ideas and convictions, was increasingly portrayed as a mere reflection of material conditions, as their product, and often as their legitimation. Quite generally, the primacy of social history over intellectual history was — and is — the operative presupposition for most of the best work in our field. Decisively helped by my new setting in an innovative History Department, and teaching shoulder to shoulder with my colleagues in Medieval and Renaissance history, Alan Bernstein and Don Weinstein, a graduate program could be developed to pursue that "total history" which seeks to close the gap

---

2. (Tübingen, 1989[3] [1977]); English version, *Masters of the Reformation* (Cambridge, 1981).

3. *Luther: Mensch zwischen Gott und Teufel* (Berlin, 1987[3] [1982]); English trans., *Luther: Man Between God and the Devil* (New Haven, 1989).

between the history of ideas and social history. We must rise above both "elitism" and "determinism": against the withdrawal of the history of ideas to the high plains of theological vision *and* the necessitarian view that history is only the struggle for gain, power, prowess and prosperity, against this stubborn tendency to slight the evidence that we deal with an epoch when reform always comprised individual *and* communal, religious *and* social renewal, the dialectic between social and intellectual history offers us an integrating analytical principle.

The most concise expression of both the division of labor and the common goal is, it seems to me, as follows: conditions of life (comprising economic, demographic, geographic, and dietary data as well as crises such as famine, war, and social disorder) become historical factors shaping a communal mentality only when recorded, evaluated, and articulated by intellectual leaders. This formulation has a double critical edge: first, it insists, against traditional intellectual history, that ideas are never sufficiently grasped when the study of treatises and documents is not extended to the analysis of their social matrix and their societal impact. The edge against traditional social history is that the study of matrix and impact cannot be short-circuited, but must bow to the iron rule of the sequence: conditions-program-impact. This very sequence requires that equal attention be given to intellectual history in order to understand both spokesmen and leaders: the approach underlying all essays in this volume.

Once one descends from the breathless heights inhabited by individual great thinkers to the "low" countries, such a movement of programmatic simplicity as the Modern Devotion takes on a new importance. In their suspicion of intellectual speculation, we find the thoughts and experience of "middling people" without academic training. As a looking-glass at the time, "lower" strata in society, marginalized and persecuted groups such as the Jewish communities in the Diaspora, increasingly laid claim to my attention. Here we discern how ideas serve to protect "civilization" against the threat from "without," and thus leave unexpected imprints by revealing what they intended to obliterate. Furthermore, the pervasive attraction of antisemitism alerts us to the danger of differentiating too rigidly between "high" and "low" culture: the chilling myths of a Jewish threat were alive "and well" among the simple folk as much as among the intellectual elite. My earlier work, *The Roots of Anti-Semitism*,[4] finds its sequel in part III, "The Growth

---

4. *Wurzeln des Antisemitismus: Christenangst und Judenplage im Zeitalter von Humanismus und Reformation* (Berlin, 1981); English trans., *The Roots of Anti-Semitism in the Age of Renaissance and Reformation* (Philadelphia, 1984).

of Antisemitism," which highlights the critical acceleration in the transformation of Christian anti-Judaism to gentile antisemitism.

In recent years I have also devoted much of my scholarly energy to the study of John Calvin. He most certainly deserves a prominent place in any history of the Reformation's impact, not only as the city reformer of Geneva, but also as the leader of the dispersed refugee communities. It is indeed due to his signal importance that I find it wise to dedicate to him a separate volume.

With their impressive bilingual gifts, Dr. Andrew Gow and Jeff Tyler successfully shouldered the exacting task of translating the three articles originally published — and conceived — in German. Peter Dykema could apply his experience as the accomplished editor of the vast volume on Anticlericalism (1993) in keeping a firm hand on all dimensions of this collection, including the necessary indices. Behind the final product stands a heartwarming lineage — what one once dared to call the *traditio ancillarum* — three who together tested and typed successive drafts: Suse Rau, Elsie Vezey, and Luise Betterton.

Most of the research for these articles was undertaken during my first ten years at the University of Arizona (1984-94). Here the withering sun no longer tests the mettle of Desert Fathers but sheds a probing and uncompromising light on the ideas and ideals that once seemed to emerge so naturally from the fertile matrix of the Low Countries, that fluid land of *grachten* and dikes, between the Ijssel and the Rhine.

Tucson, Arizona   Heiko A. Oberman
Laetare 1994

I. POINTS OF DEPARTURE

Via Antiqua and Via Moderna: Late Medieval Prolegomena to Early Reformation Thought

I. A Matter of Definition

When in the first part of the fourteenth century the Oxford master Thomas Bradwardine (†1349) launched his formidable offensive *Contra Pelagium* in a massive work completed in 1344, the very assumption of his campaign was the common front of the Pelagians of all times. For him, the ancients and the moderns formed one unbroken phalanx: "Sicut antiqui Pelagiani . . . ita et moderni."[1] To leave no room for doubt, he clarified his battle plan as directed against "tam veteres quam recentes."

When, one century later, Lorenzo Valla (†1457) applied the same terminology in the revealing 1444 preface to Book 4 of his *Elegantiae*, Bradwardine's innocuous categories of time had become a very different kind of animal: He would rather be a farflying bee like the ancients — meaning the Church Fathers — than a creepy ant like the moderns: The

---

1. *De causa Dei contra Pelagium et de Virtute causarum*, ed. H. Savile (London, 1618), Praefatio, b 1^r.

"*Via Antiqua* and *Via Moderna*: Late Medieval Prolegomena to Early Reformation Thought," *Journal of the History of Ideas* 48 (1987): 23-40. Reprinted in *From Ockham to Wyclif*, ed. A. Hudson and M. Wilks, Studies in Church History, Subsidia 5 (Oxford, 1987), pp. 445-63.

first produces food, whereas the second steals it away![2] These "ants" who deny the great achievements of antiquity deserve as little status as their name *moderni* can claim space in a good Latin dictionary: "Qui sunt isti, quaeso 'moderni' — si 'moderni' latinum vocabulum est."[3] Each of these statements by Bradwardine and Valla contains the seeds of historical confusion. Whereas the Oxford don does not use the pair *antiqui-moderni* to contrast epochs, he de facto attacks tenets in the doctrines of predestination and justification which would become the trademark of the theology of the *via moderna*. Vice versa: though Valla explicitly assails the "Moderni," he does not have the *via moderna* or one single school in mind but rather the bigotry of *all* barbarous school-men who condemn the use of classical culture.

In the century between Bradwardine and Valla, a third and very different meaning had become attached to the vocabulary, when in the newly founded German universities, instead of Parisian *nationes*, philosophical *viae* were introduced. Among the older foundations, Cologne (1388) became a stronghold of the *via antiqua* and Erfurt (1392) of the *via moderna*. But increasingly *both* "viae" were inscribed into the statutes. In Basel five years after its founding (1460) the *via antiqua* receives equal status with the earlier *via moderna*, and in Tübingen (1477) both *viae* are acknowledged from the very beginning. How little the designation *moderna* or *antiqua* has here to do with categories of time may appear from the fact that in Heidelberg (1386) the *via moderna* is known as the *via Marsiliana* (after Marsilius of Inghen, †1396) and that in the Wittenberg statutes of 1508 even three *viae* are admitted, named for school leaders: the *Via Thomae*, the *Via Scoti*, and the *Via Gregorii*, thus called after Gregory of Rimini (†1358).

Even this short summary allows for two conclusions: 1. The previous assumption must be qualified which suggested that the "odor" of Hussite heresy that haunted the *via antiqua* after 1415 and the ensuing exodus of the German masters from Prague (the first German university, founded in 1348) could explain the ascendency of the *via moderna*: the

---

2. "Veteres illi theologi videntur mihi velut apes quaedam in longinqua etiam pascua volitantes, dulcissima mella, cerasque miro artificio condidisse. Recentes vero formicis similimi, quae ex proximo sublata furto grana, in latibulis suia abscondunt. At ego (quod ad me attinet) non modo malim apes quam formica esse, sed etiam sub rege apum militare, quam formicarum exercitum ducere." Lorenzo Valla, "Praefatio in quartum librum Elegantiarum" (1444), in *Opera Omnia*, 1 (Basel, 1540; repr. Turin, 1962), 117-18.

3. *Opera Omnia* (Basel, 1540), fol. 434. This quest is pursued in W. Zimmermann (ed.), *Antiqui und Moderni*, Miscellanea Mediaevalia 9 (Berlin, 1974).

via moderna is already well entrenched before the Hussite Crisis. Erfurt is a case in point and Cologne provides the "mirror" example, when the university in 1425 blocked all efforts to add the *via modernorum*. If an external, institutional cause is to be found, it is rather to be seen in the proscription of any authoritative use of Ockham by statute of the Parisian faculty of arts on 25 September 1339, not to be revoked until after 1346.[4] But such institutional explanations for the spread of the *via moderna* are essential only when the attraction of the substance of its thought is in doubt — as has been the case for too long a time.

2. Whereas in the fourteenth century *modernus* still meant "recens" or "contemporary" in the sense encountered in Bradwardine,[5] the German wave of university foundations provided for a new technical meaning: *via moderna* became a school not to be identified with just the one name of Ockham but associated with a whole range of "school leaders." When the Erfurter philosopher Bartholomäus of Usingen (†1532) in the programmatic disputation of 1497 designated Ockham as "venerabilis inceptor viae modernae," then we should translate *inceptor* as "initiator" rather than as *the* "teaching authority."[6] Gregory of Rimini was held in high regard by Usingen — as well as by his colleague and ally Jodocus Trutvetter (†1519) — and Pierre d'Ailly was even called "philosophus maximus et theologus profundissimus." It is therefore misleading to designate the *via moderna* as Ockhamism.[7]

---

4. For the best-documented and carefully argued interpretation of the 1339 Ockhamist crisis in Paris see two related articles, W. J. Courtenay and K. H. Tachau, "Ockham, Ockhamists, and the English-German Nation at Paris, 1339-1341," *History of Universities* 2 (1982): 53-96; W. J. Courtenay, "The Reception of Ockham's Thought at the University of Paris," in *Preuve et raisons à l'université de Paris: Logique, ontologie et théologie au XIVe siècle*, ed. Z. Kaluza and P. Vignaux (Paris, 1984), pp. 43-64.
    5. See W. J. Courtenay, "The Role of English Thought in the Transformation of University Education in the Late Middle Ages," in *Rebirth, Reform and Resilience — Universities in Transition 1300-1700*, ed. J. M. Kittelson and P. J. Transue (Columbus, 1984), pp. 103-62; 146, n. 5.
    6. Wolfgang Urban, "Die 'Via Moderna' an der Universität Erfurt am Vorabend der Reformation," in *Gregor von Rimini, Werk und Wirkung* . . . (see n. 58, below), pp. 311-30. To explain the title "inceptor sacrae scholae invictissimorum nominalium" in the Bologna 1496 (1522) edition of the *Expositio aurea*, Helmut Junghans suggests that "Ockham irrtümlicherweise im 15. Jahrhundert als inceptor im Sinne von Begründer gefeiert wurde, weil man den akademischen Titel nicht mehr kannte" (*Ockham im Lichte der neueren Forschung* [Hamburg, 1968], p. 148). This hypothesis deserves the razor of Ockham. Cf. Philotheus Böhner, *The Tractatus de successivis Attributed to William Ockham* (New York, 1944), p. 3.
    7. Cf. my article "Headwaters of the Reformation," in *Luther and the Dawn of the Modern Era*, ed. H. A. Oberman (Leiden, 1974), p. 56.

Particularly German Protestant research prefers to retain this identification, which certainly would make it easier to dissociate Luther from the *via moderna*.[8] With the large number of school authorities goes a variety of ways to describe the chief tenets of the *via moderna*. In the sources we find as equivalents "nominalists" and "terminists," depending on whether epistemology and (meta)physics or dialectics and logic is stressed as the neuralgic point.[9] But since the search for the *proprietas sermonis* or proper *modus loquendi* provides for the means to argue the case of conceptualism, I suggest that we continue to render *via moderna* as "nominalism."

II. The Omnipotence of God

The present state of codification of late medieval thought does not encourage us to draw upon it as a potentially illuminating backdrop for the Reformation in general nor for the differences between Luther and Zwingli specifically. If we look at what is going to be for the foreseeable future the canon or bible in this field, *The Cambridge History of Later Medieval Philosophy*, published as recently as 1982,[10] we discover that *the* programmatic struggle in this very period, namely, the one between the *via antiqua* and *via moderna*, is completely bypassed, while either *via* is mentioned only twice, but without any content definition or description. First-rate in its presentation of the development of logic and natural philosophy, this standard volume de facto offers the history of the degree of fidelity to Aristotle, moreover importing a modern distinction between metaphysics and theology which cuts out a major portion of the most hotly debated issues at this time. Instead we are served with a number of ill-advised slogans such as a critique of the fourteenth century

---

8. See most recently — and most outspoken! — U. Köpf, in *Verkündigung und Forschung* 2 (1984): 31-59. A significant adjustment in Adolar Zumkeller, *Erbsünde, Gnade, Rechtfertigung und Verdienst nach der Lehre der Erfurter Augustinertheologen des Spätmittelalters* (Würzburg, 1984), p. 1.

9. Thus Luther can refer to his "party" in Erfurt as "terministen," whereas Melanchthon is described (by Camerarius) as embroiled in Tübingen in the debates between the Platonic "reales" and the Aristotelian "nominales": "*Nominales appellati fuere et moderni.*" Appendix 4.1 and 4.2 only in the first edition of my *Werden und Wertung der Reformation: Vom Wegestreit zum Glaubenskampf* (Tübingen, 1977), pp. 424-25.

10. *The Cambridge History of Later Medieval Philosophy*, ed. N. Kretzmann, A. Kenny, and J. Pinborg (Cambridge, 1982).

for abandoning the "harmony of faith and reason" or for a bigoted view of Aristotle "as a pagan" and his followers as "hostile to the faith."[11] The later Middle Ages and particularly the Franciscans and Austin Friars are caricatured here as defenders of fideistic simplicity against the demands of scholarly rules of demonstration. Though the subtitle suggests the reach from "the rediscovery of Aristotle to the disintegration of scholasticism 1100-1600," in fact the storm is all over in 1300 as far as the history of medieval progress is concerned: forty years of research, not only on the Harvard-Tübingen axis but also in the Wisconsin tradition, reaching from Weinberg to Clagett and Courtenay, is contained and confined to the realm of logic and natural philosophy without reflecting its findings with respect to epistemology, metaphysics, and theology.

The critique of metaphysical speculation advanced by the fourteenth-century Franciscan masters and the fifteenth-century *via moderna* is not geared, as James Weisheipl assumes, toward separating and protecting "simple faith" from "scholarly demonstration." Rather, exactly the other way around, it serves to develop a truly scholarly mode of demonstration: faith in God as person and free agent, rather than as a "First Cause" and "Unmoved Mover," is invoked to transform the myth of ontologically necessary laws of nature into models for the investigation of reality, models, or concepts to be adjusted to the findings of experience and experiment.

The designation of Aristotle as a pagan is not born out of hostility to the great Greek philosopher: the late medieval masters continued to be his avid readers and commentators. But the epithet "pagan" allowed them to pursue alternative hypotheses — and, as they proudly claimed, to be better Aristotelians than was St. Thomas, who forced Aristotle into the baptismal font, no longer able to speak for himself. Since we are given to divorce characteristics of Renaissance humanism from late medieval scholasticism, it can easily be overlooked that the nominalist desacralisation of *the* philosopher is not narrow-minded iconoclasm but is to be taken seriously as the search for the historical Aristotle. This quest can combine harsh critique of the "blind pagan" in matters theological with due respect for his achievements in the *artes*. Such dual vision, which can be traced through to Luther,[12] is an essential part of the larger story of the "querelle des anciens et des modernes."

11. James A. Weisheipl, O.P., "The Interpretation of Aristotle's *Physics* and the Science of Motion," *Cambridge History*, pp. 521-36; 522.

12. See Gottfried Rokita, "Aristoteles," *Archiv für Begriffsgeschichte* 15 (1971): 51-93; Separatum, *Luther: Sol, Ratio, Erudio, Aristoteles. Probeartikel zum Sachregister der Weimarer Lutherausgabe*, Abt. Schriften (Bonn, 1971).

To dramatize the contrary trend, one telling example may suffice: in the late fifteenth century the influential Thomist professor in Cologne, Lambertus de Monte Domini ('s Heerenberg near Arnhem, the Netherlands; †1499), advanced the proposal to have Aristotle beatified!

As Charles Trinkaus[13] and Michael Screech[14] have shown, such eminent humanists as Valla and Erasmus could demand the utmost respect for Cicero and Socrates without ever allowing their readers to forget the demarcation line drawn by the incarnation.

The indicated misunderstanding of the innovation of late medieval philosophy would not have to concern us here if we could assume that the Reformation marked a new epoch which left medieval thought behind it as the "dark ages," together with the superfluous squabbles of irrelevant, speculative scholastics. However, notwithstanding the snide and sniping propaganda of humanists and reformers, such a view of discontinuity may serve confessional interests but not our grasp of historical reality: one of the most basic of differences between Luther and Zwingli concerns the understanding of the omnipotence of God, and that is by no means a new debate. This issue forces us back to the famous condemnation in 1277 of 219 articles in theology and natural philosophy by the Bishop of Paris, Stephen Tempier. For our purposes we single out article 147, which condemned as erroneous the view "quod impossibile simpliciter non potest fieri a Deo. . . ," the impossible cannot be performed by God.

The condemnation of this article did not cause — as is often suggested — but rather legitimized and supported the late medieval appeal to God's *potentia absoluta* by such eminent schoolmen as Duns Scotus, Ockham, Aureoli, Buridan, Oresme, Gregory of Rimini, Pierre d'Ailly, Marsilius of Inghen, and Gabriel Biel. The import of the emphasis upon the *potentia absoluta* can only be understood together with its dialectical complement, the *potentia Dei ordinata*. The basic argument is that what God actually has chosen to do *de potentia ordinata* in creation and recreation — that is, in the realms of natural philosophy and theology — he very well could have chosen to decide differently *de potentia absoluta*. The older scholarship from Alexandre Koyré to Gordon Leff and from Etienne Gilson to Erwin Iserloh argued that the distinction between the

---

13. See *The Scope of Renaissance Humanism* (Ann Arbor, 1983), esp. pp. 151-55, 443-44.

14. See his review article "Erasmus, Athens, and Jerusalem," in *Erasmus of Rotterdam Society Yearbook* 3 (1983): 166-75, an acute critique of the findings of Marjorie O'Rourke Boyle, *Christening Pagan Mysteries: Erasmus in Pursuit of Wisdom* (Toronto, 1981).

potentia absoluta and *ordinata* led to sterile and unproductive debates, made God into an arbitrary tyrant, and put the very existence of the world and its history up for grabs, placing them beyond the ken of humankind. In the *Harvest of Medieval Theology* I believe I have shown that the distinction is not understood unless presented as "dialectics."[15] William Courtenay has convincingly countered the charge of arbitrariness by pointing out that the *potentia Dei absoluta* "referred to the total possibilities *initially* open to God, some of which were realized by creating the established order; the unrealized possibilities are now only hypothetically possible."[16] The *potentia ordinata*, that is, reality as the object of human exploration, is therefore not threatened by a whimsical God but unfolds the complete and definitive plan of God for his creation.

To cut through the complex layers in which critics have shrouded the new dialectic, the insistence on the absolute power of God has a twofold yield, one in the realm of physics and one in the realm of theology. If God is no longer tied to creation by "deterministic" causation but related to it by volition, that is, by his personal decision, then all metaphysical arguments based on necessary causal links — as is indeed typical of the cosmology of Aristotle and the *via antiqua* of Aquinas — lose their cogency, if not their credibility. The actual situation is the exact reverse of what the modern critics of nominalism argue: it is not God who is arbitrary but rather human beings in their explanations of problems in natural philosophy, when these are not tested and supported by experience and experiment. Edward Grant is right in regarding the appeal to God's absolute power as "a powerful analytic tool in natural philosophy."[17]

In theology a parallel advance is achieved. Whereas in the realm of natural philosophy physics is freed from the shackles of metaphysics, in the realm of theology metaphysics is shown to be sheer speculation when not verifiable in God's self-revelation, which for the later Middle Ages means Scripture and tradition. If there does not exist a metaphysically necessary ladder along which the first cause has to "connect with" the second cause, the laws of nature can be derived no longer from illuminating the physical world from "above," but from this world itself. The same applies to theology, but vice versa. The truth about God can

15. (Cambridge, Mass., 1963), pp. 34-35.
16. William J. Courtenay, "Nominalism and Late Medieval Religion," in *The Pursuit of Holiness in Late Medieval and Renaissance Religion: Papers from the University of Michigan Conference*, ed. C. H. Trinkaus, with H. A. Oberman (Leiden, 1974), pp. 26-59; 39.
17. *Studies in Medieval Science and Natural Philosophy* (London, 1981), pp. 211-44; 217.

no longer be derived from "below": the second causality does not erect a Jacob's ladder which allows us to transcend the natural phenomena by reasoning back to the first cause, God. Not the reliability but the predictability of the established order is in doubt.

In a significant variant, the *potentia absoluta* of God could be extended from denoting the sheer potentiality of the infinite range of God's potential action to the realm of miracles when God de facto bypasses the common laws of nature. We can notice this shift in Pierre d'Ailly.[18] This new application of the older dialectic[19] is at once useful and risky. *Risky* insofar as God's ability to dispense with the established legal order could — when applied to church and state law — enhance the doctrine of "Divine Right" and thus legitimize papal and royal absolutism.[20] It may well be that John Calvin had this application in mind when he protested that the Parisian figment of the *potentia absoluta* drives a wedge between God's power and God's justice and thus makes God *exlex,* that is, into a tyrant.[21] *Useful* in that the dialectic of the

18. See *Harvest,* p. 38. Francis Oakley sees ambiguity already with Ockham: *Omnipotence, Covenant, and Order: An Excursion in the History of Ideas from Abelard to Leibniz* (Ithaca, 1984), pp. 52-56. William J. Courtenay has called attention to a statement by Gregory of Rimini which might have accelerated a development initiated by Scotus. See his article "The Dialectic of Divine Omnipotence," in *Covenant and Causality in Medieval Thought,* 4 (London, 1984), 13; 32, n. 42; 36, n. 52. For a revealing extension by Biel's successor in Tübingen's *via moderna,* Wendelin Steinbach, see his Hebrews commentary (1516/17) in *Wendelini Steinbach: Opera Exegetica Quae Supersunt Omnia,* ed. H. Feld, 2 (Wiesbaden, 1984), 85.19-23.

19. This development does not go from "clarity to unclarity." Already in the 1430s the dialectic could be applied in one respect and rejected in others. Though Bradwardine can admit that "cooperation" in justification is necessary "secundum legem statutam" — required by the Augustinian adage "qui fecit te, sine te, non iustificat te, sine te" — he passionately rejects it when applied to the question whether revealed future events are bound to take place (*De causa Dei* 1.43.407 D; 3.49. 805 B). Gregory of Rimini is clearly aware of possible abuse when he underscores twice that God's action *de potentia ordinata* should be understood "ad intellectum *recte* intelligentium," or safeguarded by the clause "ad *bonum* intellectum communis dicti de potentia ordinata dei" (*I Sent. Dist.* 42-44, q.1; fol. 162 N; ed. D. Trapp and V. Marcolino, 3 [Berlin, 1984], 368.6; q.2 fol. 166 E; 3.316.4-5).

20. Oakley, *Omnipotence, Covenant, and Order,* pp. 93-118; Courtenay, "The Dialectic of Divine Omnipotence," 17-18.

21. "Itaque Sorbonicum illud dogma, in quo sibi plaudunt papales theologastri, detestor: quod potentiam absolutam Deo affingit. Solis enim lucem a calore avellere, imo suum ab igne calorem, facilius erit, quam Dei potentia separare a iustitia. Facessant ergo procul a piis mentibus monstrosae illae speculationes: plus aliquid Deum posse quam conveniat, vel eum sine modo et ratione quidquam agere" (*De aeterna Dei praedestinatione* [1552], in *Calvini Opera* [CO] 8.361). Cf. *Inst.* III, 23, 2 (1559): "Neque tamen commenturn ingerimus absolutae potentiae: quod sicuti profanum est,

moderni was not only intended to establish the contingency of the created order but also to free physics from the embrace of metaphysics so as to allow the investigation of the world by means of reason and experience. Once God's miraculous intervention was squarely placed outside the *lex statuta*, "secular" research could focus on the *common* course of nature by means of (practical) reason and (sense) experience.

What light, however, does this debate throw on early Reformation thought? With this question we come to our main theme. It is crucial for the further argument to realize that Martin Luther was reared and trained philosophically in Erfurt. This did not make him an Ockhamist. Just as Ockham had stood on the shoulders of Scotus and outgrew him, so Luther reached beyond Ockham and Biel: for him, philosophy — which for Aquinas was still the willing handmaiden of theology — had become the wily whore, when fashioning and faking a liaison between the human mind and God's inner being. The only reliable source for knowing about God's revelation and redemption is the Word of God, which in terms of logical necessities surpasses all understanding. In part IV, I intend to show that Zwingli differed from Luther's approach just as widely as the *via antiqua* deviates from the *via moderna*.

III. *Deus Ludens:* Luther and the *Via Moderna*

"It is useless to debate with the scholastics" — thus Luther concludes a recently recovered list of theses for a Wittenberg disputation (set for 7 July 1542). The key concepts of Scripture, such as sin and promise, faith, and justification, are beyond them. Hence to discuss theology when confronted with such ignorance is nothing else than to try to make an ass play the lyre.[22] This perhaps more eloquent than elegant proverb,

---

ita merito detestabile nobis esse debet. Non fingimus Deum exlegem, qui sibi ipsi lex est." Pierre d'Ailly finds this distinction already with Lombard and some *antiqui*: ". . . quaedam deus potest de potentia quae non potest de iustitia" (*Quaestiones super libros sententiarum cum quibusdam in fine adjunctis* [Straßburg, 1490; repr. Frankfurt, 1968], 1, q. 13 D). He needs this appeal to authority — impatiently brushed aside before (1, q. 6 T) — since he has to defend his new definition of the *potentia ordinata* "magis large" as that which God can do "stante veritate legis seu scripturae divinae" (1, q. 1 JJ).

22. "Summa, frustra disputatur cum scholasticis de his rebus sibi incognitis et inusitatis. Impossibile est apud eos intelligi, quid sit peccatum, promissio, fides, iustificatio, imputatio, lex et impletio eius. Non sunt haec in eorum libris, sed contritio, satisfactio et opera humanis viribus gratiam Dei merentia. Ignorant, imo negant

among Erasmus's very first selections for his *Adagia*,[23] seems to make any further discussion of Luther's relation to scholasticism redundant and irrelevant. The demarcation line is firmly drawn: any comparison must be confrontation. And yet on closer consideration Luther's main charge, though directed against *all* schools, bespeaks his own schooling when he argues that theology will be warped when its chief concepts are taken "ex philosophia rationis."[24]

Philosophical reasoning presents a God in keeping with its own tongue and language instead of listening to the vocabulary of Scripture.[25] Luther refers here to Nehemiah 13:24, "loquebantur iuxta linguas populi et populi," to mark the contrast with listening to the *proprietas sermonis* and the genuine *modus loquendi* of Scripture. A few years earlier he had illustrated this point in a classroom lecture with a story about Pope Leo X. Probably during the Fifth Lateran Council the pope invites two philosophers for dinner to argue for and against the immortality of the soul. After a long and sharp debate, the pope is to designate the winner: You who defended the immortality of human beings may well have the better arguments, but your opponent will please the people more: "his speech makes for a happy face."[26] This domestication of God Luther calls "Epicurean" since it presses faith into the harness of natural reason and remodels God into an extension of human desire. It is just as the inhabitants of Sodom who did not take the coming judgment of God seriously but laughed about him as if he were a *Deus ludens:* "Sed fuit [Dominus] in oculis generorum suorum 'quasi ludens'" (Gen. 19:14, Vulg.).

The *Deus ludens* of the Genesis text forces Luther into a seemingly rambling exposition, which cannot be unraveled without a firm grasp of the late medieval debate about the dialectics of the *potentia absoluta* and *ordinata*. The loaded theme[27] of the *Deus ludens*, inter-

---

peccatum originale post baptismum et tantum de actualibus disputant. Hac ignorantia stante velle Theologiam tractate est aliud nihil quam asinum velle lyra canere" (Luther, "Contra Satanam et Synagogam Ipsius," WA 59.722.23–723.6).

23. *Collectanea* (1500), nr. 125. See *Collected Works of Erasmus*, 31, *Adages* (Toronto, 1982), 344-45.

24. ". . . quae non potest ea capere et tradere, quae sunt Christi et Spiritus eius" (*WA* 59.722.1-2).

25. *WA* 59.722.5-8, with reference to Neh. 13:24.

26. *WA* 43.67.15-21. Lecture on Genesis (19:14); c. March 1539. Cf. *WA Tischreden* 4 (nr. 4407).

27. For the significance of this issue, see my analysis of the history of "curiosity": *Contra vanam curiositatem: Ein Kapitel der Theologie zwischen Seelenwinkel und Weltall* (Zurich, 1974), pp. 48-49. As far as I can see, the only other reference to this

preted as the God who is laughed out of court and replaced by the Epicurean figment of human dreams and wishes, concerns by no means just one issue or one opponent.[28] Rather, it enables Luther to summarize his view of the essentials of Reformation thought: here we must highlight two converging lines of argument. The first we can call the "Erasmian front," since it resumes the central theme of Luther's attack of 1525.[29] In *De servo arbitrio* the hidden God, who is naked *(nudus)* while not dressed in his revelation,[30] is the God *de potentia absoluta.* To this God applies the Socratic proverb: "Quae supra nos, nihil ad nos."[31] In contrast the God that concerns us is the God revealed in Jesus Christ: the faithful should embrace the "ordinatam potentiam, hoc est, filium incarnatum."[32]

Luther passage is to be found with Francis Oakley, whose important study is at this point misleading in dating and interpretation. See *Omnipotence, Covenant, and Order* (see n. 18, above), pp. 57; 138, n. 49.

28. The *ira Dei,* and the approaching *dies irae,* is believed neither by "the Pope and his cardinals" nor by Luther's own former close associates, the antinomians: "Nos quoque contionamur de filio Dei, venturo ad iuditium, et aeternis flammis subiecturo impios. Sed haec cum vel legit vel audit Papa cum suis cardinalibus, rident tanquam in re impossibili. Quid, inquiunt, si coelum ruat?" (WA 43.67.11-14). Cf. "Memorabilis profecto historia, praedicanda in Ecclesia Dei saepe, quantumcunque simus iustificati, ne in Antinomorum insaniam incidamus, qui legem ex Ecclesia tollunt, quasi vero in Ecclesia omnes sint sancti, nec opus sit talibus exemplis irae divinae. Mundus quidem tales Doctores amat . . ." (*WA* 43.67.34-38). The lucid article by Ernst Koch, "Johann Agricola neben Luther. Schülerschaft und theologische Eigenart," seems to me to provide the key to the question why Luther at the end of his exposition of Gen. 19:14 feels the need to warn specifically against Jean Gerson. Agricola's *Drey Sermon* (Wittenberg, 1537), which caused the final break with Luther, invokes the authority of the great Parisian chancellor; see Koch, *Lutheriana: Zum 500. Geburtstag Martin Luthers, Archiv zur WA (AWA),* 5 (Cologne, 1984), 131-50; 149.

29. In the parallel passage Luther explicitly refers to "De servo arbitrio." See WA 43.458.35-40.

30. WA 43.685.6-7. For the most recent, careful analysis, see Jun Matsuura, "Zur Unterscheidung von deus revelatus und deus absconditus in 'De Servo Arbitrio'," in *AWA* 5.67-85.

31. "Quae supra nos, nihil ad nos. Dictum Socraticum deterrens a curiosa vestigatione rerum coelestium et arcanorum naturae. Refertur proverbii vice a Lactantio libro tertio, capite vigesimo: Ex his, inquit, unum eligam, quod ab omnibus sit probatum. Celebre hoc proverbium Socrates habuit: Quod supra nos, nihil ad nos. Torqueri potest et in illos, qui de negociis principum aut theologiae mysteriis temere loquuntur. Vertere licebit et in contrarium: Quae infra nos, nihil ad nos, ubi significamus res leviusculas, quam ut nobis curae esse debeant." Erasmus von Rotterdam, *Ausgewählte Schriften,* 7, ed. Theresia Payr (Darmstadt, 1972), 414, 416. Cf. Lactantius, *Divinae Institutiones* 3.20, in *Corpus Scriptorum Ecclesiasticorum Latinorum,* 19.246.15.

32. WA 43.73.3.

Charles Trinkaus has called attention to a passage in the *Hyper-aspistes,* where Erasmus concedes that God sometimes saves some people in an extraordinary way *de potentia absoluta.*[33] Paul's conversion on the road to Damascus is indeed an example of God's prevenient and sovereign grace, but this is an exceptional intervention. It is implied that such overriding and overpowering of human choice and decision is rare and by no means proof against God's *usual* respect for human decisionary responsibilities, that is, for the morally more suitable mode of salvation *de potentia ordinata.*[34] From the perspective of Erasmus, Luther has "men saved exclusively by God's *potentia absoluta,*" according to Trinkaus.[35] From the perspective of Luther, Erasmus makes the revealed God into a *Deus ludens* by removing the morally offensive dimension of divine operation to the "exceptional" realm of the *potentia absoluta.*[36]

The second line of argument we can best call the "Zwinglian front," though at this point, a decade after the death of the Zurich reformer (1531), other sacramentarians are named explicitly. Luther's point of departure is again the visit of the angels with Lot to announce the coming judgment of Sodom (Gen. 19:12-14). Luther's goal is to deal with one of the most formidable biblical arguments, which led to the failure of the Marburg Colloquy (1529) and thus broke the common front of the early Reformation movement: it is the text from John 6:63, "The flesh is of no avail," used to show that a "physical presence" of Christ in the eucharist is out of the question.

---

33. Leiden edition *(LB)* 10.1527. Trinkaus, *The Scope of Renaissance Humanism* (see n. 13, above), 174-301; 282. Erasmus can fall back here on the solution to the problem of predestination as presented in the *via moderna* — traceable from Ockham to Biel. See *Harvest* (n. 15 above), pp. 191-92.

34. In his "Quaestio Disputata" (1517) Gabriel Biel's editor and successor in the Tübingen *via moderna,* Wendelin Steinbach, formulates the exegetical principles which subordinate the search for the *proprietas sermonis* to ethical considerations. The clause "propter hominis profectum" is also the chief argument of Erasmus contra Luther: "Scriptura aliquas loquuciones admittit, alias non admittit. . . . In scripturis omnia erant propalanda, que Deo vere conveniunt, propter hominis profectum, ut timeat et diligat. . . . Hec congruit nobis significare in scripturis, non ea, que facile possent esse scandalo pusillis" (*Opera Exegetica,* 2 [see n. 18, above], 424.11, 18, 19; 425.17-18). The key to Steinbach's knowledge about what "Deo vere convenit" implies is reflected in his revealing definition of the *iustitia Dei:* "Iusticia est voluntas divina volens ex sua libera sponsione seu pacto dare tantum pro tanto, ut condecet suam bonitatem et hominis merita vel demerita secundum taxam racionis recte in Deo" (*ibid.,* 357.16-18). This passage — completely in keeping with his mentor Gabriel Biel — provides an illuminating backdrop for Luther's point of departure.

35. *Scope of Renaissance Humanism,* p. 295, n. 28.

36. See Luther's evaluation in 1525: *WA* 18.715.2-3.

For interpreters not familiar with the terminology used, the following argument must remain obscure: God could have governed this world by direct intervention — as he did indeed do, when he punished culprits and sometimes still does punish murderers — foregoing the proper legal procedures by the civil magistrate, when he created Adam and Eve without carnal union or when he gave bread to the Israelites in the desert without their having to work for it. But it pleased God in his majesty to use human beings and angels and to make them his cooperators.[37] This expression "but it pleased the divine majesty" *(sed divinae maiestati placuit)* is the standing formula for the self-binding commitment[38] which marks the establishment of the *potentia ordinata*. Since the advent of Christ — though Luther does not indicate the exact moment in time[39] — God no longer wishes to act according to his absolute power but according to his *potentia ordinata*, that is, through the ministry of angels and human beings.[40]

Since what applies to God's creatures is valid for his whole creation — thus Luther concludes against the sacramentarians — one dare not say that *all* externals are matter and flesh and therefore "to no avail." To some externals God has chosen to attach his promise and power by commitment of his word, through which he has bound and committed himself.[41]

37. "Omnino enim hoc verum est, quod Deus mundum hunc visibilem gubernat non tantum per homines, sed etiam per Angelos. Posset quidem occidere fures sine carnificis opera, et sine Magistratus civilis sententia: sicut nonnunquam facit, praesertim cum homicidis. Sic posset homines creare sine coniunctione maris et foeminae, sicut creavit Adam et Euam: sed divinae maiestati placuit hominum ministerio et opera uti: Ut scilicet ostenderet mirabilem et divinam suam potentiam in creaturis suis, quas non voluit esse ociosas. Ideo Paulus vocat nos omnes 'cooperarios Dei'. Utitur enim nostro ministerio ad varias res, sic etiam Angelorum ministerio utitur, quos instruxit tanta potentia, ut propria virtute seu concreata possint perdere terras et populos, si Deus sit apud eos" (*WA* 43.68.17-27).

38. See here especially Berndt Hamm, *Promissio, Pactum, Ordinatio: Freiheit und Selbstbindung Gottes in der scholastischen Gnadenlehre* (Tübingen, 1977), pp. 279-90; 388, n. 200.

39. See, however, *WA* 43.73.3: "Ordinatam potentiam, hoc est, filium incarnatum. . . ."

40. "Manet igitur regula, de qua supra etiam dixi [cf. 68.24], quod Deus non amplius vult agere secundum extraordinariam, seu, ut Sophistae loquuntur, absolutam potestatem: sed per creaturas suas, quas non vult esse otiosas. Sic dat victum, non ut Iudaeis in deserto, cum coelitus daret Manna, sed per laborem, cum diligenter facimus opus vocationis nostrae, nec vult amplius homines ex gleba fingere, sicut Adamum, sed coniunctione maris et foeminae utitur, quibus benedicit. Hanc vocant Dei ordinatam potestatem, cure scilicet utitur ministerio vel Angelorum vel hominum" (*WA* 43.71.7-14).

41. "Ideo ante omnia hoc considerandum est: an externa ista fiant secundum

Sometimes God acts *de potentia absoluta* outside the chosen chan-
nels of the laws of nature, of angels, human beings, and sacraments, as
when the friends of Daniel are not burned in the fiery oven or when
unbaptized children are saved. But such action of the hidden God as
Luther clarified this point in *De servo arbitrio* does not concern us. To
draw on such exceptions is to go against God's explicit will — that God
once upon a time *(tum)* acted in such a way himself does not free us
from the obligation to act in accordance with God's *potentia ordinata*.[42]
Therefore, when the sacrament is received to which God has committed
his power, "genuflexo tacitus adora ista externa."[43]

IV. *Homo Ludens:* Zwingli and the *Via Antiqua*

In turning to Zwingli I should like to point to two revealing passages in
his last writings which, as far as I see, have gone unnoticed. They are
commentaries presented in the "Zürcher Prophezei"[44] in the years 1528-
1529.[45] Easily overlooked in his interpretation of Jeremiah 27 is Zwingli's
greatest concession ever.[46] He approaches Luther's position as far as he

---

institutionem et voluntatem Dei, vel non. Si verbum seu institutio Dei non adest, tunc
recte dicis externa nihil prodesse ad salutem, sed etiam nocere. Sicut Christus Matthaei
15. dicit: 'frustra me colunt mandatis hominum.' "

"Sed si rides externa ista niti verbo, et divino mandato instituta esse, ibi
genuflexo tacitus adora ista externa, et dic: hoc non iubet fieri meus Pastor, non Petrus,
non Paulus, sed meus Pater in coelis, igitur in humilitate obediam, et credam obedien-
tiam hanc profuturam ad salutem" (*WA* 43.70.23-32).

42. "Si qua autem nonnunquam fiunt extra ministerium vel Angelorum vel
hominum, ibi recte dixeris: Quae supra nos: nihil ad nos. Nobis enim ad ordinatam
potestatem respiciendum, et ex ea iuditium sumendum est. Potest Deus salvare sine
Baptismo, sicut credimus infantes, qui nonnunquam parentum negligentia, aut alio casu
Baptismum non consequuntur, non ideo damnari. Sed nobis in Ecclesia secundum
ordinatam Dei potestatem iudicandum et docendum est, quod sine Baptismo illo externo
nemo salvetur. Sic ordinata potentia Dei est, quod aqua humectat, ignis urit etc. Sed in
Babylone in medio igni Danielis socii incolumes vivebant. Haec fuit potentia Dei
absoluta, secundum quam tum agebat, sed secundum hanc nihil nos iubet. Vult enim nos
facere secundum ordinatam potentiam" (*WA* 43.71.17-28). This "tum" interprets *WA*
43.685.23-24, and therefore clarifies the conclusion of E. Jüngel; see n. 57, below.

43. *WA* 43.70.29.

44. See *Corpus Reformatorum (CR)* 100; *Zwinglis Werke (ZW)* 13.289-90.

45. *CR* 101; *ZW* 14.872. See my *The Reformation: Roots and Ramifications*
(Edinburgh, 1994), pp. 196-97.

46. In the *Amica Exegesis* (1527) definite steps are made in this direction.
Walther Köhler finds here "in aller Form den Begriff der Realpräsenz," but must add

possibly can: "The very [!] body of Christ is in the Eucharist and is also truly eaten, when bread and wine are presented."[47] And yet since the elements are only *externa*, faith alone can receive the eucharistic Christ: "non possunt ergo externa ulla eam [fidem] dare aut facere."[48] Take this faith away and people will burst out in laughter at the sight of the naked elements: "iocus ac risus sunt. . . !"[49] Hence, one may add, no adoration of the externals — no genuflexion.[50] If Luther would have read these words published in the year of Zwingli's death, they surely would have reminded him of the *Deus ludens,* the God laughed out of court by the Sodomites.[51]

In the programmatic treatise *De Providentia* (1530) there is one eloquent sentence which is shorthand for the theologian of the *via antiqua*. It is proper to ask, Zwingli argues here, about such acts of God as the rejection of Esau and the election of Jacob — why he has done them and why he has done them in this way: "cur facta aut sic facta sint."[52] This Anselmian confidence in the ability of human reason to unravel the divine mystery would have been inconceivable in the *via moderna*. In his Isaiah commentary (published 1529) Zwingli gives account of this assumption in the interpretation of 42:8, where it is said that God alone

---

that it remains a "praesentia in mente." *Zwingli und Luther: Ihr Streit über das Abendmahl nach seinen politischen und religiösen Beziehungen,* 1 (Leipzig, 1924), 483.

47. "Christi verum corpus in caena; vere etiam editur, cum panis ac vinum praebentur" (CR 101; ZW 14.597.15-16).

48. ZW 14.596.29-30.

49. ZW 14.597.4-5; cf. 14.596.24-25.

50. For the best summary to date of the Marburg alternatives, see Walther Köhler, *Zwingli und Luther* (see n. 46, above), 2 (Gütersloh, 1953), 133-38. Gottfried W. Locher's brief sketch of the later Zwingli has the advantage that Köhler's characterization of Zwingli's position as "idealistisch" (138) is further clarified as "platonisch-augustinisch" in the tradition of the *via antiqua*. See G. W. Locher, *Die Zwinglische Reformation im Rahmen der europäischen Kirchengeschichte* (Göttingen, 1979), p. 335.

51. Since Johannes Eck (†1543) is apparently not familiar with Zwingli's OT commentaries, he does not discuss the new "praesentia realis fidei." Eck eliminates this faith, sees only the elements, and hence joins the ranks of the laughers: "Veteri Christiana religione obliterata" is the description of Zwingli's reformation, which threw out more and more to retain at the end only "baker's bread" on the altar — "non nisi pistorium panem": *Repulsio Articulorum Zwinglii,* 1530, as quoted in the new critical edition of Zwingli's *De Convitiis Eckii,* CR 93, pars 3; ZW 6, III (Zurich, 1983), 250f.

52. ZW 6, III.188.21 (see n. 51, above). Compare Steinbach's typical nominalistic critique of Anselm: "Hinc posset forte concedi, quod necesse sit redemptorem esse Deum et hominem, stante ordinacione divina de sic redimendo homine, ad sensum sepe dictum" (2.140.8-10; cf. 137.20–138.2).

is omnipotent: "I will not transfer my majesty to anyone else." Of course, Zwingli first directs this text against Luther's doctrine of the eucharist by pointing out that God does not allow his divinity to be so limited by the incarnation that he could be ubiquitous and hence physically present on all altars everywhere. Much more important than this application against Luther, however, is the range of philosophical presuppositions displayed here. The being of God and the necessary conclusions we have to draw from this are established with the arguments of the *via antiqua*: "Ubique autem esse, intima ac sola numinis est proprietas. Hinc enim dimanat omnipotentia."[43] Hence not only the existence of God, but also the mode of his existence can be proven. This omnipotence of God is indivisible and non transferable. The chain of argumentation leads from conclusion to conclusion — with the typical logical bridges "necesse est," "ergo," "hinc enim," and "non potest" — thus passing over the demarcation line from the *potentia ordinata* to the *potentia absoluta*. This can be undertaken by Zwingli because for him there is no such demarcation line at all.[54]

The reason for the basic divergence between Luther and Zwingli in the interpretation of the eucharist has been searched for in many directions, from anthropology to christology. When we look beyond single theological *loci* to the difference in "mentality," it is to be underscored that, although they were born only seven weeks apart, a whole epoch stands between the two reformers: Zwingli expected the Reformation to bring modern times; Luther expected the end of times. For Luther — in a seemingly medieval fashion — the devil and the antichrist play a central role. It is revealing that Zwingli makes the explicit point in his Daniel commentary (1528) that the antichrist is not a single person but many, since all those who persecute Christ[55] are to be regarded as "antichrists." The underlying reason for the lessening of the threatening

53. CR 101; ZW 14.337.1-15; 9-11.

54. Zwingli knows the *pactum* concept, but this is the beginning of reformed covenant theology, which could develop because the *pactum* is not the eternal self-limitation of God but the historical — often conditional — "alliance" of God with human beings and hence the basis of reformed ecclesiology. See the commentary to Ezekiel 16:61; ZW 13.706.9-13. Cf. the discerning study by J. Wayne Baker, *Heinrich Bullinger and the Covenant: The Other Reformed Tradition* (Athens, Ohio, 1980), pp. 2-5; 24.

55. "Et iam multi sunt antichristi. Expones, quid intelligat [Rev. 12,13] per antichristum. Quasi dicat: Ne putetis me loqui de aliqua persona certa, que veniat ad consumacionem seculi. Sed hoc voco antichristos, quicunque Christum persequuntur. Nunquam sic sevitum est a tyrannis sicut in Christianos. Nemo truculencius sevit in Christianos quam antichristi" (CR 101; ZW 14.750.23-28).

power of the devil and antichrist lies, it seems to me, in the fact that with Zwingli there is no self-limitation on God's part of his own omnipotence. With this observation we touch the heart of the issue between the two leading reformers.

V. Epilogue: *Querelle des Anciens et des Modernes*

Three conclusions seem to be warranted: eucharistic debate of the sixteenth century is not to be reduced to a sudden relapse to the low point of late medieval scholasticism after some ten years of emancipation.[56] Rather, this world of discourse and frame of reference can illuminate the multitude of arguments and side issues to the diverging receptions of basic school alternatives. The historian must leave it to the philosopher to establish whether this school allegiance *determines* the positions taken, be it by agreement or by rejection.[57] But he must realize that without thorough familiarity with the late medieval vocabulary employed, he will be unable to grasp, interpret, and render his documents *e mente auctoris*. Since the historian at times will know more about the author than the author about himself, the scholarly canon *e mente auctoris* even applies when the author himself claims to have eradicated the past and in this sense to be *totus modernus*.

Second, the investigation of one of the major themes of late medieval thought, the pursuit of the implications of the omnipotence of God, has made marked progress in the last two decades. William Courtenay and Francis Oakley in this country and Berndt Hamm and Manfred Schulze abroad[58] have extended the scope of our knowledge about the

---

56. For a critique of this thesis with respect to Luther, see my *Werden und Wertung der Reformation* (Tübingen, 1979), p. 368, n. 91; Engl. trans., *Masters of the Reformation: The Emergence of a New Intellectual Climate in Europe* (Cambridge, 1981), p. 288.

57. The use of the uncommon expression *Deus absolutus* should not discredit the observation of E. Jüngel: "Luthers Lehre vom verborgenen Gott ist nicht einfach die Fortsetzung der spätnominalistischen Lehre vom deus absolutus, wenngleich sie erst auf deren Hintergrund recht verständlich wird: nämlich als deren schärfste Kritik." "Quae supra nos, nihil ad nos. Eine Kurzformel der Lehre vom verborgenen Gott — im Anschluss an Luther interpretiert." *Evangelische Theologie* 3 (1972): 197-240; 220.

58. See esp. Manfred Schulze, "'Via Gregorii' in Forschung und Quellen," in *Gregor von Rimini: Werk und Wirkung bis zur Reformation*, Spätmittelalter und Reformation Texte und Untersuchungen 20 (Berlin, 1981), pp. 1-126.

prehistory of key concepts in nominalist thought and its diverse impact on (natural) philosophy and theology. As far as the fourteenth-century intention of the distinction between the *potentia absoluta* and the *potentia ordinata* is concerned, there exists a firm scholarly consensus: it marks the voluntary self-limitation of the omnipotent God and hence the non-necessary contingent nature of the established order of creation and redemption. The older view of the nominalist God as the arbitrary tyrant by whose whim the present order can be suddenly overturned seemed discredited once and for all.

The recent awareness of the impact of legal patterns of thought could, however, reopen this debate. When the *potentia ordinata* becomes known as the *lex statuta,* the *potentia absoluta* is apt to be regarded as the domain of divine paralegal action and can become the paradigm for papal and royal absolutism, for pope or king as *legibus absolutus* or *exlex*. In view of our modern high regard for the parliamentary tradition, this development can be and has been regretted as a retarding obstacle on the path toward "modern" constitutionalism. At the present I cannot dwell on the anachronism implied in this critique. The actualization of God's absolute power, however, also has marked advantages. In the early modern search for the laws of nature — which could begin after the "book of nature" came to replace Holy Scripture as a scientific source — the absolute power of God could be invoked to distinguish between miracles and the *regular* course of nature. Hence, experience and experiment could concentrate on the laws of nature. In the realm of ethics and biblical theology, the holiness of God as *totaliter aliter* could be domesticated in the service of a generally valid moral code.[59]

In Erasmus we have a free example of how the morally threatening story of St. Paul's conversion can be diffused when God's acceptance of an impious persecutor of the truth is regarded as an exception *de potentia absoluta*.

With Luther, we find the acceptance of God's actual deployment of his absolute power in the general governance of this world. But at the same time this God is hidden as naked force and should remain so. The God that concerns the faithful is the God of the *potentia ordinata* made manifest in Jesus Christ.[60]

For Zwingli there is no such distinction between the hidden majesty of God and his self-limitation. At least one word should be added at this

---

59. See Steinbach, *Opera Exegetica*, 2, 137.20-138.2; 294.12-22; 400.14-401.2.
60. Cf. Kenneth Hagen, "From Testament to Covenant in the Early Sixteenth Century," *Sixteenth Century Journal* 3 (1972): 1-24; esp. 15-20.

point about John Calvin: whereas Zwingli's background is properly described as the *via antiqua* and Luther's as the *via moderna,* Calvin proves to hold the middle ground on the question of God's omnipotence. This points to his association with the *via Scoti,* which I find particularly evident in the doctrines of predestination and justification. In the traditional view, the so-called "extra-Calvinisticum" formed the chief cornerstone — or stumbling block! — in his theological thought. On closer consideration, Calvin's view of God's operation outside and beyond the incarnation rather proves to be an "extra-patristicum," indeed an "extra-catholicum."[61] As I have pointed out elsewhere,[62] not this "extra-Calvinisticum" as such, but the thoroughgoing application of the underlying assumption is typical of Calvin: God operates not only beyond the incarnate Son but also beyond the confines of the visible church,[63] the eucharist, and the law. This extra dimension is in the terminology of the *via moderna* the realm of the *potentia absoluta,* at one point referred to by Calvin as the "ius mundi regendi . . . nobis incognitum."[64]

In contrast to Zwingli, Calvin emphasizes God's commitment to the *externa* as the chosen operational instruments. In contrast to Luther, Calvin utilizes the full potential of the realm which before d'Ailly used to be the *potentia absoluta.* Calvin's comparatively progressive — while more dynamic — view of state and society is intimately related to his steady look beyond the officially ordained institutions and vessels of grace.

John Calvin provides an excellent counterproof for the thesis that the "operationalization" of the *potentia absoluta* — that is, the transition from speculation about what God *could* have done to what he *actually* does *extra ordinem* — should be regarded as detrimental to the emancipation of European civilization.

---

61. See the clear analysis of the development and significance of this concept by E. David Willis, *Calvin's Catholic Christology,* Studies in Medieval and Reformation Thought 2 (Leiden, 1966), esp. pp. 8-25; 60.

62. See my article "The 'Extra' Dimension in the Theology of Calvin," *Journal of Ecclesiastical History* 21 (1970): 43-64; original German version in *Geist und Geschichte der Reformation: Festgabe Hanns Rückert zum 65. Geburtstag,* ed. H. Liebing and K. Scholder (Berlin, 1966), pp. 323-56.

63. Thus explicitly, Willis, *Calvin's Catholic Christology,* pp. 144-52.

64. *Inst.* I,17, 2, *Opera Selecta,* 3.205.12-13; cf. ". . . quanvis nobis absconditae sint rationes" (*ibid.,* 205.19). "Vray est qu'il ne fait pas cela d'une puissance absolue, comme disent les Papistes" (*Supplementa Calviniana,* 1.605.19-20). "Deum enim exlegem qui facit, maxima eum gloriae sua parte spoliat, quia rectitudinem eius ac iustitiam sepelit. Non quod legi subiectus sit Deus, nisi quatenus ipse sibi lex est. Talis enim inter potentiam eius ac iustitiam symmetria et consensus, ut nihil ab ipso nisi moderatum legitimum et regulare prodeat" (CO 8.361; cf. sermon on Job 32:2, in CO 34.339).

Third and last, what claim can the foregoing exercise in intellectual history make on our time and interest? As always, our real battles are fought in book reviews, and therefore I must quote one eminent specimen to sharpen the challenge implied in this question. In his discussion of the merits of a recent book on the confessional significance of marriage in the Reformation era,[65] Thomas A. Brady, Jr., takes issue with Steven Ozment's *When Fathers Ruled*[66] with a carefully phrased statement which pitches the social historian against *les anciens,* the intellectual historians of "yesterday":

> Reformation studies are plagued by books and articles which advance this or that sampling of sources, often pamphlets or treatises, as representative, typical or particularly revealing of the motives, mentalities and anxieties of an earlier age. One then infers revolutions which never happened, relying on the romantic-idealist notion that the meaning of a process may be grasped truly only at its origin. Such procedures have allowed historians to discover revolutionary change in the Reformation era at almost every hand, while sober analysis of archival sources usually dispels the myth. It is not that the method of interpreting the life of a society through a sampling of its ideas, whether Marx's "leading ideas" or humbler ones, is wrong; it is dreadfully incomplete.[67]

Whatever further significance may and must be attached to the event; Marburg 1529, that is, the eucharistic debate between Luther and Zwingli, stands out as *the* example of the irreducible impact of intellectual history. The divisive nature of the discord cannot be contested: notwithstanding all the political pressure and economic interests involved, the Protestant leaders did not compromise or yield to the obvious need for establishing a united front. Our investigation has shown how deep and how far the roots of their differences reached into the past. With this in mind, Brady's conclusion must be turned around in order to describe the *complementary* function of the *anciens*: Without their input, social history is not wrong: "it is dreadfully incomplete."

65. T. M. Safley, *Let No Man Put Asunder: The Control of Marriage in the German Southwest: A Comparative Study, 1550-1600* (Kirksville, Mo., 1984).

66. (Cambridge, Mass., 1983).

67. *Sixteenth Century Journal* 15 (1984): 225-27; 226. Although he directs it in the form of a question, Robert M. Kingdon, *Renaissance, Reformation, Resurgence,* ed. P. de Klerk (Grand Rapids, 1976), p. 96, raises the very same issue: "My dissatisfaction [with a Calvin study by André Biéler] no doubt reflects the viewpoint of an historian who is never sure of the real impact of ideas and prefers to seek social causes for social developments."

Preface to
Devotia Moderna: Basic Writings

This volume is published at an auspicious moment. In an external sense it arrives in time to commemorate the third and most influential foundation by Geert Groote (†1384): After the Sisters of the Common Life (1379), and in its wake the Brethren, the Windesheim Congregation near Zwolle was established in 1387. There is, however, a more substantial reason for welcoming this volume. In religious history it is not uncommon that a considerable period of time is needed to gain a proper perspective on the significance of a movement; in the case of the Modern Devotion, some six hundred years were needed to remove at least some of the major obstacles. An internal reason for regarding this volume as timely is that scholarship in this field is now at the very beginning of what promises to be its most creative phase of research. As often in the history of Western thought, this is the third phase: following the nineteenth-century claims for the significance of the Modern Devotion, climaxing in views that regarded this Dutch movement as the center of the Christian Renaissance or as the forerunner of both the Renaissance and the Reformation north of the Alps, in a much-needed correcting phase, scholarly energy had to be invested in retrieving the solid historical basis of the documents themselves.

At this point in time we are about to move away from a situation in which much space and energy had to be invested in establishing what

Preface to *Devotio Moderna: Basic Writings*, by John Van Engen, Classics of Western Spirituality (New York: Paulist Press, 1988), pp. 1-3.

the Modern Devotion was and what it was not. To get a handle on a movement that for such a long time proved elusive, it is essential to realize that its period of growth and strength stretched over almost one and a half centuries and may not have reached its zenith until the end of the fifteenth century. Since a century lasts one hundred unique years, ten decades of breathtakingly rapid shifts in social conditions and intellectual assumptions, it is mandatory that any characterization of the movement be provided with a time index. Of no less import is the realization that during this period the movement spread from the Ijssel Delta in the Netherlands to northern and southern Germany, Belgium, France, and Switzerland, so that together with the category of time the importance of space and place must also be taken into consideration. However, before the extent of growth and change can be measured, and the glorious but tough questions of the past as to the relation of the Modern Devotion to the Renaissance and the Reformation can be re-opened, the principles and ideals of the founding period have to be clarified by concentrating on the work of the three great men — Geert Groote (†1384), Gerard Zerbolt of Zutphen (†1398), and the charismatic organizer, Florens Radewijns (†1400).

In searching for a connection with Renaissance humanism and the Reformation, past studies concentrated on doctrines and on the ideological profile of the Modern Devotion — and it would be wrong to deny that there is indeed a "program," individually developed and shared by the founding fathers of the movement in the fourteenth century. But as our present knowledge of the sources indicates, the best available working definition is a functional description, namely, that the movement had its common thrust in the search for a new meditation technique for the working classes, directed toward the reformation of the soul and the rejuvenation of the spirit as the basis for renewal of the communal life, whether within or outside monastic walls.

This last statement is not without special significance: within *or* outside the monastic walls. The Modern Devotion in its first two historical forms of expression, namely, as the community of the Sisters and the Brethren of the Common Life, propagated a life without vows and therefore without the official monastic rules as prescribed by canon law. Even when, after 1387, the movement was regularized under the rule of St. Augustine, this original vision was kept alive in the characteristic interpretation of the vows (1) as the necessary forms of the communal devotion, and (2) as the means by which other monastic houses are not won over and incorporated to strengthen their own organization but brought to reform from within, in order to have a greater spiritual yield for the world "outside." In the suspicion against vain curiosity and the "hot air" of academic learning — *scientia inflat!* — we should note not merely the undeniable element of anti-intellectualism but also the awareness that the inhibiting rules of classroom logic and textbook dialectic have in common with the *consuetudines* or life-style of the monastic orders that the true *praxis pietatis* (i.e., the fertile soil for the tender roots of spiritual experience) will dry out. The movement would never have had such an impact, however, if it had been just a protest movement springing from antimonastic or anticlerical sentiments — which often explain better the excitement and praise of later interpreters than of the late medieval authors themselves. The reform of the soul is seen as the road to reform of late medieval monasticism, and beyond that of the prelates and of the clergy in general — and thus indirectly as the road to the quickening of the church at large.

Modern interpreters will be quick to point out that the movement was a failure, soon overshadowed and bypassed by Renaissance humanism and Reformation reorientation. But in one sense, no movement of rejuvenation of any sort has ever been a long-term "success," including Christianity itself. In another sense, the Modern Devotion has continued to survive under many other names, such as Jansenism or Puritanism, and it fed into that resurgence in vitality which we vaguely call "reform Catholicism," particularly in its plethora of new monastic foundations. Above all, it performed its most lasting service as a reminder that the greatest threat to true devotion is the professionalization of religion.

Captivitas Babylonica:
Johann von Staupitz's Critical Ecclesiology

I. Olim Praecursor Extiti

Staupitz scholars have reacted, in recent years, with some justification to the view that their work is nothing but a preliminary approach or warmup to the study of the Reformation. In more general but parallel terms, the later medieval period has been taken seriously only since it ceased to be interpreted as the dying echo of the high Middle Ages or as a pre-reformation and a prelude to the events of the Reformation, and started to be studied as an historical era in its own right. The writings of Johann von Staupitz, OESA (c. 1468-1524), began to receive serious scholarly and editorial attention only after the topic "Luther and Staupitz," along with its inherent direct comparison of the two figures, had been expanded to include the question of Staupitz and the Augustinian Order. This approach offers a less confrontational framework in which to place these men and their works.

However, the older parochial and confessional search for "forerunners" of the Reformation — based on the outmoded notion that the later Middle Ages were merely the prehistory of the Reformation — is

---

"*Captivitas Babylonica*: Johann von Staupitz's Critical Ecclesiology," translated by Andrew Colin Gow from the original German article "Captivitas Babylonica. Die Kirchenkritik des Johannes von Staupitz," in *Reformatio et Reformationes: Festschrift für Lothar Graf zu Dohna zum 65. Geburtstag*, ed. Andreas Mehl and Wolfgang Christian Schneider (Darmstadt, 1989), pp. 97-106.

grounded, at least in one instance, in the sources, namely in the case of Johann von Staupitz. At the end of his last letter to his "successor" Luther, the former vicar-general of the Observant Augustinians characterizes his relationship to the Reformation, saying of himself "I was the one" "qui olim praecursor extiti sanctae evangelicae doctrinae et quemadmodum etiam hodie exosam habui captivitatem babylonicam"[1] ("who became the forerunner of the holy gospel and still, as always, hate the Babylonian Captivity"). These words are meant to convey the message "I, who once took the stage as a precursor of the holy gospel, still to this day, in accordance with my views at that time, condemn and despise the Babylonian Captivity." The close relationship between *olim* and *hodie*, as well as the content of the phrase "Babylonian Captivity", are comprehensible only in light of the challenging final sentence in Luther's last letter to Staupitz, dated 17 September 1523. Luther ended this missive with the words "ut alienus a Cardinale tuo et papatu fias, sicut ego sum, imo sicut et tu fuisti"[2] ("I will not cease to hope and pray that you will abandon your Cardinal [Matthäus Lang] and the papacy as I have done, and indeed, more to the point, as you yourself once did").

Staupitz expresses clearly in this last letter his mistrust of the Reformation as a mass movement: criticism of the church is all too rarely made for reasons of faith (i.e., guided by the "yardstick" of faith)[3] and too many take the call of the gospel as a means of justifying fleshly license.[4] He also directs a pointed critique at Luther's rejection of monastic vows. Adiaphora or neutral things neither commanded nor forbidden

1. *WA Br* 3.264.34-36 (nr. 726; Salzburg, 1 April 1524).

2. *WA Br* 3.156.37f (nr. 659). I understand *alienus* in the sense of *alienare*, which in medieval documents pertaining to church law always refers to excommunication; however, see n. 11, below. On the interpretation of the insignificant-seeming interjection *immo* see my article " 'Immo': Luthers reformatorische Entdeckungen im Spiegel der Rhetorik," in *Lutheriana: Zum 500. Geburtstag Martin Luthers von den Mitarbeitern der Weimarer Ausgabe,* ed. Gerhard Hammer and Karl-Heinz zur Mühlen, Archiv zur Weimarer Ausgabe der Werke Martin Luthers 5 (Cologne, 1984), pp. 17-38.

3. "Intervenit proh dolor fere in singulis humanis exercitiis abusus, et rari sunt, qui fide metantur omnia . . ." ("Evil rears its ugly head, I am afraid, in almost every human activity, and there are very few who measure everything by the yardstick of faith . . .") *WA Br* 3.263.15-16. Cf. Rom. 12:2.

4. "Dominus Ihesus tribuat incrementum, quatenus evangelium, quod nunc auribus percipimus, quod in ore multorum volvitur, tandem vivamus, siquidem ad libertatem carnis video innumeros abuti evangelio" ("The Lord Jesus grants this growth [of the gospel], because we are finally living the gospel, which we now hear with our own ears, and which is on the lips and in the mouth of many, even though I see untold numbers abusing the gospel for the sake of fleshly freedom"). *WA Br* 3.264.24-26. Cf. Gal. 5:13.

ought not to be treated as issues touching the faith. An opinion still common in scholarship is that Staupitz thereby gave up on Luther and his program. On the contrary, he did not disassociate himself from his "former" pupil Luther. Rather, Staupitz emphasizes that they had both remained on the road they had once chosen together. To Luther's anxious question whether Staupitz had distanced himself from the gospel and simultaneously from himself, Brother Martin, Staupitz gave an unequivocal answer: I love you not only with the intimacy of Jonathan and David — "surpassing the love of women" (2 Sam. 1:76) — but even today believe what once made me a forerunner: I hate the Babylonian Captivity. Yet exactly what Staupitz abhorred cannot be deduced immediately from this statement.

II. *Pater et Praeceptor*

It is not difficult to discover how Luther perceived Staupitz's perseverance in true evangelical faith: Luther often commented on this theme. He owed to Staupitz not only the courage to embark on a doctorate in theology, and his liberation from the unbearable weight of anxiety concerning predestination, but also the solution to his central theological concern, the nature of true penance. Luther assured his spiritual and academic advisor, on 30 May 1518, in a letter attached to the *Resolutiones:* From you I learned, as though it had been straight from heaven — "velut e caelo sonantem" — the Biblical meaning of true penance.[5]

In a profound and broadly conceived study, Lothar Graf zu Dohna and Richard Wetzel have clearly delineated Staupitz's doctrine of penance, which was based on the idea that God's love ignites an all-consuming fire in us — a revolutionary departure from medieval tradition.[6] As a result, we can now work out exactly what Staupitz had to offer in his new definition of penance. When Luther addresses Staupitz in his last letter as *pater* and as *praeceptor,* it is no mere flourish of gallant courtesy. The reformer repeated the same sentiment in his own mother tongue at the end of his life, on 27 March 1545, explaining, as he wrote to Prince-Elector Johann Friedrich, that Staupitz "erstlich main Vater ynn

---

5. WA 1.525.10-12.
6. "Die Reue Christi: Zum theologischen Ort der Buße bei Johann von Staupitz," *Studien und Mitteilungen zur Geschichte des Benedikter-Ordens und seiner Zweige* 94 (1983): 457-82.

dieser lere gewest ist und ynn Christo geborn hat"[7] ("was at the very beginning my Father in this doctrine and gave birth to me in Christ"). There can be no doubt: Luther sees himself as Staupitz's pupil, and no attempt to downgrade this relationship of dependency to one of mutual influence can be squared with the sources.

III. *Captivitas Babylonica*

It is much more difficult to dig out to what extent and in which ways Staupitz saw his role as that of a spiritual father or, from the perspective of history (and salvation history), as a forerunner of the Reformation. The only key that will fit this hermeneutic lock is Luther's farewell letter of 1 April 1524 — assuming that we understand *olim* and *hodie* to be inseparable, as they have been shown to be. If we grant this, then Staupitz's perseverance and loyalty to the path of the gospel are expressed in the idea that his continued hatred of the *captivitas Babylonica* had not become separate from his earlier activities aimed at preparing the way for genuinely evangelical doctrine; rather, his role as forerunner is documented by his continued abhorrence of papal tyranny over the church.

It is quite possible that Staupitz's reference to the Babylonian Captivity is an echo of Luther's epochal, programmatic, Latin treatise of 1520, or, even more likely, of the boldly provocative treatment of papal power written in preparation for the Leipzig Disputation and published in 1519. Here Luther for the first time declared explicitly and in public that if Rome is not obliged to defer to Holy Writ, and if the pope has the exclusive right to interpret Scripture, then the right to examine papal doctrine in the light of biblical teaching and commandments is annulled: "Absit, absit ista plus quam Babylonica captivitas." ("To hell with this more than Babylonian Captivity").[8]

---

7. *WA Br* 11.67.7-8. (nr. 4088).
8. *WA* 2.215.2. Luther had already come very close to this conclusion in his interpretation of Psalm 9b (verse 9b) in his Psalms commentary: "Regnabit [antichristus] enim in Babylone ipsaque Roma et omnia vasa desiderabilia . . . in suam captivitatem ducet, sicut figurat captivitas Babylonica Israelis . . . Exemplis ista probaremus pulchre, nisi nostro saeculo per se abundarent." *Operationes in Psalmos 1519-1521*, part II: "Psalm 1 bis 10 (Vulgata)," ed. Manfred Biersack, Archiv der Weimarer Ausgabe der Werke Martin Luthers *(AWA)* 2 (Cologne, 1981), 600.10-12; 19-20. Cf., however, the conclusion of the *Resolutiones* (1518) — the foreword of which was addressed to Staupitz — where Rome is identified with "vera illa Babylon"; XXV in *WA* 1.573.25.

It is important to note the possibility that Luther and Staupitz may have drawn on a meaning of the *captivitas Babylonica* available to them both in the medieval tradition, one that has not yet received sufficient attention in scholarship.[9] Any such study would have to begin with the two most important teachers of the western church, Augustine and Jerome, who were the first sponsors of this tradition. The opposition between Jerusalem and Babylon is, after all, one of the main themes of Augustine's *The City of God*.[10] In his much-publicized letter to Asella (XLV), when he was forced in 385 C.E. to flee Rome, Jerome declared, almost as a formula of anathema, "ut de Babylone Hierosolyma regrediar nec mihi dominetur Nabuchodonosor, sed Iesus filius Iosedech" ("I leave Babylon and return to Jerusalem so that I will be a subject not of Nebuchadnezzar, but of Jesus the son of Joseph") — to which Jerome added a fraught paraphrase of Psalm 137: "How stupid I was, when I tried to sing the Lord's song in a strange land."[11] Augustine's vision of the *peregrinatio* (pilgrimage) of the entire church of Christ is thus applied to all those she has rejected.

A precedent closer in time and even in diction was available to Staupitz in the tradition he shared with Luther, that of the Observant Augustinians, specifically in the work of Johannes von Paltz (†1511). In his *Supplementum Coelifodinae*, written at the monastery of the Erfurt Augustinians in 1503, Paltz justifies his work with the necessity of strengthening all Christendom, since it is in great danger even after receiving the benefits of the jubilee indulgences.[12] In order to escape this peril, safe havens must be built for the faithful "ne iterum contingeret eos a Babyloniis abduci captivos in Babyloniam, de qua per gratiam sacramentorum et indulgentiarum erepti fuerant" ("lest it should befall them once again to be led away captive by the Babylonians to Babylon, whence they had been liberated by the grace of the sacraments and of indulgences").[13] Christians

---

9. The field has been surveyed in Hans Preuß's most important work, *Die Vorstellungen vom Antichrist im späteren Mittelalter, bei Luther und in der konfessionellen Polemik* (Leipzig, 1906), esp. pp. 22-32.

10. See the recent study by J. van Oort, *Jeruzalem en Babylon. Een onderzoek van Augustinus' De stad van God en de bronnen van zijn leer der twee steden (rijken)* (s' Gravenhage, 1986).

11. Psalm 136:4 (Vulg.); Jerome, *Corpus Scriptorum Ecclesiasticorum Latinorum* 54.327.12-16. I owe this insight to Peter Brown.

12. Paltz refers here to his preaching of jubilee indulgences on two occasions (1490 and 1502/3), both at the behest of Raimund Peraudi. See Berndt Hamm, *Frömmigkeitstheologie am Anfang des 16. Jahrhunderts: Studien zu Johannes von Paltz und seinem Umkreis*, Beiträge zur Historischen Theologie 65 (Tübingen, 1982), pp. 88-90.

13. Johannes von Paltz, *Werke 2: Supplementum Coelifodinae*, ed. Berndt

have already been liberated, but a relapse into exile is by no means unthinkable. Although Paltz understands the means by which grace is communicated, and thus the nature of the divine infusion of grace, in a way quite different from Staupitz and Luther, without a doubt he is thinking of (1) liberation from the Babylonian Captivity, which is (2) a real and direct danger to Christians as living beings and as believers.

Johann von Staupitz himself provided a precedent even closer in time and relevance in his Nuremberg Advent sermons of 1516, a Latin edition of which was published in 1517 under the title *Libellus de exsecutione aeternae praedestinationis*.[14] As Dohna and Wetzel demonstrate in their exemplary critical edition, Staupitz was in a position to draw on a medieval tradition rich in exegetical possibilities. He interprets the horrifying figure of Nimrod (Gen. 10:8-9) as a typological representative of Satan's drive for domination in the period following Noah; Satan has become the ruler of this world: *princeps huius mundi*.[15]

Building on long-established exegetical and allegorical traditions, with an express debt to the thought of Augustine and Jerome, Staupitz unmasked the long-term strategy of the devil along with his immediate war aims: "He wants to hunt down God's flock, and be said and believed to be God; for this reason he erects his kingdom *(turrim)* here on earth, in opposition to Jerusalem. After he has become king over all the world, the children of God will be forced to leave their ancestral land, and embark on a pilgrimage to Jerusalem. They cannot sing the song of the Lord in a strange land, only await with weeping the fall of Babylon and the exaltation of the holy city Jerusalem."[16]

Hamm with Christoph Burger and Venicio Marcolino, Spätmittelalter und Reformation 3 (Berlin, 1983), p. 447.26-28.

14. Johannes von Staupitz, *Sämtliche Schriften*, ed. Lothar Graf zu Dohna and Richard Wetzel; *Lateinische Schriften II: Libellus de exsecutione aeternae praedestinationis mit der Übertragung von Christoph Scheurl "Ein nutzbarliches büchlein von der entlichen volziehung ewiger fürsehung,"* ed. L. Graf zu Dohna, R. Wetzel, and A. Endriss, Spätmittelalter und Reformation 14 (Berlin/New York, 1979).

15. "Tunc enim monarchia dei ad apparentiam cessat, et diabolus princeps huius mundi regnare coepit." *Ibid.* 258.201. Staupitz did not have to "discover" the meaning of the *captivitas Babylonica* in Luther's work, but drew on a tradition to which they both had immediate access. Cf. Luther's later use — compared to Staupitz's — of the Nimrod myth. In his Psalms commentary (Ps. 9b:11), he refers to "Nimbroth" ("coepit esse potens": Gen. 10:8) in order to apply the text of the psalm not (yet) to the person of the antichrist but to his work, his tyrannical style of government. AWA 2 (as above, n. 8), 603.6-12; 11. Yet in *De captivitate Babylonica,* Luther states with clear finality: ". . . scio nunc et certus sum, Papatum esse regnum Babylonis et potentiam Nimroth robusti venatoris." WA 6.498.4-6.

16. "Venari de pecude dei vult ac dici aestimarique deus, hic erigit turrim contra

Christ, however, who in his role as "prince of peace" is Nimrod's opponent, does not allow his people in exile to perish, but visits and strengthens them through his servants, "the patriarchs, prophets, apostles, disciples, preachers and saints: the world is no longer and never again will be so lost that there are not at least a few such (messengers) to comfort it."[17] The power of love has triumphed already in the coming of Christ; there is no need to wait for his future return — that is the meaning of the perfect tense used to describe the *dénouement* of the cosmic drama.[18] The contemporary translation of Staupitz's humanist friend Christoph Scheurl reads:

> Als aber Christus die einhellig herschaft angenomen hat, do ist der fürst diser welt verurteilt und verdamet, Babylon zerbrochen und sein herzog verjagt.[19]

The theme of this most immediate of sources is not the "Babylonian Captivity", but rather the liberation from Babylonian tyranny, which is already a reality for the church, the body of Christ and the elect *(praedestinati),*[20] who are united to Christ through love.[21]

IV. *Et Hodie Fieri Cernitur*

Although the church — as the body of Christ — has been torn from the power of the devil, "Babylon broken and her Prince chased away," as

---

Ierusalem; adepta quoque monarchia terrae, filii dei relinquunt sua et — peregrinantes in Ierusalem — non possunt cantare canticum domini in terra aliena, sed lugentes praestolantur casum Babylonis et exaltationem Ierusalem sanctae." *Libellus* (n. 14 above), 260.203. Cf. n. 11, above.

17. "Servi dei fuerunt et sunt patriarchae, prophetae, apostoli, discipuli Christi, praedicatores et sancti homines; nec umquam desertus est mundus adeo, nec erit umquam, quin tales in consolationem habeant." *Libellus* 262.205.

18. "Quando autem Christus monarchiam accepit, princeps huius mundi iudicatus est, damnatus est, Babylon destructa, et princeps eius eiectus." *Libellus* 262.206.

19. *Libellus* 263.206.

20. Cf. David C. Steinmetz, *Luther and Staupitz: An Essay in the Intellectual Origins of the Protestant Reformation,* (Duke Monographs in Medieval and Renaissance Studies 4 (Durham, N.C., 1980), 42, 133-34.

21. On the differences between Luther and Staupitz concerning justification and sanctification, see my article " 'Tuus sum, salvum me fac': Augustinréveil zwischen Renaissance und Reformation," in *Scientia Augustiniana: Studien über Augustinus, den Augustinismus und den Augustinerorden,* Festschrift Adolar Zumkeller, OSA (Würzburg, 1975), pp. 349-94; 386-87.

Scheurl put it, nonetheless Babylon's rule can be grasped "even today": "et hodie fieri cernitur."[22] This rule of terror finds expression in the separation and variety of languages and customs, in the division of kingdoms, in war, hatred, theft, and murder.

The question of how far the raging of the antichrist reaches into the ranks of believers and thus affects the church in the here and now is not addressed in any systematic fashion. Staupitz does admit that the sins of the great prelates cause much scandal that can lead true believers astray, but only those believers who open themselves to this kind of behavior and make the sins of others their own. All criticism of the church is made subject to the principle that the righteous accuse themselves first, and only he who is without sin should cast the first stone.[23] In short, the "captivity" is interpreted in the Advent sermons of 1516 as the devil's drive for dominion, which was overcome and left behind by Christ's triumph over sin. This "diabolical captivity," the chaining of the devil, is so central a comfort to besieged Christendom that the "Babylonian Captivity," by comparison, receives hardly any attention.

Seen from this historical perspective, Staupitz's confession at the end of the path he had shared with Luther — on 1 April 1524, shortly before his death — is far more than mere imitation or the polite adoption of a concept already used by Luther. Staupitz's critique of the church has once again, as in his youth,[24] gone so far as to attack the pope. In his answer to Luther's final plea "ut alienus a . . . papatu fias, sicut ego sum, imo sicut et tu fuisti" ("that you will abandon . . . the papacy as I have done, and more to the point, as you yourself once did"), he stresses the continuity of his own thought.[25] In the Advent sermons of 1516, Staupitz gathered together in numerous versions all the elements connected in the medieval exegetical tradition with the opposition between Jerusalem and Babylon. However, in all instances, he subordinates this tradition to the preaching of "the final execution of eternal providence."[26]

22. *Libellus* 260.203.
23. *Libellus* 290.241-42.
24. For an analysis of the ecclesiology of the young Staupitz as he appears in his Tübingen sermons of 1498, see my article *"Duplex Misericordia:* Der Teufel und die Kirche in der Theologie des jungen Johann von Staupitz," in the Festschrift for Hans Anton Schmidt, *Theologische Zeitschrift,* Sonderheft 45 (1989) 2/3, 231-43; translated by Andrew C. Gow in this volume as *"Duplex Misericordia:* The Devil and the Church in the Early Theology of Johann von Staupitz."
25. *WA Br* 3.156.37-38. See, however, the argument of Johann Sallaberger, "Johann von Staupitz, Luthers Vorgesetzter und Freund, und seine Beziehungen zu Salzburg," *Augustiniana* 28 (1978): 108-54; 141.
26. The same can be said of the Salzburg sermons of 1518 and 1519. These

The ecclesiastical battles of the years 1517 to 1524 left their horrifying mark on all concerned. At the end of this period, Staupitz must
have heard in Luther's pleading prayer that Staupitz be today as formerly
"alienus a papatu" (hostile to the papacy), the deep horror of Jerome,
who applied the phrase of the Psalms "in a strange land" to the wander-
ings of the pilgrim church in its forced exile. The continuity of Staupitz's
thought does not, however, require that it be identical to Luther's. Therefore, that Staupitz did not come to the same conclusion as Luther and
abandon the papacy, despite having started out with the same analysis
of the church's situation, ought not to be misinterpreted as a sign of
weakness. He who once took the stage as a "forerunner" was not lacking
"even today" in the courage needed to repudiate the devil publicly. Rather,
he was certain that the "prince" had already been routed by Christ.

The difficulty — past and present — experienced by those who are
rooted in the ancient and medieval doctrine of God's omnipotence in
dealing with hard historical "facts" is demonstrated clearly by Luther:
"Yet the devil is lord in this world, and I was myself entirely unable to
believe that the devil was lord and god of the world until I discovered
that it is an article of faith: the ruler of the earth is the god of this
world."[27]

---

have been prepared by Wolfram Schneider-Lastin for the Staupitz edition (*Deutsche
Schriften I*, Spätmittelalter und Reformation 15). The difference is more in genre and
purpose than in theological position. In these sermons as well, God's mercy is the
foundation that bears the entire church.

27. "Aber der Teuffel ist herr jnn der welt, und ich habe es selbs nie können
gleuben, das der Teuffel solt Herr und Gott der welt sein, bis ichs nu mals zimlich
erfaren, das es auch ein artickel des glaubens sey: Princeps mundi, Deus huius seculi."
Wider die Antinomer (1539); WA 50.473.34-37.

Duplex Misericordia:
The Devil and the Church in the Early
Theology of Johann von Staupitz

I

In his wide-ranging survey of medieval theology, Martin Anton Schmidt has blazed a new and original trail that leads straight to the heart of four hundred years of medieval doctrinal tradition. Starting with Bernold of Constance, OSB (†1100), and ending with Nicholas Cusanus (†1464), Schmidt has devoted careful attention to the primary sources and made a thorough survey of the scholarly literature. His extensive essay is a standard reference work for scholars of all persuasions and a reliable guide to medieval intellectual history.[1]

Schmidt's independent and novel work can be summed up in three points.

(1) Four of the nine chapters are devoted to the period *after* Thomas

---

1. "Die Zeit der Scholastik," in *Handbuch der Dogmen- und Theologiegeschichte, 1: Die Lehrentwicklung im Rahmen der Katholizität*, ed. C. Andresen, A. M. Ritter, K. Wessel, E. Mühlenberg, and M. A. Schmidt (Göttingen, 1982), pp. 567-754.

"*Duplex Misericordia*: The Devil and the Church in the Early Theology of Johann von Staupitz," translated by Andrew Colin Gow from the original German article "*Duplex Misericordia*: Der Teufel und die Kirche in der Theologie des jungen Johann von Staupitz," in *Theologische Zeitschrift: Festschrift für Martin Anton Schmidt*, ed. Theologische Fakultät der Universität Basel (Basel, 1989), pp. 231-43.

Aquinas, and thus to the later Middle Ages.[2] More importantly, whereas traditional Protestant and Catholic scholarship long misunderstood or misrepresented this era as either a prelude (to the Reformation) or an epilogue (to the heyday of scholasticism), Schmidt takes great pains to address the theology of the later Middle Ages on its own terms, in all its conceptual depth and far-reaching influence.

Second, medieval mysticism is neither excluded nor treated as a stepchild to scholasticism, but developed as a separate and equally valid tradition — with a sharp eye for the characteristic intellectual dynamic of the mystical *itinerarium mentis*.[3] Schmidt establishes more than merely structural parallels between scholasticism and mysticism: in his description of the structures of scholastic theology, even in its most abstract details, it becomes clear that theologians were constantly listening for the voice of experienced faith; conversely, the affective theology of mysticism conveys precise doctrinal points.

(3) In the wake of that new wave of critical voices directed at the church in the age of conciliarism, the question as to the character and constitution of the church became an independent *locus de ecclesia*. This new issue in turn began to reshape the older *loci* formed by ecclesiastical tradition. Within and parallel to the new recognition of the *via moderna* and what contemporaries experienced as the nominalist revolution, the double question arose concerning not only the nature of the church — the church must be more than a *Platonica civitas*[4] as the *via antiqua* would have it — but also the church's visible constitutional reality, its palpable administrative apparatus, and its audible preaching.[5]

In addressing the critique directed against the established church by the young Johann von Staupitz, I will pass beyond the chronological

2. "Die Zeit der Scholastik," pp. 683-754.

3. Schmidt's historical analyses are persuasive in that they are based on his own detailed textual analyses. Two other examples of his method are "*Gratia* und *Gratitudo*: Zu Dionysius des Kartäusers Traktat ‹De Munificentia et Beneficiis Dei›," in *Zeitschrift für deutsches Altertum* 108 (1979) 95-112; and "*Jesus Christus simul Rex et Amicus* (Bonaventura, *Itinerarium Mentis in Deum* IV,5)," in *Gottesreich und Menschenreich: Ernst Staehelin zum 80. Geburtstag*, ed. M. Geiger (Basel/Stuttgart, 1969), pp. 47-67.

4. In his Apology on Art. 7 of the Confession of Augsburg ("Von der Kirchen", "On the Church"), Melanchthon adopts this term from Luther to dismiss the idea that evangelical doctrine saw the church as an object of faith that did not exist in concrete terms. See *Die Bekenntnisschriften der evangelisch-lutherischen Kirche* (Göttingen, 1986[10]), 238.21-22. Cf. Luther, *WA* 7.683.11 (1521).

5. Not only is the basic outline of John Hus's theology sketched out here, but this perspective also includes an evaluation of the critique of the church as justified by the doctrine of predestination, measured against the yardstick of concrete reality.

boundaries of that epoch of medieval theology studied by Martin Anton Schmidt. However, my study remains entirely within Schmidt's broad thematic sphere of interest[6] in that it concentrates on a significant late medieval theologian who bequeathed to posterity a unique combination of scholasticism and mysticism, and who made a lasting impression on what would be a world-historical era noted for its critical approach to the church — the Reformation.

II

Dated Salzburg, 1 April 1524, just nine months before his death (28 December), Staupitz's last letter to Luther is a theological time-bomb. This former vicar-general of the Augustinian Observants in Germany set out his personal position on the history of the church in one sentence, a sentence that still baffles scholars. It has evoked a multitude of conflicting interpretations in the intervening centuries. In the most controversial and most important passage of this letter, Staupitz says of himself "I was the one" ". . . qui olim praecursor extiti sanctae evangelicae doctrinae et quemadmodum etiam hodie exosam habui captivitatem babylonicam"[7] (". . . who became the forerunner of the holy gospel and still, as always, hate the Babylonian Captivity"). Staupitz is laying claim to continuity in his work, and although he was not exactly a man to hang his cloak according to the wind, he did undergo major upheavals in the course of his career. After a hectic period as vicar-general of the German Observant Augustinians, he vacated his professorial chair in Biblical Theology at the University of Wittenberg in 1512 and chose as his successor Martin Luther. In 1515, Staupitz made Luther District Vicar, entrusting him with the management of the most important cloisters. In 1518, when Luther and Cajetan came into conflict, Staupitz supported his former pupil, now professor at Wittenberg. After resigning his position as vicar-general of the "reformed congregation of the Augustinian Eremites in Germany" in August of 1520, Staupitz went to Salzburg as cathedral preacher. In 1522,

6. Cf. Schmidt's new interpretation of Staupitz's consolatory treatise on death, *Von der Nachfolgung des willigen Sterbens Christi*, which he published in 1515 at Leipzig. Martin Anton Schmidt, "Rechtfertigungslehre in Staupitz 'Nachfolgung'," in *Kontinuität und Umbruch: Theologie und Frömmigkeit in Flugschriften und Kleinliteratur an der Wende vom 15. zum 16. Jahrhundert*, ed. J. Nolte, H. Tompert, and C. Windhorst (Stuttgart, 1978), pp. 142-144.

7. *WA Br* 3.264.34-36 (nr. 726).

he received a papal dispensation that allowed him to join the Benedictine order and become abbot of St. Peter's, the Benedictine monastery at Salzburg.

Concerning Staupitz's function as a "forerunner" of the Reformation, until the 1960s the two leading Staupitz scholars, one Protestant and one Roman Catholic, refused to recognize the validity of Staupitz's self-assessment. In 1962, Ernst Wolf summarized the result of decades of research by suggesting that Staupitz's "alienation from Luther" only increased in Salzburg — not surprisingly, because "Staupitz never really managed to understand his 'pupil' completely."[8] Two years later, Reinhoud Weijenborg made the same argument, but more pointedly, in a volume that — surely by coincidence — bears the imprint "Rom bis Tetzel," claiming that Staupitz "hardly understood Luther's teaching. . . . As abbot [of St. Peter's], he completely disassociated himself from the Lutheran movement."[9]

Although prompted by entirely different motivations, Wolf and Weijenborg achieved some kind of ecumenical concord by doubting Staupitz's claim for two reasons. First, they both highlighted Staupitz's later alienation from Luther and rejection of his teachings, a development that is said to have occurred after 1520; second, they insisted that Staupitz had, at bottom, misunderstood Luther and his doctrines. To Weijenborg, Staupitz's intellectual "edge" simply was not keen enough; indeed, his works were "theologically superficial."[10] Wolf approaches the problem from the opposite perspective, emphasizing Luther's theological depth and breadth, the dimensions of which Staupitz could not grasp. "Alienation" and "rejection" suggest psychological states of mind; however, the historian is duty-bound to counter with Staupitz's own clear and final declaration of love: "In te constantissimus mihi amor est, etiam supra amorem mulierum, semper infractus"[11] ("Above all love for women, my love for you is unchanging and forever unbreakable"). One needs to have read only a little of the work of this former vicar-general of the Augustinians, and only a few of his letters, to know that this is no mere ornament, but a genuine expression of his feelings. The phrase "olim praecursor" (formerly a forerunner) must not be separated from the words "etiam hodie" (even today). The point of this letter is not continuity of doctrine, but the concord of hearts.

8. "Staupitz hat seinen ‹Schüler› im Grunde nie eigentlich zu verstehen vermocht." *RGG* 6³(1962), col. 343.

9. Staupitz "[hat] Luthers Lehre kaum durchschaut. . . . Als Abt distanzierte er sich vollkommen von der lutherischen Bewegung." *LThK* 9 (1964), col. 1026.

10. *LThK* 9, col. 1026.

11. *WA Br* 3.268.8-9 (nr. 726).

The other, nonpsychological explanation is equally wrong. Instead of casting doubt on the authenticity of Staupitz's declaration, it questions the basic intellectual capacity and theological judgment of Luther's teacher. Now that there is a critical edition of Staupitz's main theological works,[12] there is no longer any excuse for doubting Staupitz's independence and creative ability in dealing with Scripture, the Church Fathers, and medieval tradition. The critical queries and objections that Staupitz makes within the framework of his clear loyalty to Luther's cause show that at the end of his life, his critical faculties were in no way diminished. He concerned himself, probably under the cloud of the troubles at Wittenberg, with exactly the same questions that moved Luther. Staupitz was so disturbed by the two obvious problems associated with the rapid introduction of the reformed liturgy — terrified consciences and misunderstood freedom — which had forced Luther to return posthaste from the Wartburg to Wittenberg, that it seems as though Staupitz never read the *Invocavit* sermons, and Luther must therefore have appeared to him to be the leader of the Wittenberg movement.

Be this all as it may, Staupitz recognized the decisive breaking point very clearly. Nonetheless, his relations with Luther and his trust were unchanged: "Now I have written myself dry. I wish I could talk with you for a single hour and lay bare to you the innermost thoughts of my heart."[13] Staupitz did the next-best (and most likely) thing, sending to Luther the young *baccalaureus* Georg Führer — "my brother" and "your pupil" — with the request to help him quickly attain the Master's degree at Wittenberg:[14] there is no hint of alienation or rejection, on either side. Luther promptly complied with Staupitz's request.

Unquestionably there were basic differences between Luther and Staupitz;[15] but they ought not to be used to contradict Staupitz's claim to

---

12. See Johannes von Staupitz, *Sämtliche Schriften: Lateinische Schriften, I: Tübinger Predigten,* ed. R. Wetzel, Spätmittelalter und Reformation 13 (Berlin/New York, 1987); *II: Libellus de exsecutione aeternae praedestinationis mit der Übertragung von Christoph Scheurl: Ein nutzbarliches büchlein von der entlichen volziehung ewiger fürsehung,* ed. L. Graf zu Dohna, R. Wetzel, and A. Endriss, Spätmittelalter und Reformation 14 (Berlin/New York, 1979).

13. "Sat scripsi, utinam vel unica hora liceret tibi colloqui et aperire secreta cordis." *WA Br* 3.264.29-30 (nr. 726).

14. *WA Br* 3.264.30-33 with n. 17.

15. Cf. my contribution to the Festschrift for Adolar Zumkeller: " 'Tuus sum, salvum me fac': Augustinréveil zwischen Renaissance und Reformation," in *Scientia Augustiniana,* ed. C. P. Mayer and W. Eckermann, Cassiciacum 30 (Würzburg, 1975), pp. 349-94.

the position of Luther's *praecursor* — guide or forerunner. It has not yet been clearly understood that Staupitz is no more claiming to be identical with Luther than the precursor John the Baptist can be said to have taught the same things as Jesus of Nazareth. Above all, it is vital to recognize that the figure and function of the "forerunner" had developed during the Middle Ages, under Joachimite influence, from a personal to an instrumental office. And in this letter, Staupitz does not claim to be Luther's forerunner, but the forerunner of the doctrine of the holy gospel.[16]

Since the word *praecursor* suggests a clear claim to some kind of connection but does not specify its details, we are all the more dependent on the second part of the sentence. Here the suggested continuity is the common rejection of the Babylonian Captivity. Here again we stumble over a gap in scholarship: it is by no means certain just what Staupitz meant by this phrase.[17] Staupitz knew very well how Luther would understand these words, since the Wittenberg reformer had devoted his programmatic work of 1520 to this topic; as early as June of 1519, he had termed the pope's claim to exclusive authority to interpret Scripture a Babylonian Captivity.[18]

Moreover, in a letter of 27 June 1522, Luther painted for Staupitz a startling and personal portrait of the *captivitas Babylonica* as a call to meet the challenge of the approaching end time. He now adds to his unmasking of the pope's tyranny over Scripture and the sacraments:

Destruendum est mihi, mi Pater, regnum illud abominationis et perditionis Papae, cum toto corpore suo. Atque id agit iam sine nobis, sine

16. Here we must note that the abbot Joachim (†1202), whose teaching on the Trinity had been considered heretical since his condemnation in 1215, was once again accepted and read in the fourteenth century as an "orthodox" authority. This can be documented not only from the works of Pierre d'Ailly but also, as has recently been demonstrated, from the works of Heinrich von Langenstein. According to M. H. Shank, "By 1390, Langenstein was praising Joachim in public for his attempts to forecast the Last Things from Scripture." In: *"Unless You Believe, You Shall Not Understand": Logic, University and Society in Late Medieval Vienna* (Princeton, N.J.: Princeton University Press, 1988), p. 168. On d'Ailly's reception of the apocalyptic Joachim, see my evidence in *Werden und Wertung der Reformation* (Tübingen, 1989³ [1977]), p. 70, n. 50; English version: *Masters of the Reformation: The Emergence of a New Intellectual Climate in Europe*, trans. Dennis Martin (Cambridge: Cambridge University Press, 1981), p. 56, n. 42.

17. In another context I have attempted to shed some light on the medieval prehistory of the *captivitas Babylonica* from the exegetical tradition defined by Augustine and Jerome to Johannes von Paltz. See my article "Captivitas Babylonica: Die Kirchenkritik des Johann von Staupitz," in *Festschrift Lothar Graf zu Dohna* (Darmstadt, 1989), pp. 97-106; Engl. trans. in this volume, above, pp. 26-34.

18. WA 2.214.33–215.2.

manu . . . at ego indies magis provoco Sathanam et suas squamas, ut acceleretur dies ille Christi destructurus Antichristum istum.[19]

Even without our help, God has already started to crush the tyranny, based on misery and terror, of the pope — "However, I see my task as provoking the devil and his satellites more and more every day, in order to hasten the Last Day, when Christ will destroy the antichrist." Staupitz, therefore, had every reason to know how Luther had learned gradually to interpret the "captivity" of the church. However, this does not mean that Staupitz had followed Luther every step of the way in his exegesis: we cannot interpret his abhorrence of the "captivity" as a "Lutheran" reaction. If we discount as the last resort of a desperate interpreter the suggestion that Staupitz was being disingenuous out of dishonesty or weakness, then the only possibility left is to understand the term *captivitas Babylonica* — as used by a man who had been able to leave the Augustinian order for the Benedictines only with papal permission — as expressing abhorrence for the tyranny exercised by the pope over the interpretation of Scripture and the sacraments, but without taking Luther's final step, that is declaring the Pope to be antichrist, the apocalyptic enemy of the church.

Just such a differentiation between critique of the papacy and total rejection — as alternative reactions to the *captivitas Babylonica* — occurs in a letter written by Staupitz on 4 January 1521, to his successor as vicar-general, Wenzeslaus Linck (who assumed his duties 20 August 1520). Staupitz developed a less radical but nonetheless pointed critique, making a suggestive pun on the papal name of Giovanni de'Medici (Leo, the lion), applying the roaring of the lion (1 Pet. 5:8; in the Vulgate "diabolus tanquam leo rugiens circuit," used in the traditional monastic evening prayers to refer to the raging of Satan) to Leo X's plan to "devour" Staupitz.[20] As early as the beginning of December 1520, Erasmus reported from Louvain that a Roman instruction to Cardinal Archbishop Matthäus Lang was circulating at Cologne; the eminent churchman was instructed to force Staupitz to recant.[21] Although Staupitz wrote to his fellow Augustin-

---

19. *WA Br* 2.567.19-20 (nr. 512). On the meaning of the expression "provoco Sathanam et suas squamas," see my article "Teufelsdreck: Eschatology and Scatology in the 'Old' Luther," in this volume, below, pp. 51-68, esp. 62-64. As it turns out, Luther's words "Atque id agit iam sine nobis, sine manu . . ." characterize Staupitz's position; "at ego . . ." emphasizes Luther's own strategy.

20. *WA Br* 2.246, n. 2.

21. *WA Br* 2.246, n. 2. See *The Correspondence of Erasmus*, 8, *1520-21*, translated by R. A. B. Mynors, annotated by Peter Bietenholz (Toronto/Buffalo/London, 1988), pp. 107-8. Cf. Allen, *Opus Epistolarum Des. Erasmi Roterodami*, 4, *1519-21* (Oxford, 1922), 399.92-96 (nr. 1166).

ian Linck on 4 January 1521 that he had been able to escape the clutches of Rome by refusing to retract theses that had been proposed not by himself but by Luther, by 9 February Luther knew that Staupitz had given in and submitted himself to papal authority. In response, Luther entreated Staupitz: "Unde, si te Christus dilexerit, coget te ad revocationem huius scripti, cum in ista bulla damnarit omne, quicquid de misericordia Dei hactenus et docuisti et sapuisti"[22] ("Therefore, if Christ loves you, he will force you to retract your signature [on the papal condemnation; i.e., your recognition of papal jurisdiction over such matters], for this damnable Bull condemns everything that you have ever taught and understood about the mercy of God").

This conclusion, so convincing from Luther's theological perspective,[23] is entirely off the mark for Staupitz. The key portion of this essay is devoted to the first important theological model proposed by the young Staupitz, in order to show that he was able to combine the mercy of God *(misericordia Dei)* with critique of the church in so seamless and complete a fashion that even at the end of his life he was able to hate the Babylonian Captivity of the church without declaring war on the pope as the antichrist.[24]

22. *WA Br* 2.263.17-19 (nr. 376; written 9 February 1521). Since according to Staupitz's letter to Linck (see n. 20), "this Bull" condemned theses of Luther's, the reference may well be to the forty-one theses appended to the Bull that threatened Luther with excommunication (24 July 1520). The actual Bull of excommunication *Decet Romanum Pontificem* contains not a single phrase of Luther's. Moreover, although it was decreed 3 January 1521, it was made ready only on 28 January; it reached the papal nuncio Aleander at Worms sometime after 10 February. See Martin Brecht, *Martin Luther,* [1:] *Sein Weg zur Reformation 1483-1521* (Stuttgart, 1983[3] [1981]), pp. 406-7.

23. Already in his *Operationes in Psalmos* (foreword dated to 27 March 1519), Luther formulated his position in a powerful burst of polemical principle: "Ubi Antichristus . . . hic nulla misericordia prorsus." *Operationes in Psalmos 1519-1521,* part II: Psalms 1–10 (Vulg. numbering), ed. G. Hammer and M. Biersack, Archiv zur Weimarer Ausgabe der Werke Martin Luthers 2 (Cologne, 1981), pp. 602-8.

24. Although Martin Brecht has made a superb compilation, given the predetermined boundaries of his Luther biography, of the data relevant to Staupitz's attitude to Rome in the years 1520-1521, there are palpable tensions in Brecht's interpretation. On the one hand, Staupitz is said to have recognized expressly the pope's right to pass judgment ("Ausdrücklich erkannte er den Papst als Richter an"): *Martin Luther* (as in n. 22), p. 407. On the other hand, Brecht speaks of the "partial" submission, which had depressed Luther. *Martin Luther,* p. 408. However, Luther bewailed Staupitz's *complete* submission without qualifiers: "Vere nonnihil me contristavit ista tua submissio . . ." ("That wretched acquiescence of yours makes me very sad indeed"). *WA Br* 2.264.47 (9 February 1521). Furthermore, Staupitz did not "expressly" recognize the pope as the highest authority. Nonetheless, Luther's judgment was correct, more so than he knew. When he writes *submissio,* Luther is thinking of

III

The main theme of Staupitz's "Tübingen Sermons of 1498"[25] was the mercy of God *(misericordia Dei)*. In the first of the thirty-four sermons on the prologue to the book of Job, the theme is the "Magna utique misericordia dei nobis in Iob ostensa" ("God's great mercy as shown to us in the case of Job"). This mercy consists of God's refusal, at the same time as he was giving the law to the Jews, to withhold his *misericordia* from the heathens, as he made manifest through Job.[26] David C. Steinmetz hit the nail on the head when he entitled his as-yet-unsurpassed work on the theology of Johann von Staupitz *Misericordia Dei*.[27] His opinion of the "Tübingen Sermons," however is not entirely favorable. In a more recent work, Steinmetz deplores "the strict homiletical" and "artificial framework" of the "Tübingen Sermons."[28] However justified this evaluation may be for users of the often opaque and sometimes misleading edition of Georg Buchwald and and Ernst Wolf,[29] the new critical edition, which clearly separates citations from Staupitz's own material, ought to allow the reader to form a much clearer impression of the lively progression and natural order of Staupitz's thought.

We now turn to sermons 16-23, because in them the theme of *misericordia* is treated in considerable depth and breadth, while at the same time the right to criticize the church, and the limits of this critique, are clearly sketched out within the framework of a description of the devil's offensive strategy. Beginning with Job 1:12 — "Ecce universa, quae habet, in manu tua sunt; tantum in eum ne extendas manum tuam"! (Vulg.) —, and, as elsewhere in the sermons, making intense use of Gregory the Great's commentary on Job, Staupitz makes it very clear from the start that although the devil is in subjective terms God's

---

a signature, whereas — if we are not mistaken — this *submissio* was so much a part of the foundation of Staupitz's theology that Luther's contrasting of "before" and "after" the Bull threatening excommunication is pointless: "Quod si ante bullae istius notitiam et Christi ignominiam sic fecisses, nihil contristasses" ("Had you done thus before knowing about this Bull and Christ's humiliation, there would be no grounds for sadness"). *WA Br* 2.264.48-50.

25. The year 1498 is just as doubtful as the information that these were "sermons" preached at Tübingen. On these questions, see the balanced analysis of R. Wetzel in the introduction to his critical edition: *Tübinger Predigten* (as in n. 12), pp. 3-11.

26. *Sermo Primus*, in *Tübinger Predigten* 48.26-28.

27. *Misericordia Dei: The Theology of Johannes von Staupitz in Its Late Medieval Setting* (Leiden, 1968).

28. *Luther and Staupitz: An Essay in the Intellectual Origins of the Protestant Reformation*, Duke Monographs in Medieval and Renaissance Studies 4 (Durham, N.C., 1980), p. 50.

29. Staupitz, *Tübinger Predigten* (Leipzig, 1927); preface by O. Scheel.

"enemy," in objective terms he is merely an executive instrument of the divine Judge. The devil is allowed to tempt people only so that miserable sinners will have occasion to discover their state and seek refuge in divine compassion.[30] The principle which he would later develop in his 1516 Advent sermons is fundamental here as well: "miseria misericordiam provocat" ("misery calls forth mercy").[31]

The true meaning of diabolical attacks on humanity, however, is inaccessible unless we recognize that Staupitz conceived of God's mercy as a *duplex misericordia,* a twofold mercy: one aspect concerns temporal goods, which must all perish; the other, heavenly gifts, which endure forever.[32] Through temptation, Job — and, with him, all human beings subject to temptation — learns to distinguish between these two types of *misericordia.* When a human being, both a Christian and a sinner, loses his temporal goods, God having thus unmistakably refused him the first, that is, temporal mercy, it becomes clear, Staupitz argues, that God has decided to comfort people dispossessed in this fashion with the second, heavenly *misericordia:* "In hoc ergo manifesta est dei misericordia, quod iustos et fideles servos variis temptationibus submittit" ("In this, therefore, God's mercy is manifest, because he makes his just and faithful servants undergo many temptations").[33] Therefore, when God gives the devil the right to dispose of any and all of Job's property, excepting only Job's person, the Devil has received the power, or rather a mission, to tempt, but not to overcome.[34]

In sermons 16 and 17, Staupitz develops the theme of the devil's (delegated) authority within the worldly sphere connoted by God's first type of *misericordia,*[35] demonstrating how much more important the second type of mercy is — through which God clothes the naked sinner and adorns him with heavenly gifts. In the following sermons, Staupitz turns to the question that is our real concern: To what extent is the devil permitted to exert his influence on the church? *De facto* the devil is given

---

30. "Ideo autem temptationem miserorum admittit, ut miseros se cognoscant et misericordiam petant aut ad ipsum recipiendam consentiant." *Tübinger Predigten* (n. 12 above), 277.81-83.

31. *Ibid.* 227.330. Cf. *Libellus de exsecutione* (n. 12 above), cap. X, para. 63ff.; 150ff.

32. "Sed nunc adverte, quare per temptationes ad illam misericordiam disponat; est enim duplex misericordia: quaedam est in terra . . . alia in coelo." *Tübinger Predigten,* 278.92-94.

33. *Ibid.* 279.130-32.

34. *Ibid.* 282.225-27.

35. "Ideo non plus potest diabolus, quam nobis expedire deus cognoscit." *Ibid.* 286.70-71.

the opportunity *(libertas)* to tempt human beings by the negligence of those who are officially responsible for barring his way.[36] But just how far can he go, and what can be done to counter his attack?

Staupitz gradually directs the reader toward the spiritual drama of the devil's attacks on the holy House of the Lord. The point of departure is the recognition that the laity tend toward moral laxity if they are not held to the straight and narrow path by the disciplined example of their priests. But if the priests themselves start to behave licentiously, those who needed to strengthen themselves with the good example provided by their clerics will certainly license themselves to do whatever they want as well. The consequences would not be quite so disastrous if only the prelates, the superiors of the priests, had not themselves submitted to worldly temptations. Wherever the great prelates live in sin, the devil's sphere of influence will expand to terrifying dimensions: those who have the authority to reprimand and correct sinners are ineffective moral leaders, because they themselves sin without fear of punishment.[37]

The tone of Staupitz's admonitions becomes harsher. If he had failed to make it sufficiently clear, he now states unmistakably that he is turning from general thoughts about the effects of sin on the church to a description of the miserable state of the church in his own time. The "salt test"[38] is stated in no uncertain terms: "You are salt to the world. And if salt becomes tasteless, how is its saltiness to be restored? It is now good for nothing but to be thrown away and trodden underfoot" (Matt. 5:13). The church is full of just such weak, tasteless salt: many bishops, archdeacons, and cathedral canons sin so openly and with impunity that no one has the courage to confront them in public, to accuse them, and to name their sins. The reason: *they* are the judges responsible for punishing sins, for the betterment and discipline of morals.

Then Staupitz unveils the central formula, a paradox capable of astonishing even those who have made a careful study of his teachings on *misericordia:* "O Deus, quanta misericordia toleras, ut inimici tui iudices tuorum constituti sunt!" ("O God, how great your mercy must be for you to allow your enemies to sit in judgment over your children!").[39] He is convinced that no human being and no human piety are

36. As Staupitz concludes in *Sermo* 23; *ibid.* 349.6-8.
37. "Cum vero et illi perperam agunt, recipit multam nimis auctoritatem temptandi diabolus, quid scandalum difficulter amovibile vulgus recipit, cum ille qui culpas corrigendas ore dicit sine omni poena delinquit. . . ." *Ibid.* 304.71-74.
38. "Videamus, sine sal infatuatum sit in ecclesia" ("Let us see whether the salt of the church has lost its bite"). *Ibid.* 307.143.
39. *Ibid.* 307.147–308.148.

capable of bearing this burden. "Those who love you so much that for
your sake they do not refuse their respect even to the cruel and raging
wolf, the vicar of Christ who has been called to your service — they love
above all measure, because they respect their enemy, the devil's
Ganymede, for your sake."[40] Just as the higher prelates are the only ones
allowed to absolve sinners from grave crimes, God's righteousness shows
in his reserving for himself the punishment of the gravest of all sins. For
this reason, one ought to call for and counsel patience,[41] since the public
castigation of abuses — such as priestly concubinage — scandalizes
simple believers, who already have to put up with enough scandal. But
one may well weep over the disarray of the church.[42]

In these evil times ("hoc tempore malo") there is only one way to stay
firm in faith: to hold fast to the preaching of the Word, for the word of God
is just, even if it is announced by morally reprobate preachers.[43] Preaching
communicates the right way of living. It is important to make sure even

---

40. "Qui enim sic te diligunt, ut nec iniustum lupum rapacem in tuo servitio
constitutum vicesque gerentem Christi tui propter te honorare contemnunt, videntur
amplius aliquo modo dilexisse, quoniam et inimicum suum satellitem diaboli propter
te venerantur." *Ibid.* 308.152-56.

41. Here we come across the apocalyptic interpretation of the papal principle
"Papa a nemine iudicatur" ("the pope is to be judged by no man"). I cannot devote
any more attention to the theme of *patientia,* a topic which is not only "naturally"
suggested by the story of Job, but which also is directly linked to Staupitz's idea of
spiritual tranquility *(Gelassenheit)* — for Staupitz, the heart and soul of the true
Christian life. For more on this topic see A. Endriss, "Nachfolgung des willigen
Sterbens Christi," in *Kontinuität und Umbruch* (as in n. 6, above), pp. 93-141, esp.
126ff. *Patientia* as a form of tranquillity also demarcates — as it always had in the
mystical tradition — the limits which criticism of the church may not exceed.

42. ". . . prohibet autem me offensio simplicium. . . . Sed flere libet ecclesiae
damna. . . . *Tübinger Predigten* (n. 12 above), 312.259-62. Staupitz reminds Luther
of this duty — to protect the *simplices* — in his final letter: "Cur igitur turbantur
simplicium corda. . . ." *WA Br* 3.763.13.

43. ". . . non derelinquet eos, sed est semper praesto ad docendum, quid agere
debeant, et haec per praedicatores, sint boni sive mali; verbum tamen dei, quod praedicant verum est. . . ." *Tübinger Predigten,* 315.349-51. I will not elaborate on the idea, so
important for the way the Observants saw themselves, that God will appoint other,
uncompromised preachers in accordance with Rev. 20:1, who will reprimand, set straight
(corrigere), and teach *(informare):* "qui auctoritate apostolica praedicant." Staupitz bases
this interpretation on Lyra; of course he is not thinking only of the orders named by Lyra,
the Franciscans and Dominicans *(ibid.* 315.353-59 with n. 130), but also of the
Augustinians. Here we encounter the sense of mission shared by the Observant Augustinians and the controversy concerning the Observance, which culminated in the years
1509-1511 See my overview in *Luther: Mensch zwischen Gott und Teufel* (Berlin, 1987[3]
[1982]), pp. 148-51; English version: *Luther: Man between God and the Devil* (New
York, 1992[2] [1989]), pp. 140-43.

small children attend church so that as adults they will not find it unusual. Christian life is upheld by the word of God: "Let the preachers be silent for six years, and then you will see how true this is."[44]

The texts cited here speak so clearly for themselves that no further commentary and only a few conclusions are necessary: if God's *misericordia* is so immeasurably large that he allows the church to be entirely subject to sin, weak and perverse in all its highest offices, and if God allows the devil to spread his poison into the innermost regions of the church, then the true believers are also obliged to bear it and tough it out by preaching God's word. Thus we find in the early work of the young Staupitz, in his observations on the *misericordia Dei*, the foundations of the principles that will allow him, in the 1520s, to see the state of the church clearly and call it as he sees it — a Babylonian Captivity — and yet to remain in captivity and bear it patiently.

Luther accused Staupitz in 1521 of condemning, with his obeisance to the pope, "everything he had ever taught or understood about the *misericordia Dei*."[45] Even the younger Staupitz of the "Tübingen Sermons" would have answered clearly: No, I did not condemn these things, precisely because of the *misericordia Dei!* Whether or not the six years in Salzburg, far away from Protestant territory, were enough to provide an answer to his "six-year test" is impossible to say: "Let the preachers be silent for six years. . . !" The answer to this question belongs to the *secreta cordis* ("innermost thoughts of the heart") that Staupitz would so dearly have loved to share with Luther in a last learned and loving colloquium.[46]

---

44. "Vita namque christiana, ut dixi, solo verbo dei conservatur. Cessent praedicare sex annis praedicatores ecclesiae, et apparebit quod dixi." *Tübinger Predigten,* 315.371–316.373.

45. See n. 22.

46. *WA Br* 3.264.29-30.; cf. n. 13; see also Luther's revealing dream concerning Staupitz: "Hac nocte somnium de te habui, tanquam recessuro a me, amarissime me flente et dolente, verum te manu mota mihi dicente, quiescerem, te reversurum esse ad me; hoc certe verum factum est hoc ipso die." *WA Br* 1.515.75-78.

II. THE IMPACT OF LUTHER

Teufelsdreck: Eschatology and Scatology in the "Old" Luther

Luther himself did not see his activities broken into periods (e.g., "young Luther"; "mature Luther"; "older Luther"), nor did he see his preaching as the beginning of a "movement:" Rather, Luther preached as one standing between God and the devil at the end of time. One should not apologize, by way of psychogrammatic history or periodizations of Luther's life, to explain away verbal vituperation as that of an old and unhappy man. Even as early as 1515 Luther was using scatological language against that great foe, the devil. Luther's method was to shout down the foe with the admonition "Das frissestu!" and to sling back its own filth *(Teuffels Dreck)*. Thus the traditional picture of Luther as old, vile, and bitterly resigned is misleading and should be revised. This article pursues some of the implications of such revisions for both theologians and social historians, taking into account twentieth-century ecumenical concerns.

I. The "Old" Luther

The very formulation of the title marks progress in Luther research by the mere inclusion of quotation marks around the word "old." For the

"Teufelsdreck: Eschatology and Scatology in the 'Old' Luther," *Sixteenth Century Journal* 19 (1988): 435-50.

uninitiated the old Luther is the innocuous reference to the last phase in the reformer's life. The quotation marks call attention to the fact that what seemingly is an historical category, de facto functions as a travelers' advisory and more often even as an apologetic construct, on the rebound from an equally myth-ridden designation, namely the "young" Luther.

Though it is often unclear whether the term "young" Luther refers to the so-called Reformation breakthrough and the emergence of early Reformation theology in Luther's study and lecture hall, or whether it also includes his first public impact, it is safe to say that it relates to the years when this so-called young man was well into his thirties. With the "old" Luther we have not even a vague idea what is precisely meant in terms of age and life span.

Such a clarification has not been seriously attempted — as a matter of fact, the very term reveals a lack of interest, for two seemingly very different reasons. To begin with, in an effort to correct the long-standing emphasis on the theological significance of Luther, the more recent social history of the Reformation has emphasized the impact of Luther on public opinion, assumed to be limited to the early years. This view is well presented by R. W. Scribner in his fine book *The German Reformation,* from which three eloquent quotations suffice to delineate his position. First, Scribner stresses that onto Luther were "projected very traditional ideas about the expected *reformator,* the holy man, the prophet, the saint sent by God."[1] Here the verb *projected* is to be underlined, since Luther's inner "difficulties" are interpreted as "typical of a monastic piety based on spiritual athleticism, something which few lay folk either experienced or aspired to."[2] Hence, Scribner's conclusion does not come as a surprise; the Reformation "attained wider significance because it quickly outran Luther's ideas, and achieved a near-revolutionary impetus of its own."[3] The old Luther thus must seem irrelevant to later Reformation history — Luther is merely the spark in the kindling wood, not the fire itself.

This dissociation of Luther's intention from his impact had been prepared for by the church historians who were so long the chief laborers in the vineyard of Luther studies. The history of Luther research in this century is the story of concentration by contraction, moving in ever smaller concentric circles from the large grasp of European Reformation history around the turn of the century to an increasing preoccupation

1. *The German Reformation,* Studies in European History (Atlantic Highlands, N.J.: Humanities Press, 1986), p. 4.
2. *The German Reformation,* p. 8.
3. *The German Reformation,* p. 24.

with the German Reformation, then with Luther's thought, and finally with the Reformation breakthrough and the young Luther. Here the "old" Luther no longer functions and is indeed ignored, not because of the assumption that the reformer has stopped being a factor in Reformation history, but because after the full articulation of Luther's theological program and its confessional formulation in Augsburg 1530, he ceases to be required reading for the delineation of a Protestant position over against medieval Catholicism.

As a matter of fact, the lopsided interest of social historians and church historians alike has reached such graspable proportions that a Luther scholar working in libraries as far removed from each other as Stanford from Harvard, and Amsterdam from Jerusalem, has had to come prepared with a sharp butcher's knife to open the uncut pages of the later volumes in the Weimar edition. This lacuna, to be sure, applies to many more sources for the later sixteenth century and is more generally indicative of the need to enlarge the scope of our research from Saxony and the City Reformation to the third reformation — the reformation of the refugees. But there is no doubt in my mind that in each case the measuring of the distance between intention and impact, inception and reception, program and propaganda, reform and revolt, must claim the place of absolute priority in Reformation research. Valid results can only be achieved, however, when the data on both sides of the ledger are taken seriously and conclusions are reached on the basis of a mutual respect and with a sense of dependency on the scholar "on the other side of the house" — now too often thoroughly missing.

As far as the reduction of Luther's significance to the young Luther is concerned, there are clear and encouraging signs that this development has been recognized as a misleading distortion. Heinrich Bornkamm, as so often before, also in this case a trailblazer, published in 1979 *Luther in Mid-Career,* which, though de facto covering the decade between the diets of Worms and Augsburg, was intended to reach the Truce of Nuremberg 1532, which Bornkamm saw as the basis for "Luthers ganzes späteres Wirken."[4]

The two-volume 1983 *Festgabe,* in which forty-two Luther scholars from East and West Germany cooperated under the editorship of Helmar Junghans, is fully dedicated to the life and work of the older Luther. Partly for political reasons, as one may surmise, the demarcation line is drawn after the Peasants' War: the twenty last years of Luther's life, from 1526 through 1546, are treated as one period in *Leben und Werk Martin*

---

4. See the preface of Karin Bornkamm in *Martin Luther in der Mitte seines Lebens* (Göttingen: Vandenhoeck & Ruprecht, 1979), p. 9.

Luthers von 1526 bis 1546.[5] Though even the explicit assignment to concentrate on the later Luther did not force all authors to overcome their predilection for the young Luther, this festival volume has the considerable merit of opening up whole dimensions of Luther's thought and actions which were hitherto underexposed, and it documents particularly well the extent to which the senior Luther continues to be fully involved in the political power play pertaining to the survival of the Reformation in imperial Germany.

The second volume of Martin Brecht's comprehensive Luther biography follows the lead of Bornkamm in choosing the year 1532 as the end of the "older" and the beginning of the "old" Luther. Whereas Brecht characterizes the middle phase with the subtitle *Ordnung und Abgrenzung der Reformation 1521-1532,*[6] which he justly regards as the characteristic elements of the second phase, the sharp-sighted Luther scholar will find it hard to close his eyes to the fact that exactly the same description can apply to his third volume, dedicated to the last twenty-five years. As Bornkamm before him, Brecht sees the peace in the empire of 1532 as the fulfillment of Luther's political and theological program, which Luther is dedicated to "consolidate" in the future.[7]

The danger is that this vision of Luther as the *Defensor Pacis* can be readily used to condone the verbal ferocity of the old Luther's invectives against Papists, Jews, and Turks and to excuse these as a necessary and perhaps even courageous defense of peace in the empire. No such apologetic tendency can be discerned with the one scholar who explicitly dared to pursue the theme of the old Luther with all his scatological vituperation, so repugnant to modern taste. In the Luther year 1983, Mark U. Edwards, Jr. published *Luther's Last Battles: Politics and Polemics 1531-46,* in which he did not hesitate to indict Luther's style as "vulgar and abusive." Though intent on avoiding psychohistory, de facto Edwards relates this characterization of Luther senior to a psychogram, to an X-ray of his soul which makes ever so clear why Luther scholars have been brief in their allusions to the later writings.

---

5. Two volumes (Göttingen: Vandenhoeck & Ruprecht, 1983). Though Bernard Lohse suggests the same division, he appropriately suggests "statt von dem alten Luther von Luther in seinem Spätwerk zu reden." "Der alte Luther," in *Martin Luther und die Reformation in Deutschland: Vorträge zur Ausstellung im Germanischen Nationalmuseum Nürnberg 1983,* Schriften des Vereins für Reformationsgeschichte 194 (Schweinfurt: Weppert GmbH, 1988), pp. 135-51; 136.

6. *Martin Luther,* vol. 2, *Ordnung und Abgrenzung der Reformation 1521-1532* (Stuttgart: Calwer Verlag, 1986), pp. 9-10.

7. *Ordnung und Abgrenzung,* 411.

Exactly because of the fact that this psychogram is so plausible that it might well sway a future generation of Reformation scholars, Edwards's conclusion deserves to be quoted in full: "The older Luther was a man who saw the world engaged in a metaphysical struggle between good and evil. He was a man gripped by apocalyptic hopes and fears; a man who had given his name to a movement that had taken, for him, a painful and frustrating direction." Edwards sees Luther as a "worried observer," who "tried to maintain his influence," but who became deeply "disappointed" since "he found himself misunderstood": "So as his own death neared, bringing with it both promised relief and fear for the fate of the movement after his death, he became ever more pessimistic, praying not only for his own release but for the end of the world."[8]

This psychogram is at once alluring and delusive: alluring in that there is no effort to salvage Luther as the divine pastor or God-sent preacher. Edwards has succeeded to un-Saint Luther and draw him back into everyday life. But his psychogram is also delusive insofar as it tries to explain Luther's verbal vituperation as the expression of an old, disappointed, embittered man who sees the fruits of a life's work wasted by devilish powers and devious opponents.

This critique of the "old" Luther is by no means a sniping assault, but rather the expression of regret, born out of esteem for the achievements of the reformer. Yet, if Luther were to look at this psychogram as in a mirror, he would hardly have been able to recognize his own features. This discrepancy as such is no historical proof that Edwards's psychoanalysis of Luther is erroneous. After all, since Denifle, Grisar, and Reiter this view has been advanced by many a scholar, though here stated most eloquently and more convincingly, while presented in more political terms. The mirror test does indicate, however, that we should grant Luther a second hearing, unencumbered by modern assumptions about invective and mental stress.

Before we can take up this task, we may be well advised to clarify the time span which can be associated with the old Luther. Of the proposals listed, the range of years 1526-1546, suggested by Helmar Junghans, makes sense only to the extent that it provides the much-needed shift away from an overemphasis on the early years of Luther's development. Useful as this reorientation is, the year 1526 as point of

8. *Luther's Last Battles* (Ithaca, N.Y.: Cornell University Press, 1983), p. 208. However, on the programmatic nature of Luther's invective, cf. Josef Schmidt, "Luther the Satirist: Strategies and Function of His Satire," in *The Martin Luther Quincentennial,* ed. Gerhard Dünnhaupt (Ann Arbor: Michigan Germanic Studies, 1984), pp. 32-47.

departure is not argued on the basis of Luther's stages of growth, but merely on that of what Junghans called "the present state of scholarship" — which if seriously applied would rather point to the year 1530, the period after the Augsburg Confession.

Much more appealing is the decision of Bornkamm and Brecht to opt for the year 1532, since it has the advantage of relating Luther's life to the political history of the Reformation. The major drawback of this watershed is, however, that soon after the Truce of Nuremberg in 1532, which indeed delighted Luther, this event is so fully relegated to the background of Luther's consciousness that he no longer refers to it in later letters, sermons, or treatises. Edwards's suggestion to assign Luther's so-called "last battles" to the years 1531 through 1546 runs into the problem that except for the front against the Turks (as Luther indicates explicitly, he had started his offensive already in April 1530),[9] the other battles can be retraced not only to the "young," but even to the "youngest" Luther — by which I mean the period before 1517.

If one has no ulterior motives and wants to be guided by biographical considerations, the study of the last ten years of Luther's life have a special claim on our attention, since Luther wrote on the 23 August 1535: "I am aging not in years but in energy, no longer able to do any useful work in the mornings. Pray for my blessed departure from this horrible age."[10] Though such a sense of waning energy is not singular,[11] Luther is now increasingly aware of the fact that time is running out, and the end of his life is approaching. This very awareness, however, that time is "running out," has been the *cantus firmus* in a much larger sense of the word ever since the end of 1518, and marks the real inception of Luther's "last" battles. To this theme we must turn now.

II. The Politics of Polemics

The legend is slow to die that Luther in his old days became an apocalyptic, convinced he was living at the end of time amidst the struggle

---

9. "Ego incipio totis animi affectibus in Turcam et Mahometum commoveri . . ." *WA Br* 5.285. 7-10 (24 April 1530).

10. "Ego non annis, sed viribus decrepitus fio, ad labores antemeridianos paene totus inutilis factus. Tu ora mihi pro beato transitu ex isto pessimo saeculo. . . ." *WA Br* 7.239.10-12.

11. See Luther's wonderful play on words in the letter to Melanchthon of 12 May 1530: "Caput meum factum est capitulum." *WA Br* 5.316.17.

between God and the devil and pessimistic about the chances of the cause of the Reformation in this world. Indeed, this legend is very much alive, notwithstanding the ample evidence to the contrary throughout Luther's works. Elsewhere I believe I have shown that Luther as the reformer cannot be understood unless he is seen located between God and the devil, who have been involved in a struggle — not in a *metaphysical* but a *real* battle — ever since the beginning of the world — a battle which now "in these last days" is reaching a horrible climax. As the assiduous reader of Augustine and Bernard, Luther knew that after the first phase of persecutions in the Roman empire and the second phase of attacks by heretics assailing the church from without, in the third phase the enemy would come from within, when the antichrist would successfully disguise himself as the *vicarius Christi*.

We encounter here doubtlessly three basic elements in the tradition usually referred to as "apocalyptic" eschatology: the struggle between God and the devil, the approaching end of time, and the appearance of the antichrist. With varying degrees of profundity, recent research has established that this type of eschatology is by no means only a medieval or especially a late medieval phenomenon, but reaches well into the seventeenth century. Jaroslav Pelikan has traced "some uses of Apocalypse in the magisterial reformers."[12] Bernd Moeller has gathered further evidence for the eschatological orientation in early Reformation preaching,[13] and Paola Zambelli has edited a precious volume with a Luther quote in the title " *'Astrologi hallucinati'*: Stars and the End of the World in Luther's Time."[14]

This very advance allows us to be more precise in delineating Luther's particular type of apocalyptic eschatology. Already before 1520, when Luther was stunned by reading Hutten's edition of Valla's discovery of the falsification of the Donation of Constantine, he started to look for the signs of the third and last period in history. Thus when he answered in March 1518 Eck's *Obelisci* — Eck's critical comments on Luther's own ninety-five

---

12. In *The Apocalypse in English Renaissance Thought and Literature: Patterns, Antecedents and Repercussions*, ed. C. A. Patridus and Joseph Wittach (Ithaca, N.Y.: Cornell University Press, 1984), pp. 74-92. Pelikan's close association of Luther and Calvin — exactly at this point worlds apart — shows not the limits of the author, but of comparative exegesis as an historical tool.

13. "Was wurde in der Frühzeit der Reformation in den deutschen Städten gepredigt?" in *Archiv für Reformationsgeschichte* 75 (1984): 176-93. Luther's unique vision is homogenized with general expectations of the end time. Over against astrological *prodigia* he was particularly skeptical.

14. (Berlin: de Gruyter, 1983).

theses — he was not so much shocked by Eck's error in defending the indulgences as by the fact that apparently the time had come that a Catholic theologian was prepared to take the side of diabolical distortion: "It is a horror for me to hear such, not from a Jew, nor a Turk, nor a Bohemian, but by a Catholic theologian."[15] When one is familiar with apocalyptic language, then the sequence of the persecution by the Jews, the Turks, and the heretics makes one look for the next and decisive step or phase of the persecution "from within" — no longer just by the enemies *(inimici)*, but now also by "friends of God" *(amici)*, by Catholics.

While this discovery is dawning on Luther, he is not yet certain how to respond — What style of answer is now required? He knows that he should not be impressed by the fact that Eck can invoke the authority of Gabriel Biel: "Dumb dribblers deserve disdain."[16] At this point, he still feels that he should not answer with irony but rather with commiseration: "Facessat Ironia, miseratione potius opus est."[17] Soon afterward, not even sarcasm would suffice: the faithful are in "Babylonian Captivity" (1520).

In the year 1523 we reach a next decisive stage following the Diet in Nuremberg which had decided to mitigate some of the sharpest points of the Edict of Worms, calling for a future council to decide on basic issues. Luther responded to the imperial mandate, in which he was convinced that non-Christian, yes, indeed anti-Christian, laws were promulgated — one of them spreading misery by forbidding the marriage of priests.

At the risk of losing some of the apocalyptic power of Luther's vocabulary of urgency, I venture to render the key passage into English: "For God's sake, you princes, do something to humanize the mandate, at least on this point. No one has an idea how horribly, blasphemously *(lesterlich)*, and scandalously the devil succeeded in having his way. Hitherto this was not publicly known, but now it has been brought into the open by the gospel. Why should you want to become his ally and load your conscience? . . . I am practically forced to shout too loud and cry out, 'May God strip Satan speedily and unmask him,' in order to expose him — then it will help that [= what] we now shout so loud."[18]

---

15. "Horror mihi est audire, non a Iudaeo, non a Turco, non a Bohemo haeretico, sed a Theologo catholico. . . ." WA 1.297.33-35. For the impact of Valla's discovery, see Scott H. Hendrix, *Luther and the Papacy: Stages in a Reformation Conflict* (Philadelphia: Fortress, 1982), pp. 98ff.

16. "Frivolos declaratores oportet vilipendere." WA 1.296.30.

17. WA 1.298.21-22.

18. "Ich werde schier gezwungen alzu lautt schreyen und sagen, Gott wollte dem Satan schnell die hautt abzihen und an den tag bringen, so wirtts denn helffen was wyr itzt schreyen." WA 12.66.25-36.

"Too loud" — that is what scholars have noticed! But his "shrill voice" has been interpreted as an involuntary consequence of mental stress rather than a conscious strategy of reform.

In this urgent appeal, three crucial elements come together which have been overlooked hitherto. The three elements are: the "blasphemy" of the devil, his surreptitious mode of operation, and hence, in response, the need to call him "forth" by shouting him "down."

First we should turn to the epithet for the devil, *lesterlich,* here tentatively translated in accordance with the Greek root as "blasphemously." For Luther, however, "blasphemy" embraces the abominable, abhorrent, despicable, and revolting, because it is literally execrable, that is, cursed. This confusing range of connotations suddenly receives focus and takes on a clear meaning when we turn from the Greek to the Latin root, *detractans.* It is this root which provides the bridge to the scatological language of feces and urine so long associated with the old Luther. To establish this connection we have to reach back to the young Luther at the peak of his career as an Augustinian monk.

On 1 May 1515, Luther preached a sermon against the vice of slander or *back*biting ("contra vitium detractionis"), which, as he makes abundantly clear, refers to the *lower* back. In this Latin sermon he uses for the first time the German word *Teuffels Dreck,* and proceeds to clarify how backbiting is related to the excrements of the devil.[19] Before I quote two salient passages, I want to emphasize that we are not dealing here — to name just the obvious options — with some loose locker-room talk, with a careless exchange over the beer table, with words spoken by an old man who has lost his touch and must get attention by reaching for an anal vocabulary, or with a man who as a consequence of waning vitality and virility allows his repressed peasant background to break through the thin veneer of academic civilized behavior.

The text I turn to is not taken from the Table Talk, but from a sermon — an early sermon. In the pulpit stands in 1515 not the young, but the "youngest" Luther — who can still quote Gabriel Biel as an impressive authority.[20] He had been designated to preach the solemn ceremonial sermon before the priors and select members of his order, the Reformed Augustinians, gathered for their triennial chapter meeting in Gotha. Immediately after the sermon, Luther was elected as the right

---

19. WA 1.50.14.
20. WA 1.44.15; 45.34. Biel, *Collectorium* 4, d. 15, q. 16; ed. Werbeck and Hoffmann, 4.2 (Tübingen: J. C. B. Mohr [Paul Siebeck], 1977), 334-41.

hand of Staupitz and placed in charge of eleven monastic houses and the only two *studia* in Erfurt and Wittenberg — the very "foundation of the order."[21]

This "election sermon"[22] deals most appropriately with a passage of the Constitutions of his congregation which in chapter 44 has designated the sin of slander as work of the devil *(diabolica suggestione)*; the immediate occasion may well have been the stubborn undercurrent of critique on the part of the extreme Observants against Staupitz and (since 1511) also against Luther. The chief backbiter, as Luther points out, is the devil himself, because while he is called "Satan" in Hebrew and "Diabolus" in Greek, he is called "Detractor" in Latin.[23] Therefore a slanderous detractor is not merely a galling nuisance but a pestiferous associate of Satan — *Omnis lingua detractoris est lingua Diaboli* (50.6):

> A backbiter does nothing but chew with his teeth the excrements of other people and sniff at their filth like a swine. Thus, human feces becomes the greatest pollutant, topped only by *Teuffels Dreck*.[24]

Whereas it is typical for a human being to defecate in private, the detractor makes it a public session. He defames by changing a good odor (i.e., *bona fama*, good reputation) into evil stench, and he delights in rolling in feces; according to God's just judgment he does not deserve better: "Flee him, man . . . since the maw of the slanderer is the chasm of hell which spews stench from the abyss of all filth."[25] And now Luther breaks into German, when the great slanderer comes and says, "Sehet

---

21. "Attente demum provideant, quomodo studia, in quibus fundamentum ordinis consistit, continuentur. . . ." *Constitutiones* (Nuremberg, 1504), cap. 36. I have used the "printout" of the critical edition of Wolfgang Günter, to be published in *Johann von Staupitz: Sämtliche Schriften*, ed. Lothar Graf zu Dohna and Richard Wetzel, vol. 5, *Gutachten und Satzungen* (Berlin: de Gruyter, 1988).

22. According to the statutes, this sermon is to be preached on the first full day of the chapter meeting, after morning mass and before the elections. I call it "election sermon" because this theme is prescribed: "Post hoc [the mass and invocation of the Holy Spirit] sedentibus omnibus, fiat sermo in communi exhortatorius de electione pastoris." *Constitutiones*, cap. 32.

23. WA 1.45.17-18.

24. WA 1.50.12-14. This background lends realistic dimensions to the breakthrough — the discovery of the meaning of Rom. 1:17, on the *cloaca* of the Augustinian monastery in Wittenberg. Cf. my article "Wir sein pettler: Hoc est verum," *Zeitschrift für Kirchengeschichte* 78 (1967): 234ff.; Engl. trans. in *The Reformation: Roots and Ramifications* (Edinburgh: T & T Clark, 1994), pp. 91-115.

25. Ergo fuge eum, homo. . . . Est enim os detractoris vorago inferni, quae spirat . . . ex profundo omnium fecum. WA 1.51.5-8.

wie hat sich der beschissen" — see how he covered himself with shit — then the effective answer is, "Das frissestu!" — stuff it, eat it yourself.[26] This "scatological" counterattack is not merely a good defense — it is the only defense.

There are many more revealing aspects to this sermon, which for understandable reasons has never been translated, or for that matter quoted by Luther scholars. The main point is, however, that all true Christians stand in a large anti-defamation league and are called upon to combat the God-awful, filthy adversary, using his own weapons and his own strategy: "Get lost Satan, eat your own shit!" This same anti-defamation strategy is put in the service of the Reformation in the often reprinted and even more often plagiarized 1521 *Passional Christi und Antichristi* — which Jaroslav Pelikan regards as "fateful" because of its identification of the pope with the antichrist, but which Luther describes as "bonus pro laicis liber."[27] On the final page of his text, placed as captions under woodcuts of his good friend "Meister Lucas Maler,"[28] Lukas Cranach, Luther warns that this book cannot be forbidden by the authorities because it is not a *Schandbuch;* after all, it exposes the filth of Canon Law which distorts the truth of Christ.[29] Hence, the *Passional* is not a detraction, but a detergent!

In its compendium volume, which is at the same time the graphic illustration of Luther's last and most ferocious writing against the papacy, *Wider das Papsttum zu Rom, vom Teufel gestiftet,* Luther addresses the pope as "du unverschampts lügen maul, lester [!] maul, Teufels maul,"[30] because he has produced stinking shit laws that smell to heaven, namely his *Drecket* and *Drecketal.*[31] This woodcut sequence of 1545, usually referred to as the *Papstspotbilder* and regarded as conclusive proof for the anal vulgarity of a sick and bitter old man, opens with the presentation of the birth of the antichrist out of the lower intestines of the devil, and concludes with two woodcuts showing the most effective way to deal with the pope, by directing a *Pfurtz,* or fart, against his ban, and releasing feces in his tiara. In this way, as the Latin caption advises: *Adoratur Papa Deus Terrenus.*[32] In the thirty years between the election

26. *WA* 1.51.24-25.
27. See the letter of 7 March 1521 to Spalatin. *WA Br* 2.283.24-25. Cf. Pelikan, as in n. 12, above.
28. *WA Br* 2.349.99.
29. *WA* 9.715.1-4.
30. *WA* 54.277.3-4.
31. *WA* 54.271.26-27.
32. *WA* 54. Appendix, reproductions 1 and 10-11.

sermon of 1515 and the pictorial satire of 1545, the one new element is the antichrist and his identification with the pope. The association of the devil with defecation, and the use of feces to combat him, have remained the same, and thus have absolutely nothing to do with disappointment or senility in the last years of life.

The foregoing was the extensive but necessary explanation of *lesterlich* as the disdainful epithet for the detestable operation of the devil. This loaded term, however, is but the first of three expressions in the passage quoted from the "young" Luther, written in the year 1523. Now, the next two can be more readily understood. The antichrist can only operate secretively, without public exposure, till through Luther's mission his disguise is exposed and "nu durchs Evangelion er fur bricht."[33] Luther never refers to himself as the "Reformator," but he does claim that through him the light of the gospel has come to shine again. Rather, the gospel's *primary* function is not — as assumed today, and as was indeed the case in the City Reformation — to change *obvious* injustice by introducing social legislation to establish *biblical* justice, but to unmask *hidden* injustice, thus saving the souls of duped Christians and opening the eyes of the secular authorities for their mandate to establish *civil* justice.

Hitherto, the antichrist and the curia could operate under the cover of darkness and thus catch the souls of Christians unawares. Now his invasion of the church is publicly exposed. To point to this diabolic mimicry and disguise, Luther can use the expression found in Erasmus's *Adagia:*[34] *monstrum ali.*[35] In German texts he will invariably speak about the devil and his *Schuppen.* These are the scales on this snakelike dragon, his typical disguise toward his seemingly so pious servants which when stripped away will reveal the evil profile of the master himself.[36] The word of God scrapes the scales off the devil, which exposes him and shocks the enemies of the gospel who unwittingly are under his command — or, as Luther can invert the image, who are "ridden by him."[37] Here we discern the apocalyptic "network" in which the offensive but crucial sentence in Luther's later answer to Erasmus is to be understood.[38] The

33. WA 12.66.27-28.
34. *Adagia* 2.5.98 (485).
35. WA Br 1.209.24; 2.258.13-14.
36. See the article "Schuppe," in Jacob and Wilhelm Grimm, *Deutsches Wörterbuch,* 12 (Leipzig, 1899), 2012-25.
37. Your vengeance is not only directed "an euern lieblichen Verfolgern, sondern viel mehr am Teufel der sie reitet." WA 15.72.12-13. (1524).
38. Cf. human beings as the *iumentum* ridden by God or the devil, in *De Servo*

gospel shocks the misguided, captivated Christians out of their blind ignorance so that they can now be converted.[39]

The very ferocity of Luther's language, his high pitch, has the double purpose of unmasking the devil and shouting to God *(clamare, schreien)*, so loud that he will intervene to skin the devil and expose him for all to see.[40] This double purpose in crying aloud the gospel, to confront the devil and pierce the ear of God, has a twofold impact. It provides for a time of grace before the coming of the *Dies irae* (and *Dies gratiae*), for the *interim* in which the blind servants of the devil can be converted: it creates space for what we usually call "the Reformation." But since the preaching of the gospel evokes the reaction of the antichrist all the more, it also brings closer the final *adventus,* the second coming and the last day of the world. Thus on the one hand "the prophet at the end of time" stands shoulder to shoulder with all the saints, the last of the just (cf. Gen. 18:23-33), to form a wall of protection against the impending wrath of God.[41] On the other hand, the very appearance of the gospel accelerates the events in the last phase of the end of time, and thus the prophet invokes and announces the intervention of God which will bring the *true* Reformation.

The so-called "disappointment" of Luther is not a reaction to the historically *perceived* impact, but part and parcel of Luther's understanding of the *expected* impact of the gospel. This applies already to those early years which we like to refer to as the "triumphant epoch" of Reformation progress. Thus Luther can write in the fall of 1523 to the Christians in Riga, Reval, and Dorpat that he hopes that the gospel there will find better roots than in the old empire:

> With us, the better part of the people wants neither to hear nor to tolerate the gospel; the more amply God offers to us his gift of grace, all the more furiously react the princes and the bishops, and start with "alle breyte schupen des Behemoth sich da widder [zu] streuben [und] lestern [sic!]. . . .[42]

Arbitrio, WA 18.635.17-22 (1525). Cf. the earlier version in a sermon dated 9 October 1524: "Tu es der hengst [horse] diabolus te equitat. Aut sub diabolo es aut spiritu sancto." *WA* 15.714.31-32; quoted by Martin Brecht, *Martin Luther,* 2 (as in n. 6, above), 220.

39. *WA* 15.73.15-17.

40. *WA* 12.66.34-36.

41. ". . . ponamus nos murum contra Deum pro populo in isto die furoris sui magni." *WA Br* 2.479.36-37. Letter of 19 March 1522 to Link. On the same day to Grebel, 476. 21-22. Cf. *WA* 15.362.24-27.

42. *WA* 12.147.13-148.7; 147.15.

This does not mean that Luther expects success elsewhere to come more readily than in Germany. In a second letter to Riga of some eight weeks later, at the beginning of 1524, he writes explicitly:

> After all, it is not to be expected that either with us or with you the gospel, which now shines anew, will fare any better than it did at the time of Christ and the apostles, or, for that matter, since the beginning of the world.[43]

On the contrary, Luther states soberly, it will get worse before the last day, it will get worse "as it undoubtedly will and must come to pass."[44] Such expectation does not allow for disappointment about failure, but only for surprise about success.

III. The Prophet of the End Time

In the foregoing we have tried to show that the traditional picture of the old and therefore vile and bitterly resigned Luther is untenable and misleading. In this epilogue I should like to pursue some of the implications of this revision. The first implication for Luther research, in the more technical introspective sense of the word, is obvious: we will fail to grasp his self-understanding if we do not see him as emerging from the beginning of his public career onward as the apocalyptic prophet at the end of time, placed in the increasing power struggle between God and the devil.

I should like to point to two further implications for the redirection of research in the two major schools in Reformation studies; for brevity's sake I shall personalize these by using the names of Bernhard Lohse and Robert Scribner. The Hamburg church historian Lohse — one of the foremost Luther scholars in Germany — is a worthy representative of that respectable and fine tradition in Luther scholarship which has patiently surveyed and precisely identified all the stages and all the loci in Luther's thought. Yet by not realizing that a modern concept of "Reformation" is employed — replacing Luther's understanding of God's plan and timetable — Luther becomes the mastermind and architect of "the Reformation *movement*" instead of the forerunner and the prophet,

43. WA 15.360.19-21.
44. WA 15.362.16-17.

who in the short interim left before the final intervention of Christ raises his voice to call for the Day of the Lord and erects the shield of the gospel to buy time for conversion.

His denominational reading of the "Reformation" does not prevent Lohse from criticizing Luther at some crucial points. As a matter of fact, in a recent article Lohse shows himself deeply embarrassed by what he calls "Luther's polemics," referring to the antipapist works of the old Luther in the years 1541-1545. To improve the contemporary ecumenical climate, he calls for a public recantation of Luther's designation of the pope as the antichrist. Ashamed by this *faux pas,* he urges Lutherans to respond in kind to the confession of guilt, formulated by Pope Paul VI at his opening of the second session of Vatican II. After all, Luther attacked the pope with a "matchless mordancy" beyond all propriety: "Luther hat mit einer nicht mehr zu überbietenden Schärfe den Papst als Antichristen abgelehnt."[45]

It cannot be my task here to probe the validity of an ecumenical strategy advocated by German Lutherans or, for that matter, by spokesmen for the American dialogue between Lutherans and Catholics. I am inclined to believe, however, that we touch here upon a structural problem in the confessional approach to the sixteenth-century Reformation in general and to Luther in particular. Notwithstanding its impressive and lasting achievements by way of critical editions, scholarly journals, and invaluable monographs, the phalanx of scholars on "this side of the house" has a penchant toward the exploration of the past in terms of the needs of the present, which proves then to carry too high a price when Luther and the historical record are adjusted to the needs of contemporary Christianity.[46]

Of structural significance is the assumption that Luther's apocalyptic strategy of exposure-by-confrontation is the kind of external, timebound polemics which one can strip away in order to get to the "real

45. *Luther* 57 (1986):143-48; 147. In 1980 Lohse had already expressed his embarrassment about Luther's antipapist furor and characterized *Von Papsttum zu Rom* as "totally and extravagantly polemical"; its pictures "must also have stimulated the lowest instincts of those who saw them." *Martin Luther: An Introduction to His Life and Work* (Philadelphia: Fortress, 1986), p. 89. Note that the "battle between God and Satan" is relegated to a subsection of "Luther's View of History" and dealt with in less than half a page. *Martin Luther,* p. 195.

46. I bypass here the minor historical question whether Pope Paul VI indeed "asked for forgiveness" when he decided not to revoke the ban of Luther, for which many had pressed. Historically seen, his formulation with its conditional phrasing, "Si quae culpa est . . . ," falls far short of the declaration of guilt in the message of Pope Hadrian VI, conveyed to the Nürnberger Diet on 3 January 1523. *Deutsche Reichstagsakten,* Junge Reihe 3.396.15-25; 397.1-8; 397.14-398.9.

Luther." To reduce Luther's strategy to bad manners and foul language is not unlike asking a child to leave the dinner table to go brush his teeth and clean his nails; or perhaps even more apropos, to ask a furious colleague first to calm down and then to rephrase his intentions. Luther's so-called "polemics" are to be equated with his intentions, and his vocabulary can only be translated — and if one feels the need, *then* to be excused — after it has been acknowledged that it is part and parcel of the total apocalyptic "framework."

In short, one cannot apologize for Luther's attack against the pope without apologizing simultaneously for his attack against the devil and with that for his preaching of the gospel as the initiation of the Reformation and for his posture as the chosen prophet at the end of time. Unfortunately, Luther's ferocity is by no means *unüberbietbar*: Luther can very well be matched and indeed surpassed in his mordancy against the pope, namely by all those who repeat his words without sharing his apocalyptic web of assumptions, of which verbal assault is an essential and deliberate part.

Turning now from the church historians to those "on the other side of the house," I should like to question again one of the most eminent of the school representatives, in this case the spokesman for the social history of the Reformation, Robert Scribner. I select one representative statement which is intended to explain why Luther's message could play only a limited role in the ensuing Reformation movement: "Luther's difficulties were more typical of a monastic piety based on spiritual athleticism, something which few lay folk either experienced or aspired to."[47] As every good writer is bound to do, Scribner makes here a tempting appeal to the reasonableness of the average reader. Avoiding the theological jargon of the traditional church historians, this is an anthropological shortcut by direct appeal to the modern reader's assumption that what he "feels" himself today is also germane to the sixteenth century. The existence of one monolithic monastic piety is assumed which is to be so clearly identified by the reader with spiritual lofty, unattainable, olympic ideals that "of course" it was alien to the experience and aspirations of the common man. *This* so-called "common man," however, is a construct.

The critique which Thomas Brady directed two years ago over the head of Steven Ozment, at the whole field of intellectual history, namely that there lurks a grave danger in trying to construct a whole trend or revolution on the basis of one or two documents,[48] applies here all the more. After all, the category "few lay folk" risks the quantification of a

47. *The German Reformation*, p. 8; cf. n. 2, above.
48. See *Sixteenth Century Journal* 15 (1984): 225-27; 226.

social group which, by definition, is and remains voiceless without the literary evidence of its spokesmen. I for my part do not hesitate to see in much of what nowadays is called "simple" superstition — in the pilgrimages, in the support for a Drummer of Niklashausen as well as in the Peasant Revolt — proof of the "spiritual athleticism" of the common man. That at least is the clear evidence of its spokesmen.

What precisely "spiritual athleticism" entails in each case must be measured within the context of the economic and social reality in which each group operates. The current trend to replace the increasingly unknown printed sources by unpublished archival materials does not guarantee a more reliable access to reality. It cannot eliminate the hazardous but unavoidable jump from the observed singular expression, event, experience, or set of circumstances to a general historical assessment. For the two schools on either side of the house, common sense will continue to be the indispensable creative element required in writing that history, which leads from singular observations to general conclusions. In our case, this same common sense credits the so-called common man — once divested of the disdainful connotation of simple credulity — with more discretionary power than presently assumed. The usual medieval Latin equivalent for the common man is *idiota*, the unlettered or layman — in either case a far cry from our "idiot."[49]

But there is more than this formal debate of method. Luther's lifelong battle from 1515 through 1545 against the hitherto hidden and hideous power of the greatest detractor of all times, the devil, cannot and should not be reduced to propaganda "For the Sake of Simple Folk." In one of the most precious chapters in his important book on Reformation propaganda, Scribner deals with our theme under the heading of popular culture. After placing Luther in the context of a whole series of late medieval and early Reformation scatological satires, he reaches the conclusion: "The Reformation tried to present itself in the form of a popular movement."[50] Applying Mikhail Bakhtin's conclusion about Rabelais to his own sources, Scribner sees in the use of feces "a reduction of the sublime to the mundane,"[51] and makes the penetrating observation — well beyond anything church historians have written on the theme — that "the material

49. Cf. Yves Congar, "Clercs et laics an point de vue de la culture an moyen âge: 'Laicus' sans lettres," in *Studia Mediaevalia et Mariologica* (Festschrift Carolo Balic O.F.M.) (Rome, 1971), pp. 316ff.

50. *For the Sake of Simple Folk: Popular Propaganda for the German Reformation*, Cambridge Studies in Oral and Literate Culture 2 (Cambridge, 1981), pp. 59-94; 94.

51. Bakhtin, *Rabelais and His World* (Cambridge, Mass.: MIT Press, 1968), pp. 19-21; Scribner, *For the Sake of Simple Folk*, pp. 81-82.

bodily principle was used to desacralize the numinous and withdraw it from the realm of religious veneration." And indeed Scribner dares to go one step further in explaining the early impact of Luther in this way: "If Reformation popular propaganda was highly successful, it was because it relied so heavily on what was taken for granted in popular culture."[52]

Three observations are in order. In the first place, it seems to me that Scribner links too exclusively popular culture with a gross language "readily recognizable to the common folk of the time." Though not easy to document, common sense suggests that, at least until the eighteenth century, body language guarantees communication with people on all social levels.

The second observation concerns the fact that the so-called "spiritual athleticism" of the monks is by no means so far removed from what "lay folk either experienced or aspired to." As Luther's election sermon of 1515 clearly documents, monastic language apparently lent itself to communication in that kind of body language which today we associate with scatology.

And finally, the foregoing documents that Luther's so-called "vulgar polemic" is not a marketing device, and clearly refutes the thesis that the Reformation "tried to present itself" in the form of a popular movement. In Luther's case, the language is the message. Whereas the prophet at the end of time never expected the Reformation to become a truly "popular movement," his language was so chosen that Satan would hear him loud and clear — which requires, I suppose, non-elitist communication, understandable to all.

To conclude: Luther has been hailed in this century as the "theologian of the word." That is completely justified — but applies not only to the Word in that fundamental sense of the word as gospel *(sine vi sed verbo!)*, but also to the word as that powerful weapon *(vis verborum!)* with which Satan is challenged, by which his threat is exposed, the simple folk protected, and above all the coming of the last day accelerated: ". . . at ego indies magis provoco Satanam et suas squamas, ut acceleretur dies ille Christi destructurus Antichristum istum."[53] Thus by slaying the great Detractor, Christ transforms the *dies irae* into *dies gratiae*.

It is not just the *Old Luther* who sees the world coming to an end; already the young Luther has seen that the world has *grown old*.

---

52. *For the Sake of Simple Folk*, p. 94. More helpful than Bakhtin is Michael Screech in his treatment of "scatological laughter" in *Rabelais* (London: Duckworth, 1979), pp. 50ff.

53. Last appeal of Luther to Staupitz, from Wittenberg, 17 June 1522, in *WA Br* 2.567.35-36. Cf. the programmatic conclusion of the sermon preached during the last visit outside Saxony in Schmalcalden, his "testament" proclaimed hours before falling mortally ill on 18 February 1537; *WA* 45.47.12-38.

The Nationalist Conscription
of Martin Luther

There exists a national, cultural, and theological exploitation of Martin Luther which consistently distorts the reformer solely for its own purposes. In the process the man himself is lost from sight, as contemporary concerns overtake him, pass him by, and leave him far behind. Gudrun Tempel, a German emigrant in London, raised the question of the search for Germany with acute insight when she entitled her book *Germany, But Where Is It?*[1] It is a land without fixed boundaries, she warned, and it is thus boundless and boundlessly dangerous to Europe, to the world, and to progress and enlightenment. Given this absence of national boundaries, national cohesion is in Germany more than elsewhere dependent upon common symbols, cultural achievements, and a successful quest for religious roots — in short, upon the myth of moorings.

Where is Germany now? In Luther's land? Since the fall of the Third Reich little has been heard from the national enthusiasm that embellished itself with gems pilfered from the German Reformation.

1. Gudrun Tempel, *Deutschland? Aber wo liegt es? Wiederbegegnung mit einem Vaterland* (Reinbek, 1962).

"The Nationalist Conscription of Martin Luther," published in *Piety, Politics, and Ethics: Reformation Studies in Honor of George Wolfgang Forell*, ed. C. Lindberg, Sixteenth Century Essays and Studies 3 (Kirksville, Mo., 1984), 65-73.

Understandably so, for shame brings silence. A survey of the literature on Luther during the Nazi era leaves the impression that the Reformation was the very birth hour of the brown-garbed nationalist movement itself; that Nazism was Luther's gift to "his beloved Germans." "I, the German prophet," he once wrote, "seek salvation and blessedness not for myself but for the Germans."[2] Even though the ring of Nazi propaganda has died away, this picture of Luther remains alive. There is no place in it for the fact that Luther uttered his prophecy as an indictment: "Every German should on this account rue having been born a German and being called a German."[3]

The nationalist view was at least correct in seeing that Luther was no European, particularly not "European" in the sense of the House of Hapsburg, which controlled Europe from Iberia to the Balkans. Luther considered himself a German; and the German patriotic movement, which was just then beginning to move beyond mere protests against Roman influence and papal exploitation, bid with high hopes for his favor. Indeed, the sixteenth century saw the first signs of a national consciousness, against which the Spanish king and Hapsburg emperor, Charles V, collided, scraping his dignity on all sides. This occurred from Alsace to the Burgundian Netherlands — everywhere that hometown or fatherland strove to win freedom from foreign lordship.

We ought not ignore the national-patriotic thrust in Luther's thought nor its influence on his conception of reform, even though these were brought into such ill repute by the National Socialists. The connection

2. "Aber weil ich Deudschen Prophet bin (Denn solchen hoffertigen namen mus ich mir hinfurt selbs zu messen, meinen Papisten und Eseln zur lust und gefallen), so wil mir gleichwol als einem trewen Lerer gebüren, meine lieben Deudschen zu warnen für irem schaden und fahr und Christlich unterricht zu geben. . . . Welcher Deudscher nu meinem trewen rat folgen wil, der folge. Wer nicht wil, der lasse es. Ich suche hie mir nicht das meine, sondern ewer, der Deudschen, heil und seligkeit. Mir künd für meine person nicht bas geschehen, denn das mich die Papisten fressen, zurissen, zubissen, odder wie sie mir sonst aus dem sundlichen, tödlichen madensack hölffen. . . . Denn ich weis, wo meine sache stehet und wo ich bleiben sol, Gott sey gelobt. Mügen sie meinen dienst nicht zu irem besten annemen, so dancke in der leidige Teufel, wo sie mir ein tröpflin liebe odder gnade erzeigen. Dürffen sie meiner lere nicht, so darff ich irer gnaden viel weniger, und lasse sie zürnen und toben inn aller Teufel namen, so lache ich inn Gottes namen." *WA* 30 III.290.28-32; 291.7-19; *LW* 47. 29-30. "Dis wil ich meinen lieben Deudschen zur warnung gesagt haben. Und wie droben, also bezeuge ich hie auch, das ich nicht zu krieg noch auffrur noch gegenwere wil jemand hetzen odder reitzen, sondern allein zum Friede." *WA* 30 III.320.20-22; *LW* 47.54-55. *Warnung an seine lieben Deutschen,* 1531.

3. "Es muss gewiss einen jeden Deutschen gereuen, dass der deutsch geboren ist und als Deutscher gelten wird." *WA* 30 III.285.15-16; *LW* 47.22.

between the Reformation and national consciousness may not be overlooked. This truth, though a partial truth, must be kept in mind in order to guard against the legends about the "German Luther" and the "German soul" that to this day have distorting consequences upon German self-understanding. In this respect, too, the Reformation is indeed a German event.

The National Socialists celebrated in Luther the national hero, but they did not create this image of him. Religious conviction and national pride had for centuries entwined themselves around his image, especially during the Bismarck era. Luther's role as a symbol of national unity is well documented by the celebrations of his four-hundredth birthday in 1883; a swelling tide which, I fear, few of his present-day critics would have been strong enough to resist.[4]

The first warnings against the misuse of Luther as the champion of German culture were expressed in 1917, the darkest year of World War I. He was, it was argued, rather a man of religion and, first and foremost, a biblical theologian. The Protestant weekly *Die christliche Welt* diverged most radically from Imperial Protestant triumphalism. Its editor, the prominent Marburg theologian Martin Rade, emphasized that "Luther's center of gravity lay not in his German manner, his German sensibility or his actions, but solely in his faith, in his Christianity."[5] Rade, in a popular Luther edition which appeared in 1917, also demanded that Luther be taken for "what he intended and wanted to be; not the creator or author of a new culture — for all that he may have done for education, literature, art, science, morality, and politics. Luther was a preacher of the Word, a professor of divinity, a *theologian*. That is all he was — but he was that wholly and completely."[6]

Rade's was hardly, of course, a representative voice. In 1917 there also appeared a popular selection of Luther's letters, writings, songs, and

4. Cf. Max Lenz, *Martin Luther: Festschrift der Stadt Berlin für ihre Schulen zum 10. November 1883* (Berlin, 1883), cited by Gottfried Maron, "Luther 1917: Beobachtungen zur Literatur des 400. Reformationsjubiläums," *Zeitschrift für Kirchengeschichte* 93 (1982): 177-221, 183.

5. "Luthers Schwerpunkt lag eben nicht in seiner deutschen Art und in seinem deutschen Empfinden oder gar Handeln sondern schlechterdings in seinem Glauben, in seinem Christentum." *Die christliche Welt* 31 (1917): 753, cited by Maron, "Luther 1917," p. 203.

6. "Was er sein sollte und wollte. Nicht als Anfänger und Vollender einer neuen Kultur, mag er für Bildung, Literatur, Kunst, Wissenschaft, Moral, Politik noch so viel bedeuten. Luther war Prediger des Worts, war Professor der Gottesgelehrtheit, war *Theologe*. Weiter nichts, aber dieses ganz und vollkommen." Martin Rade, *Luther in Worten aus seinen Werken,* Die Klassiker der Religion 10/11 (Berlin, 1917), p. xv, cited by Maron, "Luther 1517," p. 203.

"Table Talks" of which forthwith fifty thousand copies were printed for immediate distribution throughout Germany. The editor, a certain justly forgotten Tim Klein, conjured up the German Luther in what seems now a cacophany of persecution mania and arrogance. As Luther's motto, Klein wrote, "No nation is more despised than the Germans. The Italians call us 'beasts,' and France, England, and all other nations heap ridicule upon us." The German feeling of national inferiority would, he promised, be transformed, in God's name: "Who knows what God wants to make, and will make, out of the Germans?"[7]

It remains to be shown how thoroughly Tim Klein perverted a remark from Luther's "Table Talk" from its intended meaning. Klein's own intention is nonetheless clear enough from the hymn of praise that in nine stanzas opened this popular edition. It was written by the national poet of German-speaking Switzerland, Conrad Ferdinand Meyer. I cite here two revealing and representative stanzas; the first portrays Luther standing steadfast before the alien ruler, Emperor Charles V, at the Diet of Worms in 1521, while the second rounds out what we must call "the nationalist conscription of Luther."

> Herr Kaiser Karl, du warst zu fein,
> den Luther fandest du gemein —
> gemein wie Lieb und Zorn und Pflicht,
> wie unsrer Kinder Angesicht,
> wie Hof und Heim, wie Salz und Brot,
> wie die Geburt und wie der Tod —
> Er atmet tief in unsrer Brust,
> und du begrubst dich in Sankt Just . . .

> Herr Luther, gut ist eure Lehr,
> ein frischer Quell, ein starker Speer:
> Der Glaube, der den Zweifel bricht,
> der ewgen Dinge Zuversicht,
> des Heuchelwerkes Nichtigkeit!
> Ein blankes Schwert im offnem Streit!
> Ihr bleibt getreu trotz Not und Bann
> und jeder Zoll ein deutscher Mann.[8]

7. "Es ist keine Nation mehr verachtet denn die Deutsche. Italien heisst uns Bestien; Frankreich, England und alle anderen Länder spotten unser." "Wer weiss, was Gott will und wird aus den Deutschen machen." *WA TR* 2.98.11-14, nr. 1428; *LW* 54.151. *Luther: Deutsche Briefe, Schriften, Lieder, Tischreden,* Ausgewählt und lebensgeschichtlich verbunden von Dr. Tim Klein (Munich, 1917), p. 2.

8. Lord Emperor Charles, you were too refined,
   You found Luther rather common —

In spite of banishment and excommunication, Luther is every inch a German man! In plain words, the man of God, hunted and banished by the unholy team of pope and emperor, anchors his rod and staff in the German faith. There he stands, Martin Luther, the first German Christian! Germany, awaken! Already present here are the images that would transmute the reformer into a symbol for that part of the nation which felt drained and humiliated by the Treaty of Versailles. They become a people, a united nation, by means of defying the whole world as Luther once did at Worms.

About this same time, at the end of World War I, a new wave of Luther scholarship was breaking ground for what today is rightly honored with the name of "Luther Renaissance." Led by Karl Holl (†1926), a Swabian professor in Berlin, this wave turned its back on vulgar nationalism and stressed the centrality of Luther's Reformation discovery.[9] After 1933, however, led by Emanuel Hirsch, a Holl disciple, Holl's students practically as a single unit joined the camp of the German-Christians, Hitler's Christian supporters. Their scholarly achievements and academic prestige lent honor and plausibility to the nationalist interpretation of Luther, though for this the Holl school by no means bears the blame alone. A whole series of prominent Luther scholars fell into line, and their influence reached far beyond the universities. Indeed, some of the ablest workers on the standard modern edition of Luther's writings, the Weimar edition, were collaborators with this "German hour of the church," as one theologian called Hitler's seizure of power. Count-

---

As common as love, anger and duty,
As common as our children's faces,
As farm and home, as salt and bread,
As birth and as death.
Luther still breathes deep in our breasts,
While you buried yourself. . . .

Lord Luther, your teaching is good,
A bubbling spring, a strong lance:
The faith that purges doubt,
And gives trust in eternal things,
That smashes hypocrisy!
A shining sword in a fair fight —
You remain staunch despite danger and the ban,
Every inch a German man.

Klein, *Luther: Deutsche Briefe,* pp. 67.
9. Cf. Johannes Wallmann, "Karl Holl und seine Schule," *Zeitschrift für Theologie und Kirche* 4 (1978): 1-33.

less popular editions taught the nation about Luther and led it to his writings — or at least to a carefully limited selection of them. Luther's harsh writings against the Jews were the core of the selections because — it was said in 1936 — "it is an intolerable situation that this important and still perfectly valid national religious confession [against the Jews] by the great German Reformer is known at most by name by nearly all Germans but is only read by a few."[10] After the doctrine of race had furnished the scientific foundation, the historical and religious legitimation for hatred of the Jews and for the final solution was extracted out of Luther's warnings against the "Jews and their lies."

The terrible events of the Nazi supremacy apparently developed organically out of the consequences of World War I and no doubt correspond to them in such a way that in retrospect even the irrational becomes comprehensible. The agitated and frenzied atmosphere of the postwar years is revealed by a seemingly minor, everyday incident which, though it did not find its way into the history books, speaks volumes about the mood of those times. At Christmas time in 1922 some theological students at Paris sent a Christmas greeting to their counterparts at nineteen German universities "in order," they wrote, "to convey to their German comrades feelings of brotherly and Christian affection."[11] Few of the addressees responded, not least because on 11 January French and Belgian troops occupied the Ruhr. The incident nonetheless had an enlightening sequel. During the summer semester of 1923, two of these Parisian students came to meet with divinity students at Göttingen. When news of their visit spread among the Göttingen students, groups began to assemble in front of the meeting place and to whip themselves into a frenzy through nationalist songs and anti-French slogans. The French students were told to leave Göttingen and were forced to buy second-class railway tickets but to travel fourth-class. The *Göttinger Tagblatt* complained about an "act of national dishonor," referring not to the demonstrators but to the host who was arrested the same day for "lodging alien spies." A week later the University Senate issued a weak-kneed statement which, though it criticized the form of the demonstration,

10. "Es ist ein unerträglicher Zustand, dass dieses wichtige und heute noch vollauf gültige völkisch-religiöse Bekenntnis — (gegen die Juden) — des grossen deutschen Reformators bei fast allen Deutschen höchstens dem Namen nach bekannt und nur von wenigen gelesen ist." *Luthers Kampfschriften gegen das Judentum,* ed. W. Linden (Berlin, 1936), p. 7.

11. ". . . um ihren deutschen Kameraden ihre Gefühle brüderlicher und christlicher Zuneigung auszudrücken." *Karl Barth — Martin Rade: Ein Briefwechsel,* ed. Chr. Schwöbel (Gütersloh, 1981), p. 184, n. 3.

praised the good faith of the demonstrators. The latter had acted in "justifiable defense."[12] The atmosphere of anxiety and defensiveness in those years and the crabbed search for a foundation in German culture and morality against violent and hostile forces provided a ready soil for the nationalist appropriation of Luther. The Nazis did not have to discover or create Luther as a German national reformer — he was already there, rifle at the ready.

The National Socialist image introduced, however, two innovations to make Luther serve current national interests. These two changes, which have had lasting consequences until today, were: Luther "the apolitical leader" and Luther "the antisemite."

On Reformation Day, 1935, Professor Hermann Werdermann, who belonged to the "Glaubensbewegung Deutsche Christen," gave the festival address at the Teachers' College in Dortmund. Werdermann entitled his talk (which the "Research Group for 'Positive Christianity'" printed for distribution throughout Germany) "Martin Luther and Adolf Hitler: A Historical Comparison."[13] Werdermann, a proud Nazi Christian, tried to show that Hitler stood on Luther's shoulders. When Hitler in *Mein Kampf* cited Jesus' words, "no man can serve two masters," he was citing, said Werdermann, not just the Bible but something uniquely German — Luther's German Bible.[14] And the wondrous power of Hitler's words, when he "speaks so grippingly in the German tongue to German hearts," is expressed by the Führer in "Martin Luther's German." Hitler is today, "as Luther was then, the tutor of the whole German nation."[15]

It was at this point that the German Christians had to introduce a major new interpretation. For them Luther is, to be sure, the Führer, but he is always the spiritual Führer and never the political one. Luther fits neatly into his role in Hitler's struggle because both leaders, it was said, had opposed "without reservation the illicit mixing of religion and politics."[16] The Nazi Christians here reinterpreted Luther against his own intentions, his own statements, and the evidence of his deeds. Luther had taught with such energy the distinction between the Kingdom of God

12. "Akt nationaler Würdelosigkeit," "Beherbergung feindlicher Spione," "in berechtigter Abwehr." *Karl Barth — Martin Rade*, pp. 190-92.

13. *Martin Luther und Adolf Hitler: Ein geschichtlicher Vergleich* (Gnadenfrei in Schlesien, 1935, 1937²).

14. Werdermann, *Martin Luther und Adolf Hitler*, p. 4.

15. "volkstümlich in deutscher Sprache zu deutschen Herzen redet," "Martin Luthers Deutsch," "wie Luther einst, der Erzieher der ganzen deutschen Nation." Werdermann, *Martin Luther und Adolf Hitler*, pp. 9, 12.

16. "unbedingt gegen Verquickung von Religion und Politik." Werdermann, *Martin Luther und Adolf Hitler*, p. 17.

and the Kingdom of This World because he wanted to call Christians to political action in an age when piety was conceived only as a retreat from the world's dirty business. Under the Third Reich, by contrast, Luther was made to teach that true Christians withdraw from the world and can, with good conscience, leave Germany's political fate to the Führer. This misinterpretation was pregnant with consequences that live on in the "anti-Luther slogans" of today's peace movement.

The Nazi Christians' second revision of Luther's image seems more difficult to refute. In his speech of 1935, three years before *Kristallnacht,* Professor Werdermann established for Luther and Hitler a common goal: the "Jewish solution." Werdermann unequivocally stated, "In his treatment of the Jewish Question, Adolf Hitler continues and completes Luther's work."[17] After the war, at the Nuremberg Trials, Julius Streicher, editor of the Nazi agitational journal *Der Stürmer,* offered just this linkage between Luther and Hitler in his own defense.

Luther's conscription as advocate for the Final Solution has to a very large extent shaped the image of the Wittenberg reformer both in Germany and abroad. One thing must be clearly understood: Luther was anti-Jewish in his repeated warnings against the Jews as bearers of an anti-Christian religion which had established itself both within and outside Christianity. But Luther was not an antisemite or racist of any kind because — to apply the test appropriate to his time — for him a baptized Jew is fully Christian. Conversely, he said that among us Christians in Germany there are horrifyingly many who in their hearts deny Christ. Those are the true Jews! Not race but belief in the law, in good works, makes Jews.[18]

The monstrous myth that Luther was completed by Hitler enjoyed a tremendous propagandistic success in the Third Reich — and not only among Protestant Christians. Very likely, it weakened catastrophically an already weak will to resist Hitler. And in our own day, while the flames of antisemitism have died down in Germany, the anti-Jewish Luther remains a weapon for intolerance and political agitation around the globe.

There is another form of "applying" Luther which is far more sophisticated than the crude nationalistic embrace. The moral quality of this "application" makes it easy to misidentify. This form unlike the

17. "Adolf Hitler (ist) in der Behandlung und Lösung der Judenfrage der Fortsetzer und Vollender Luthers. . . ." Werdermann, *Martin Luther und Adolf Hitler,* p. 9.

18. Cf. Part III of my *The Roots of Anti-Semitism in the Age of Renaissance and Reformation* (Philadelphia, 1984).

others we have mentioned, did not grow out of efforts to honor in Luther the national symbol or the hero; rather, it accuses the reformer and in him the nation and above all the German spirit. In 1945, the year of accounting and reflection, Thomas Mann spoke the judgment of a German emigré on Luther. He is, said Mann, "a gigantic incarnation of Germanness. I don't love him, I must freely confess. The purely German, the separatist anti-Roman, the anti-European in Luther I find alien and troubling — even when it appears in the form of Evangelical liberty and spiritual emancipation. . . . Luther was a hero of liberty, but in the German manner, for he understood nothing of liberty."[19] With Mann we have come full circle. The abuse of Luther began with the creation of a national symbol as a cultural ornamentation of the new Reich with the Protestant Luther and the application concludes with Mann's pinpointing the barbarian German in the person of Luther. What is constant is the failure to listen to Luther the prophet.

The national interpretation of Luther is not just a product of the nineteenth and twentieth centuries. In his own lifetime there already were efforts to make him a national symbol. The suppressed imperial knights, the exploited peasantry, and the acquisitive princes tried in 1522, 1525, and 1527 to politicize, revolutionize, or nationalize the Reformation. Luther could have integrated these conflicting interests, each of which tried to harness him for special purposes, only if he had acted differently at the Diet of Worms in 1521; that is, if he had followed the dictates of political reason. Political reason demanded surrendering the struggle against Rome's *religious* power in favor of battle against its *financial* power. Luther stood at Worms at the peak of his political influence; at that moment he could very well have proclaimed and borne aloft the cause of national unity. He refused, however, the role of national hero.

Luther was a "German event," not because of any basic summons to national mobilization but because he called the Germans to repentance and suffering, the true marks of a Christian. And such a call could not awaken a nation. In his famous political manifesto to the German nobility, Luther smashes the dream of a free Christian state in Germany:

---

19. "eine riesenhafte Inkarnation deutschen Wesens. . . . Ich liebe ihn nicht, das gestehe ich offen. Das Deutsche in Reinkultur, das Separatistisch-Anti-romische, Anti-Europäische befremdet und ängstigt mich, auch wenn es als evangelische Freiheit und geistliche Emanzipation erscheint. . . . Er war ein Freiheitsheld — aber in deutschem Stil, denn er verstand nichts von Freiheit." Thomas Mann, *Politische Schriften und Reden*, 3 (Frankfurt, 1968), 166-67 (Thomas Mann, *Werke* 6 [Fischer Bücherei], p. 118).

"Never," he warns, "have men on this earth committed themselves to a Christian cause, for the resistance has always been too great and too strong."[20]

Luther, who wanted to be a prophet of repentance, did not become one. Luther, who refused to be a national symbol, became one. Today he is still being manipulated, either in the Federal Republic as a cultured creator of language or in the German Democratic Republic as a progressive historical force.

Any genuine celebration of Luther demands the cooperation of scholars who can grasp and interpret the German reformer in a larger, supranational frame of reference. Luther called for absolute receptivity in the realm of faith and for unremitting activity in the political realm of social justice: these are the signs of the *communio sanctorum* which transcend *all* national boundaries. To precisely this understanding of Luther, in all its breadth, significance, and subtlety, the work of George Wolfgang Forell makes a distinguished and lasting contribution.[21]

20. "Es ist noch nie eine christliche Sache von Menschen auf Erden gutgeheissen worden, sondern alle Zeit ist der Widerstand zu gross und stark gewesen." *WA* 6.469.9-11; *LW* 44.217.

21. It deserves to be known and to be documented that courageous dissidents kept this vision of Luther alive as late as 1937:

"Hie steh ich" — der in Worms es sprach,
stand trotz den Feinden allen. —
"Hie steh ich" — viele sprechen's nach
und wanken, weichen, fallen.

"Ich kann nicht anders" — sprach der Held
an Gottes Wort gebunden. —
"Man muss halt, leider!" — sagt die Welt,
und ist bald überwunden.

"Gott helf mir" — so betet er,
den Sieg in sichern Händen. —
"Ich helf mir selbst!" — kein Beten mehr!
Wie mag solch Trotzen enden?

Und "Amen!" noch voll Zuversicht:
Ja! Ja! So soll's geschehen!
Warum willst du und ich denn nicht
auch somit Luther stehen.

                                                          T.G.

Evangelisches Gemeindeblatt der Stadt Sulz am Neckar, nr. 10 (October 1937). These initials cannot be identified since they were intended as cover for the "anonymous" author.

III. THE GROWTH
OF ANTISEMITISM

Three Sixteenth-Century Attitudes toward Judaism: Reuchlin, Erasmus, and Luther

I. Introduction: The Plight of the Historian

During the sixteenth century, Europe made a hesitant but significant transition to modern times. This generalization does not apply to all of Europe nor to all facets of life, but in northern Europe we can notice a marked step forward in the understanding of human rights and in the advocacy of tolerance.[1] Reuchlin, Erasmus, and Luther contributed to this development, each in his own way. From this advance, however, the Jewish communities hardly profited; the ideal of tolerance bypassed the Jews, geared only toward the coexistence of Christian factions within the fractured unity of a basically Christian society. In point of fact the ideal of tolerance grew very much at the expense of the Jews in northern Europe, particularly in Germany — at the expense of their social role, their legal status, and their religious liberties. Reuchlin, Erasmus and

1. Erich Hassinger, *Religiöse Toleranz im 16. Jahrhundert: Motive — Argumente — Formen der Verwirklichung*, Vorträge der Aeneas-Silvius-Stiftung an der Universität Basel 6 (Basel and Stuttgart, 1966); Hans R. Guggisberg, "Veranderingen in de Argumenten voor religieuze tolerantie en godsdienstvrijheid in de zestiende en zeventiende eeuw," *Bijdragen en Mededelingen betreffende de Geschiedenis der Nederlanden* 91 (1966): 177-95.

"Three Sixteenth-Century Attitudes toward Judaism: Reuchlin, Erasmus, and Luther," in *Jewish Thought in the Sixteenth Century*, ed. B. D. Cooperman (Cambridge, Mass., 1983), pp. 326-64.

Luther contributed to this development as well; and again, each in his own way. Before we turn to the questions of how such diverse roles can be assigned to the same people, or how it can be justified to mention in one breath three such dissimilar historical figures, I have to comment upon the state of research in this highly sensitive field.

If I had to rank the factors that continue to obstruct our grasp of the interaction of the history of the Jews and the history of European society in the sixteenth century, I would not start with a complaint about the lack of sources and of reliable interpretive articles. Nor would I be inclined to mention the abundance, the baffling and at times indeed disgusting number of books and articles seemingly concerned with our theme but de facto utilizing the plight of the Jews to document the priority of economic forces which are claimed to underlie or even to determine Christian-Jewish relations in early modern Europe. In these cases research in depth is replaced by research into debts and indebtedness which, however, fails to solve the riddle why, symbolically speaking, the Fuggers merely met with scattered protests but not with pogroms. To be sure, economic considerations are necessary[2] when used in the service of that kind of intellectual history which one might call motivation research. It is important to note that the lower-strata *Flugschriften* crying out for reform of society are often rabidly anti-Jewish, whereas positive statements are found among publicists close to the emperor or to those *Landesherren* who exercised the right to protect and tax the Jews in their territories. Nevertheless, the many exceptions all around warn us not to regard economic factors or social status as an historical determinant for the attitude to the Jews.

There exists today a more subtle and hence more formidable obstacle to research in our period, a silent and suppressed undercurrent in the treatment of our theme. To put the matter as simply as possible: We are writing history in the wake of the Nazi massacres. Historians have forced one another to hold out for an unconfessional presentation of the past; and at least we have learned to read the danger signs of treatments by colleagues who fall short of this scholarly ideal. Yet we are still so haunted by a nightmare which continues to be daylight reality that in our field it is hard to find a middle ground between aggressive accusations and escapist apologies. If the historian's first task is to act as the final advocate for the dead, it is nearly impossible for him to distinguish

---

2. See the important article on the fourteenth century by Stuart Jenks, "Judenverschuldung und Verfolgung von Juden im 14. Jahrhundert: Franken bis 1349," *Vierteljahrschrift für Social- und Wirtschaftsgeschichte* 65 (1978): 309-56.

between his role and his conscience; if the historian's second task is to act as public prosecutor, it is nearly impossible for him not to judge the past in order to prevent recurrence in the future. And worst of all, if it is true that both tasks, the advocate's and prosecutor's, presuppose a careful hearing of the sources as eyewitnesses, it requires a more-than-human effort not to follow the relativizing escape route of "attenuating circumstances" — attenuating for a single man like Martin Luther or for all northern Europe's hesitant history of tolerance, said to be the finest fruit of Renaissance humanism.

Under the impact of the all-too-recent epoch in the history of the diaspora, the typecasting by enlightened historians of the beginning of this century has fashioned a new orthodoxy: Reuchlin is the hero of emancipation, Pfefferkorn the fanatic, Luther the bigoted anti-semite, and Erasmus the father of tolerance and human dignity. Historians should bear in mind that even minor revisions in this script are suspect of heresy. At this point it is high time to abandon our concern with the historian and turn to history itself.

II. The Fictitious Triumvirate

In the scholarly tradition of the nineteenth century the Renaissance and the Reformation were still understood as kindred movements which together led Europe toward the emancipation from medieval patterns in life and thought. Today it is by no means obvious to rank Reuchlin, Erasmus, and Luther together. Without being blind to interaction, derivations, and alliances, we are acutely aware of the difference in motives and goals of these two, perhaps even three, programs of renewal. There is admittedly a significant element of historical truth in the typology of Johann Eberlin von Günzburg's (†1533) *15 Bundsgenossen* (1521), which presents Reuchlin and Erasmus as forerunners of Luther: They have the "ersten stain gelegt alles hails."[3] We shall have to return to this point to grasp how Eberlin could have come to this view. But seen from close quarters the three "forerunners" prove to have far less in common than what sets them apart.

Johannes Reuchlin (1455-1522), Desiderius Erasmus (1466[9?]-

---

3. Published first by Pamphilus Gengenbach (Basel, 1521). Johann Eberlin von Günzburg, "Der erst bundtsgnoß," *Ausgewählte Schriften*, 3 vols., ed. L. Enders, Neudrucke deutscher Literaturwerke des XVI. und XVII. Jahrhunderts: Flugschriften aus der Reformationszeit 11 (Halle, 1896-1902), 1.3.

1536), and Martin Luther (1483-1546) differ in a number of respects. The first and seemingly most pedestrian is the fact that they flower and reach their zenith in three successive decades. And these are decades of crucial events and shifts in Europe's intellectual climate. Furthermore, Reuchlin is a son of southern Germany whose geographical ambiance runs basically from Pforzheim to Stuttgart and Tübingen. Erasmus, on the other hand, is in touch by letter and horse with the educated all over Europe, always at once in exile and at home. As he likes to put it: "My *patria* is where my library is," but particularly along the Rhine, for him the "fruitful mother carrying news and culture." As Reuchlin explicitly indicates in his letters of recommendation on behalf of Melanchthon to the Elector Frederick dated 25 July 1518, he is very much aware that Erasmus is not a German: "In Germany I do not know anyone better [for this Greek chair than Melanchthon] except for Erasmus, and *der ist ein Holländer.*"[4] Luther, too, traveled widely but except for one trek on foot over the Alps to Italy he stayed within the boundaries of the empire, preferring solid land to rivers, which for him had no positive meaning; at times swollen as if at the order of the devil, rivers thwarted his missions or prevented him from returning to his family. And third, on that decisive point where career and motivation coincide Reuchlin is the literate jurist and German Pico,[5] Erasmus the philological ethicist, and Luther the prophetical and professional *Doctor Sacrae Scripturae.* Even in that momentous endeavor which Eberlin of Günzburg described as their common effort, namely the interpretation of Scripture on the basis of the original texts instead of the Vulgate, they differ most. Reuchlin is the only one to be truly *trilinguis,* with command of Hebrew, Greek, and classical Latin. Erasmus for a time tried his hand at Hebrew, but soon gave up, invoking the shortness of life and the pressures of his many scholarly projects.[6] Luther came to know and respect Hebrew: "Lingua Ebraica est omnium optima . . . ac purissima . . . ,"[7] and he pitched its

---

4. *Corpus Reformatorum,* vol. 1: *Philippi Melan[ch]thonis Opera quae supersunt omnia* 1, ed. C. G. Bretschneider (Halle, 1834; repr. New York, London, and Frankfurt a.M., 1963), 34.

5. Lewis W. Spitz has coined an expression which applies as well and would have pleased Reuchlin even more: "Reuchlin: Pythagoras Reborn," in *The Religious Renaissance of the German Humanists* (Cambridge, Mass., 1963), pp. 61-80.

6. See his letter to John Colet (Paris, December 1504); *Opus Epistolarum Des. Erasmi Roterodami* [= Allen], ed. P. S. Allen, 12 vols. (Oxford, 1906-1965), 1.405.35-37. Cf. Michael Andrew Screech, *Ecstasy and the Praise of Folly* (London, 1980), p. 10.

7. "Lingua Ebraica est omnium optima ac in thematibus omnium copiosissima ac purissima, quia ab aliis linguis nihil prorsus mendicat. Sie hat ir eigen farb." *WA TR* 1, nr. 1041, p. 525, ll. 42-44; September-November 1532.

nonspeculative clarity against Greek[8] without ever being so much at home with the language of Aristotle and Origen as later lore has it.

All these differences in age, origin, vocation, and ability were later overlooked by Eberlin and many scholarly generations to follow because of the wartime pact uniting Reuchlin, Erasmus, and Luther against the *viri obscuri,* the past masters of scholasticism (Ortwin Gratius) in alliance with the Dominican protectors of orthodoxy (the inquisitor Jacob Hochstraten). This alliance was still so firmly entrenched in the centers of power that it achieved a common lot for all three: Reuchlin and Luther were condemned in 1520; Erasmus's works were put on the *Index librorum prohibitorum* of Pope Paul IV in 1559 and, with some alterations, in subsequent editions as well.[9] Here indeed we may well have touched upon a significant feature, not in stance but in joint common effect, since nothing furthers the cause of intellectual freedom more than the proscription of books which continue to be read and respected.

Yet Reuchlin, Erasmus, and Luther cannot be remodeled into a triumvirate merely because all three met with ecclesiastical censure: their motivations were too different. Reuchlin for one stood up for Hebrew wisdom, never attained by the pedestrian techniques of scholasticism.[10] Erasmus — in contrast with his disciples, the city reformers, and after his own *Sturm und Drang* — came to lean back from antischolastic and anticlerical satire; he feared that such would not further the cause of the *bonae litterae.* Luther early declared himself against the "infelices Colonienses," the calamitous Doctors of Cologne.[11] But his line of attack differed from those of both Reuchlin and Erasmus; he did not assail

---

8. *WA TR* 2, nr. 2771a; cf. nr. 2779a.

9. See particularly Myron P. Gilmore, "Italian Reactions to Erasmian Humanism," in *Itinerarium Italicum: The Profile of the Italian Renaissance in the Mirror of Its European Transformations: Dedicated to Paul Oskar Kristeller on the Occasion of His 70th Birthday,* ed. H. A. Oberman and T. A. Brady, Jr., Studies in Medieval and Reformation Thought 14 (Leiden, 1975), pp. 61-115; 84.

10. Ludwig Geiger, *Johann Reuchlin: Sein Leben und seine Werke* (Leipzig, 1871). Cf. James H. Overfield, "A New Look at the Reuchlin Affair," *Studies in Medieval and Renaissance History* 8 (1971): 165-207; 206; cf. 181. Of the older literature see esp. Gustav Kawerau, "Reuchlin," in *Realencyklopädie für protestantische Theologie und Kirche,* 16 (Leipzig, 1905³), 680-88. For earlier English literature see Werner Schwarz, *Principles and Problems of Biblical Translation: Some Reformation Controversies and Their Background* (Cambridge, 1955), pp. 61-91; esp. 70, n. 2.

11. *WA Br* 1.23.28. Letter to Georg Spalatin, February 1514; *Gutachten* on Reuchlin's case, probably based on Reuchlin's most recent publication, the *Defensio contra calumniatores suos Colonienses* (Tübingen, 1513).

magistri nostri for matters of classical style or uncultured simplicity but in the name of biblical doctrine.[12] In 1522 Luther even made a point of saying that his own fight against scholasticism did not concern its lack of eloquence or erudition. As far as these two were concerned, he confessed: "Sum et ego barbarus."[13]

The one sound reason for regarding the triumvirate of legend and lore as an intellectual phalanx is their shared confidence that a fresh investigation of the biblical sources would yield that wisdom which, once recovered, was to restore pristine truth and thus renew church and society. Concomitant with this audacious vision is a shared anti-Judaism which could feed upon popular conceptions but — far from being merely a medieval survival — was with significant variations an organic part of their reform program with wide-reaching consequences for what was to develop into modern antisemitism. It is in their attitude to Jews and Judaism, I submit, that we can discern most clearly in what respects Reuchlin, Erasmus, and Luther did, or did not, transcend their times, and how beneath what later came to be proudly looked upon as a program for religious tolerance lay sobering origins.

---

12. In 1518 Luther called himself indeed Reuchlin's "successor." *WA Br* 1.268.9-10. 14 December 1518. Max Brod, the most recent biographer of Reuchlin — and exceptional in that he makes explicit that he treats Luther from the perspective of centuries of persecution — praises Reuchlin for not having fallen for this "ingratiation" and "fake claim" of Luther. *Johannes Reuchlin und sein Kampf* (Stuttgart, 1965), p. 122. But on reading this letter itself it is clear that Luther means with "successor" that he is the next on the blacklist of the "sophists"; by no means, however, next in line as concerns his scholarly gifts. Nor was Luther a disciple of Reuchlin in a programmatic sense. Schwarz concludes, however, in too unnuanced a fashion: "Yet Reuchlin was opposed to every aspect of Luther's doctrine. He died a member of the Roman Catholic Church. His aim was, to use a phrase of Erasmus, "to restore the old," and he did not see the danger that this implied for the Church of his time." *Principles and Problems,* p. 86. Another significant parallel between Reuchlin and Luther has gone unnoticed. The Elector Frederick of Saxony, who decisively protected Luther against Rome (Cajetan) and "Reich" from 1518 is already in 1513 regarded by Reuchlin as a protector against ecclesiastical interference: "Quo ardentius ad te Saxonesque tuos confugio . . . ut me contra quorumlibet latronum in cursus semper tuearis." Letter dated 13 August 1513, accompanying Reuchlin's translation of the "Life of Constantine the Great"; *Johann Reuchlins Briefwechsel,* ed. L. Geiger (Stuttgart, 1875; repr. Hildesheim, 1962), p. 190.

13. *WA* 10 II.329.10; 1522.

III. Reuchlin and the Jews:
Emancipation and the Birth of a New Antisemitism

We have overcome our longtime preoccupation with *The Letters of Obscure Men,* which encouraged the view of two warring camps, the "humanists" versus the "scholastics." Paul Oskar Kristeller[14] and Charles Trinkaus[15] have pointed to the medieval roots of Renaissance humanism in Thomism and nominalism. We know that we have only begun to trace the indebtedness of leading humanists to the "schoolmen." Reuchlin himself was not in doubt about the opposition's chief motive: he expected to be attacked for jeopardizing the authority of the Vulgate. Yet recently it has been argued that the "Obscure Men" attacked in Reuchlin not primarily his humanism but his Jewish sympathies: ". . . the anti-Reuchlinists were made up of a disparate group of anti-Semites from the many walks of life: they included some scholastics, but also a few humanists and even several kings."[16]

One implication of this antisemite thesis must at least be considerably qualified: Reuchlin's campaign was not pro-Jewish, let alone pro-semite. I am well aware that we have to tread here most carefully, since there is no "dictionary clarity" and consensus about the precise content of such terms in relation to sixteenth-century attitudes. After all, how does one grade degrees of anti-Judaism in a Christian world which is unable to decide whether it finds more self-confirmation in Jewish mass conversion or in the stubborn blindness of those stricken by God? As George Santayana put it: Fanaticism is "redoubling your effort when you have forgotten your aim." The dangerous fanaticism of Christian anti-Judaism is rooted in the inability to decide between these two aims of mass conversion and mass expulsion. What then are the characteristics

14. See esp. *Medieval Aspects of Renaissance Learning: Three Essays by Paul Oskar Kristeller,* ed. E. P. Mahoney, Duke Monographs in Medieval and Renaissance Studies 1 (Durham, N.C., 1974).
15. *In Our Image and Likeness: Humanity and Divinity in Italian Humanist Thought,* 1 (London, 1970); idem, "Erasmus, Augustine, and the Nominalists," *Archiv für Reformationsgeschichte* 67 (1976): 5-32; idem, *The Poet as Philospher: Petrarch and the Formation of Renaissance Consciousness* (New Haven and London, 1979), esp. 111.
16. J. H. Overfield, "A New Look at the Reuchlin Affair" (n. 10, above), p. 206. Cf. a few years later more cautiously: "A number of letters [in Gratius's *Lamentationes obscurorum virorum;* Cologne, 1519] also depicted the Reuchlinists as anti-Christian pagans who hurt the Church by aiding the Jews"; idem, "Scholastic Opposition to Humanism in Pre-Reformation Germany," *Viator* 7 (1976): 391-420; 398, 419. For Ortwin Gratius of Deventer (c. 1480-1542) as victim of "unjust attacks" see Jozef Ijsewijn, "The Coming of Humanism to the Low Countries," in *Itinerarium Italicum* (n. 9, above), pp. 193-301; 277, 290.

of anti-Judaism: confiscation of Jewish books or a resident-alien tax? Neurotic suspicion of Jewish conspiracy, or outright slander based on the stories of host desecration or of ritual murder in order to use Christian blood for treating Jewish illness? Is the mere fact that one does not call for slaughter as in previous centuries, and allows expulsion with all movable possessions a sign of leniency?[17] Let us look at the writings of Reuchlin and his opponent Pfefferkorn with these questions in mind.

I do not intend to deal with the "Reuchlin Case," which developed only after publication of the *Augenspiegel* in Tübingen (1511) when, instead of the Talmud, the author's orthodoxy becomes the main issue, and a fortiori not with the two volumes of the *Epistolate obscurorum virorum* published by Crotus Rubeanus in 1515 and by Ulrich of Hutten in 1517. Of Reuchlin's preceding works,[18] the *Vocabularius breviloquus* (Basel, 1478) does not yield any statement pertaining to our theme. This leaves us with the illusive but most significant *De verbo mirifico* (Basel, 1494), the *Tütsch Missive* (Pforzheim, 1505), the *De rudimentis hebraicis* (Pforzheim, 1506) with its programmatic preface, and finally the imperial *Opinion* or "Gutachten" against the confiscation of Hebrew books (1510), published in the *Augenspiegel*[19] together with a defense in Tübingen a year later.

Reuchlin's *De verbo mirifico*[20] is the first we must take in hand. The "Wonder-Working Word" has been read in a number of ways: as a proof of the necessity of the study of Hebrew, as a defense of the Christian Cabala, as a personal expression of Reuchlin's mystical concerns, and most recently — and most convincingly[21] — as a program

---

17. See Yosef Hayim Yerushalmi, *The Lisbon Massacre of 1506 and the Royal Image in the Shebet Yehudah,* Hebrew Union College Annual Supplements 1 (Cincinnati, 1976), p. 2.

18. Josef Benzing, *Bibliographie der Schriften Johannes Reuchlins im 15. und 16. Jahrhundert,* Bibliotheca Bibliographica 18 (Bad Boddet and Vienna, 1955). Cf. Guido Kisch, *Zasius und Reuchlin: Eine rechtsgeschichtlich-vergleichende Studie zum Toleranzproblem im 16. Jahrhundert,* Pforzheimer Reuchlinschriften 1 (Constance and Stuttgart, 1961), p. 71.

19. J. Benzing, *Bibliographie der Schriften Reuchlins,* p. 26.

20. Reprint of the Amerbach edition of *De verbo mirifico* (Basel, 1494), together with *De arte cabalistica* (Hagenau, 1517; Stuttgart–Bad Cannstatt, 1964). The second edition of *De verbo mirifico* was published in the same year, 1494, by Thomas Anshelm, the patron of the so-called "Tübingen Academy." See my critique of this epitheton in *Werden und Wertung der Reformation: Vom Wegestreit zum Glaubenskampf* (Tübingen, 1979[2]), pp. 19-24.

21. It is the continuation of "Pico's attempt to subordinate the occult sciences to religion through the agency of Kabbalah." Charles Zika, "Reuchlin's *De Verbo Mirifico* and the Magic Debate of the Late Fifteenth Century," *Journal of the Warburg and Courtauld Institutes* 49 (1976): 104-38; 138.

to recover the divine gift of the occult sciences which enables human beings to master the forces of nature by means of the Cabala. Irreverently we bypass Reuchlin's own theme to look at his mis-en-scène repeated later in his *De arte cabalistica* (1517): a disputation between Sidon, the former Epicurean and spokesman for pagan philosophy; Baruch, the learned Jew; and Capnion speaking for Reuchlin, the Christian.

In the form of a "sectarum controversia"[22] but much sharper than in the similar dialogue in Lessing's *Nathan der Weise*, Capnion establishes the superiority of the Christian faith, and both calls for, and achieves, the penance[23] or conversion of Sidon and Baruch, to be followed by baptismal rites of purification. Just as Sidon has to disavow his Epicurus, Baruch must renounce his Talmudic sources: "Resipiscentia vestra haec esto: A Thalmudim Baruchia, tuque Sidoni ab Epicuro . . . receditote. Lavamini, mundi estote."[24] Of course, this is not the crude conversion rite which medieval disputations between Christians and Jews had intended to achieve; rather, it is the initiation into the art of the *magus*. Yet this is the art of the Christian *magus*, bound by the faith of the Christian church. This tie has consequences since Capnion combines his respect for Hebrew and its cabalistic interpretation with a rejection of the Talmud and, what is more, with a vehement attack on the Jews:

> You [Jews] have subverted the Holy Books; therefore you rattle off your prayers in vain, in vain you invoke God, in vain because you speak to Him in self-made prayers, not in the way God wants to be

22. *De verbo mirifico*, fol. a 2^r. Johannes Franciscus Pico, nephew of Reuchlin's greatest Italian example, later (1512) quite appropriately summarizes this "Dialogue" with the words: ". . . de verbo mirifico secundum tria dogmata, scilicet philosophorum, Judaeorum et Christianorum, ubi continetur nomen sacrum id est tetragrammaton ineffabile, quin potius pentragrammaton effabile." Geiger, *Reuchlins Briefwechsel*, p. 88.

23. The word used by Reuchlin, *resipiscentia*, does not necessarily mean "penance"; some ten years later it will be used by Erasmus in his *Novum Instrumentum* as the Latin equivalent of the Greek word *metanoia*, "conversion." In his *Breviloquus* (1494; Benzing, *Bibliographie der Schriften Reuchlins*) Reuchlin describes *resipere* as 'iterum sapere': "proprie ille resipit, qui penitens forefacti redit ad satisfactionem. . . ." See the Index, s.v. *resipere*.

24. *De verbo mirifico*, fol. b 5^v; cf. c 6^r. The unique features of Reuchlin's "three rings" may appear most clearly in comparison with the trilogue in Cusanus's *De Pace Fidei* (shortly after the fall of Constantinople in 1453). See the edition by John P. Dolan, *Unity and Reform: Selected Writings of Nicholas de Cusa* (Notre Dame, Ind., 1962), pp. 195-237; cf. 185-94.

worshipped. At the same time you hate us, us the true worshippers of God. You hate us with a never-ending hatred. . . .[25]

In the "German Open Letter"[26] completed ten years later in 1504, this animosity has become thematic. Reuchlin explains the *Elend,* that is, the exile of the Jews, in terms of their self-invoked collective guilt punished by God with such blindness that they cannot find the way to penance, "die weg der buß, das ist ruw und leid,"[27] the way to that contrition which means conversion to the church. But only the learned Jew will find this solution; only the scholar who is trained in the secret art of the Cabala will understand that the Hebrew letters for the name of the Almighty mean *Jeschuh,* Jesus. In short, this treatise is the practical application of *De verbo mirifico,*[28] except for the fact that the turnabout, Baruch's change of heart, *resipiscentia,* is here unambiguously described as conversion, a real option only for the happy few, for those Jews initiated into the mysteries of the wonder-working word.

The misery of the Jews is not the consequence of man-made injustice but of God-willed punishment, to be escaped only through conversion. He concludes by pointing to the Good Friday prayer for the *perfidi Iudaei:* "I pray God that He will illumine and convert them to the right faith so that they are liberated from captivity by the devil. . . . Once they

25. ". . . vos legitima sacra mutastis: ideoque frustra murmuratis, frustra deum invocatis quem non ut ipse vult colitis, sed inventionibus vestris blandientes etiam nos dei cultores livore immortali oditis. . . ." *De verbo mirifico,* fol. b 5ᵛ.

26. Benzing, *Bibliographie der Schriften Reuchlins,* p. 25. Cf. Kisch, *Zasius und Reuchlin,* p. 16-22.

27. Cf. Kisch, *Zasius und Reuchlin,* p. 19.

28. Geiger finds in this treatise "das Princip einer milden Duldung der Juden". *Reuchlin: Sein Leben,* 164. He points to the "praiseworthy" fact that Reuchlin does not call for the eviction of the Jews: *Reuchlin,* p. 208. The same observation is made by Kisch, *Zasius und Reuchlin,* p. 20. See, however, Reuchlin: If the Jews burden society with their usury "essent per superiores nostros emendandi et reformandi seu expellendi. . . ." *Doctor Johannsen Reuchlins . . . Augenspiegel* (Tübingen, 1511), fol. H 2ᵛ; repr. ed., Quellen zur Geschichte des Humanismus und der Reformation in Faksimile-Ausgaben 5 (Munich, [1961]). It is to be remembered that Reuchlin's first sponsor and protector, Count Eberhard im Bart, had in his testament stipulated that the Jews be evicted from his dominions — carried through since 1492. Reuchlin was Eberhard's council and together with Gabriel Biel was a member of the Rome delegation which requested papal authorization for the University of Tübingen (1477). Eberhard's founding letter excluded Jews from this city. For the most recent data on Reuchlin's life see Hansmartin Decker-Hauff, "Bausteine zur Reuchlin-Biographie," in *Johannes Reuchlin 1455-1522: Festgabe seiner Vaterstadt Pforzheim zur 500: Wiederkehr seines Geburtstages,* ed. M. Krebs (Pforzheim, [1955]), 83-107. For Eberhard's anti-Jewish policy see Lilli Zapf, *Die Tübinger Juden: Eine Dokumentation* (Tübingen, [1974]), pp. 15-16.

acknowledge Jesus as the true Messiah everything will turn to their good in this world and in the world to come. Amen."[29]

Now we turn to the revealing preface in *De rudimentis,* dated 7 March 1506. Here we have at once a summary of his earlier views and a prophetic forecast of the events to come, those events which were to make and break his career as "Praeceptor Germaniae" — a title and task he had to bequeath to his grandnephew Melanchthon. This preface is easily summarized: Reuchlin expresses his readiness to stand up against all three parties concerned: the humanists, the scholastics, and the Jews. His point of departure is the thoroughgoing damage done to the study of Scripture not only by the "sophists" but also by the students of eloquence and poetry.[30] The *literati* may well think that he, Reuchlin, with his concern with grammar, deals with *puerilia,* not befitting an educated man.[31] But the study of grammar has been the very basis of his achievements in philosophy, since the knowledge of Hebrew is the precondition for initiation into the Cabala.[32]

29. Cf. Kisch, *Zasius und Reuchlin,* p. 20. Reuchlin has made good on his concluding offer to further the social integration of converted Jews by "placing" them as Hebrew teachers in monasteries: They should serve the purpose of spreading the knowledge of Hebrew, which in turn is the necessary basis for introduction to the Cabala. See the revealing autobiographical letter to Ellenbog of 19 March 1510 in *Nikolaus Ellenbog: Briefwechsel,* ed. A. Bigelmair and F. Zoepfl, Corpus Catholicorum 19/21 (Münster, 1938), pp. 54-55.

30. "Persaepe mihi cogitanti de communi sacarum literarum jactura, Dionysi frater, quae cum multitudine sophismatum annis superioribus, tum maxime nunc propter eloquentiae studium et poretarum amoenitatem non modo negliguntur, verum etiam a quam plurimis contemptui habentur, in mentem venit tandem opportuni cujusdam remedii, ne sanctae bibliae scriptura vel aliquando tota pereat. . . ." Geiger, *Reuchlins Briefwechsel* (n. 12 above), pp. 88-89.

31. "Fateor itaque, circa literarum rationem puerorum esse studia, et esse me etiam eo nunc provectum, ut partim me philosophum, partim jurisconsultum arbitrentur his de causis maxime, tum quod ex Capnione nostro quem edidimus 'De verbo mirifico' non nihil quod verae philosophiae accedat, sibi persuadeant posse exanclari, tum quod jam annos complures super fortissimis Suevis confoederatos principes dignitatem triumviratus non ambitione sed electione mera sim consecutus, eumque honorem usque in hunc diem servare me sentiant inconcussum atque sanctum"; Geiger, *Reuchlins Briefwechsel,* p. 90. The lukewarm support of Reuchlin by a majority of the humanists in the ensuing battle can indeed be explained by their preoccupation with the Greek and Latin authors. As Hans Widmann has pointed out, the great Hebrew master failed to find a market for his *De rudimentis.* "Zu Reuchlins Rudimenta Hebraica," in *Festschrift für Josef Benzing,* ed. E. Geck and G. Pressler (Wiesbaden, 1964), pp. 492-98. Apparently not only the scholastic centers like Cologne, but also the humanist sodalities did not hail Hebrew studies at this "early" date.

32. "Inscriptio hujus libri est: 'De rudimentis hebraicis', eo quod non jam doctis, sed rudibus ac erudiendis ea volumina composuerim, deinceps altiora deo annuente

While the humanists may merely laugh at him and lose their respect, the Jews will assail him and the sophists will fall upon him like growling dogs.[33] What enormity, they will cry out. This man dares to criticize the holy Vulgate and to call into question the inspired work of such holy men as Jerome and Lyra.[34] Since Reuchlin correctly assessed these opponents — as history amply illustrates — the following statement combines the power of rhetorical rhythm with the ring of truth: "Quamquam enim Hieronymum sanctum veneror ut angelum, et Lyram colo ut magistrum, tamen adoro veritatem ut deum. (Though I admire Jerome as an angel and highly esteem Lyra as a master, I bow before the truth as before God)."[35]

This impressive declaration of independence is indeed the basis of all truly historical research. It includes at the same time the obligation to apply Reuchlin's dictum to the great master himself. His own golden rule for the iconoclastic emancipation from reverence yields the admission that for him "the Jews" are collectively guilty for their lasting rejection by God, with the rare elitist exemption made for the cultured Jew who abandons the Talmud to accept the Christian Cabala. Though Reuchlin acknowledges his indebtedness to Jakob Jehiel Loans, "the learned and widely read" physician to Emperor Frederick III, who taught him the Hebrew alphabet,[36] he knows that the Jews are not going to respond favorably to his undertaking.[37] This Christian syntax, thus Reuchlin concludes his Preface to Book 3, is all the more necessary "since our [German] Jews are unwilling to teach Christians their language either due to ill-will or to inability, but basically because a Talmudic saying

---

daturus, quae ad arcanae Pythagorae disciplinam et artem Cabalisticam deserviunt, a nemine prorsus intellecta, nisi Hebraice praedocto." Geiger, *Reuchlins Briefwechsel*, p. 93.

33. ". . . ego miseratus tam sanctas literas, indolui, mea aetate studiosos diutius hebraicae linguae scientia carere: quapropter illorum ingenio favens ausus sum, licet supra modum forsan temere, primus omnium et tam grave pondus meis humeris imponere et simul me offerre latratibus mordacium; utinam judaicis solum." Geiger, *Reuchlins Briefwechsel*, p. 90.

34. "At gravius insurgent, credo, invidi contra Dictionarium nostrum in quo multorum frequenter interpretationes taxantur. Proh scelus, exclamabunt, nihil indignius patrum memoria, nihil admissum crudelius, cum ille homo audacissimus tot et tam sanctos viros divino spiritu afflatos labefactare contendat. Hieronymi beatissimi scriptura, Gelasio Papa teste, recepta est in ecclesia, venerabilis pater Nicolaus de Lyra, ordinarius expositor Bibliae, omnibus Christi fidelibus vir integerrimus probatur." Geiger, *Reuchlins Briefwechsel*, p. 97.

35. Geiger, *Reuchlins Briefwechsel*, p. 98.

36. Cf. Geiger, *Reuchlins Briefwechsel*, pp. 91-92.

37. Geiger, *Reuchlins Briefwechsel*, p. 93.

forbids them to do so."[38] Once again the Talmud stands between the Jews and their conversion, between the Jews and their eternal salvation.

When Reuchlin in his legal "Gutachten" or *Opinion* of 1510 advises against the proposed confiscation of the "Jewish books" he argues — as Guido Kisch in his precious *Zasius und Reuchlin*[39] has shown — like Bartolus before him on the basis of Roman law, of the *Codex Iustinianus.* As a jurist he concludes that the Jews are not slaves but *concives,* fellow citizens, not heretics but a tolerated *secta,* and finally, for the Christian, neighbors. The Jewish books should not be burned; rather, the Jews should be converted by persuasion, "durch vernünfftig disputationen, senfftmüttigklich und güttlich."[40]

The lasting significance of Reuchlin's "Gutachten" is easily lost in the cloud of his later retractions. He heralds the two-kingdoms doctrine which Luther was to make his mainstay albeit ultimately without benefit for the political status of the Jews. The basis of Reuchlin's argument is precisely that the Jews in civil law are *concives,* fellow citizens "inn ainem burgerrecht und burgfriden." At the same time they are "unsers glaubens fiendt," enemies from the perspective of the Christian religion.[41] Once assaulted as a heretic in the pay of the Jews, Reuchlin claims in the *Augenspiegel* (Tübingen, 1511) to have been thoroughly misunderstood in his defense of the Jewish books, and proves amenable to the solution that "the blasphemous parts" of the Talmud be confiscated and stored in Christian libraries.[42] In this way at once the interests of ecclesiastical inquisition and of scholarly investigation are safeguarded.[43]

---

38. ". . . nolui etiam huic decori tuo deesse quin hebraica nunc sacerdos, addisceres, praesertim cum nostrates Judaei vel invidia, vel imperitia ducti Christianum neminem in eorum lingua erudire velint idque recusant cujusdam Rab[b]i Ami auctoritate, qui in Thalmud . . . ita dixit: 'Non explanantur verba legis cuiquam gentili eo quod scriptum est: Qui adnunciat verba sua Jacob, praecepta sua et judicia sua Israel non fecit similiter omni genti.' Nobis autem in statu gratiae aliter mandatur [Matt. 10:27]. . . ." Geiger, *Reuchlins Briefwechsel,* p. 100.

39. Kisch, *Zasius und Reuchlin* (n. 18 above), pp. 23-36.

40. *Augenspiegel,* fol. E 4ᵛ. Cf. Johannes Reuchlin, *Gutachten über das jüdische Schrifttum,* ed. and trans. A. Leinz-von Dessauer, Pforzheimer Reuchlinschriften, 2 (Constance and Stuttgart, 1965), pp. 106-7.

41. *Augenspiegel,* fol. J 3ʳ.

42. ". . . conservandus esset saltem apud ordinarios, ut docti apud nos in lingua hebraea aliquando possent eum habere, et ubi Iudaei aliqua futuris temporibus confingerent, possent cum opus esset probati apparere in reprobatione eius et condemnatione." *Augenspiegel,* fol. F 3ʳ.

43. Not all the Jewish books are to be burned, but some are to be preserved: "Ad hoc respondeo intelligendum esse dictum meum quod non debeant comburi universaliter et omnes, sed quod aliqui essent conservandi. . . ." *Augenspiegel,* fol. H 2ʳ. I differ at this

Has the great spokesman for Jewish emanicipation been brought to heel by intimidation or is the *Augenspiegel* a reliable commentary upon the "Gutachten" of the year before? It must be said that if we are prepared to trust Reuchlin himself as "sui ipsius interpres" his sole concern remained what it had been from the beginning: not the Jews, nor the Talmud as such, but free scholarly access to the sources of the Christian Cabala. Reuchlin combines the plea for civil emancipation of the Jews with social discrimination and religious ostracism.

IV. Pfefferkorn: A Convert's Shrill Voice

For over a century no one has made a detailed study of the tracts of Josef Pfefferkorn (1469-1522/23);[44] the frenzies of this fanatic seemed sufficiently documented. Baptized Johannes Pfefferkorn in 1504, he published by 1507 in Nuremberg and Cologne his *Judenspiegel* in German and Latin.[45] A series of pamphlets reprinted in various cities followed: *Die Judenbeichte* (1508), *Wie die blinden Juden yr Ostern halten* (1509) with as a first climax the *Judenfeind*,[46] adorned by an epigram of Ortwin

---

point from Wilhelm Maurer, who concluded in his otherwise excellent study: "Bildungs-einheit statt Judenmission — das ist im Grunde Reuchlins Programm, durch das er das Anliegen der Judenemanzipation vom Ende des 18. Jahrhunderts schon vorweg nimmt." *Kirche und Synagoge: Motive und Formen der Auseinandersetzung der Kirche mit dem Judentum im Laufe der Geschichte* (Stuttgart, 1953), p. 38.

44. See the bibliographical data given by Kisch, *Zasius und Reuchlin,* p. 75, n. 3.

45. Translated as *Speculum adhortationis Judaice ad Christum.* For this international forum I prefer to use the Latin edition with the explicit: Editum Colonie per Iohannem pefferkorn [sic] olim Judeum modo Christianum. Anno domini 1507, feria tertia post Decollationem sancti Joannis baptiste.

46. Meier Spanier has questioned the authenticity of Pfefferkorn's pamphlets. The Latin works are excluded *in toto:* "Er konnte kein Latein." "Zur Charakteristik Johannes Pfefferkorns," *Zeitschrift für die Geschichte der Juden in Deutschland* 6 (1936): 209-29; 210. But the German pamphlets are also said to betray external guidance. His Hebrew and Talmud knowledge were not a bit better: "Er wußte eben nicht mehr als irgendein anderer ungebildeter Jude der damaligen Zeit; vom Talmud verstand er gar nichts. . . . ," "Characteristik Johannes Pfefferkorns," p. 212, Finally, all typically German "folksy" colloquial sayings, "von denen einige uraltes deutsches Sprachgut," are also proof of Cologne "humanist" origin. "Characteristik Johannes Pfefferkorns," p. 222. Our *Speculum adhortationis Judaice* (*Judenspiegel;* Latin and German edition, 1507) is almost completely assigned to Ortwin: "Die erste Schrift . . . dürfte fast ganz ein Werk des Ortuin Gratius sein." "Characteristik Johannes Pfefferkorns," p. 221. A collection of the German and Latin Pfefferkorn writings is

Gratius (1509), soon as anti-Reuchlinist the object of scorn in the world of learning.

It is in the *Judenspiegel* of 1507 that Pfefferkorn formulates the portentous proposal that the Talmudic books are to be confiscated and burned — the only passage noted by Reuchlin's biographer, Ludwig Geiger, and hence one of the few statements ever quoted in secondary literature.[47] The first part of the *Judenspiegel* fully suffices to explain why Pfefferkorn's readers must have lost all inclination to read any further: the convert turns on his own with the resentment of one who, having painfully broken away from his anchorage, has now fully imbibed the anti-Jewish hostility of his new environment. Based on the Vulgate which Reuchlin is about to call into question, Pfefferkorn wants to convert his "brethren according to the flesh" with that mixture of proofs and charges known from centuries of Christian "mission." Four points deserve our full attention.

Pfefferkorn advocates as a "good work" for Christians, particularly for princes and magistrates, that the obstacles to conversion be removed by confiscation of all Hebrew books except the Scriptures.[48] "On first sight someone can object," thus Pfefferkorn anticipates Reuchlin's arguments,

> that my proposal is both imprudent and morally wrong since I seem to suggest that the authorities take away possessions of the Jews against

---

being gathered at the Institut für Spätmittelalter und Reformation in Tübingen to facilitate future research. It should be noted that the Latin versions are not in keeping with late medieval scholastic Latin. Perhaps intentionally so; but in that case the riddle is unsolvable. As far as Pfefferkorn's "Bildungsstand" is concerned, Josef was several years in Prague the houseguest of Rabbi Meir Pfefferkorn and must, in view of his successful mission to the sister of Emperor Maximilian, have possessed better credentials than assumed by Spanier. Cf. Heinrich Graetz, *Volkstümliche Geschichte der Juden*, 3 vols. (Berlin and Vienna, 1923), 3.170-220; 175 and 185.

47. This limitation is noted, however, by Salo Wittmayer Baron, *A Social and Religious History of the Jews*, 16 vols., 2nd ed., rev. and enlarged (New York, 1952-1976), vol. 13; *Inquisition, Renaissance, and Reformation*, pp. 184-91; 186.

48. "Ergo omnes huiusmodi fallacias et fabulas continentes libros [Talmoth] auferte ab oculis eorum, et in ignem mittite. Ita magnum facietis opus charitatis, cum occasione errorum sublata eos inducetis in viam rectam. Postquam amiserint hos libros, tum convertent se eo promptius et facilius ad sacras literas," *Speculum adhortationis Judaice* [= *Speculum*], fol. C 4ᵛ. Actually Pfefferkorn makes three proposals. Usury should be forbidden, since to be a usurious Jew is more attractive than to be a poor Christian; fol. C 1ʳ–C 2ᵛ. Second, Jews should be forced to attend Christian sermons: This is merely a return favor since without the (preaching of the) Jews Christians would still be worshiping idols: "adhuc adoraretis idola"; fol. C 4ʳ. Third, the Jewish books should be confiscated and burned: "ita magnum facietis opus charitatis"; fol. C 4ᵛ.

their will *(ab invitis)*, illegally and contrary to law *(contra ius et fas)*. Yet I insist that no one's possessions should be taken; on the contrary, something is *given* to the Jews. But let me ask first: Why are the Jews so severely persecuted by you [Christians]? As everyone knows, they have to pay heavy taxes for their protection and public safety; they are burdened like packhorses, though they are, by nature, as free as birds in the air.[49] You bring hardly convincing arguments for your greed by claiming that in this way you want to achieve their conversion; you want to make believe that everything the Jews have to suffer from you is for their betterment. Why shouldn't you now for once do something you cannot profit from which really serves them, their conversion and eternal benefit?[50]

Our first point is that Pfefferkorn combines the awesome plan which would inscribe his name in the historical record with a daring critique of the manceps-tradition,[51] the "Reichskammerknecht" interpretation and "Rechtsbasis" for exploitation.[52]

The second point worth noting is that Pfefferkorn not only visited Reuchlin and saw him at work in his study but basically accepted Reuchlin's views as described in *De verbo mirifico*: Not just in the words but in the very letters of the Hebrew Scriptures the occult knowledge is stored which provides dominion over the forces of nature.[53] Therefore

---

49. "Notorium est quod magnis vectigalibus censibus teloneis pecunia pro tuitione et securitate onerantur, quasi servum pecus et hec prestare coguntur, quamvis sint liberi quasi avis. . . ." *Speculum* (n. 45 above), fol. C 4ᵛ–D 1ʳ.

50. Cf. *Speculum,* fol. C 4ᵛ–D 1ʳ.

51. See Guido Kisch, *The Jews in Medieval Germany: A Study of Their Legal and Social Status* (Chicago, 1949), pp. 129ff.; 145-53.

52. The principle on which Reuchlin bases his "concives", thus according the Jews the legal status of "fellow citizens," had by the end of the Middle Ages lost its — relatively seen — positive aspects when nobility and city magistrates vied with the emperor for the "protection" taxes, usually only yielding a residency permit for six years. See the documents published by Friedrich Battenberg, "Zur Rechtsstellung der Juden am Mittelrhein in Spätmittelalter und früher Neuzeit," *Zeitschrift für historische Forschung* 6 (1979): 129-83; "Urkundenanhang," pp. 171-83; and the transition as described by Renate Overdick, *Die rechtliche und wirtschaftliche Stellung der Juden in Südwestdeutschland im 15. und 16. Jahrhundert, dargestellt an den Reichsstädten Konstanz und Eßlingen und an der Markgrafschaft Baden,* Konstanzer Geschichts- und Rechtsquellen 15 (Constance, 1965), pp. 158-64.

53. "Homo qui vetus testamentum intelligit, novum legit, ex vetere novum dilucide cognoscit, neutra parte labascens. Dum nova veteribus novis vetera componit, necesse est ut oblectetur, quoniam ex figuris spiritum videt, spiritum oculis mentis quasi corpus oculis corporis cernens. Ita Iudeis accidit, quoniam ipsi acutius et comprehensibilius ad intelligendum sua dispositi profundius plerisque ceteris inquirunt et examinant scripturas. Cum et apud eos vera sint sacrarum scripturarum fundamenta

Pfefferkorn does not subscribe to the "Gutachten" of the University of Mainz which suggested that all Jewish books including the books of Moses should be confiscated.[54]

Third, Pfefferkorn's confiscation plans stand in the context of the expectation of the imminent end of the world. At least a major revolution is at hand, injustice is growing fast and God's justice is about to strike. Before God's intervention, the Jews will convert en masse — he himself is merely the beginning of a mass movement — provided they are treated properly. This includes, "of course," confiscation since this serves their betterment.[55]

As is also the case with Luther, there is here a basic ambivalence[56] and oscillation between a concerted conversion effort in view of God's eschatological timetable and a fear-ridden hatred because the stubborn, unrepenting Jews involve the Christians in a guilt-by-association soon to be horribly punished. Though the reasoning in Luther's plea for conversion by cordiality and decency in *Jesus Was Born a Jew* of 1523[57] is

---

originaliaque primordia a deo tradita per servos eius, hebraica lingua perscripta et multe particule sunt et clausule in sacris literis in libris Moisis presertim secrete adhuc et obstruse, que tamen possent prodire in lucem per eos. Ego certum puto imo nec dubito, quoniam [quin] omnis scientia, que naturali ratione comprehendi potest, veluti astronomia et cetere, in sacra maxime scriptura in litteris hebraicis mirabiliter complexa et occultata sit. Non verbis solum, sed (ut dixi) litteris, praeterea Sancta Mysteria ex singulari earum litterarum vix aliis cognoscibilium extra Judeos proprietate. Quapropter hebrei omnia hec perscrutantur funditus, et conversi ad religionem christianam conferent ea tandem ad intellectum fidei, unde dominus noster Iesus Christus laudari queat et cognosci. . . ." *Speculum,* fol. D 3ᵛ.

54. Geiger, *Johannes Reuchlin: Sein Leben,* p. 283. Cf. Graetz, *Volkstümliche Geschichte,* 3.188.

55. "Vos autem fratres Judei secundum carnem et o christiani fratres spiritu ausculantte, . . . aurem paulisper accommodate. Late et vulgo dicitur iudeos mansuros eorumque stirpem et religionem (cum horum multa interierint) in finem usque mundi, tum erit ovile unum, una fides, unus pastor. Ex meis nonnullis propositis et animo multa repetenti meditatis videtur prope adesse novissimus mundi dies. Dico ego ad hoc, quantum intelligo et sentio, Judeorum gens, non unus solum aut alter convertetur ad fidem Christi, si a christianis ita tractentur et habeantur, ut dixi et consului . . . an venturus sit dies novissimus brevi aut multo post conversionem iudeorum nihil certi scio . . . omnino sic fore credo, quod mutatio humanarum rerum orietur et consurget brevi in mundo, maxime in populo christiano." *Speculum,* fol. D 4ʳ.

56. This ambivalence is also part and parcel of the confiscation plan itself: "non quasi vi sed in emendationem Judeorum." *Speculum,* fol. D 1ʳ. Furthermore, it is necessary for us, for the church: ". . . quandiu idola hec (sic enim nominare placet hos falsos et blasphemos libros) non tolluntur e medio et internitioni [sic] dantur, nunquam ecclesia christiana in quiete et pace erit aut perdurabit." *Speculum,* fol. D 1ʳ.

57. For Luther see the concluding passage of his famous 1523 treatise (see n. 110, below): "For they have been led astray for so long that one must deal gently

quite different from Pfefferkorn's in 1507,[58] the same shift from conversion hope to bitter hostility is to be noted in the further development of both.[59] Generally it can be said that, so long as the conversion of Jews served Christian needs either by signifying or by forestalling the end, Christian Europe would remain a dangerous habitat for Jews, and especially so in times of heightened religious fervor.

A fourth and final observation leads us away from Cologne on the eve of the Reformation to Nuremberg and Ingolstadt in the forties when a new peak of anti-Judaism is reached. Pfefferkorn warns the Christians — and respect for his daring should not be withheld at this point — that they weaken their own case by their base credulity in circulating stories about Jewish ritual murder. With this popular belief in Jews killing children to get at the healing power of their blood, "we make ourselves ridiculous and the Christian faith a matter of mirth and contempt."[60]

---

with them. . . . In this way some may be won over. Instead of this we try to drive them by force. . . . So long as we treat them like dogs how can be expect to work any good among them? Again when we will not let them work or do business or have any human fellowship with us, and so force them into practising usury, how can that do them any good? If we really want to help them, we must be guided by Christian love, not by popish legalism. We must receive them cordially and allow them to trade and work among us, hear our Christian teaching and witness our Christian life style. If some of them prove obstinate, what of that? We are not such good Christians ourselves." WA 11.336.19-34; translation according to *Luther's Works,* American edition, 45 (Philadelphia, 1962), 229, cited by E. Gordon Rupp, *Martin Luther and the Jews,* Robert Waley Cohen Memorial Lecture, 1972 (London, 1972), pp. 11-12. For Pfefferkorn note: "Igitur vos, o charissimi christiani, obtestor per nomen Iesu redemptoris nostri, qui cum publicanis et peccatoribus manducavit, qui a peccatrice sanctos pedes suos lachrymis eius lavari et a samaritana petere potum non dedignitus est, recipite iudeos benigne, oculos commiserationis in eos coniicite, misereminique populi dei, quem in miseriis et exilio cernitis. Adversus eos mites et moderati sitis suaviter eos doceatis instituatis non modo in fide, verum etiam illis opera misericordie et virtutum impartiamini. Ipsi enim inordinato et incomposito regimine moralis vite secundum naturam motumque sensualem potius vivunt. Hec via est quam dominus Iesus monuit et docuit, ut tandem in unum ovile [John 10:16] cum pastore nostro Iesu Christo, qui animam suam posuit pro ovibus suis, conveniamus rabidis luporum morsibus non derelicti. Quod vobis concedat pius pater et misericors dominus. Amen." *Speculum,* fol. D 3ᵛ-4ʳ.

58. ". . . veniet dominus noster Jesus Christus qui non cum Iudeis fuerat temporis in carne. . . ." *Speculum,* fol E 3ᵛ. ". . . meditemur passionem domini Jesu assidue, sequamur doctrinam eius, in fide integra perseveremus, contemptum eius non feramus aut patiamur, ulciscamur pro viribus." *Speculum,* fol. E 3ᵛ.

59. Cf. WA 51.195-96; 15 February 1546; sermon preached three days before his death.

60. If Jews kill children at all, it is out of revenge but not to get blood for medical purposes: "Fugite ergo et vitate orationem hanc ridiculam, falsam, et (si recte conspicere vultis) nobis christianis non parum contemptui existentem." *Speculum,* fol. D 1ᵛ.

Early in the year 1529 an anonymous treatise was published on this same risky theme: "Whether it is true and credible that Jews secretly kill children and use their blood."[61] It is now well established[62] that this treatise is the work of Andreas Osiander (1498-1552), a Lutheran minister in Nuremberg, one of Luther's chief strongholds in the South, which opted the next year publicly for the Reformation by signing the *Confessio Augustana*. It has not been noted that Osiander uses Pfefferkorn's warning in building his own case against the ritual murder charge. For Osiander this accusation is not based on fact or reason but more likely on greed and envy. After all, Moses not only forbids murder but also the taking of blood. Furthermore, why would Jews have to commit murder in order to get at blood; and if it is to be Christian blood, what about the Jews in Turkey? Were not also the early Christians accused of ritual murder? In all known murder cases not Jews but Christians were guilty. In every future case a series of primary suspects should be investigated who all have an interest in making Jews responsible for their own crime: a poverty-stricken feudal

61. Gottfried Seebaß, "Verzeichnis der Werke Andreas Osianders," in *Das reformatorische Werk des Andreas Osiander*, Einzelarbeiten aus der Kirchengeschichte Bayerns 44 (Nuremberg, 1967), pp. 6-58; 17, n. 80. In the *Bibliographia Osiandrica: Bibliographie der gedruckten Schriften Andreas Osianders d. Ä. (1496-1552)*, ed. G. Seebass (Nieuwkoop, 1971) this treatise is dated as "1540?" with the comment, "Originaldruck nicht gefunden." "Verzeichnis," p. 124, n. 29. My Erlangen colleague, Professor Gerhard Müller, kindly provided me with a copy of the only known print, which is in American "Privatbesitz." Moritz Stern edited this text with a preface under the title *Andreas Osianders Schrift über die Blutbeschuldigung* (Kiel, 1893).

62. Emanuel Hirsch, *Die Theologie des Andreas Osiander und ihre geschichtlichen Voraussetzungen* (Göttingen, 1919), pp. 276-80; Seebaß, *Das reformatorische Werk des Andreas Osiander*, pp. 82-85. For Osiander's attitude toward Judaism see his revealing request to the town council of Nuremberg (17 February 1529) to allow a Jewish teacher to visit and train him in Aramaic: "Dieweil nun unwidersprechlich ist, das die Juden baide, das gesetz und propheten, baß [besser] verstehn dan wir Christen, ausgenomen, das sie die person nicht fur Christum halten, die wir darfur erkennen, und sonst auch vil guts verstands und grosser gehaimnus haben, deren sie ytzo selbs nicht geprauchen, als die nichts mer studirn, sonder nur dem wucher und andern posen stucken anhangen, were es ye wol werd, das die Christen solchs zu sich prechten, nicht allain wider die Juden, sonder auch fur sich selbs zu geprauchen, welchs aber nicht geschehen kan noch mag on verstand der caldaischen sprach. Dieweil aber bißher in vil hundert jaren kain Christ dieselben konnt hat, es were dan der graff Picus von Mirandula, der zu frue gestorben, ists offenbar, das wir die von Juden mussen lernen: dan das sie ymand von im selbs solt lernen, ist unmuglich, dieweil wir weder grammatica noch vocubularien darzu haben, die gegrundt wern." *Andreas Osiander d. Ä. Gesamtausgabe*, 3: *Schriften und Briefe 1528 bis April 1530*, ed. G. Müller and G. Seebaß (Gütersloh, 1979), p. 337, ll. 14-25. This request may well have started the rumor that Osiander was a Jew. See the excursus of Seebaß, *Das reformatorische Werk*, pp. 82-85.

overlord or one of his civil servants; the clergy interested in a new miracle and the concomitant attraction of pilgrims; indebted citizens, witches, or abusive parents — they all want to put the blame on the Jews.[63]

Osiander, one of the foremost Hebrew scholars of his day, was an enthusiastic disciple of Reuchlin and came to share Reuchlin's respect for the hidden power and secret knowledge stored in Cabala and Talmud. And again, as before with Reuchlin, this implied for him not a lesser effort at conversion but rather the correction of misleading Talmudic errors. Yet Osiander goes beyond Reuchlin, in that he not only respects the learned Rabbi, the Baruch-figure of *De verbo mirifico,* but also the common Jew, the collective assailed and caricatured in popular Christian stories.

It is exactly this aspect which infuriated Johannes Eck (1486-1543), for a time even host to Reuchlin in Ingolstadt (December 1519). By way of response, Eck wrote a booklet expressly designed to lend scholarly credence to popular anti-Judaism in which he manages to surpass in crudity, fury, and defamation all preceding publications of the Reformation era: *Ains Judenbüchlins Verleging [Widerlegung].*[64] Two Jews from Sulzbach try to aid Tittingen Jews accused of the ritual murder of young Michael Pisenharter shortly after Easter 1540.[65] They present in their

63. "Zum zwelfften so sein die taufften Juden hin und wider an mancherley orten in mancherley weg von geschickten gelerten und weysen leuten bespracht [i.e., verleumdet] worden und hat doch keiner nie bekant das er etwas darvon wisse oder das er glaube das es war sey. Nun werden nicht allein die Juden getaufft die auß gottes gnaden die warheyt erkennen. Sonder auch ye zuzeyten die so unter den Juden jrer mißhandlung halben veracht, verstossen, und verbannet sein. Nun hat ye kein teyl ursach die sach zu verlaugnen wann etwas dran were. Dan die rechtglaubigen solten es ja Christo dem herrn zu ehren bekennen und oeffnen, damit die Christen gewarnet und weg gesucht wurden das man solchs ubel unterkeme. Die andern aber so auß haß der Juden Christen werden, solten es freylich auch nich verschweygen von jren feynden und verfolgern. Als dann der Pfefferkorn zu Coeln den Juden zu wider vil angezeygt und eroeffnet hat — obs alles war gewest oder nit, ist hie nicht not anzuzeygen. Het er aber von der kinder mord etwas gewust, wie were es jm und seinen Prediger munchen ein freud gewest das selb anzuzeygen, und aller welt bekant zu machen." *Ob es war und glaublich sey, daß die Juden der Christen kinder heymlich erwürgen und jr blut gebrauchen ein treffenliche schrifft auff eines yeden urteil gestelt* (s.a., s.l. [1540]), fol. b 1ᵛ–b 2ʳ.

64. Ingolstadt, 1541. Durch Joh. Ecken. I used the copy of the 1542 edition at the University Library, Freiburg.

65. Johann Casper Ulrichs includes this "event" in a survey which he concludes with the words: "Wir beschliessen nun diese Mord Geschichten mit vielem Eckel, und gestehe[n] gerne daß aus so vielen Mordthaten, die man ehedem den Juden aufgebürdet hat, die allermeisten schändliche und unverantwortliche Zulagen seyen. Es dienet auch der Christenheit nicht zur Ehre, daß man aus diesen angegebenen Martyrern Heilige gemachet hat." *Sammlung Jüdischer Geschichten, welche sich mit diesem Volk in dem XIII. und folgenden Jahrhunderten bis auf MDCCLX. in der Schweitz von Zeit zu*

defense Osiander's "Gutachten" of 1529, which the Bishop of Eichstätt, ex officio chancellor of the University of Ingolstadt, refers to his vice-chancellor Johannes Eck, for twenty-five years the most significant and learned spokesman for the Counter-Reformation. For Eck it is immediately clear that the author must be a "Lutherischer predicant" (whom he rightly suspects to be Osiander) so blinded by his heresy that he makes the Jews out to be better than Christians — Lutherans, that is.[66]

With the same repetitiousness with which Reuchlin had discredited Pfefferkorn as "der Tauft Jud" in the *Augenspiegel,* Eck calls Osiander "Judenschützer" or "Judenvater" who has the gall to denounce the authorities for their financial greed instead of denouncing the Jews for their guilt. Osiander must have received a good bit of the Jewish golden calf to line his pockets. After all, the Talmud explicitly commands the Jews to kill Christian children.[67] When that man argues that no baptized Jew has ever reported such a thing, Eck replies that the appeal to Pfefferkorn does not prove a thing, since Pfefferkorn can only speak for himself.[68] It is equally inadmissible to introduce Reuchlin's authority; the *Augenspiegel* makes perfectly clear that "der ehrlich Doctor" differed from Pfefferkorn only in a matter of words: Reuchlin never denied that there are Talmudic prayers directed against the Christians.[69] Eck himself knows about a ritual murder case in Freiburg during 1503 and furthermore about many well-attested published cases. Why have the Jews been thrown out of so many countries and cities? Eck goes on to relate the European history of banning Jews over fifty years from the Spanish expulsion until his own day, which serves as proof of a common Christian stance and of Christian common sense.[70]

The peak of fury is reached when Eck piles nineteen caustic characteristics of the Jews into one sentence, summarized in the designation: a blasphemous people, "ein gotslesterlich Volck."[71] Not in keeping with our present state of research and therefore quite unexpected is Eck's final

---

Zeit zugetragen. Zur Beleuchtung der allgemeinen Historie dieser Nation herausgegeben (Basel, 1768), pp. 92, 87.

66. Eck, *Ains Judenbüchlins Verlegung,* fol. G 2^v.

67. Eck, *Ains Judenbüchlins Verlegung,* fol. G 3^r.

68. Eck, *Ains Judenbüchlins Verlegung,* fol. N 4^{r-v}.

69. Eck, *Ains Judenbüchlins Verlegung,* fol. H 3^v.

70. Eck alludes to well-recorded events at Freiburg, "a community with a long tradition of special hostility to Jews." Steven W. Rowan, "Ulrich Zasius and the Baptism of Jewish Children," *Sixteenth Century Journal* 6/2 (1975): 3-25; 7; German translation: "Ulrich Zasius und die Taufe jüdischer Kinder," *Zeitschrift des Breisgau-Geschichtsvereins ("Schau-ins-Land")* 97 (1978): 79-98; 82.

71. Eck, *Ains Judenbüchlins Verlegung,* fol. J 3^r.

conclusion. "Der Judenvater" who wants to whitewash the Jews is a natural product of Wittenberg and "the latest fruit on the Lutheran tree":[72] the devil speaks through you, Lutherans, in order to exculpate the Jews from ritual murder.[73] The inversion of this charge had been expressed before. Josel von Rosheim reports that the Jews had been made responsible for the "out-break" of the Reformation.[74] Eck, however, reverses these roles by pointing to the spiritual havoc caused by Luther: "Luthersohn" and "Judenvater" are but two sides of one coin. One example suffices for him: Destructive insistence on the scriptural principle leads to the equally irrational and heretical respect for the Hebrew Scriptures.[75]

Eck construes here an identification of Luther's Reformation with philo-Judaism which is wholly untenable as far as Luther himself is concerned. At the same time, he rightly alerts us to the fact that it is equally impermissible to deal with "Luther and the Jews" in terms of a *solus Lutherus,* so long pursued by a Luther scholarship which isolates Luther from the wider context of Wittenberg theology and from the social and intellectual history of his times.

V. The Surprising Intolerance of Erasmus

In the following two sections on Erasmus and Luther we can be brief, not because these two prolific authors would not provide us with ample material but because we must restrict our presentation to points where the sources require a partial or total reorientation.

Three points are to be noted in respect to Erasmus's view of the Jews. In the first place the signal contribution made by Guido Kisch in his booklet on Erasmus's view of the Jews[76] has not yet left its imprint

72. ". . . kumt auch da ain newe frucht herfur ains luterischen, der schön machen will der juden kindermord." Eck, *Ains Judenbüchlins Verlegung,* fol. N 4r.
73. Eck, *Ains Judenbüchlins Verlegung,* fol. Q 4r.
74. Cf. Selma Stern, *Josel von Rosheim: Befehlshaber der Judenschaft im Heiligen Römischen Reich Deutscher Nation,* Veröffentlichung des Leo-Baeck-Instituts (Stuttgart, 1959), p. 83.
75. Why then, Eck shrewdly insists, did not the *Confessio Augustana* (1530) reject the Vulgate and argue on the basis of the Hebrew text! *Ains Judenbüchlins Verlegung,* fol. Q 1r-v.
76. *Erasmus' Stellung zu Juden und Judentum,* Philosophie und Geschichte 83/84 (Tübingen, 1969). After the appearance of this article, Cornelis Augustijn published "Erasmus und die Juden," *Nederlands Archief voor Kerkgeschiedenis* 60 (1980): 22-38. More clearly — and most appropriately — Augustijn underscores that

on Erasmus scholarship.[77] Kisch's conclusion, summarized in the words "der tiefverwurzelte, maßlose Judenhaß" (a deeply rooted, boundless Jew-hatred),[78] is indeed not easily reconciled with our equally deepseated respect for the *philosophia christiana* of this great Dutchman, his plea for peace and tolerance, and his vision of the *bonae litterae* as the basis of a new human dignity. Yet Kisch has not overstated his case, but rather understated it by not collecting all evidence. Erasmus saw "the Jews" collectively at work as allies of Pfefferkorn and accused them of being the masterminds of the Peasant Revolt. France is "the most spotless and most flourishing part of Christendom," because France alone is "not infected with heretics, with Bohemian schismatics, with Jews, with half-Jewish marranos."[79] A baptized Jew remains a half-Jew; but the "creep" Pfefferkorn is not merely a half-Jew but a Jew and a half. And when a person is disliked, as in the case of the papal nuncio Aleander, the explanation is obvious: The man must be a Jew.

With the critique of Pfefferkorn Erasmus combines a warning against baptizing Jews: If we could look inside Pfefferkorn we would find not one but six hundred Jews;[80] we should show more caution in

---

"Iudaei" often refers to legalistic Christians. Yet, I cannot agree with his conclusion that Erasmus respects the individual Jew *sub specie aeternitatis*: "Das Judentum hat als Religion keine Zukunft. Die Juden schon!" "Erasmus und die Juden," 37. Erasmus's expectation that ultimately all Jews would be converted is not a specific view on his part. The whole tragedy of toleration based on conversion is formulated by Erasmus himself: ". . . quia Paulus praedixit fore ut Judaei tandem aggregentur ad ovile Christi, toleramus impaiam ac blasphemam gentem. . . ." "Declarationes ad Censuras Facultatis Theologiae Parisiensis," *Opera Omnia* (Leiden, 1703-1706, repr. ed., London, 1962), IX, 909AB; quoted by C. Augustijn, "Erasmus und die Juden," 37, n. 95. Simon Markish does not go beyond Augustijn in bringing new arguments. *Erasme et les Juifs* (Lausanne, 1979).

77. In the Toronto edition of Erasmus's letters, exemplary both in its translations and in its annotations, we find an exceptionally long note to letter 541, which is addressed to Wolfgang Capito and dated 26 February 1517. Erasmus's warning against the revival of Judaism, "the most pernicious plague . . .," is explained in terms of "a deep Paulinism rather than any notable interest in, or concern about, the Jewish community. . . ." *Collected Works of Erasmus: The Correspondence of Erasmus* [= *EL*], trans. R. A. B. Mynors and D. F. S. Thomson, annotated by J. K. McConica (Toronto, 1974ff.), 4.266-67; note to l. 154. Though Kisch (see nn. 76, 78) is referred to in the preface to Letter 694, which at the end of the same year is addressed to Pirckheimer (2 November 1517), Erasmus's view of the Jews in connection with Pfefferkorn — here designated as a Dominican (!) — is characterized as "unprecedented as far as his earlier correspondence is concerned." *EL* 5.164.

78. Kisch, *Erasmus' Stellung zu Juden und Judentum*, p. 29.

79. Allen (n. 6 above), 2.501.10; *EL* 4.279.12-15; 10 March 1517.

80. Allen, 3.127.24.

admitting others into the Church.[81] To contain the new upsurge of Judaism Erasmus is prepared to discard the Old Testament. In this way the New Testament and the unity of Christians can be kept intact. "If only the Church would not attach so much importance to the Old Testament — it is a book of shadows, given just for a time *(pro tempore datum)*!"[82] We will have to redefine our concept of tolerance significantly in order to claim for Erasmus the historical respect he really deserves.

Our second observation concerns the type of tolerance in which Erasmus did believe and for which he labored. The tolerance intended by Erasmus is the freedom of the Christian scholar to publish his findings regardless of schools and party alignment. This vision explains his seemingly contradictory statements about Reuchlin made within three years of each other. In the Louvain 1519 edition of the *Colloquies* he makes a point of stating: "I am no Reuchlinist . . . never have I given him support; and he would not have wanted it."[83] To the enlarged re-edition of the same *Colloquies* (Basel, 1522), already in press, Erasmus hastens to add in the summer of 1522 his *Apotheosis Capnionis,* his glorification of Reuchlin who has just died.[84] In this "In Memoriam" Reuchlin is honored as a second Jerome — for Erasmus the highest praise conceivable.[85] Yet, far from being presented as the protagonist of Jewish emancipation Reuchlin is depicted by Erasmus as the victim of Satan, Satan who attacks some of the most eminent contemporaries just as he once assailed Jesus Christ — through the Scribes and the Pharisees.[86] His identification is clear; his loyalty to

81. Allen, 3.127.37-38.

82. Allen, 3.253.25-26. Cf. *EL* 5.347.26-28.

83. Erasmus's concern is of course to deny his complicity in the publication of the *Illustrorum Virorum Epistolae* of May 1519, particularly after Hochstraten's publication in April 1519 of the *Destructio Cabale* in which he also attacked Erasmus's *Novum Instrumentum;* see Allen, 4.120-122; 121.13, 16-17. Erasmus's denial contains a double untruth since Reuchlin not only asked Erasmus explicitly to champion his cause (Allen 1.556.22-28; *EL* 2.285.25-33 [April 1514]), but second, Erasmus had actually written on Reuchlin's behalf to Cardinal Riario (†1521), generally thought to be *papabilis.* Allen, 2.73.135-38; *EL* 3.91.145-48 (15 May 1515).

84. In Bad Liebenzell on 30 June 1522. See Hans Rupprich, "Johannes Reuchlin und seine Bedeutung im europäischen Humanismus," in *Johannes Reuchlin* (n. 28, above), pp. 10-34; 33. Cf. Allen, 5.124.46 and corresponding note.

85. His name is to be inserted in the saints' calendar just as in the library his books ". . . proxime divum Hieronymum." *Desiderio Erasmo da Rotterdam: L'apoteosi di Giovanni Reuchlin,* ed. and trans. G. Vallese (Naples, 1949), p. 130, ll. 210-11.

86. "Quod olim fecit Sathanas per Scribas et Pharisaeos in Dominum Iesum, hoc et nunc facit per Pharisaicos quosdam in optimos quosque viros, ac de genere mortalium suis vigiliis bene merentes. Nunc ille metit optiman messem pro semente

Reuchlin is owed not to the great Christian cabalist but to the sturdy student of the *bonae litterae,* suffering like Erasmus under the Dominican obscurantists.[87] Erasmus was indeed a protagonist of tolerance. Yet his concept of "tolerance" was too erudite to temper his own virulent anti-Judaism. This apparently belonged for him to another world of reference. As critique Erasmus could coin the often quoted phrase: "Si christianum est odisse Iudeos, hic abunde Christiani sumus omnes."[88] But this critique never served as a criterion.

Finally, there is a strong, theological anti-Judaism[89] underlying Erasmus's very program,[90] which cannot simply be identified with racial anti-Judaism, or what we nowadays would call social or political "anti-semitism." It is his antilegalism, his campaign against formal religion and its multiplication of observances, which allows the easy alternation between "Pharisees" and "Scholastics," between "Jewish" and "legalistic." This anti-Judaism insists on the duality of body and soul or, in terms of reform ideology, on the tension between external religion and internal truth which would become a major theme for his younger disciples, the city reformers. Yet the very facility with which the terms "Pharisaic," "Jewish," and "Judaistic" are used nearly interchangeably, and invariably with negative connotations, suggests that this symbolic language refers to the continuous threat of the old Israel, a life threat to the values of the Erasmian trinity of scholarship, society, and religion: unpartisan scholarship, a learned society, and genuine piety.

In view of the foregoing three points it should no longer surprise

---

quam fecit. Interim nostrae partes erunt illius memoriam habere sacrosanctam; illius nomen ferre laudibus; ac subinde illum salutare verbis huiusmodi: O sancta anima, sis felix linguis sanctis, perdito malas linguas, infectas veneno gehennae." *Desideris Erasmus von Rotterdam,* p. 134, ll. 247-57.

87. Cf. his letter to John Fisher dated 1 September 1522; Allen, 5.123.19-20.

88. To Hochstraten, 11 August 1519; Allen, 4.46.142-43.

89. For the parallel phenomenon with Jerome, Erasmus's favorite Church Father, see Horst Dieter Rauh, *Das Bild des Antichrist im Mittelalter: Von Tyconius zum Deutschen Symbolismus,* Beiträge zur Geschichte der Philosophie und Theologie des Mittelalters, N.F. 9 (Münster, 1979[2]), pp. 132-33.

90. Though a constant theme in Erasmus's writings, a most concise formulation is found in *Commentarii in Psalmum 'Beatus Vir'* [Psalm 1] *Finis,* often overlooked while attached to the second edition of the *Enchiridion* (Basel, 1518): "Sub lege sunt servi, in lege liberi. Iudaei . . . nihil habentes praeter insipidam litteram, legis onere gravantur. . . . Superstitio litterae contrahit animum, spiritus et caritas dilatat." *Opera Omnia* [n. 76, above], V, p. 182B. Cf. "Item, qui summo legis cortici insistit, non meditatur in lege Domini. Cortex insipidus est plerumque tum adeo non frugifer, ut pestilens etiam ac letalis, teste Paulo." p. 183A.

us that the amalgam of peace, concord, and erudition which constitutes the new tolerance as a typical Christian virtue is restricted to a Christian society, excluding Judaism as "the most pernicious plague and bitterest enemy that one can find to the teaching of Christ."[91] When Erasmus wanted the whole world to know "I am no Reuchlinist" he obviously was afraid of being implicated in a heresy trial. He spoke out of fear. And yet he spoke the truth: he was no Reuchlinist.[92] Erasmus feared above all that with the renaissance of literature not only paganism but also Judaism would become a new intellectual force,[93] and this "pernicious plague," already making headway,[94] was for him the direct consequence of the revival of Hebrew studies.[95]

VI. The Eve of the Reformation

It is not too harsh to say that in medieval and early modern times phases of intensified religious fervor and programs for reform of the *Corpus Christianum* always spelled doom for the Jews. In the sixteenth century there are, as far as I see, three major factors which coalesced to lead to a new peak of anti-Judaism.

1. The pamphlet war, leading up to the explosion of the so-called "German Peasants' Revolt" of the years 1524-1526, made renewal of society through the justice of God thematic and added to the traditional *gravamina* against extortion of the empire by the church a general critique of the powers that be, particularly with regard to tithing and taxing.[96] The protection of the Jews by the emperor and the patrician faction

91. To Capito, 26 February 1517; Allen, 2.491.138-39; EL 4.267.154-55.

92. See Charles Zika, "Reuchlin and Erasmus: Humanism and Occult Philosophy," *Journal of Religious History* 9 (1977): 223-46; 229.

93. "Nunc audimus apud Bohemos exoriri novum Iudaeorum genus, Sabbatarios appellant. . . ." *De Amabili* [Allen: *Liber de Sarcienda*] *Ecclesiae Concordia*, dedicated to Julis Pflug and dated 31 July 1533. Erasmus, *Opera Omnia* (n. 76, above), V, p. 505D-506A. Cf. "Dicuntur et hodie repullulascere Sabbatarii, qui septimi diei otium incredibili superstitione observant." *Ecclesiastae, sive de Ratione Concionandi*, lib. III, dedicated to Christoph von Stadion, dated 6 August 1535. Erasmus, *Opera Omnia* V, p. 1038B.

94. "Nuper exierunt in vulgus aliquot libelli merum Iudaismum resipientes," Allen, 2.491.147-48.

95. ". . . ne renascentibus Hebraeorum literis Iudaismus meditetur per occasionem reviviscere." Allen, 2.491.137-38.

96. Oberman, *Werden und Wertung*, pp. 199-200; 263-66.

among the city fathers who opposed the expulsion of Jews led to the easy identification of tithing with usury. In a large number of early "Flugschriften," obviously intended to mobilize popular discontent against conservative territorial or city policies,[97] the Jews are depicted as an intolerable threat to life and goods,[98] and usually as thirsting after the blood of young Christian children.[99] Eck's treatise on this theme is but a late and dismal climax.

2. Favored by the high authority of St. Jerome, the story of the antichrist and the history of the Jews came to be placed on converging

97. Cf. Johannes Teuschlein, "Auflosung ettlicher Fragen zu lob und ere christi Jesu auch seiner lieben mutter Marie wider die verstockten plinten Juden und alle die jhenen so sie in jren landen und stetten wider recht enthalten füren und gedulden neülich geschehen," printed by Fryderich Peypus, (Nuremberg, 1520).

98. "Als es aber jetzo in der welt steet/ dz gemeinlich alle stend beladen seind mit dem teufflischen geytz/ so wil uns nützer sein/ dz wir sie von uns weysen/ dan gedulden." "Auflosung ettlicher Fragen," fol. C 2ʳ. "Seitmal nun die juden uns sovil schaden bringen an leib/seel/ eer und gut/ so lernet uns das natürlich gesetz/ das wir sie nach unserem vermügen solfen verweisen." Fol. C 3ʳ. "Darumb auch etwa der herr durch Titum und Vespasianum/ als seinen verwalter gerochen der juden missethat durch außtreybung von dem jren." Fol. C 3ᵛ. "Sehen wir aber an die sitten der menschen geistlicher und weltlicher/ finden wir das sie sich vol gefressen haben durch juden gut das der kropff der selbigen geschenck gar schwerlichen von jn gezogen mag werden/ deßhalb die juden solcher ort nit leichtlich vertriben." Fol. C 4ᵛ. Mary, answering a prayer: "Du bittest mich umb das/ so thu du auch meinen willen/ treib von dir/ mein und meynes lieben suns grosse feindt." Fol. C 5ʳ.

99. In one case the ritual murder charge is not contradicted in order to defend the Jews but to sharpen the accusation; they do not thirst after Christian blood for "medical" purposes but out of blank hatred: "Es ist gleublich was ich uch sag/ den ir gantzer ostertag/ allein dorumb ist uff gestifft/ das er ir find uff erd antrifft/ Wie parro der vor was ir here/ mit allem volck erdranck im mere/ . . . So sy nun kein parro haben/ des nemen sy ein christen knaben/ Dem sy vergiessen do syn blut/ alß obs ein findt dem andren dut." "Enderung und schmach der bildung Marie von den juden bewissen, und zu ewiger gedechtniß durch Maximilian den römischen keyser zu malen verschaffet in der löblichen stat kolmer, von dannen sy ouch ewig vertriben syndt" (anonymous, s.a., s.l.; cf. Emil Weller, *Repertorium Typographicum,* Nördlingen, 1864; nr. 1), fol. D 5ʳ. "Ich habs von einem ein verstandt/ wie das sy gsyn in hispaier landt/ do sy das under in erkandt/ In eim concilium betracht/ das die iuden handt gemacht/ Das ieder fliß sich wer do mag/ das kein iud den ostertag/ Begang on christen blur do by/ das alle zytt ein zeichen sy/ Allen die dar syndt gesessen/ unnd handt matz kuchen do selbst gessen/ Das sy das christen blut erman/ mit uns ein ewige findtschafft zu han." Fol. D 6ᵛ. "Darumb in soelches blutes krafft/ bestettiget wurdt ir bruderschafft/ Der christen hatt kein groesseren findt/ den fur wor die iuden sindt/ Die unser blut all tag begeren/ das sy gern unser herren weren/ Sy durstet alle zytt und stundt/ noch unserem blut — der recht blut hundt/ Dorumb sol mans ouch mit in tryben/ das sy solch schelmen moegen blyben/ Wir ziehen ein schlangen in dem geren/ der im syn gifft nit lasset weren/ Den es sich alle stundt dut meren/ wider christum unßeren lieben herren." Fol. E 1ʳ.

lines. The antichrist is expected to be circumcised in Jerusalem and to find his first worshipers among the Jews. In the beautiful picture book, *The Antichrist* (first published in Strasbourg in 1480 and often reprinted), the Jews are the first to gather around him and cry out that "yr got sy kumen."[100] "Gog" and "Magog" from Ezekiel 38 and 39 signify either the fearsome re-emergence of the ten lost tribes or of the ferocious infidels, the Mohammedans or Turks, for whom the Jews are the natural allies and undercover agents.[101] The older interpretation which regarded the story of the antichrist as the lore of the common people must be corrected: the "Endchrist" is the product of learned exegesis, of exegetes who were less arbitrary and speculative than they would seem from a modern perspective; they are rather the *speculatores,* the watchmen on the walls of the true Jerusalem trained to interpret the signs of the times and to relate them to scriptural data.[102]

A heightened sense of the approach of the last times, by no means to be confused ipso facto with the pursuit of the millennium, sharpens the profile of the antichrist and makes an immediate mobilization of all Christian forces mandatory. As we have seen in the case of Pfefferkorn, this means a massive campaign for the mass conversion of the Jews described by St. Paul as the fulfillment of history (Rom. 11:25-32). Yet this missionary concern is but a small step away from an equally radical dissociation, rigorous "Apartheid"[103] and even expulsion, as propagated

---

100. *Der Antichrist und Die Fünfzehn Zeichen vor dem Jüngsten Gericht: Faksimile der ersten typographischen Ausgabe eines unbekannten Straßburger Druck-ers, um 1480,* 2 vols. (Textband, Kommentarband), ed. C. P. Burger et al. (Hamburg, 1979), Textband, 5.2. Cf. especially the commentary by Christoph Peter Burger, "Endzeiterwartung im späten Mittelalter: Der Bildertext zum Antichrist und den Fünfzehn Zeichen vor dem Jüngsten Gericht in der frühesten Druckausgabe," Kommentarband, pp. 18-53; 36, 39, 43.

101. Burger, "Endzeiterwartung," 47ff.

102. See my article "Fourteenth-Century Religious Thought: A Premature Pro-file," *Speculum* 53 (1978): 80-93; 90-91. For rich materials see Hans Preuß, *Die Vorstellungen vom Antichrist im späteren Mittelalter, bei Luther und in der konfes-sionellen Polemik: Ein Beitrag zur Theologie Luthers und zur Geschichte der christli-chen Frömmigkeit* (Leipzig, 1906), pp. 12ff.; and Joshua Trachtenberg, *The Devil and the Jews: The Medieval Conception of the Jew and Its Relation to Modern An-tisemitism,* Harper Torchbooks, The Temple Library TB 822 (New York, 1966; New Haven, 1943), pp. 32-43.

103. George, Duke of Bavaria (1486-1529) and Bishop of Speyer (1515-1529), argues on the basis of the wrath of God in a hitherto overlooked harsh "Mandat" (4 April 1519) against the Jews, for him "rather dogs than human beings." As with Pfefferkorn we find here the charge against the secular authorities of bribery by the Jews: "Quo circa officii nostri esse visum est tante hominum seu potius canum perversitati quocumque modo resistere aut obviam ire, et eo magis cum seculares

by sundry pamphlets of the twenties, earlier by Pfefferkorn and later by Eck.

3. Eschatological urgency incites to immediate reform. The parallelism assumed between the first and the last *adventus* of Christ made it clear that as John the Baptist had quoted the prophet Isaiah (40:3) we are again to heed his voice crying out in the desert: "Prepare a way for the Lord; clear a straight path for him" (Matt. 3:3).[104] Insofar as preparation for the Second Coming is interpreted as the need for reform of the church, the contrast between the "Spirit" and the "Letter" takes on a fundamental significance, based on St. Paul's saying: "The letter kills, the spirit gives life" (2 Cor. 3:6). Though variously interpreted by Erasmus and Luther — for the first in line with Origen and Jerome an exegetical device and directed against ceremonial external laws, for the latter as with St. Augustine basic to the doctrine of justification and the contrast between the gospel and the law as such — this new Paulinism was bound to cement the identification of "legal" and "external" with "Judaistic" and "Jewish."

The gusts of social and apocalyptic fervor fanning the never-extinguished medieval brushfires of anti-Judaism find in this Paulinist reform theology an ideological confirmation, lending a durability to anti-Judaism which outlasts by far the times of immediate social and eschatological duress. With this conclusion I do not join the ranks of those who regard economic factors as the basis for an ideological "Überbau";[105] after all, the indicated social discontent and apocalyptic anxiety are themselves riddled with "ideology." Moreover, one glance at the timetable of expulsions from German cities reveals that after 1520

---

prefecti quorum esset [officium] hec nephanda ob christi gloriam prohibere, non solum hec non prohibeant, sed interdum (judeorum donis corrupti) etiam tolerent et quantum in ipsis est non sine gravi peccato tutentur. . . . Cum autem verendum sit ne divinam propter hoc indignationem incurramus . . . pro contumeliam creatoris respublica ledatur, fames, terremotus et pestilentia (qua etiam nunc laboratur) fiat, dum nimis pacienter christi dei nostri opprobria sustinemus. . . . Volumus . . . sub excommunicationis pena publice moneatis et requiratis ne posthac judeis cohabitent sive cum eis manducent neque servitia aliqua illis prestare aut proles eorum mercede lactare vel nutrire aut medicinam ab eis recipere presumant aut frequentiorem cum eis conversationem habeant. . . ." *Mandat gegen die Juden* (Hagenau: Heinrich Gran, 1519), Univ. Bibliothek Tübingen, Gb 599.2°.

104. See my characterization in *Forerunners of the Reformation: The Shape of Late Medieval Thought* (New York, 1966), pp. 4-14.

105. Cf. Peter Herde, "Probleme der christlich-jüdischen Beziehungen in Mainfranken im Mittelalter," *Würzburger Diözesan-Geschichtsblätter* 40 (1978): 79-94; esp. 88.

only a handful of cities decreed expulsion — Prague (1541), Kaufbeuren (1543/1636), Schweinfurt (1555), and Nordhausen (1559) — whereas in the preceding period from 1388 (Strasbourg) through 1520 (Weissenburg) some ninety cities took such action against the Jews.[106] True, the imperial Diet at Augsburg required by order of 4 September 1530 that all Jewish men should wear a yellow ring on their coat or cap,[107] but this was an effort to guarantee some kind of uniformity for long-existing territorial laws rather than an innovative measure of discrimination against the Jews. Hence the new "Paulinism" with its peculiar brand of anti-Judaism follows *after* and does not precede or create the rising tide of Jewish repression. Luther's attitude toward the Jews should be considered within this larger context.

VII. Luther's Voice Raised against the Jews

When we now turn to Luther's attitude to Judaism we have been introduced to a larger context than is usual in the impressively extensive literature on the theme "Luther and the Jews."[108] As before in the case

106. See the "Table of Expulsions" drawn up by Phillip N. Bebb, "Jewish Policy in Sixteenth Century Nürnberg," *Occasional Papers of the American Society for Reformation Research* 1 (1977): 125-36; 132-33. Mr. Bebb explicitly warns that his data and dates are only approximate. His list is to be completed — e.g., the Donauwörth expulsion in 1517 — with the data presented by Helmut Veitshans, *Die Judensiedlungen der schwäbischen Reichsstädte und der württembergischen Landstädte im Mittelalter,* Arbeiten zum historischen Atlas von Südwestdeutschland 5 (Stuttgart, 1970), pp. 12-43; 38.

107. "Desgleichen sollenn die Judenn ein Gelbenn Ring an dem Rock ader kappenn allenthalb unverborgenn Zu Irer erkannthnus offenntlich tragen." *Urkundenbuch zu der Geschichte des Reichstages zu Augsburg im Jahre 1530,* ed. K. E. Förstemann, 2: *Von der Übergabe der Augsburgischen Confession bis zu dem Schlusse des Reichstages* (Halle, 1835; repr. Osnabrück, 1966), p. 347. For the efforts to enforce — and endure! — the badges in Strasbourg and Regensburg see Ḥaim Hillel Ben-Sasson, "Jewish-Christian Disputation in the Setting of Humanism and Reformation in the German Empire," *Harvard Theological Review* 59 (1966): 369-90; 372-73.

Still in Augsburg Charles V confirmed on 15 October 1530 the "privileges" of Württemberg in being 'unencumbered' by the imperial protection of the Jews. This horrifying, anti-Jewish "Mandat" — in the literature misleadingly quoted as "kaiserlicher Freiheitsbrief" — is published by August Ludwig Reyscher, *Vollständig historisch und kritisch bearbeitete Sammlung der württembergischen Gesetze,* 4 (Tübingen, 1831), pp. 60-65.

108. See particularly the comprehensive presentation by Johannes Brosseder, *Luthers Stellung zu den Juden im Spiegel seiner Interpreten: Interpretation und Re-*

of Erasmus, we limit ourselves to such areas where corrective interpretation seems called for. There are three such points to be made.

1. We cannot completely bypass the issue of changes in Luther's thought since this has dominated Luther research for over a century. In 1523 Luther is concerned about removing obstacles in order to facilitate Jewish mass conversion, whereas his harsh writings of the late thirties and forties heap invectives on the Jews for their stubborn and malicious blindness. But this change, significant both from a modern perspective and from the perspective of his Jewish contemporaries, is not indicative of a change of heart as far as those Jews are concerned who want to retain their religious identity and remain outside the Christian fold.

A key document is the revealing letter of 11 June 1537 to the ubiquitous advocate of oppressed Jewry, Josel of Rosheim.[109] Luther rejects Josel's request to intercede with the Elector on behalf of the Jews, who by edict of August 1536 had been ordered to leave Saxony. Notwithstanding Capito's plea on Josel's behalf, Luther says, politely but firmly, "no," because the acts of charity he had called for in 1523[110] had not only proven to be ineffective as a means of conversion but had on the contrary confirmed the Jews in their error. The fact that Jesus the Christ was a Jew, which was formulated in 1523 as a Christian self-critique with a clear edge against the papal church,[111] is now turned

---

zeption von Luthers Schriften und Äußerungen zum Judentum im 19. und 20. Jahrhundert vor allem im deutschsprachigen Raum, Beiträge zur Ökumenischen Theologie 8 (Munich, 1972). For the most recent literature see C. Bernd Sucher, *Luthers Stellung zu den Juden: Eine Interpretation aus germanistischer Sicht,* Bibliotheca Humanistica & Reformatorica 23 (Nieuwkoop, 1977). Unreplaced and probably irreplaceable is the analysis provided by Reinhold Lewin, *Luthers Stellung zu den Juden: Ein Beitrag zur Geschichte der Juden in Deutschland während des Reformationszeitalters,* Neue Studien zur Geschichte der Theologie und der Kirche 10 (Berlin, 1911; repr. ed., Aalen, 1973). Rabbi Lewin must be highly commended for his unusual degree of fairness (in my view even "leaning over backwards") which gained for him the annual prize of the Protestant faculty of the University of Breslau. Together with his family he fell victim to the Nazi terror after "the American consulate in Berlin refused to grant him a visa. . . ." Guido Kisch, "Necrologue Reinhold Lewin 1888-1942," *Historia Judaica* 8 (1946): 217-19; 219.

109. *WA Br* 8.89-91; Lewin, *Luthers Stellung zu den Juden,* pp. 62ff.; Stern, *Josel of Rosheim* (n. 74, above), pp. 125-30; 137-38.

110. Cf. *Daß Jesus Christus ein geborner Jude sei* (1523), *WA* 11.314-36; 315. 14-24; 336.22-37.

111. "Aber nu wyr sie nur mir gewallt treyben und gehen mit lugen teydingen umb, geben yhn schuld, sie mussen Christen blutt haben, das sie nicht stincken, und weys nicht wes des narren wercks mehr ist, das man sie gleich fur hunde hellt, was sollten wyr guttis an yhn schaffen? Item das man yhn verbeutt, unntter uns tzu erbeytten, hantieren und andere menschliche gemeynschafft tzu haben, da mit man sie tzu

directly against the Jews: Pre-Christian antisemitism, that is, the Gentile hatred of the Jews, highlights the miracle of divine intervention so that the Christians were prepared to acknowledge a Jew as their savior.[112] Hence the Jews should give up their hopes and stop looking for the end of their captivity and dispersal over the earth. Luther announces a special treatise on this matter — de facto developing into those five final writings[113] which only Eck matches in fury. Basic to Luther's anti-Judaism[114] is therefore the conviction that since the coming of Jesus there is no future for the Jews as Jews.[115]

2. As we saw, Erasmus had good reason to deny that he was a Reuchlinist. The same applies to Luther. In his "Gutachten" on the Reuchlin case of February 1514,[116] Luther indeed declared Reuchlin's orthodoxy to be beyond suspicion. Yet his critique of the burning of the books was argued in quite a different way.[117] Since, as the prophets foretold, the Jews are to curse and blaspheme Christ, their very God and King, even a first-year theological student can see that to purge the Jews

wuchern treybt, wie sollt sie das bessern? Will man yhn hellfen, so mus man nicht das Bapsts, sonder Christlicher liebe gesetz an yhn uben und sie freuntlich annehmen, mit lassen werben und erbeytten, da mit sie ursach und raum gewynnen, bey und umb uns tzu seyn, unser Christlich lere und leben tzu horen und sehen." WA 11.336.24-33. Cf. WA, 11.314.26-31 to 315.1-13.

112. WA Br 8.90.21-28; as one among other arguments this is mentioned already in 1523; WA 11.331.3-8.

113. Daß Jesus Christus ein geborner Jude sei (1523), WA 11.314-36; Wider die Sabbather an einen guten Freund (1538), WA 50.312-37; Von den Juden und ihren Lügen (1543), WA 53.417-552; Vom Schem Hamphoras und vom Geschlecht Christi (1543), WA 53.579-648; Von den letzten Worten Davids (1543), WA 54.28-100. The impact of Luther's "no" on Saxonian politics is documented by the "Ausschreiben" of the Elector Johann Friedrich of the year 1543 confirming the "Mandat" of 1536, published at the end of the last century: Dr. Burkhardt, "Die Judenverfolgungen im Kurfürstentum Sachsen," Theologische Studien und Kritiken 70 (1897): 593-98; 597.

114. Cf. the harsh judgment of Peter Maser, "Luthers Schriftauslegung im Traktat 'Von den Juden und ihren Lügen' (1543). Ein Beitrag zum 'christologischen Antisemitismus' des Reformators." Judaica 29 (1973): 71-84, 149-67.

115. See WA 42.448.25-42 to 451.1-34. For future research it should be noticed that in the Genesis commentary (1535-1545) we find the main exegetical arsenal for arguments of the aging Luther against the Jews. Cf. n. 124, below.

116. WA Br 1.23-24. It is Luther's first letter to Frederick's later confidential secretary, Georg Spalatin. Cf. Irmgard Höss, Georg Spalatin 1484-1545: Ein Leben in der Zeit des Humanismus und der Reformation (Weimar, 1956), pp. 75-78.

117. I bypass Luther's first observation, that while evil within the church is crying out to heaven, these Dominicans start to clean the streets outside, a theme which he pursued in 1523. WA Br 1.23.20-30.

from blasphemy is to contradict God and to call him a liar. Besides, if Jews are to be converted that is not a matter of people fooling around with burning, banning, and such mere external doings; God converts from within.[118] Not just the middle or the late Luther, but the earliest Luther recorded, holds that there is no future for the Jews as Jews — in this "Gutachten" supported with the contrast "internal-external" which we encountered as a typical element of the Augustinian theme of the "Spirit and the Letter." Though on first sight Luther argues with Reuchlin that no external force is to be applied, Reuchlin had tried to defend the Talmud against the charge of blasphemy whereas Luther takes this blasphemy as an unshakable, divinely ordained fact.

3. Related to this is a third point. Luther is also no Reuchlinist in view of his explicit scepticism concerning the Cabala.[119] Notwithstanding his great interest in Reuchlin's *De verbo mirifico* and his immediate reading of *De arte cabalistica*[120] he rejects the Cabala as suitable only for curious and idle scholars, "curiosi et ociosi."[121] Theologically he regards it as superstition to hold that the Hebrew letters contain divine power: Words only have impact when received in faith.

As far as method is concerned, Luther's nominalist training had taught him to find the *proprietas verborum,* the exact meaning of words, in their precise usage as clarified by the grammatical context. The very same reason which soon afterward made him oppose the biblical exegesis of the Zurich and Strasbourg theologians — nearly all trained in the *via antiqua* — with respect to the eucharistic words of institution[122] underlies his rejection of the Cabala as a reliable exegetical device. Generally it can be said that the nominalistic interpretation of words and their conventional and contextual significance gainsays all "word-works" of the magus, irrespective of whether it concerns black or white magic.[123]

4. Luther is not a Reuchlinist; neither is he a "Lutheran." This surprising conclusion deserves at least a short explanation. As we saw, Eck regards Osiander as a "Luthersohn" and "Judenvater," a natural fruit on Luther's tree. It is clear from the foregoing that this view is untenable. Luther's prescriptions and "remedies" may have changed — and change

---

118. *WA Br* 1.23.39-42; 41.

119. For a detailed and convincing treatment of this issue see Siegfried Raeder, *Grammatica Theologica: Studien zu Luthers Operationes in Psalmos,* Beiträge zur historischen Theologie 51 (Tübingen, 1977), pp. 59-80.

120. *WA Br* 1.149.11-13 to 150.14-15. 22 February 1518.

121. *WA* 5.384.12; quoted by Raeder, *Grammatica Theologica*, p. 79.

122. Cf. Oberman, *Werden und Wertung*, pp. 368-69.

123. Cf. *Werden und Wertung,*pp. 208-9, 224.

they did, considerably so — but his diagnosis remained the same from the beginning: the blasphemy of the Jews is punished with blindness and dispersal; they will never have a country of their own.[124]

Osiander, however, is not an isolated Nuremberg deviant from the Wittenberg party line. We have good reason to assume that Melanchthon was as embarrassed as some of the leading city reformers by the ferocious anti-Judaism of the later Luther. We know that he protected Osiander against Luther's wrath by suppressing the evidence that Osiander had sent an apology for Luther's utterances to the Venetian scholar Elias Levita.[125] It is even more important to take notice of the position of Justus Jonas (1493-1555),[126] Luther's lifelong colleague, marriage witness, and, above all, the translator of Luther's treatises on Judaism. The independence of Jonas's position may well have gone unnoticed because he praises and recommends Luther's views as if his own were a mere explication of Luther's attitude toward the Jews; ultimately he leaves Luther far behind and ends up with a position which nearly coincides with modern biblical exegesis. In the 1524 preface to his Latin translation of Luther's treatise of the preceding year[127] his deviation is not yet obvious and only a matter of emphasis. Jonas underscores the common lot of Jews and Christians in having been misled — the Jews by Talmudic trifles, the Christians by scholastic figments.[128] Just as Christians have been won for the Reformation by the recovery of Holy Scripture, so Jews will see the light of truth by returning to the unadulterated witness of Moses and the prophets. Christians should pray for the Jews, "particularly since also among us not all

124. Since all interest has been focused on Luther's treatises on the Jews some most revealing passages from his lectures have escaped attention. For the dispersal of the Jews as tangible evidence of God's wrath see the commentary to Gen. 12:3; WA 42.448.25-42 to 451.1-34; esp. 448.34ff.

125. April 1545; see Seebaß, Das reformatorische Werk des Andreas Osiander (n. 61, above), p. 82; cf. Corpus Reformatorum, 5: Philippi Melan[ch]thonis Opera quae supersunt omnia, ed. G. C. Bretschneider (Halle, 1838; repr. New York, London, and Frankfurt a.M., 1963), pp. 728-29.

126. See Walter Delius, Lehre und Leben: Justus Jonas 1493-1555 (Gütersloh, 1952). Only part of the Jonas letters is available in Der Briefwechsel des Justus Jonas, 2 parts, ed. G. Kawerau, Geschichtsquellen der Provinz Sachsen und angrenzender Gebiete 17 (Halle, 1884/85; repr. Hildesheim, 1964).

127. Libellus Martini Lutheri, Christum Ieum [sic] verum iudaeum et semen esse Abrahae, è Germanico versus, per I. Ionam (Wittenberg, 1524); cf. WA 11.309-10.

128. Jonas added a dedicatory letter to his Latin translation in which a common middle ground is suggested, since the Jews have to draw away from Talmudic distortions "like we from Scotistic and Thomistic nonsense": "Videmus plane contigisse Iudaeis, ut haud aliter a verbo Dei et simplicitate scripturae avocati sint Thalmudicis nugis ac nos Scotisticis et Thomisticis somniis." Briefwechsel des Justus Jonas, 1.93.4-6.

Christians deserve that name."[129] Yet Luther's chief argument is taken up when the rabbis are accused of leading the Jews astray with their fantasy of the perpetuation of the messianic kingdom: "Do they want to make us believe that this kingdom has been transferred to the moon?"[130]

In his second preface to the Latin translation of Luther's treatise against the Sabbatarians, written fifteen years later (1539),[131] Jonas boldly disregards the fact that Luther's position has hardened, already presaging the vitriolics to come. As if bending over backward to neutralize Luther's irritated impatience, he develops a new, positive vision of the Jews. The papists are now presented as far more removed from the Scriptures than even the most unworthy offspring of Abraham: The recovery of the gospel "in our days" has opened our eyes to the fact that there were never more significant doctors of theology than among the people of Israel;[132] the opening of the gospel has led to the discovery that we, Christians, are guests in Abraham's house, and latecomers to the promises of God, Gentiles grafted on the tree of Israel, made into one body with the Jews under the one Head, Jesus Christ.[133]

The final conclusion of Jonas may not seem to be so different from the early Luther: We owe it to the Jews to save as many as possible "as if from shipwreck."[134] Yet a new sense of historical obligation to a common past and a new biblical vision of a common future are unmistakable. Luther confirms our conclusion when he informs Jonas on 21

129. "Sed orandum est nobis pro hac gente, praesertim cum inter nos quoque non omnes Christiani sunt, qui titulum Christianismi gerunt." *Briefwechsel des Justus Jonas*, 1.93.12-14.

130. "Quin in lunares urbes regnum Iudaeorum translatum comminiscuntur?" *Briefwechsel des Justus Jonas*, 1.93.11-12.

131. WA 50.311.

132. "Nos autem, quibus Deus hoc seculo aperuit libros sacros, quibus contigit hoc tempore aspicere claram lucem evangelii, iam cognitum habemus, nullos unquam doctores theologiae verae praestantiores sub sole vixisse, quam in illo populo Israel. . . ." *Briefwechsel des Justus Jonas*, 1.323.19-22.

133. ". . . et ecclesiam Iudaeorum olivetum pinguissimum et uberrimum esse, imo hortum balsami generosissimi, cuius fragrantissimo odore delectatus est Deus, nos vero gentes campos illos, unde oleastri desumpti in veras olivas translati sunt, sicut et Paulus ad Romanos hac similitudine utitur. Nos gentes hospites utique sumus et peregrini, qui ad communionem tantarum opum et benedictionum in Christo Iesu vero Messia admissi sumus, olim sine Deo in hoc mundo, nunc facti mysteriorum Dei participes et cum Abraham et patriarchis, tantis Dei viris, sub uno eodemque capite Christo unum facti sumus corpus." *Briefwechsel des Justus Jonas*, 1.323.22-30.

134. "Ideo cum tam nobilis et sanctus populus sunt Iudaei, ex quorum plenitudine nos omnes accepimus, profecto perpetuam nos gentes eis debemus gratitudinem, ut quantum omnino fieri potest, quosdam ex eis adhuc quasi e medio naufragio servemus." *Briefwechsel des Justus Jonas*, 1.324.7-10.

December 1542 that he goes his separate way against Jonas's advice to tone down and temper his anti-Jewish utterances.[135] Luther himself had already come to despair of the mass conversion of the Jews — Christians can "mit gutem Gewissen an ihnen verzweifeln."[136] Convinced that their dispersal is the central issue, he swears that, as soon as the Jews return to Jerusalem to re-establish the temple, priesthood, and statehood, the Christians will follow them "und auch Juden werden."[137]

VIII. Epilogue: The Arduous Road to Peaceful Coexistence

We began this lecture with Europe's slow trek toward tolerance, a journey hesitantly commenced in the sixteenth century and pursued very much at the expense of the Jews, particularly in Germany. Is this progress due to any of the three: to Reuchlin, the "trilinguis," admirer of the Cabala and proponent of the Jews as *concives*; or to Erasmus, the patient editor of the Fathers and propagandist for peace and concord; or perhaps to Luther, the nominalist exegete and mighty prophet of a truly "secular" state, freed from supervision by the church?

It seems obvious that it is the humanist line to be drawn from Reuchlin and Erasmus to Hobbes, Voltaire, and Lessing, which points to modern concepts of equality and human rights. No one has presented

---

135. "Hactenus in Ludeorum me mersi furias, postquam tu quiescendum esse consuluisti, dum aliam viam tentaretis." *WA Br* 10.226.19-21. For Jonas's complex efforts also to translate Luther's harshest tract "Von den Juden und ihren Lügen" in March 1543, see *WA* 53.414. I doubt that the editor J. Luther is right in assuming that Jonas did not translate "Vom Schem Hamphoras" because of linguistic problems: *WA* 53.573.

136. "Und summa: Weil diese Funffzehen hundert jare im Elende (da noch kein ende gewis ist noch werden kan) die Jueden nicht demuetigen noch zur erkentnis bringen, So muegt jr mir gutem gewissen an jnen verzweiveln. Denn es unmueglich ist, das Gott sein volck (wo sie es weren) so lange solt on trost und weissagung bleiben lassen." *WA* 50.336.1-6.

137. "Oder ist solches nu verseumet und nicht geschehen, So lasst sie noch hinfaren jns land und gen Jerusalem, Tempel bawen, Priesterthum, Fuerstenthum und Mosen mit seinem gesetze auffrichten und also sie selbs widerumb Jueden werden und das Land besitzen. Wenn das geschehen ist, so sollen sie uns bald auff den ferssen nach sehen daher komen und auch Jueden werden. Thun sie das nicht, So ists aus der massen lecherlich, das sie uns Heiden wollen bereden zu jrem verfallen gesetze, welches nu wol Funffzehenhundert jar verfaulet und kein gesetze mehr gewest ist. Und wir solten halten, das sie selbs nicht halten noch halten konnen, so lange sie Jerusalem und das Land nicht haben." *WA* 50.323.36-37 to 324.1-8.

this view more convincingly and eloquently than Peter Gay in his magnificent interpretation of the Enlightenment. One passage taken from *The Rise of Paganism* may at once illustrate and document this prevailing point of view. Amid the deadlock of Catholicism and Protestantism a third force, thus Gay, provided Europe with a new option: "The Humanists [had] prepared the way for that solution; their realism made possible a secular view of political power and a secular, or at least no longer specifically Christian, justification for political obligation; their critical philology, combined with their admiration for antiquity, prepared educated men to read Christian documents with skeptical detachment, and pagan philosophies with sympathy; their appeal to nature laid the foundation for . . . a style of thought that ordered the world by natural law, natural morality, and natural theology."[138]

Yet it is exactly the test case of Judaism which, I submit, when seen from afar might appear to confirm Gay's findings but under closer scrutiny represents a major obstacle to them, and a chief reason to look for new answers. Gay's misconception is not singularly his own, nor is it a chink in the armor of his own wide-ranging research. Our common misunderstanding is due rather to the predominance of German Reformation research, which in this century was first focused single-mindedly on Luther and during the past ten years concentrated with equal determination on the City Reformation. Not until we acknowledge the significance of what I am inclined to call — after Luther and the City Reformation — "the Third Reformation" will we be in a position to complete our story.

The City Reformation is a significant but brief episode of about ten years' duration from 1523 to 1534 which reached its climax in the late twenties and was over by 1549. The "Third Reformation" owes its very emergence to the weakening of the political and religious status of the city, for which the Imperial Interim of 1548 spelled final doom.[139] The Third Reformation is the reformation of the refugees banished from their cities in southern Germany, in France, and soon in the Netherlands. It is a movement of much longer duration and deeper penetration than that of the cities. This refugee reformation entails a reinterpretation of government in church and

---

138. *The Enlightenment: An Interpretation: The Rise of Modern Paganism* (New York, 1977²), p. 297.

139. Cf. Gustav Bossert, *Das Interim in Württemberg,* Schriften des Vereins für Reformationsgeschichte 46/47 (Halle, 1895), pp. 95-105. Thomas A. Brady, Jr., *Ruling Class, Regime and Reformation at Strasbourg, 1520-1555,* Studies in Medieval and Reformation Thought 22 (Leiden, 1978), pp. 275ff. Erdmann Weyrauch, *Konfessionelle Krise und soziale Stabilität: Das Interim in Straßburg (1548-1562),* Spätmittelalter und Frühe Neuzeit, Tübinger Beiträge zur Geschichtsforschung 7 (Stuttgart, 1978), pp. 159ff.

state, and a rereading of the Scriptures in the light of its own enforced exile.[140] One of its salient characteristics is a new attitude toward Judaism.

City reformers like Zwingli in Zurich and Bucer in Strasbourg may not have assented to Luther's intemperate outbursts against the Jews; they did, however, agree with his basic attitude.[141] Christian Hebraists like Osiander in Nuremberg and Capito in Strasbourg accumulated exegetical knowledge of the Old Testament and expressed a deep respect for rabbinical learning.[142] But only after this knowledge and this respect were kindled by the experience of the roaming refugees did the diaspora cease to be regarded as the deserved punishment for the "blind stubbornness of the Jews": the traditional explanation for the dispersal of Israel had now become self-indictment. In the late French sermons of Calvin, recently edited,[143] we find the first traces[144] of a growing awareness of

140. After reaching a state of near establishment in France, the Huguenots again experienced, in the aftermath of St. Bartholomew's Day on 24 August 24 1572, a traumatic shock comparable with the Interim's effect. See for this impact particularly Robert M. Kingdon, *Geneva and the Consolidation of the French Protestant Movement 1564-1572: A Contribution to the History of Congregationalism, Presbyterianism, and Calvinist Resistance Theory,* Trauvaux d'Humanisme et Renaissance 92 (Geneva, 1967): 200-201.

141. See Lewin, *Luthers Stellung zu den Juden* (n. 108 above), pp. 98-99; J. Cohrs, WA 54.20-21. Cf. also the ample evidence presented by John W. Kleiner, "The Attitudes of the Strasbourg Reformers toward Jews and Judaism" (Unpubl. Ph.D. diss., Temple University, Philadelphia, 1978). For Martin Bucer see esp. Rabbi Dr. Kroner, "Die Hofpredigerpartei und die Juden unter Philipp von Hessen," *Das Jüdische Literaturblatt* 11 (1882): 165-66; 169-70; Wilhelm Maurer, "Martin Butzer und die Judenfrage in Hessen," *Zeitschrift des Vereins für hessische Geschichte und Landeskunde* 64 (1953): 29-43.

142. For Osiander see *Andreas Osiander d.Ä. Gesamtausgabe* (n. 62, above) 3.335-40, and literature cited in the footnotes there. For Capito see James M. Kittelson, *Wolfgang Capito. From Humanist to Reformer,* Studies in Medieval and Reformation Thought 17 (Leiden, 1975), pp. 21-22; 25-26; 33-34; 211-12.

143. Sermon dated 8 July 1549 (Jer. 16:1-7): "Quant donc nous voyons que nous sommes pareilz aux Juifz, nous avons ung mireoir pour congnoistre nostre rebellion contre Dieu. Or quant il nous chastiera bien rudement, pourrons nous dire qu'il n'a pas assez attendu et que de nostre costé nous ne nous sommes pas monstrez incorrigibles jusques au bout? Ainsi donc, quant nous lisons ce passage, aprenons de ne point condampner les Juifz mais nous mesmes, et de congnoistre que nous ne vallons pas myeulx, et que s'il y a eu alors une telle brutalité que la parolle de Dieu n'ait de rien servy, que aujourdhuy il y en a autant ou plus." Jean Calvin, *Sermons sur les Livres de Jérémie et des Lamentations,* ed. R. Peter, Supplementa Calviniana 6 (Neukirchen-Vluyn, 1971), p. 59, ll. 12-18. Sermon dated 10 July 1549 (Jer. 16:12-15): "Et combien que nous ne soyons pas de la race d'Abraham et de ce peuple qui a esté delivré d'Egipte, neantmoins pource que nous representons ce peuple lá, ceste delivrance ne nous doibt point sortir des aureilles." Calvin, *Sermons,* 78, ll. 27-29. Sermon dated 6 September 1550 (Lam. 1:1, Introduction): ". . . sy on faict comparaison avec ceux dont parle icy le prophete on trouverra que nous sommes beaucoup pires que ceulx lá de son temps." Calvin, *Sermons,* p. 183, ll. 34-35 to 184, l. 1.

144. For a different conclusion on the basis of earlier materials see A. J. Visser,

the parallels between the persecution of all true Christians and the diaspora of the Jews.[145]

In a two-pronged movement from Zurich and Geneva via Bullinger and Beza, the Third Reformation extends the message of the one covenant for Jews and Gentiles. It proclaims the fidelity of the God of Abraham, Isaac, and Jacob, who does not reverse his promises. In the course of the seventeenth century, first in the Netherlands, then in England, and finally in a number of early settlements in the New World, the Jews are granted protection and certain civil rights. In 1657 the Dutch demanded that their Jews be recognized as full citizens abroad[146] — an act of emancipation which, in sharp contrast with the short-term effects of the French Revolution elsewhere, was never revoked.

Presentation of the precise shape of the "Third Reformation" would

---

Calvijn en de Joden., supplement to *Kerk en Israel* 17 ('s Gravenhage, 1963), esp. p. 18. In a less than profound article (first published in *Judaica* 2 [1946]: 203-8) Jacques Courvoisier concludes: "... was Calvin zu diesem Thema sagt, ist für diese Sache nicht von großer Bedeutung." "Calvin und die Juden: Zu einem Streitgespräch," in *Christen und Juden: Ihr Gegenüber vom Apostelkonzil bis heute*, ed. W.-D. Marsch, K. Thieme (Mainz and Göttingen, 1961), pp. 141-46; 146.

145. With this new evaluation of the phenomenon of "diaspora" corresponds an optimistic Jewish interpretation. See the evidence compiled by Hayim Hillel Ben-Sasson, "The Reformation in Contemporary Jewish Eyes," in *Proceedings of the Israel Academy of Sciences and Humanities* 4 (1969-1970; Jerusalem, 1971), pp. 239-326; 286-87. From the Jewish perspective the refugee-Reformation is just another sign of the breaking apart of the *corpus christianum*. But as in the case of the Hussite movement, it is not merely a negative sign: "... the anti-hierarchical, anti-monastic and iconoclastic tendencies characterizing the Hussite movement [are considered] to be a change in the right direction. . . . The rise of Luther in Germany occurred at a time when Jews were in particular need of encouragement." "The Reformation in Contemporary Jewish Eyes," p. 255.

146. See J. van den Berg, *Joden en Christenen in Nederland gedurende de zeventiende eeuw*, Verkenning en Bezinning 3, nr. 2 (Kampen, 1969); cf. the elaboration "Eschatological Expectations concerning the Conversion of the Jews in the Netherlands during the Seventeenth Century," in *Puritans, the Millennium and the Future of Israel: Puritan Eschatology 1600-1660*, ed. P. Toon (Cambridge and London, 1970), pp. 137-53. See also Robert M. Healey, "The Jew in Seventeenth-Century Protestant Thought," *Church History* 46 (1977): 63-79; 64. On 13 December 1619 the states of Holland and Westfrisia permitted the cities to make their own legislation governing their relations with "the Hebrew nation." The document is published by J. Meijer, *Hugo de Groot: Remonstrantie nopende de ordre dije in de fanden van Hollandt ende Westvrieslandt dijent gestelt op de Joden* (Amsterdam, 1949), p. 101. The key document in this edition is the liberal proposal of Hugo Grotius. Most revealing is, however, the anonymous reaction (c. 1617) from the Jewish side to the proposed legislation. *Hugo de Groot*, Appendix C, pp. 141-43. Cf. also W. J. M. van Eysinga, "De Groots Jodenreglement," *Mededelingen der Koninklijke Nederlandse Akademie van Wetenschappen*, Afd. Letterkunde 13 (Amsterdam, 1950), pp. 1-8.

require a separate lecture and, indeed, a separate monograph.[147] The one point I wish to stress is that this movement honors Luther's basic Reformation writings of 1520 as its theological charter, that its Old Testament insights are essentially derived from the Christian Hebraists, all students of Reuchlin, and that in the seventeenth century it could absorb Erasmian ideas all the more readily because of its own origins in the City Reformation, so heavily indebted to Erasmus of Rotterdam. Interpreted by the Third Reformation, Reuchlin, Erasmus, and Luther were divested of their anti-Judaism and could now function together in a positive fashion which none of them had envisioned.

In light of the preceding remarks, I dare to conclude with one thesis and one hypothesis. My thesis is: The first significant advances toward tolerance were not achieved by Gay's "new paganism," nor by the *philosophes* of royalist France, nor by the elitist Deists of the English Enlightenment, not to mention the much-overrated *Aufklärung* of Lessing in Germany. There was such a thing as the "rise of paganism." However, the rise of paganism meant de facto the rise of the Gentiles, without benefit for the Jews.

And finally, my hypothesis: What is inculcated by centuries of religious fury in the minds of the elite and the uneducated populace alike can only be eradicated or, indeed, exorcised by an equally powerful and fervent antidote. If this does not occur, as recent European history has proven, the flames of religious bigotry subsist under the new secular paganism, and the horrid phantoms of the past re-emerge out of the smoldering ashes of anti-Judaism to haunt us in the stubborn, mercurial, and unsuppressible form of antisemitism.

In the very cities and regions from which the Jews had been expelled, the witch-hunts started which bound Europe under their spell throughout pre-industrial times. The new paganism of the Enlightenment had its finest hour in building the dams of human dignity solid enough to contain the floods of this irrational fear of the devil.[148] It could not

147. H. R. Trevor-Roper in his effort to unravel the mysterious bonds between Calvinism and the Enlightenment has pointed to a later but structurally parallel phase: "We find that each of those Calvinist societies [sixteenth-century Heidelberg, seventeenth-century Holland, Puritan England, Huguenot France, eighteenth-century Switzerland, and Scotland] made its contribution to the Enlightenment at a precise moment in its history, and that this moment was the moment when it repudiated ideological orthodoxy." "The Religious Origins of the Enlightenment," in *Religion, the Reformation and Social Change and other Essays* (London, Melbourne, Toronto, 1967), pp. 193-236; 205.

148. The most powerful antidote which medieval thought itself had provided remained an untapped source — until this very day. See Oberman, *Werden und Wertung,* pp. 211ff.

reach, however, beyond the phenomenon of witchcraft; it could not fathom nor control the preceding wave of anti-Judaism which, if left to agnostic indifference, would continue to inundate the inner recesses of Westerners and their society.[149]

When the "Third Reformation" turned anti-intellectual, anticultural, and pietistic — and thus turned against the legacy of Reuchlin, Erasmus, and Luther — it lost its impact on Europe's intelligentsia and could no longer perform its early mission. But it was prophetic in insisting that without an enduring foundation for coexistence between Jews and Christians — in their words, without the recovery of the one covenant for Jews and Gentiles — there will be no future for Western society.

149. Cf. Alexander Bein, "Der moderne Antisemitismus und seine Bedeutung für die Judenfrage," *Vierteljahrshefte für Zeitgeschichte* 6 (1958): 340-60.

The Stubborn Jews:
Timing the Escalation of Antisemitism
in Late Medieval Europe

I. From *Horror Vacui* to *Horror Absurditatis*

There can be no doubt that modern German historians have started to rewrite the history of the nineteenth century in light of the *Tausendjähriges Reich* of Nazi terror. The Holocaust in particular occasions a critical test of what used to be regarded as the success story of Jewish emancipation in Germany. But even though modern presentations of German history tend to include a special section on the emancipation of the Jews in the hundred years or so between 1780 and 1871, the preoccupation with "progressive" Prussia goes to such an extent that one crucial year in this history is generally slighted and seemingly forgotten.[1] In 1823, the Grand Duke of Saxe-Weimar, Karl August, who had given Saxony the first German constitution, promulgated a so-called *Ausführungsbestimmung* (on 20 June), which henceforth legalized marriages between Christians and Jews.

1. See Reinhard Rürup, "Deutschland im 19. Jahrhundert 1817-1871," in *Deutsche Geschichte,* 3, ed. R. Rürup, H.-U. Wehler, and G. Schulz (Göttingen, 1985), pp. 3-200, esp. 88.

"The Stubborn Jews: Timing the Escalation of Antisemitism in Late Medieval Europe," in *Leo Baeck Institute Year Book XXXIV* (London, 1989), xi-xxv. This is an expanded and annotated version of a lecture delivered under the auspices of the New York Leo Baeck Institute at the 102nd Annual Meeting of the American Historical Association in New York on 28 December 1987.

Johann Wolfgang von Goethe reacted to the news with the proposal that the Lutheran bishop should immediately lay down his office rather than allow a Jewess to have her marriage solemnized in the Church of the Holy Trinity: "Wollen wir denn überall im Absurden vorausgehen. . . ?" (Must we always be the front-runners in absurdity!). Ludwig Geiger, to whom we owe the still irreplaceable biography of Johannes Reuchlin,[2] evaluates Goethe's response in his forgotten but fine collection of essays, *Die Deutsche Literatur und die Juden*,[3] with that same impressive but misplaced magnanimity, which was already the Achilles' heel of his early Reuchlin study: for him the great Goethe merely chided the Saxonian thirst for innovation. By declaring mixed marriages to be "absurd," however, the cultural hero of enlightened Germany not only protested against progress, but condemned it with the most cutting curse conceivable in the "Age of Reason."

In the Middle Ages "absurdity" came to stand for deviation from the consensus of the church; in classical sources it is derived from "absonans," not in keeping with the tune or the choir, and in both epochs it figuratively connotes the irrational. With his *horror absurditatis*, Goethe follows in the footsteps of his revered enlightened predecessor, Desiderius Erasmus. In one of his most revealing, outspoken, and programmatic letters, Erasmus, on 24 June 1530 from his new abode in Freiburg, laid out his confessional position to the papal *nuncio*, Lorenzo Campeggi. After explaining that once his favorite Froben-city had opened its gates to the Reformation he had to leave Basel, he nevertheless characterizes his own position as the no-man's-land between the fronts; literally: between the armies, "in utrisque castris." He proceeds to describe the desperate situation of the church of his day, which calls for a "Deus de [sic!] Machina subito apparens" to convert all — interestingly enough, through the good offices of the emperor.

Since it is God himself who allowed such a fatal illness to break into his church, only his wrath can explain that so many and such insignificant, yes, indeed, low-caliber people, so quickly fell away from the church. How speedily did the eucharistic heresy spread, and with how much blindness do these unfortunate Anabaptists run to their deaths!

The absurdity charge which Goethe leveled at Saxony is applied by Erasmus to all of Germany with a psychoanalysis of the German soul, destined to be reinvented time and again in the centuries to come: it is

---

2. Ludwig Geiger, *Johann Reuchlin: Sein Leben und seine Werke* (Leipzig, 1871).

3. Ludwig Geiger, *Die Deutsche Literatur und die Juden* (Berlin, 1910), p. 95.

typical of the mentality of the Germans (literally, Germans seem to be so mixed up) that as soon as someone comes along marketing a sufficiently absurd view they will immediately go for it: "Atque ita videtur affectus Germaniae populus ut si quis exoriatur, qui dogma aliquod absurdius proferat, ilico sint amplexuri."[4]

The purpose of this perhaps surprising and seemingly indirect access route via Goethe and Erasmus to our theme is to point to the multiple levels on which our sources can and must be interpreted in order to bridge the deep and indeed awesome gap between literary sources and historical reality. On one elusive but basic level we discern the common focus of Erasmus and Goethe in their *horror absurditatis* — their revulsion to the irrational and the absurd, which is for them as much a law of reason as the *horror vacui* is a law of physics. This very same *horror* underlies the medieval charge of stubborn blindness *(caecitas* and *pertinacitas)* leveled against the Jews. With its elusive while unpredictable psychological mixture of intellectual superiority and emotional impatience it could — and did — allow for the seemingly so different strategies of conversion and repression.

Seen from another perspective, the juxtaposition of Erasmus and Goethe underscores the element of truth in the much-debated thesis, renewed in our day by Peter Gay,[5] which projects Erasmus and humanism as forerunners of the *philosophes* of the Enlightenment in their common stance against religious bigotry and irrational dogmatism. As argued in *The Roots of Anti-Semitism*,[6] this intriguing construction on the level of the history of ideas should take into account the conscious, explicit, and programmatic anti-Jewish sentiment of Erasmus of Rotterdam, which I am inclined to identify with antisemitism. Gay's thesis of continuity can be upheld insofar as this thrust in Erasmus's thought is clearly reflected in the views of the spokesmen for the Enlightenment.

Yet the very reaction of Goethe reminds us not of the scope but of the limits of progress in 300 years: his views show a remarkable resem-

---

4. Percy and H. M. Allen (eds.), *Opus Epistolarum* (Oxford 1906-1947), 7.451.124-25. What Erasmus regarded as a teutonic fallacy, John Calvin describes as a weakness of all mankind; there are always some fools to fall for *absurditas:* "nulla est tam monstruosa absurditas, cui non apertae sint quorundam aures." Commentary on 2 Tim. 2:18; *Corpus Reformatorum,* 80.369. In an argument, Calvin delineates in the *Institutes* the boundaries of his understanding of the eucharist with the words "absurda relicio." *Institutio religionis christianae* (1559), IV, 17, 32.

5. Peter Gay, *The Enlightenment. An Interpretation* (New York, 1977[2]).

6. Heiko A. Oberman, *The Roots of Anti-Semitism* (Berlin, 1983[2]; Philadelphia, 1984).

blance to those of Johannes Reuchlin, who combined a deep respect for the *Hebraica veritas* and its cabalistic treasures with a mixed program of conversion and social control. Reuchlin's so-called defense of "the Jewish books," which has made him a hero in all histories of emancipation, is de facto not concerned about Jews but about Christian truths hidden in Jewish sources, and is therefore not part of a campaign for toleration of non-Christian views, but rather a concentrated effort to gain free access to Jewish books for Christian scholars.

The learned Ludwig Geiger, who did so much to propagate the view of Reuchlin as the defender of the Jews, misread in the case of Goethe also the various expressions of respect for the Jewish tradition as an interest in the legal rights of Jews in early nineteenth-century Germany. It is by no means redundant to apply this lesson particularly to the late medieval–early modern period: no amount of interest or even admiration expressed for the Jewish tradition suffices to construe it as a plea for improvement of the legal rights and actual living conditions of the Jewish *concives,* to use Reuchlin's preferred legal term.

A hidden but pernicious parallel between the statements of Goethe and Erasmus serves to uncover a point which is usually bypassed in scholarly presentations but is well deserving of our attention. Both giants in the history of culture, and as such opinion makers in Europe's burgeoning ruling class of the informed intelligentsia, tried to discredit opposing views with reference to what they regarded as typical territorial or national characteristics. Goethe points to the avidity of Saxony always to claim pride of place in the race for foolish absurdity. Erasmus even goes one step further in his (Dutch) caricature of the "ugly German" who is bound to go for ideological extremes.

We should not underestimate such seemingly innocent chauvinistic universals, because they exploit deep-seated reservoirs of xenophobia. They play an often unconscious role also in Holocaust studies insofar as they tend to place the roots of the *mysterium iniquitatis* squarely in the German soul. Thus one can perhaps try to salvage the optimistic view of the basic goodness of humankind, but one pays the price by falling into the pit of a *Blut und Boden*–theory. Always more easily believed than documented, Erasmus's argument is, historically seen, sheer absurdity. His explanation of the rapid spread of heresy in Germany as an endemic German characteristic can easily be gainsaid by pointing to the rapid spread of Calvinism twenty years later in France and the Netherlands, and of puritanism in Scotland and England after another twenty years. Erasmus would have been well advised to stick to his vague reference to the *ira Dei* or his much more pertinent explanation in terms of a widespread anticlericalism, the "odium in Ecclesiasticos omnes . . . fere laicorum omnium commune."[7]

With this dangerous game of national characteristics, we have touched upon that other dimension of the passages quoted from Goethe and Erasmus, namely, not their common focus but their contrast. Goethe's reaction in 1823, some ten years before his death (1832), illustrates both the late date of emancipation and the stubborn resistance it met even among its potential propagators. It would be another thirty years before, in 1859, for the first time, a Jewish professor was to be styled *Ordinarius* — the mathematician Moritz Stern in Göttingen; and it took until 1860 before the first Jew was appointed to a court of law — Gabriel Riesser in Hamburg. Uriel Tal alerts us to the fact that when the Jews complained about discrimination, "they often had no interest whatever in obtaining such posts. The complaint itself, however, served to strengthen their Jewish identity."[8]

Emancipatory legislation marks a significant advance. Yet how far legal equality is removed from social emancipation is clearly mirrored in the history of the *Verein zur Abwehr des Antisemitismus*. In its revealing struggle from 1890 through 1933 it never reached, as well documented by Barbara Suchy, "its proclaimed goal of becoming superfluous, never giving up hope that in the end the 'better elements' of the German people would prevail against prejudice and race hatred. . . ." We hardly need Suchy's conclusion: "It is all too obvious that the history of the *Abwehrverein* is no success story. . . ."[9]

Reinhard Rürup's most recent conclusion is to my mind too optimistic — if not misleading — when he argues that the emancipation of the Jews in Germany in the nineteenth century was an "ausgesprochene Erfolgsgeschichte" and that "nothing in 1870 suggests that this history would end within two generations in the catastrophe."[10] This misreading

7. Allen, *Opus Epistolarum*, 7.450.90-92.

8. Uriel Tal, *Christians and Jews in Germany. Religion, Politics and Ideology in the Second Reich, 1870-1914* (Ithaca-London, 1957), p. 327.

9. Barbara Suchy, "The Verein zur Abwehr des Antisemitismus (I) — From Its Beginning to the First World War," in *Leo Baeck Institute Year Book XXVIII* (London, 1983), p. 205. See also the second part of her essay "From the First World War to Its Dissolution in 1933," in *Leo Baeck Institute Year Book XXX* (London, 1985).

10. Rürup, "Deutschland im 19. Jahrhundert," *Deutsche Geschichte*, p. 90. For details see the earlier *Emanzipation und Antisemitismus: Studien zur 'Judenfrage' der bürgerlichen Gesellschaft* (Göttingen, 1975). Cf. most recently idem, "The Tortuous and Thorny Path to Legal Equality. 'Jew Laws' and Emancipatory Legislation in Germany from the Late Eighteenth Century," in *Leo Baeck Institute Year Book XXXI* (London, 1986), pp. 3-33.

of the sources by a historian of substance can only be explained in terms of an overemphasis on the importance of legislation, which has its clear parallel in the field of the history of medieval antisemitism with its preferential treatment of papal and imperial decrees.

Goethe and Erasmus differ in their assessment of the speed with which new ideas spread. It is irrelevant that in each case Goethe and Erasmus were wrong in their estimates — the one in his feeling that Saxony was ahead of its time and out of step with the clock of civilization, and the other in his feeling that the rapid spread of ideological fury is a uniquely German feat. The disparity in the "growth-rates" between the sixteenth-century Reformation and the nineteenth-century emancipation can of course be explained in Erasmus's moral terms by pointing out that hatred is a more potent historical factor than tolerance and respect. For our purposes, however, it is important to realize that ideas drafted in the study, promulgated in the courtroom, and propagated from the academic lectern have a much longer fuse than sermons in packed churches or rabble-rousing speeches in the marketplace, skillfully addressing the audience in terms of its needs, fears, and hopes. After all, what has been shaped in a long history of instruction and propaganda is not easily changed by new legislation "from above."

In contrast with the assumption of Erasmus that the common folk are given to the avid pursuit of new ideas, the most striking phenomenon in the history of the relations of Christians and Jews in the later Middle Ages is rather conceptual inertia and lack of novel ideas. Whereas our secondary literature is bristling with "radical departures," "new directions," "sudden shifts," and even "revolutions," the history it claims to describe is singularly barren of innovation: the Christian "remedy" for dealing with the spiritual and social "disease" of the "stubborn Jew" is an ever-changing dosage of two unchanging ingredients — conversion and repression.

II. *Cum Nimis Absurdum:* Conversion or Segregation

Not until the middle of the sixteenth century do we find some semblance of innovation in papal strategy in dealing with the "stubborn Jews." When Pope Paul IV promulgated, on 14 July 1555, the *Cum nimis absurdum* decree to establish the first ghetto in Rome, destined to last until the end of the papal state in 1870, he used a terminology which suggests that his purpose was conversion rather than segregation. In an extensive study, Kenneth R. Stow has argued that this was indeed the driving motivation behind this change in papal strategy.[11]

As is customary with papal decrees, such a document is usually referred to by its first two words. But *Cum nimis* reveals more of its content when identified by the first three words: "Cum nimis absurdum. . . ." It takes as its point of departure the consideration that it is sheer "absurdity" that Jews, in perpetual servitude because of their own guilt, should be allowed to exploit Christian piety by gaining social equality and economic domination. After all, the Roman Church tolerates the Jews as evidence of the true Christian faith by which they should be moved to see their errors and convert, *Sedis apostolicae pietate et benignitate allecti:* "It is therefore appropriate *(propterea convenire)* that as long as they persist in their errors they are made to feel and see that they are slaves and the Christians free men through Jesus Christ our God and Lord. . . ."[12] To put an end to the absurdity of the inversion of the social order, and to break through the ingratitude blocking the road to conversion, the Jews have henceforth to be confined to ghettos — defined as separate places with but one entry and one exit.

It is a moot question to debate whether *Cum nimis absurdum* documents a papal strategy of conversion or segregation. It is both, in that segregation and repression are to break the back of the ungrateful and stubborn resistance to conversion. On the basis of his patient analysis of the papal tax records, Stow repeated his conversion thesis five years later:

> The popes of the first half of the century were felicitously able to combine fiscal and theological needs in their approach to Jewish taxation. The popes of the latter half chose to dismember a balanced and effective taxation program, at least as it applied to the Jews, and in its stead they substituted a fiscal soaking that could serve theological ends alone. Whatever other goals the papacy was pursuing simultaneously, and it assuredly was, it was also unswervingly, and despite its complete reversal of means and method at mid-century, in search of large-scale conversion.[13]

11. Kenneth R. Stow, *Catholic Thought and Papal Jewry Policy 1555-1593* (New York, 1977).

12. *Bullarium Romanum* (Turin, 1857), pp. 498-500. Text and translation available in Stow, *Catholic Thought,* pp. 291-98. I deviate in my translation as far as the indicated *propterea* clause is concerned.

13. Kenneth R. Stow, "Taxation, Community and State. The Jews and the Fiscal Foundations of the Early Modern Papal State," in *Päpste und Papsttum,* vol. 19 (Stuttgart, 1982), pp. 69-70.

The records of the first half of the sixteenth century indeed confirm that the taxation of Jews is formulated as a privilege granted to resident aliens who are allowed this because of the magnanimity of the church: throughout, the declared intention is to overcome the stubborn resistance against conversion. Long before 1555, the expression of hope for conversion has become a formula attached to all levies, as for instance in the case of Pope Leo X in 1517, when he expressed to the Jews of Umbria the hope that "the use of such magnanimity, which the apostolic see has always followed in your case, will at some point soften your bones and excise the blindness from your eyes. . . ."[14]

Kenneth Stow is convinced that the reference to conversion "was not simply a device exploited in the service of taxation strategies," and that the consideration for granting privileges was "not political, but theological"[15] — a thesis as difficult to prove as to contradict, at least by historical means. One is reminded of the bitter complaint of Johannes Pfefferkorn, in his *Judenspiegel* of 1507, that the authorities *(Obrigkeit)* pursue a Jewish policy which talks about conversion but yields them piles of money — a theme repeatedly echoed in the pamphlets of the sixteenth century.[16]

The language of conversion cannot obscure the fact that 1555 marks a strategic shift. The absurdity which Pope Paul IV is intent on removing once and for all is of a social nature, and the ghetto is set up to root out all forms of fraternizing which obscure the legal status of the Jews as slaves — thus applying the Bull of Pope Eugenius IV of 1442, *Dudum ad nostram,* which had called for a rigorous ban on all forms of social interaction.[17] This oscillation between conversion and segregation is by no means a sixteenth-century phenomenon. Just as the related expectation of the imminent end of the world or the approaching millennium, it has much earlier medieval roots.

Before we seek to establish these lines of continuity, one final comment on *Cum nimis absurdum* is in order. The decree of 14 July 1555, which initiated the scaling off of the ghetto till 1870, does not document a general papal theology or propagate a global ideal for the relationship of Christians and Jews. It is a piece of local legislation

14. Stow, "Taxation," p. 53.
15. Stow, "Taxation," pp. 55, 54.
16. *Judenspiegel* (Cologne, 1507), fol. C4^V-D1^R. Cf. Heiko A. Oberman, *Wurzeln des Antisemitismus: Christenangst und Judenplage im Zeitalter von Humanismus und Reformation* (Berlin, 1981), pp. 90ff., 113.
17. Brian Pullan, *Rich and Poor in Renaissance Venice* (Cambridge, 1971), pp. 449-50.

promulgating laws for Jews "in Statu Ecclesiastico degentibus," and hence restricted to the papal state. Pope Paul IV acted as a sovereign prince in his own territory, unable to move Florence and Milan to follow suit, whereas Venice had preceded Rome in independently ordering the Jews to be confined to a ghetto (1516) and then to withdraw to Mestre on the mainland (1527).[18] Paul IV appeals to decisions of his predecessors in the papal office, and insofar acts as pope. But he reacts as a local lord to social absurdity, which he has just *(nuper)* learned about.

This document is therefore to be placed side by side with the legislation concerning Jews of the developing early modern territorial states which had acquired, seized, or bought sovereignty in Jewish affairs and had now to find a solution for "placing" the Jews, amidst the conflicting efforts to establish a cohesive *Kulturpolitik,* and raise taxes to support the rapid growth of its administrative networks.[19] In this sense the papal decree falls under the general rule of accommodation first worked out in 1531 for Switzerland and then applied to confession-torn Imperial Germany (1555): *cuius regio, eius religio.*

III. Toward a Closed Christian Society

The mid-sixteenth-century strategy change in the papal state, while showing parallels to developments in other early modern European states, cannot be identified with the advice Luther gave Saxony in 1543 in his notorious seven points in *Concerning the Jews and Their Lies,* summarized in his last sermon a few days before his death in Eisleben in 1546. It may suffice to quote here the epilogue to the sermon of 15 February 1546: if the Jews are willing to convert and desist from blasphemy and crime, "then we will be glad to forgive them: if not, we should not tolerate and suffer them."[20]

18. See William J. Bouwsma, *Venice and the Defense of Republican Liberty: Renaissance Values in the Age of the Counter-Reformation* (Berkeley, 1968), p. 117.

19. See my contribution to the volume edited by S. N. Eisenstadt, *From Transformation to Crisis: Towards a Reassessment of Anti-Semitism in Late Medieval and Early Modern Europe* (Jerusalem, 1988).

20. "Noch wollen wir die Christliche liebe an inen üben und vor sie bitten, daß sie sich bekeren, den Herrn annemen, den sie vor uns billich ehren solten, Welcher solchs nicht thun wil, da setze es in keinen zweivel, das der ein verböster Jüde ist, der nicht ablassen wird Christum zu lestern, dich aus zu saugen und (wo er kan) zu tödten. . . . Wollen sich die Jüden zu uns bekeren und von irer lesterung, und was sie uns sonst gethan haben, auffhören, so wollen wir es inen gerne vergeben, Wo aber

Yet the much-discussed shift in Luther's attitude toward the Jews between the 1523 treatise *Jesus Christ, Born a Jew (Dass Jesus Christus ein geborener Jude sei)* calling for new, more effective conversion tactics, and his 1543 treatise *Concerning the Jews and Their Lies*, with its alternative conversion or enforced integration, shows some remarkable parallels with the 1555 change in papal politics. At first sight, there is a glaring difference in the fact that Pope Paul IV wants to establish a ghetto, whereas Luther calls for the expulsion of the Jews when they "stubbornly" reject salvation by baptism. From a sociological point of view, however, ghettos and expulsion are both forms of segregation, designed to establish a uniform, closed Christian society. Both are variants of one and the same type of *Judenpolitik*, as the easy transition to the expulsion decrees of Pope Pius V in 1569 and of Clement VIII in 1593 make clear, when, except for those in the ghettos of Rome, Ancona, and Avignon, all the Jews were removed from the papal state. In each case there is the furious reaction against the *ingrati* — the ungrateful Jews who have been unwilling to see the light of Christian mercy, shown forth by toleration.

The real difference lies in a seemingly minor detail, namely that although both advocate the burning of the synagogues, Pope Pius IV wants to retain one synagogue within the ghetto, while Luther wants to see all the synagogues destroyed as centers of blasphemy. The explanation is that despite the fact that both want to establish a closed — that is, a protected — Christian society, Pope Paul sees the solution in the establishment of a ghetto while Luther wants to abolish the *Judenviertel*, the predecessor of the ghetto, in order to force the issue: integration, or expulsion. Whereas in the papal state creating ghettos is the "harsh solution," primarily chosen in order to achieve mass conversion, Luther's plea for "a harsh treatment of the Jews" is principally aimed at the protection of Christian society itself, illustrated in the final urgent plea: "Do not burden yourself with alien sin *(fremde Sünde)* — you have sufficient to account for yourself. . . ."

As different as these two motivations may seem to be, nevertheless they clearly draw on the one common root of all forms of late medieval anti-Jewish sentiment — the urgency for the reform of church and society in light of the speedily approaching final phase of "these last days," invoked by both Pope Paul IV and Martin Luther.

This pervasive expectation was readily transformed into anti-Jewish strategies, when new "insights" and "inside reports" by New Christians seemed to legitimize increased aggression. In his fine edition of the

---

nicht, so sollen wir sie auch bey uns nicht dulden noch leiden." *Von den Juden und ihren Lügen*, WA 51.195.39-196.17.

Nizzahon vetus, David Berger could at once suggest and document that it was in the course of the thirteenth century that the "relations between Christians and Jews were indeed deteriorating."[21] Next to a whole series of other factors, like the failure of the crusades and the spreading monastic movement, the new polemical thrust is due to an increasing Christian knowledge of the Talmud,[22] a challenge to which Christian theology reacted all the more allergically as it was in the process of developing a new respect for the literal sense of the Scriptures.

There can be no doubt that from here originates one of the accelerators in the history of antisemitism in the later Middle Ages. The development from the twelfth-century dialogue to the more acrimonious polemic, so well described by David Berger for the period when "the church was not yet deadly serious about the aim of conversion,"[23] leads in stages to the ever-sharper contrast between the Israel of Holy Scripture and rabbinic Judaism, from there to the conviction that the talmudic books represent an obstacle to the conversion of the blind Jews, leading finally to the burning of the Holy Books beginning in thirteenth-century France (in Paris, 1242; Toulouse, 1319) and continuing in sixteenth-century Italy (Venice, 1553). This is the context in which the theme *Concerning the Jews and Their Lies* emerged, to use the title of Luther's fiercest writing of 1543. And this is the basis for the sixteenth-century transconfessional call for the removal of the books of the Jews, as requested by Pfefferkorn and Johannes Eck, by Luther and Pope Paul IV.

In the case of Luther, there is the additional concern about a reportedly successful Jewish counteroffensive in the 1530s, leading to the conversion of the Sabbatarians. Yet this feeds into the same insistence on the protection of Christian society as we have noticed in the ghetto decree of Pope Paul IV, which defined "absurdity" as the upheaval caused by the social ascendency of the ungrateful Jews.

With the theme of *Judenangst* we encounter the second accelerator, which can be traced through the fourteenth century, a development which

---

21. *The Jewish-Christian Debate in the High Middle Ages: A Critical Edition of the Nizzahon vetus,* introduction, translation, and commentary by David Berger (Philadelphia, 1979), p. 32. As John H. Van Engen has shown, already in the twelfth century the "dialogue" took on the more aggressive forms of *conflictum* and *duellum.* See his *Rupert of Deutz* (Berkeley, 1983), pp. 241-48, esp. 247.

22. Cf. David Berger's lucid article, "Mission to the Jews and Jewish-Christian Contacts in the Polemical Literature of the High Middle Ages," *American Historical Review* 91/3 (1986): 579, 591. To this very same point, Jeremy Cohen's "Scholarship and Intolerance in the Medieval Academy: The Study and Evaluation of Judaism in European Christendom," *American Historical Review* 91/3 (1986): 592-613.

23. Berger, "Mission to the Jews," p. 591.

Jeremy Cohen has called "the evolution of medieval anti-Judaism." This phrase is the euphemistic description of the impact of the mendicant friars who, by reaching out to the common folk, shaped a climate favoring the exclusion of all the Jews from European society, which "eventually allowed other political, social and economic trends to take their course."[24] Though one can call for refinements of Cohen's thesis insofar as he does not distinguish among the friars between the "Conventuals" and "Observants," and excludes from his purview the third largest mendicant order, the Augustinians, who were to play such a crucial role in the history of antisemitism in Germany, there can be no question that the mendicants lent a new urgency to the call to conversion, no longer primarily directed at saving the Jews, but at saving the *bonum commune* of Christian society. There is no evidence, however, that the friars created Europe's *Judenangst*. They rather fanned and exploited the widespread stories about Jewish blood libels and host desecration, which increasingly evolved into social protest of the common man against the ruling elite in cities where the Jews were under the protection of local authorities.

The fact that the Jews were a threat to society was not merely believed by the common folk influenced by the medicant friars, but by the intelligentsia as well. In a revealing German chronicle for the year 1349, which, as far as I can see, has been overlooked hitherto, we find it documented that even when popular myths of Jewish crimes are no longer believed, the killing of Jews is nevertheless fully approved. After having recorded that, in the year 1349, when the plague hit Erfurt, more than one hundred Jews were killed "per communitatem civium, invitis consulibus,"[25] and another three thousand committed suicide by self-incineration, the traditional charge is reported that the Jews had poisoned the wells. In view of the vast documentation of these and similar events, this chronicle would not deserve special mention, were it not for what the author now adds: "It is more believable that the reason for their calamity was the tremendous debts, which all classes in society, nobility and soldiers, citizens and farmers had incurred."

Yet, notwithstanding this sophisticated demythologization, the entry concludes with the exclamation: "Deo autem gratias semper, qui civitatem Erphurdensem populumque Christianum ibidem . . . sua pia

---

24. Jeremy Cohen, *The Friars and the Jews: The Evolution of Medieval Anti-Judaism* (Ithaca, 1982), p. 245.

25. *Erphurdianus Antiquitatum Variloquus incerti Auctoris, nebst einem Anhange historischer Notizen über den Bauernkrieg in und um Erfurt i. J. 1525,* hrsg. von der Historischen Kommission für die Provinz Sachsen und das Herzogtum Anhalt, ed. Richard Thiele (Halle, 1906), p. 132.

misericordia custodivit."[26] It was therefore by no means just the simple people exposed to the preaching of the friars who believed in host desecration.[27] Nor does the doubt expressed about the poisoning charge convince the enlightened author that the killing of the Jews was a miscarriage of justice. The point is that for whatever reason Jews are eliminated it serves to protect the Christian commumty: "Deo gratias!"

This anonymous chronicle, with its cool recording of numerous instances of mob action against the Jews, has an awesomely "modern" face in that the alleged crimes are questioned, but not the moral necessity of punishment. This document presages the development which Herbert A. Strauss has so aptly phrased as the nineteenth-century metamorphosis "der Ritualmordlüge zur Rassenlüge,"[28] which marks the transition to "modern antisemitism," in the precise sense of that word.

The blood libel charge, which can be traced in the empire from Oberwesel (1286) through Trent (1475) to Grevenbroich in the Rhineland (1834), not only precedes the impact of the friars, but persists long after its religious roots have been severed. It is part of that medieval tradition which no longer regards the Jews as "blind" (ceci) and therefore in need of the light of conversion, but as willfully "stubborn" (obstinati) and therefore as a corpus alienum to be excised from Christian society.

IV. The Threat of the Antichrist

Surveying the three forms of medieval repression of the Jews — by burning their books, their abodes, or their bodies — recent scholarship has been inclined to believe that the rising tide of anti-Jewish agitation is a late-medieval phenomenon with, at the earliest, late thirteenth-century roots. Yet if it is right to discern behind the critique of the Jews, as obstacles both to eternal and temporal justice, the "vision of the end" with its concomitant missionary fervor and social reform, we have to trace the roots to the twelfth century and the impact of Joachim of Fiore († 1202).

26. *Ephurdianus Antiquitatum Variloquus*, p. 133.

27. See text plus translation of the "objective report from the courtroom" of the host desecration of the year 1510, by the progressive Nuremberg printer, Hieronymus Höltzel, in Oberman, *Wurzeln des Antisemitismus*, pp. 129-33.

28. "Die preussische Bürokratie und die anti-jüdischen Unruhen im Jahre 1834," in *Gegenwart im Rückblick. Festgabe für die Jüdische Gemeinde zu Berlin 25 Jahre nach dem Neubeginn*, ed. Herbert A. Strauss and Kurt R. Grossmann (Heidelberg, 1970), pp. 27-55, esp. 49.

Two of Joachim's major themes proved to be particularly influential in shaping the general climate of thought within which the campaign against the "stubborn Jews" could gain momentum. The first theme concerns radical *reformatio,* of which in the last stage of history the monks will be the carriers who, if not replacing, will at least be outstripping the sacerdotal hierarchy of the church. The second theme, which Joachim even elevates to an article of faith, concerns the expectation of the imminent end — a theme which can be shown to be a major factor in the sixteenth-century strategies as formulated by Martin Luther and Pope Paul IV.[29]

When we turn with these assumptions in mind to the writings of Joachim of Fiore, we discover that however successful he might have been, with his expectation of the millennium to come, in combating St. Augustine's view of history, his view of the relation of Christians and Jews has lost out to the single most important Church Father of the West.

When, two years before his death, the Abbot of Fiore signed his testament "with my own hand in the year of Our Lord 1200," he authenticated a list of his writings which concludes with what he calls the two "minor works," *Against the Jews* and *Against the Enemies of the Catholic Faith (= De articulis fidei?).*[30] The importance of this listing is that Joachim distinguishes here between the Jews and the enemies of

29. See Heiko A. Oberman, *Luther: Mensch zwischen Gott und Teufel* (Berlin, 1983²), pp. 304-7; Engl., *Luther: Man Between God and Devil* (New Haven, 1989), pp. 294-97; Stow, "Eschatological Speculation," in *Catholic Thought,* pp. 225-77.

30. See the thoughtful bibliographical essay by Kurt-Victor Selge, "Joachim von Fiore in der Geschichtsschreibung der letzten sechzig Jahre (von Grundmann bis zur Gegenwart): Ergebnisse und offene Fragen," in *Atti del II Congressa internazionale di Studi Gioachimiti 6-9 Settembre 1984,* ed. by Centro internationale di Studi Gioachimiti, S. Giovanni in Fiore 1986, pp. 31-53. See further Bernard McGinn, *Visions of the End: Apocalyptic Traditions in the Middle Ages* (New York, 1979), pp. 140-41; and idem, *The Calabrian Abbot: Joachim of Fiore in the History of Western Thought* (New York, 1984); Marjorie Reeves, *The Influence of Prophecy in the Later Middle Ages: A Study in Joachimism* (Oxford, 1969), pp. 293ff. Cf. Delno C. West and Sandra Zimdars-Swartz, *Joachim of Fiore: A Study in Spiritual Perception and History* (Bloomington, 1983). For our theme, see particularly the excellent edition by Arsenio Frugoni, *Adversus Iudeos di Gioacchino da Fiore* (Rome, 1957). In the only detailed treatment, Beatrice Hirsch-Reich, in "Joachim von Fiore und das Judentum," *Miscellanea Mediaevalia* 4 (1966): 228-63; reprinted in Delno West's *Joachim of Fiore in Christian Thought,* 2 vols. (New York, 1971), 2.473-510, bases her interpretation on the (likely) hypothesis that the *Adversus Iudeos* is a "Frühwerk" (much more cautiously phrased by Herbert Grundmann, *Studien über Joachim von Fiore* [Leipzig, 1927; Darmstadt, 1966], p. 14) so that Joachim's surprising view is reduced to the unclarities of a beginner. Though Joachim does not explicitly apply here his three-status scheme, and does not distinguish between the *adventus antichristi* at the beginning and at the end of the third status, the profile of his mature thought is clear.

the church, the two designations which ever since St. Augustine had been united in the tightly knit triad: the Jews, the heretics, and the enemies (*Judei, haeretici, et inimici*).

Already in the *Liber de Concordia*, Joachim connected the need for reform and the imminence of the Day of the Lord with the mission to the Jews:[31] the carriers of the Spirit of the Third Age are the designated missionaries "per quos et Iudeorum populus convertetur ad deum," "illi ultimi predicatores per quos reliquie Iudeorum convertentur ad dominum."[32] Book 4 of the *Liber de Concordia* culminates with the prophecy:

> And the spiritual understanding [of the Scriptures] will reach the Jews and shatter as if by thunder the hardness of their hearts, so that the word of the prophet Malachi will be fulfilled: "I will send you the prophet Elijah before that horrible day of the Lord comes. He will convert the hearts of the fathers to their sons and the hearts of the sons to their fathers lest I come and smite the land with a curse" (Mal. IV:5-6). This will be completed at the end of the second and at the beginning of the third era [*status*], at about the time when the nations will trample over the holy city for forty-two months (Rev. XI:2) when the Wicked One will rule who, as the prophet Daniel put it, "is to destroy the universe in an unbelievable fashion."[33]

The historical parallels between the events in the first era, roughly speaking of the Old Testament, and those of the second era, roughly speaking of the New Testament and early church history (i.e. the seven persecutions of the Jews paralleled with the seven persecutions of the Church), are traced for the sole purpose of foretelling the things to come

---

31. "Oportet ergo mutari vitam, quia mutari necesse est statum mundi, ut quasi per transitum deserti perveniamus ad illam requiem dei nostri, quam intrare non sunt digni qui non credunt dicentibus, qui, loquentes de fine mundi, putant omnimodis insanire." *Liber de Concordia Noui ac Veteris Testamenti*, ed. E. Randolph Daniel (Philadelphia, 1983), p. 160, ll. 94-98.

32. *Liber de Concordia*, p. 158, l. 61; p. 159, l. 83–p. 160, l. 84.

33. *Liber de Concordia*, p. 422, ll. 309-17. Although Joachim declares it to be unknown how long Elijah will precede the Second Coming of Christ, he will come "in principio tertii [status]" to convert all Jews. "De ultimis Tribulationibus," ed. E. R. Daniel, in *Prophecy and Millenarianism: Essays in Honour of Marjorie Reeves*, ed. Ann Williams (London, 1980), pp. 175-89, esp. p. 189, ll. 8-9. The sequence of events on the eschatological timetable, which Augustine had been unwilling to determine *De Civitate Dei* XX, 30 is spelled out clearly in the *Tractatus super Quatuor Evangelia*. Here the ambiguities, which B. Hirsch-Reich noted, are dispelled by "incipient": ". . . antequam veniat tribulatio Antichristi, incipient converti reliquie Iudeorum. . .," ed. E. Buonaiuti (Rome, 1930), p. 143, ll. 8-9.

in the third era (with the breaking of the seven seals of the Apocalypse). Hence the conversion of the Jews is, throughout all the writings of Joachim, the central issue. His final conclusion is also his point of departure, namely, that on the Day of the Lord all Jews will be converted. This can be so clearly calculated that Joachim does not even need the traditional proof text of St. Paul in Romans 11:25.

What then can be the purpose of his *Adversus Iudeos;* why would Joachim try in this treatise to convert any Jew when all Jews will be converted collectively on the Day of the Lord, which according to him is to come so soon? The answer is that before the Day of the Lord the antichrist is to arrive, at which time the larger part of the Jews, who ever since their "killing of Christ" have been stricken with blindness, will hail the Evil One, mistaking him for the Messiah.[34] The antichrist will gather the Jews in Jerusalem and force them to obey the law of Moses and to assail the church of Christ, and that will be a time of devastation and desolation for all mankind.[35] The whole purpose of Joachim's sermon is to convince the Jews that they should not fall for the tricks of the antichrist, and avoid the misery that this will entail.[36] Yet ultimately they will be again what they always were — the people of God: "in novissimo dierum erit Israel populus Domini."[37]

In his conclusion, Joachim does quote St. Paul's vision of the conversion of all the Jews and perhaps even wants to evoke the personal history of the apostle himself in pointing out that, as in the case of St. Paul, one and the same people "are blind but will be illuminated, they are hardened and will be converted."[38] Awed by the horrible events of the last days, Joachim wants to convert the Jews not to add them to the "people of God" — they are that already — but to save them from the tricks of the antichrist.[39]

---

34. "Inde est quod, effectus cecus secundum maiorem sui partem, recepturus est Antichristum. . . ." Joachim of Fiore, *Adversus Iudeos,* p. 48, ll. 9-10.

35. "Igitur Antichristus, qui dicitur hic dux venturus assumens prevaricatores Iudeorum adherentes sibi, congregabit eos in Ierusalem, iubens eos servare legem Moysi, atque hoc modo populus Iudeorum dissipaturus est civitatem et sanctuarium, hoc est Ecclesiam Christi cum venturo duce; erit autem 'finis eius vastitas, et post finem belli statuta desolatio.' . . .", *Adversus Iudeos,* p. 48, ll. 14-19.

36. ". . . pertimescite ne inveniamini in societate illorum qui dissipaturi sunt sanctuarium et civitatem cum duce venturo, hoc est cum Antichristo. . . . Putantes enim se recipere Christum suscipient Antichristum." *Adversus Iudeos,* p. 57, ll. 14-16, 18-19.

37. *Adversus Iudeos,* p. 82, ll. 22-23.

38. ". . . consummari oportebat in populo vestro, cecitas scilicet et illuminatio, induratio et conversion . . .", *Adversus Iudeos,* p. 88, ll. 1-2.

39. "Sed cupientes aliquos vestrum etiam ante tempus illud generale saltim pro

The Strasbourg Apocalypse, *Der Antichrist,* of 1480, which was to sweep through Europe before the end of the century in three linguistic versions and numerous editions, shows that what stayed alive of Joachim's thought was the one point that was the least unique for him, namely the fact that at the moment of the coming of the antichrist the Jews would hail him as their Lord Supreme.[40] But as concerns his specific emphasis on the temporary nature of their blindness and their ultimate collective conversion, the influence of Joachim of Fiore was of only marginal significance.

From his rich agenda of the events in the third era, only the issue of the calculation of the coming of the antichrist proved to have a lasting impact: blindness became culpable, wicked, invincible stubbornness when Joachim's collective conversion of the Jews at the time of the second advent of Christ was relegated to a last event beyond real history: all attention became directed to the coming of the antichrist and his collective seduction of the Jews.

As Franz Pelster has argued, Joachim of Fiore had found his way into the inner circles of the University of Paris by 1300. In reality, however, it is "Pseudo-Joachim" who is thus received. Pelster's critical edition of the fascinating *Quaestio* by Henry of Harclay (†1317) confirms that a problem that officially deals with the issue whether the second advent of Christ can be calculated by means of astrology, de facto deals with the advent of the antichrist "qui vastabit ecclesiam."[41] It is this "Pseudo-Joachim" who will sway minds in the centuries to come.

This we have not seen clearly enough, because we have looked at the wrong sources. As far as the question of the Jews is concerned, Thomas Aquinas (†1274) and Petrus Johannis Olivi (†1298), as fascinating as they may seem, are in this respect the outsiders, who will not determine the shape of late medieval thought in its main thrust. Thomas allowed the Jews to disappear almost completely in the larger, and for him more important, category of the *infideles;*[42] and Olivi impressed his

---

ipsa vicinitate lucis de regno eripere tenebrarum, dedimus operam in hoc opusculo prevenire vos, o viri Iudei, in benedictionibus dulcedinis. . . ." *Adversus Iudeos,* p. 95, ll. 10-14.

40. Cf. Christoph Peter Burger, "Endzeiterwartung im späten Mittelalter," in *Der Antichrist und die Fünfzehn Zeichen vor dem Jüngsten Gericht* (Hamburg, 1979), pp. 18-53, esp. 39, 43.

41. Franz Pelster, *Die Quaestio Heinrichs von Harclay über die zweite Ankunft Christi und die Erwartung des baldigen Weltendes zu Anfang des XIV. Jarhunderts* (Rome, 1951), p. 41.

42. Thomas Aquinas, *Summa Theologiae,* II, 2, q. 10, art. 1-12; only the last

own views on Joachim by mobilizing the faithful *fraticelli* against the unfaithful church, with even more rigor than the very partial edition of his Apocalypse commentary by Raoul Manselli can convey.[43] With Olivi the historical Jews disappear when they are spiritualized into the allegory for the unfaithful church, the *ecclesia infidelis*.

If we are right in characterizing Joachim as the one who in his view of the Jews pitted St. Paul against St. Augustine, then the victory of the Church Father over the apostle is best documented by the eminent fifteenth-century Augustinian inquisitor and Bible scholar, Jacobus Perez of Valencia (c. 1408-1490). In his *Tractatus contra Iudaeos* and his influential *Explanationes* of the Psalms, so often reprinted in the sixteenth century, and most likely on the desk of the young Professor Martin Luther, Perez declared dialogue with the Jews to be futile and all efforts for their conversion terminated: the Jews are not merely blind but stubborn — as personified by their biblical guide, Rabbi David Kimchi, who is at once "caecus et obstinatus."[44]

The key to Perez's vituperation can be found, as if in a summary and shorthand of his views, when he identifies the Jews with the antichrist to such an extent that the Evil One himself becomes a Jew: "Erit antichristus Simul Iudaeus et Haereticus, tirannus et hypocrita . . . qui vastabit ecclesiam."[45] This means that on the Day of Judgment all his followers will be destroyed without even a chance for conversion.[46] In our search for the reason why anti-Jewish propaganda escalated to such an amazing extent in the later Middle Ages, the authentic teaching of the genuine Joachim of Fiore proves to be a red herring.

---

article, art. 12, deals specifically with the Jews, namely whether the children of Jews can be baptized against the will of their parents. Also in respect to this latter question, Thomas's opinion is set aside in a development reaching from Duns Scotus to Ulrich Zasius. See Steven W. Rowan, "Ulrich Zasius and John Eck: 'Faith need not be kept with an enemy'," *Sixteenth Century Journal* 8 (1977): 79-95.

43. Raoul Manselli (ed.), *La "Lectura super Apocalypsim" di Pietro di Giovanni Olivi* (Rome, 1955).

44. *De torrente in via bibit:* ". . . Camhi [Kimchi] 'iste caecus et obstinatus'." "Occaecavit eos malitia eorum, ne intelligerent sacramenta Dei. Imo tota Scriptura veteris testamenti, legis et prophetarum, est plena de caecitate illorum obstinationem [sic!]. Et ideo superfluum est eis respondere cum non capiant nec intelligant. Sed ne argumenta eorum maneant insoluta respondebimus propter consolationem simplicium Christianorum." Commentary to Ps. 109:7, Jacobus Perez of Valencia, *Explanationes in 150 Psalmos* (Venice, 1581), fol. 809D.

45. "Erit antichristus Simul Iudaeus et Haereticus, tirannus et hypocrita et sic vastabit ecclesiam (sed non totaliter delebit . . .)." Commentary to Ps. 90:11-13, Jacobus Perez, *Explanationes*, fol. 684A.

46. Jacobus Perez, *Explanationes*, fol. 707F.

The turmoil caused by the Western Schism and by the competing claims of three popes after the Council of Pisa (1409) must be seen as a crucial factor in changing the long-revered tradition of the calculation of the second coming of Christ to a preoccupation with the coming of the antichrist to be born in Jerusalem and sent to gather in the stubborn Jews blinded by their murder of the Messiah now bent on "vastare ecclesiam." Once the Augustinian sequence of the three enemies in the three eras — the Jews, the heretics, and the bad Christians (mali christiani) — became transformed into the Jews, the heretics, and the followers of the antichrist (antichristiani), radical reform started to take on the meaning of the extirpation of "the enemy within," which subordinated conversion of the Jews to the higher goal of the protection of church and society.[47]

We must draw the conclusion that there is not just one carrier that can be made responsible for the rising tide of antisemitism. It is not the heretical Joachimites in-the-shadows, nor just the gross preaching friars nor the uninformed common man (der gemeine Mann) who falls victim to the myth of eucharistic desecration or blood libel, but the sophisticated elite, the most refined representatives of high theology and biblical studies as well.

Modern Christian spokesmen for tolerance and the brotherhood of man prefer to believe that it was merely the base elements in Christianity that led to the upsurge of anti-Jewish agitation in the later Middle Ages. On the contrary. The Lenten season, meant to prepare for the Christian High Holidays, was throughout Europe the most dangerous period for the Jews in the fourteenth, fifteenth, and sixteenth centuries. This is indicative of the fact that it is the most spiritual thrust in Christianity, its search for reform and renewal, which makes the Christian tradition precisely in those times of revival a deadly threat to the Jews — all the more deadly when this historical fact is overlooked, repressed, or ignored.

---

47. In a well-documented study, Michael H. Shank shows the role which leading theologians of the Vienna school, such as Henry of Langenstein and Nicolas of Dinkelsbuhl, played in direct and indirect support for the eruption of anti-Jewish pogroms in Vienna, 1420-1421. See "Unless You Believe, You Shall Not Understand": Logic, University, and Society in Late Medieval Vienna (Princeton, 1988), pp. 149-69, 189-200. Of particular importance for our purposes is the identification of the Jews with the heretics — in this case the Hussites and the Waldensians.

Reuchlin and the Jews:
Obstacles on the Path to Emancipation

I. Fact and Fiction: Three Phases of Interpretation

Our view of Johannes Reuchlin (1455-1522) has been shaped and misshapen in three distinct, historical phases. In each, true insights have been articulated, revealing critical aspects of the primary sources; to this extent each phase has passed the test of time.

1. Reuchlin as "Forerunner of the Reformation"

First, Reuchlin has been portrayed as a forerunner of Martin Luther and as a herald of the Reformation. While Reuchlin was yet alive, a pamphlet appeared in Strasbourg entitled "The History of the Four Heretical Dominicans" (1521). The title page not only presents the scandal of Dominican heresy, but especially highlights the common stance of three heroes, allies in their love of truth. Reuchlin, Hutten, and Luther stand together; capital letters boldly proclaim their identity as "Patron[i] li-

---

"Reuchlin and the Jews: Obstacles on the Path to Emancipation," translated by J. Jeffrey Tyler and revised from the original German article "Johannes Reuchlin: Von Judenknechten zu Judenrechten," in *Reuchlin und die Juden,* ed. A. Herzig, J. Schoeps, and S. Rohde, Pforzheimer Reuchlinschriften 3 (Sigmaringen: Jan Thorbecke, 1993), 39-64.

bertatis," "Champions of Liberty."[1] This claim is illustrated by a sketch of Ulrich von Hutten (†1523). Although he wears the knight's armor, Hutten is adorned not with the expected warrior's helm, but rather with the laurel wreath of the *poeta laureatus,* the highly prized crown of the erudite humanist. This Strasbourg pamphlet hails the movement, which we call the Reformation, as a program or even crusade for emancipation and religious freedom, calling for mobilization against the obscurantist conspiracy of the Dominican Order.

Today, the inner connection between Reuchlin and the Reformation has been rightly called into question. Less than one year before the Strasbourg pamphlet, Luther had proclaimed the *libertas christiana* as a spiritual liberation through faith. Reuchlin — a favored guest in the house of Johannes Eck, Luther's fierce opponent — left no room for doubt or rumor; he had no sympathy for Luther's view, in his eyes a position threatening public order and private discipline. The Strasbourg portrayal of the united, courageous triumvirate reflected the hopes of many. But while both took pride in their stance as biblical scholars, Reuchlin and Luther did not stand side by side on the same front against "Rome."

Yet the common ground shared by Reuchlin and Luther cannot be overlooked. On the way to Worms in April 1521, Luther rejected the offer of an alliance with the German-national movement of Hutten and Franz von Sickingen (†1523). Likewise, Reuchlin did not support the plan of the German knights for armed intervention on his behalf. Indeed, he refused to back Sickingen's proposal to use force against the Cologne Dominicans, to compel them to pay the court costs for the Reuchlin trial (one hundred and eleven Rhenish Gulden), as the superior court in Speyer had ruled on 15 March 1514. Clearly, Luther and Reuchlin agreed on one crucial issue — the rejection of a militant, nationalistic solution.

---

1. Josef Benzing, *Bibliographie der Schriften Johannes Reuchlins im 15. und 16. Jahrhundert,* Bibliotheca Bibliographica 18 (Bad Bocklet: Walter Krieg Verlag, 1955), illus. 1, p. XIII. Such a close association between Reuchlin and Luther was not mere propaganda. See the letter of Pirckheimer to Reuchlin (Nov. 1518), in which Luther is described as "tui amantissimum"; *Willibald Pirckheimers Briefwechsel,* vol. 3, ed. Dieter Wuttke (Munich: C. H. Beck, 1989), p. 432, l. 8.

The exact configuration of these *Patroni* was flexible. In the previous year, Crotus Rubeanus, later Rector of the University of Frankfurt, displayed on his coat of arms sixteen names with those on the four corners being (from left to top): M. Lutt[er], Eras[mus], Mutianus, Io. Reüchl[in]. See Lewis W. Spitz, *The Religious Renaissance of the German Humanists* (Cambridge, Mass.: Harvard University Press, 1963), p. 130; with excellent reproduction (illus. 7), opposite p. 164.

2. Reuchlin as "Precursor" of the Enlightenment

For the portrayal of Reuchlin in modern times, Heinrich Graetz's monumental history of the Jews has proven to be most influential.[2] Alongside Graetz stands Ludwig Geiger's three formidable volumes: a history of Hebrew language studies,[3] a still unsurpassed biography of Reuchlin, and an edition of Reuchlin's correspondence.[4] As Guido Kisch has convincingly argued, this scholarly tradition "has been molded by a sentimental optimism among nineteenth-century Jews in Germany, who looked back on the Enlightenment as the torch bearer of emancipation. On this basis, Reuchlin could be perceived as a bold forerunner of the Enlightenment, far ahead of his own time."[5] To this day, whenever the

2. Heinrich Hirsch Graetz, *Geschichte der Juden von den ältesten Zeiten bis auf die Gegenwart,* 11 vols. (Leipzig, 1853-1876). I am using vol. 9, *Geschichte der Juden von der Verbannung der Juden aus Spanien und Portugal (1494) bis zur dauernden Ansiedelung der Marranen in Holland (1618),* 4th rev. ed. (Leipzig: Oskar Leiner, 1907).

3. Ludwig Geiger, *Das Studium der Hebräischen Sprache in Deutschland vom Ende des XV. bis zur Mitte des XVI. Jahrhunderts* (Breslau: Schletter'sche Buchhandlung, 1870), pp. 23-40.

4. See L. Geiger, *Johann Reuchlin: Sein Leben und seine Werke* (Leipzig: Duncker & Humblot, 1871; repr. Nieuwkoop: De Graaf, 1964); and *Johann Reuchlins Briefwechsel,* ed. L. Geiger, Bibliothek des Litterarischen Vereins in Stuttgart 126 (Tübingen: L. Fr. Fuess, 1875; repr. Hildesheim: Georg Olms Verlagsbuchhandlung, 1962); hereafter cited as Geiger, *BW,* with arabic numbering of the letters replacing Geiger's roman numerals. For a bibliography of Reuchlin's writings, see Benzing, *Bibliographie* (n. 1 above), and Hansmartin Decker-Hauff, "Bausteine zur Reuchlin-Biographie," in *Johannes Reuchlin 1455-1522: Festgabe seiner Vaterstadt Pforzheim zur 500. Wiederkehr seines Geburtstages,* ed. M. Krebs (Pforzheim: Selbstverlag Stadt Pforzheim, n.d. [1955]), pp. 83-107. See especially the two-part review article by Stefan Rhein, "Reuchliniana I: Neue Bausteine zur Biographie Johannes Reuchlins," *Wolfenbütteler Renaissance-Mitteilungen* 12 (1988): 84-94; "Reuchliniana II: Forschungen zum Werk Johannes Reuchlins," *Wolfenbütteler Renaissance Mitteilungen* 13 (1989): 23-44. Rhein has provided a comprehensive, critical account of recent international Reuchlin scholarship. For a survey of the basic biographical data in English, see Heinz Scheible, "Johann Reuchlin," in *Contemporaries of Erasmus,* ed. P. G. Bietenholz, vol. 3 (Toronto: University of Toronto Press, 1987), pp. 145-50.

5. ". . . unter dem Eindruck einer durch Aufklärung und Emanzipation unter den Juden im Deutschland des 19. Jahrhunderts hervorgerufenen sentimental-optimistischen Stimmung. Sie bildete die Veranlassung dazu, daß man in Reuchlin einen kühnen, seiner Zeit weit vorauseilenden Vorläufer der Aufklärung erblicken konnte." Guido Kisch, *Zasius und Reuchlin: Eine rechtsgeschichtlich-vergleichende Studie zum Toleranzproblem im 16. Jahrhundert,* Pforzheimer Reuchlinschriften 1 (Constance-Stuttgart: Jan Thorbecke Verlag, 1961), p. 30. See Adolf Kober's romantic description of Reuchlin's role in the liberation of the Jews: ". . . mit Reuchlin's Auftreten fiel der erste matte Lichtstrahl in das mittelalterliche Dunkel, in dem die deutsche Judenheit schmachtete. Denn er war der erste, der es in Deutschland auszusprechen wagte, 'die Juden seien Glieder und Mitbürger des deutschen Reiches', ja noch mehr, 'die Juden

name Reuchlin is mentioned, one hears the echo of Graetz's lofty assessment of Reuchlin's courageous brief of 6 October 1510: "Reuchlin's defense of the Jews was the first stuttering statement on the way to that liberating declaration of full equality; it took over three hundred years for this development to be fully articulated and to gain the force of law."[6] This view was favored by the widely held Burckhardtian interpretation of the Renaissance as the rediscovery of the individual and human dignity.[7]

In recent Renaissance research, above all in the work of Paul Oskar Kristeller, such "rebirth" no longer defines this era. "Renaissance" has come to designate merely a period of time spanning the centuries 1300-1600. And we now define "Renaissance humanism" not as a movement to fashion a new image of humanity, but rather to promote the *studia humanitatis,* reaching all the way from rhetoric to moral philosophy. An oft-quoted, striking series of negations is indicative of our tendency today to favor a de-ideologizing interpretation. Paul Oskar Kristeller characterized Renaissance humanism as "neither Christian or pagan, Catholic or Protestant, scientific or anti-scientific, civic or despotic, Platonist or Aristotelian, Stoic or Epicurean, optimistic or pessimistic, active or contemplative. . . ."[8] At the end of this essay we will have to add the characterization of Renaissance humanism as neither pro-Jewish nor antisemitic.

Yet, the "Forerunner" and "Precursor" vision of the past, generally cast aside today, contains an essential element of truth. True enough, if we regard the Enlightenment as a child of the Renaissance, we risk distorting the fundamental characteristics of each era. However, we are not excused from the historical task of explaining how Reuchlin became a lightning rod for the predominant cultural forces of his time. For Reuchlin was both celebrated as a conscientious innovator and attacked as a dangerous deviator; obviously he was ahead of his time.

---

sind unsere Nebenmenschen, wir müssen sie lieben'." A. Kober, "Urkundliche Beiträge zum Reuchlinschen Streit: Ein Gedenkblatt zum 30. Juni 1922," *Monatsschrift für Geschichte und Wissenschaft des Judentums* 67, Neue Reihe 31 (1923): 110-22; 110; quoted by Kisch, *Zasius und Reuchlin,* p. 78, n. 19.

6. "Es war gewissermaßen der erste stotternd ausgesprochene Laut zu jenem befreienden Worte vollständiger Gleichstellung, welches mehr als drei Jahrhunderte brauchte, um voll ausgesprochen und anerkannt zu werden." Graetz, *Geschichte der Juden,* vol. 9 (n. 2 above), p. 98.

7. Jacob Burckhardt, *Die Cultur der Renaissance in Italien: Ein Versuch,* 1st ed. (Basel: Schweighauser'sche Verlagsbuchhandlung, 1860).

8. Paul Oskar Kristeller, "Studies on Renaissance Humanism during the Last Twenty Years," *Studies in the Renaissance* 9 (1962): 7-23; 22.

3. *Not Luther, but Reuchlin*

Since World War II and the horrors which we have come to associate with the Holocaust, the reconstruction of the complete history of Jewish rights has acquired a further dimension unknown to Reuchlin. Whereas the "Forerunner" interpretation positioned Reuchlin and Luther shoulder to shoulder, since the 1940s they have been placed in opposite camps. At times, a continuous "German" tradition, reaching from Luther to Hitler, was suggested. And, indeed, during the Nuremberg Trials, Luther's name was invoked in order to justify and legitimate antisemitism. In fact, Reformation scholarship had been criticized by the Nazis for omitting from the record Luther's demonization of the Jews. While some Luther scholars hastened to correct this oversight, after the war the general tendency was to de-emphasize Luther's antisemitism.[9] Luther's previously privileged passages were now marginalized, while the spotlight turned brightly to Reuchlin, the authentic German defender and advocate of the Jews. Accordingly, in this third and last phase of Reuchlin research, the fundamental thrust of the first phase has been completely reversed. Reuchlin the "opposite number" to Martin Luther has replaced Reuchlin the "significant other" of Martin Luther. But in so doing, Reuchlin is again read out of context. To do justice to Reuchlin, we have to restore him to his historical setting.

II. *Ad Fontes:* The Relevant Sources

1. Homo trilinguis: *Reuchlin against Dominant Humanism*

It was only late in his life — when he was already fifty-five and for his time an old man — that Reuchlin became embroiled in a dispute with the converted Jew, Johannes Pfefferkorn, and the Dominicans of Cologne,

---

9. For a comprehensive account see Johannes Brosseder, *Luthers Stellung zu den Juden im Spiegel seiner Interpreten: Interpretation und Rezeption von Luthers Schriften und Äusserungen zum Judentum im 19. und 20. Jahrhundert vor allem im deutschsprachigen Raum,* Beiträge zur ökumenischen Theologie 8 (Munich: Max Hueber Verlag, 1972); Brosseder, "Luther und der Leidensweg der Juden," in *Die Juden und Martin Luther — Martin Luther und die Juden: Geschichte, Wirkungsgeschichte, Herausforderung,* ed. H. Kremers, 2nd ed. (Neukirchen-Vluyn: Neukirchener Verlag, 1987), pp. 109-35. This latter work shows precisely how difficult it is to combine a genuine admission of guilt with valid historical research. See further my reconstruction in "The Nationalist Conscription of Martin Luther" (chap. 6 above).

an episode which has subsequently preoccupied Reuchlin scholarship. After the Dominicans sided with Pfefferkorn and opened litigation against Reuchlin, a virulent reaction united those German humanists whom Reuchlin came to designate as his own party and praised as the "poetae et historici."[10] This humanist solidarity has blinded scholarship to Reuchlin's lonely course, his singular journey in pursuit of the Hebrew language. Admittedly, Reuchlin fully shared the enthusiasm of his fellow humanists for the rediscovery of the ancient languages. He even used the phrase "second Pentecost" to celebrate the rebirth of the true humanism (Menschlichkeit) to be disseminated by a newly united republic of scholars. But for Reuchlin, this Pentecost designated more "tongues" than Latin and Greek.[11]

Both Reuchlin's prominent predecessor, Rudolf Agricola (†1485), and his eminent successor, Desiderius Erasmus (†1536), insisted on Latin and Greek as the sole requirements for the revival of learning.[12] For Reuchlin, these two languages were acutely inadequate; to learn Hebrew is to master the language of God's own self-revelation.[13] Reuchlin's bitter disappointment that his Hebrew grammar found no market in the world of humanist scholarship documents his isolation. But this did not shake his basic conviction: ". . . if I live, I will continue to devote my life with God's help to the study of Hebrew. If I die, then at least I have made an irreversible beginning."[14]

Reuchlin's assumption of an original Hebrew revelation, preceding all sources of classical culture, not only isolated him from most leading humanists of his time, but also led him to question some of their most fundamental assumptions. His contemporaries were convinced that precisely in the classical sources — that is, in Greek and Latin, and certainly not in Hebrew — the essential models for true religion and effective political action were to be found. Hence, before Reuchlin came into conflict with the Dominican, scholastic establishment, he was by no means the typical humanist, but rather a dissenter who might cause an

10. 11 March 1512, in Geiger, *BW*, nr. 144, p. 167.

11. Reuchlin portrays the Elector Frederick the Wise as the new founder of "humanism in the German nation." 7 May 1518; Geiger, *BW*, nr. 256, p. 295.

12. 9 November 1483; Geiger, *BW*, nr. 5, p. 7. For Erasmus see the letter to Wolfgang Capito of 26 February 1517 (1516?), in *Opus Epistolarum Des. Erasmi Roterodami*, ed. P. S. Allen (Oxford: Clarendon Press, 1906-1958), vol. 2, p. 491, ll. 137f.

13. 19 March 1510; Geiger, *BW*, nr. 115, p. 123.

14. ". . . soll ich leben, so muss die hebraysch sprach herfür mit gots hillff; stirb ich dann, so han ich doch ainen anfang gemacht, der nit lychtlich würdt zergon." 31 August 1512; Geiger, *BW*, nr. 152, p. 180.

anti-humanistic relapse, a slide back into Hebrew barbarism. Once Pfefferkorn appeared on the scene and the Dominicans opened their attack, a common humanist front was forged, which tends to obscure this basic difference. Only Reuchlin's predecessor, Konrad Pellikan, and a subsequent generation of scholars — Capito, Oecolampadius, Luther, Zwingli, and Melanchthon — had an equally high regard for Hebrew and defined the "true humanist" as *homo trilinguis* — fully conversant with Greek, Latin, and Hebrew.

Henceforth two competing types of humanism evolved: one supporting a curriculum only of Greek and Latin, a second advocating three languages — Latin, Greek, and Hebrew — a bifurcation that can be traced back to Reuchlin himself. If we include the vernacular, we can even speak of a four-language focus as opposed to the more limited classical vision of the "Erasmians." This chasm between the two kinds of humanism more convincingly explains the decision among humanists for or against the Reformation than the hypothesis of a generation gap. For the evidence does not bear out that the older generation turned to Erasmus, while the younger gathered around Luther. The general trend is rather that those advocating a two-pronged humanism of Latin and Greek remained faithful to the old church, while those advancing a three- or even four-pronged humanism embraced the Reformation.

2. The Miraculous Power of Hebrew

The basis for Reuchlin's respect toward the Jews is to be found in his early work *The Miracle-Working Word* (1494) and his *Hebrew Grammar* (1506).[15] Here we discover the answer to the question why Reuchlin immersed himself so intensely in the Hebrew language. His correspondence reveals his early turn to the study of Greek and Latin[16] and his reputation manifest in both his Greek (1477) and Latin dictionary (1478), the "Mikropaedia" — a work until recently considered to be lost.[17]

15. For *De Verbo mirifico* (1494), see n. 34 below; for *De Rudimentis hebraicis* (1506), see n. 32 below.

16. See Hermann Dibbelt, "Reuchlins griechische Studien: Ein Beitrag zur Geschichte der deutschen Geistesbildung," *Das Gymnasium* 49 (1938): 16-26; and now especially Stefan Rhein, "Reuchliniana I" (n. 4 above), pp. 27-29.

17. Frank Hieronymus may well have discovered parts of Reuchlin's earlier "Mikropaedia." He has found entries and corrections made by Reuchlin covering almost a third of the alphabet in a copy of Johannes Crastonus's Greek-Latin dictionary belonging to Johannes Amerbach. These entries must predate the period of his move in 1477 from Basel to Paris. See F. Hieronymus, "Einbandschnipsel," in *Totum me libris dedo: Festschrift zum 80. Geburtstag von Adolf Seebass*, ed. A. Moirandat,

Even before the publication of his first cabalistic work in 1494, and long before the publication of his *Hebrew Grammar* in 1506, Reuchlin was already widely recognized as the leading German humanist. Some fifteen years before his *Hebrew Grammar,* on June 5, 1491, Reuchlin received the highest scholarly accolade imaginable, a letter of acknowledgment from Marsilio Ficino,[18] indicative of his high public recognition — before and until the Pfefferkorn affair. Herein the doyen of the Platonic Academy in Florence had declared his deepest respect: "now in Reuchlin true *Academia* has found a home in Germany."[19]

Already on his first Italian journey, in 1482, Reuchlin had been received by Lorenzo de'Medici (†1492) in Florence and allowed to marvel at the latter's famous library. During his second pilgrimage to Italy, in 1490, he made the acquaintance of Count Pico della Mirandola (†1494), who may well have sown the seed of Reuchlin's lifelong zeal for collecting cabalistic manuscripts.[20] While the dispute with Pfefferkorn has focused scholarly attention on the theme "Reuchlin and the Jews," it is important to realize that already twenty years before the Pfefferkorn conflict, Reuchlin had attained international acknowledgment as an eminent Latin and Greek scholar.

Unlike Erasmus, who liked to point to the year 1501 as the time of his move from philology to theology, for Reuchlin it would be inconceivable to regard this as a transition: a reliable exegete *is* the best possible theologian. In the summer of 1488, Reuchlin wrote to the Dominican cloister in Basel, seeking to borrow its precious New Testament manuscript, the *Codex Basiliensis.*[21] In his gracious request, Reuchlin affirms the fundamental right to establish the original biblical text, convinced

---

H. Spilker, and V. Tammann (Basel: Haus der Bücher, 1979), pp. 65-107; 76-90. I am indebted to Dr. Stefan Rhein for this reference.

18. To Ludwig Vergenhans, brother of the famous Chancellor of Tübingen University, Johannes Vergenhans (Naukler), and like him a jurist. See the dissertation by Erich Joachim, "Johannes Nauclerus und seine Chronik: Ein Beitrag zur Kenntniss der Historiographie der Humanistenzeit" (Göttingen, 1874), p. 3. To this work Dr. Gerhard Hammer graciously drew my attention. On Johannes Vergenhans, cf. H. A. Oberman, *Werden und Wertung der Reformation: Vom Wegestreit zum Glaubenskampf,* 3rd ed. (1977; Tübingen: J. C. B. Mohr — Paul Siebeck, 1989), pp. 17-18.

19. See Geiger, *BW,* nr. 28, p. 29. The historicity of Ficino's Platonic Academy has been questioned by James Hankins in "The Myth of the Platonic Academy of Florence," *Renaissance Quarterly* 44 (1991): 429-75 (on letter nr. 28, see p. 451, n. 75).

20. See Karl Christ, *Die Bibliothek Reuchlins in Pforzheim,* Zentralblatt für Bibliothekwesen, Beiheft 52 (Leipzig: Otto Harrassowitz, 1924), p. 4.

21. Geiger, *BW,* nr. 15, pp. 15-20 (undated; but the preceding letter is dated 24 July 1488).

that one must first confirm the authentic text of Holy Scripture as God wanted it to be recorded.[22] For it is more stirring and profitable to read the apostles in their own Greek tongue than to stumble through the distorted Vulgate translation — even if it is the received text of the church and her doctrine. Indeed, Reuchlin sharpens his point with a noteworthy play on words, replacing *translatio* with *transfuga* (a loss of substance); he likens the translation of a text to good wine, which loses its taste and quality whenever it is poured into a new vessel.[23]

Reuchlin could foresee the outcome of his insistence on the original biblical text. Those committed to the authority and prestige of the Vulgate would mobilize against him. Therefore, he had to emphasize how his innovation drew heavily upon the work of Jerome, the sainted translator of Scripture into the Latin Vulgate. Anticipating Erasmus of Rotterdam by thirty years, Reuchlin already introduced the term *Instrumentum Novum* as his description of the original New Testament.

This quest for the earliest biblical manuscript tradition appears in keeping with the *ad fontes* ideal of Renaissance humanism. But Reuchlin, in fact, followed a course distinctly his own. When he cites from the Epistle to the Galatians, "a man is justified not by works of the law, but by faith in Jesus Christ" (Gal. 2:16), Reuchlin relates "faith" to the Scriptures which Christ's first disciples recorded, written under the guidance of the Holy Spirit ("Christi sectatores primarii spiritu sancto instigati conscripsere"). The irrelevant, outdated "law" is equated with the study of history, poetry, rhetoric, philosophy, and Sibylline prophetic writings.[24] Reuchlin interprets the distinction between law and gospel in his own peculiar and indeed shocking way; the humanist's pride, the *studia humanitatis,* falls entirely under the law, superseded by the gospel. In this Reuchlin seems to be typical of the pious, educated elite north of the Alps and appears to be far more medieval than contemporary Italian humanism.

22. "Ego, mi Jacobe, mea plurimum semper interesse putavi sacras habere litteras eo charactere quo primum divinitus compositae censentur." Geiger, *BW,* nr. 15, p. 16. In his *Augenspiegel,* Reuchlin repeatedly refers to the "leakage" that occurred when the Hebrew Bible was translated into the Greek of the Septuagint and again into the Latin of the Vulgate. *Doctor Johannsen Reuchlins . . . Augenspiegel* (Tübingen: Thomas Anshelm, 1511); repr. in *Quellen zur Geschichte des Humanismus und der Reformation in Faksimile-Ausgaben,* vol. 5 (Munich: Johann Froben Verlag, n.d. [1961]); Benzing, *Bibliographie,* p. 26, nr. 93.

23. ". . . e dolio saepius derivata vina majestate minuuntur." Geiger, *BW,* nr. 15, p. 16.

24. "Igitur nobis statui ad novae tandem Legis salutares tanquam ad asylum aliquod fore confugiendum et posthabitis omnis generis scriptoribus historicis, poeticis, oratoriis, philosophicis atque propheticis. . . ." Geiger, *BW,* nr. 15, p. 16.

Indeed, on first sight Reuchlin's scholarly program does not seem to shatter the mold of late-medieval piety. Jakob Sprenger (†1495), co-author of the *Malleus maleficarum (The Witches' Hammer)*, the epitome of the so-called Dark Ages, filled Reuchlin's request for the precious Basel New Testament *Codex* without any reservations at all. In his cover letter, Sprenger underscores their collegiality; the Basel Dominicans would rather put their manuscript at risk than jeopardize their ties of friendship.[25] The *Codex* survived; the friendship did not.

In reality, Reuchlin did not oppose the *ad fontes* thrust of humanism. On the contrary, he developed and broadened this program. Though aware that he himself might not reap the full harvest of humanism, his insistence on Hebrew as the first and fundamental language was not regressive but forward looking; it proved to be a harbinger of the future.

III. The Jew: Elected but Rejected

1. *The Three Rings: Philosopher, Jew, and Christian*

The second and most productive phase of Reuchlin's scholarly life is characterized by his intensive dedication to Hebrew sources. This period extends from his second Italian journey (1490) to the years of depression, 1508 and 1509, that is, from his decisive meeting with Pico to a time of chronic sickness and paralyzing despondency. This somber period was prompted by a growing awareness that his beloved Hebrew studies were meeting with silence or scorn.

In 1492, Reuchlin had made the acquaintance of Jakob ben Jehiel Loans, the private physician of Emperor Frederick III at the royal court in Linz. Loans tutored Reuchlin in the fundamentals of the Hebrew language. There is some evidence pointing to an even earlier date for Reuchlin's discovery of Hebrew. Through his contacts with Wessel Gansfort (†1489), the first Christian Hebraist north of the Alps, Reuchlin might already a decade earlier have come to realize the importance of Hebrew for Christendom. Philipp Melanchthon (†1560) must have had this encounter in mind when he later (1552) refers to Wessel as Reuchlin's first teacher of Hebrew.[26] For his part, Rudolf Agricola, Gansfort's close

25. Summarized in Geiger, *BW,* nr. 16, pp. 20ff.; full text in K. Christ, *Die Bibliothek Reuchlins* (n. 20 above), p. 29, n. 3.
26. *Corpus Reformatorum* 11, col. 1002. See further my two articles "Wessel

friend and student, remembered how Gansfort's Hebrew lessons more frightened than enlightened Reuchlin.[27] In any case, by 1483 Reuchlin's passion for Hebrew was fully evident, eliciting a courteous but cool response from Agricola.[28]

The Hebrew instruction of Jakob Loans must have reached far beyond the doldrums of grammar exercises. Not without risk to his own name, Reuchlin publicly expressed his warm appreciation for this learned Jew in brief but poignant statements in Hebrew and Latin (1500), a remarkable testimonial to his teacher:[29] "I long," he wrote with ardor, "to set eyes on the beloved contours of your countenance," and "to hear you again expound your most pure doctrine" *(doctrinam tuam purissimam)*. This letter far transcends mere gratitude for lessons well taught. Reuchlin goes on to recount how he himself had since made great strides *(in doctrina mea)* with far-reaching implications.[30]

Gansfort: *Magister contradictionis,*" in *Wessel Gansfort (1419-1489) and Northern Humanism,* ed. F. Akkerman, G. C. Huisman, and A. J. Vanderjagt (Leiden: E. J. Brill, 1993), pp. 97-121; and "Discovery of Hebrew and Discrimination against the Jews: The *Veritas Hebraica* as Double-Edged Sword in Renaissance and Reformation," in *Germania Illustrata: Essays on Early Modern Germany Presented to Gerald Strauss,* ed. A. Fix and S. Karant-Nunn, Sixteenth Century Essays and Studies 18 (Kirksville, Mo.: Sixteenth Century Journal Publishers, 1992), pp. 19-34.

27. "Basilius quoque noster quem deterruisse te scribis, acriter me incitavit. . . ." Rudolf Agricola to Reuchlin, Heidelberg, 9 November 1493; Geiger, *BW,* nr. 5, p. 8. "Basilius" is the honorific name used for Wessel Gansfort. Geiger appears to have confused Wessel with Johannes von Wesel, whom he refers to throughout as "Johann Wesel."

I am inclined to explain the puzzling suggestion that Wessel Gansfort would have deterred *(deterruisse)* Reuchlin from studying Hebrew in terms of the shocking findings of Wessel in his search for the *veritas Hebraica.* Especially noteworthy is Wessel's assertion on the basis of the Hebrew text, that we should address God not only as *pater noster,* but also with equal justification as *mater noster.* In contrast to Latin, the Hebrew language can differentiate between feminine and masculine love. Accordingly, the Hebrew original shows that the Holy Trinity should be interpreted as God the Father *and* as God the Mother, Christ as Brother *and* Sister, the Holy Ghost as Male Friend *and* Female Friend, as *amicus* and *amica.* Wessel Gansfort, *Opera* (Groningen, 1614; repr. Nieuwkoop: De Graaf Publishers, 1966), p. 721. Cf. my "Discovery of Hebrew" (n. 26 above), pp. 28-29.

28. Geiger, *BW,* nr. 5, p. 7.

29. First printed in *Clarorum Virorum Epistolae latinae, graecae & hebraicae . . .* (Tübingen: Thomas Anshelm, 1514), fol. i3r; repr. in the Zurich edition (Froschauer, 1558), fol. 68v-69r, and in *Illustrium Virorum Epistolae, hebraicae, graecae et latinae . . .* (Hagenau: Thomas Anshelm, 1519), fol. l4v-mlr; Benzing, *Bibliographie* (n. 1 above), p. 42, nr. 136-38; *Ulrichi Hutteni Operum Supplementum: Epistolae Obscurorum Virorum,* ed. E. Böcking, 2 parts (Leipzig: Teubner, 1964-69; repr. Osnabrück: Otto Zeller, 1966), part II, pp. 81-82 and 108; hereafter cited as Böcking.

30. 1 November 1500; Geiger, *BW,* nr. 72, p. 67.

It may seem surprising that Reuchlin announces a true all-encompassing breakthrough *(perveni ad consecutionem magnam)* six years *after* the publication of *The Miracle-Working Word* (1494). But Charles Zika's convincing reinterpretation of the basic structure and purpose of *The Miracle-Working Word* makes clear that though here in 1494 the Hebrew language and the Cabala are already presented as carriers of divine power, Reuchlin's main interest concerns something else, namely the defense of the legitimacy of Christian magic. This beneficial magic, he insists, should not be confused with pernicious forms of medieval superstition.[31]

In *The Miracle-Working Word,* Reuchlin implies but does not yet pursue the mysteries of the Hebrew language. The secret knowledge of Jewish wisdom remains largely untapped, except for the name "IHSUH," Jesus, the key which unlocks the truth hidden in the Hebrew text. Twenty-three years later, in his *De Arte cabalistica* (1517), Reuchlin introduced a detailed guide, fully revealing the treasures concealed in the Cabala. His *Hebrew Grammar* (1506) was to provide the linguistic tools necessary for the penetration of these cabalistic mysteries.[32]

For our own purposes it is not "white magic" or the Cabala but Reuchlin's view of the Jews which marks the importance of *The Miracle-Working Word.* In this work, he presents a dispute between the Greek philosopher Sidon, the Jew Baruch, and the Christian Capnion, the Greek version of the name Reuchlin. This fictional debate has led to lofty praise of Reuchlin as the torchbearer of tolerance to be compared with both Giovanni Boccaccio's (†1375) and Gotthold Lessing's (†1781) Ring Parable, though it must be said that it would be more relevant to point to Nicholas of Cusa's (†1464) account of religious debate among a Jew, a Muslim, and a Christian.[33]

By focusing enthusiastically on Reuchlin's "ecumenical" spirit, scholarship has overlooked critical elements in his account. The dispute in Pforzheim culminates symbolically in Pythagorean initiation rites, but de facto in the consummation of the two central Christian sacraments

31. Charles Zika, "Reuchlin's *De Verbo Mirifico* and the Magic Debate of the Late Fifteenth Century," *Journal of the Warburg and Courtauld Institutes* 39 (1976): 104-38.

32. *De Rudimentis hebraicis . . .* (Pforzheim: Thomas Anshelm, 1506; repr. Hildesheim: Georg Olms Verlag, 1974); Benzing, *Bibliographie,* p. 24, nr. 90; *De Arte cabalistica . . .* (Hagenau: Thomas Anshelm, 1517; repr. Stuttgart: Frommann Verlag, 1964); Benzing, *Bibliographie,* p. 28, nr. 99; Böcking (n. 29 above), part II, p. 95. See Charles Zika, "Reuchlin and Erasmus: Humanism and Occult Philosophy," *Journal of Religious History* 9 (1977): 223-46; 238-41.

33. See Fritz Nagel, "Johannes Reuchlin und Nicolaus Cusanus," *Pforzheimer Geschichtsblätter,* Reihe IV (1976): 133-57.

— penance and baptism. After Capnion has established the superiority of the Christian faith, he demands conversion and achieves the repentance of Sidon and Baruch; the latter renounces the Talmud; the former repudiates Epicurus and Lucretius. Both obey his command: "Let yourselves be washed, be cleansed" *(Lavamini: mundi estote)*.[34] Hence a ritual clearly representing Christian baptism seals Capnion's triumph.

Before this climactic conversion scene, Reuchlin assails the unbaptized Baruch, unleashing the full fury of medieval, anti-Jewish ideology: "The saving power of the Word has forsaken you and chosen us. As all can see, God stands with us and on our side."[35] Why has God rejected the Jew and embraced the Christian? "Because you Jews have perverted and obscured the secrets of salvation; in vain therefore you perpetually mumble your prayers, in vain you cry out to God; you do not honor God as he commands. You flatter yourselves with forms of worship you yourselves invented; you persecute us with eternal hatred [*livore immortali oditis*], because we are the true servants of God. But from the beginning of time God has condemned hatred and what he wants to find in the human soul is the love of peace."[36] This amazing and revealing inversion of the biblical commandment of love was and will continue to characterize Reuchlin's view of the Jews, a portrayal which does not fit the Enlightenment idealization of Reuchlin's life and thought.

2. The Place of the Jews: The "Prison of the Devil"

What is mere background in Reuchlin's *The Miracle-Working Word* with its story of the conversion of the Jew becomes the principal theme of the *Tütsch Missive* (1505). In this "Open Letter," written in German, Reuchlin explains the exile *(ellend)* of the Jews as an affliction sent by God, as a punishment for their collective guilt: they repudiate God, they are God-killers. Such severe blindness besets the Jews that only a severe hand can thrust them toward the path to repentance. "True penance means both repentance and suffering" ("weg der buß, das ist rüw und leid"); harsh treatment of the Jews and true conversion to the Christian church are

---

34. *De Verbo mirifico* (Basel: Johannes Amerbach, 1494; repr. Stuttgart: Günther Holzboog, 1964), liber I, fol. b5v (repr. p. 30; cf. p. 43); Benzing, *Bibliographie*, p. 5, nr. 23. See my *The Roots of Anti-Semitism in the Age of Renaissance and Reformation* (Philadelphia: Fortress Press, 1983), pp. 26-27; p. 53, n. 24.

35. "Salubris ista potestas verborum, quae vos deseruit, nos elegit; nos comitatur, nobis ad nutum obedire cernitur." *De Verbo mirifico*, liber I, fol. b5r (repr. p. 29).

36. ". . . quod imprimis respuit divinitas, quae pacifica mentibus humanis insidere cupit." *De Verbo mirifico*, liber I, fol. b5v (repr. p. 30).

necessary for their eternal salvation.[37] Reuchlin ends the letter by invoking the traditional Good Friday prayer for the *perfidi Iudaei:* "I pray to God that he may enlighten them and lead them to genuine faith, so that they might be released from the prison of the devil" ("gefencknüs des düfels").[38]

While fifteen years later Luther would assail the Babylonian Captivity of the Church, Reuchlin is concerned with the Babylonian Captivity of the Jews. Whereas the biblical Jews were punished with an exile of seventy years, the "modern" Jews remain in the devil's prison "as long as they are Jews" ("so lang sie iuden sind").[39]

3. Contra Judaeos

In a hitherto overlooked treatise these findings are confirmed: for Reuchlin the Jews stand collectively under the wrath of God. In 1502, accompanied by his wife and servants *(cum uxore ac familia)*, Reuchlin fled from the plague in Stuttgart to the safety of a cloister in nearby Denkendorf.[40] In

37. *Doctor iohanns Reuchlins tütsch missive: warumb die Juden so lang im ellend sind* (Pforzheim: Thomas Anshelm, 1505), fol. a3v; Benzing, *Bibliographie,* p. 25, nr. 92; quoted by G. Kisch, *Zasius und Reuchlin* (n. 5 above), p. 19. See the microfiche collection: *Flugschriften des frühen 16. Jahrhunderts,* ed. H.-J. Köhler, H. Hebenstreit-Wilfert, and C. Weismann (Zug: Inter Documentation Company, 1978-87), series 1980, fiche 395, nr. 1075. Excerpts in Böcking, part I (n. 29 above), pp. 177-79.

38. Final page of the *Tütsch Missive,* fol. a5v; repr. by G. Kisch, *Zasius und Reuchlin,* p. 18; Böcking, part I, p. 179, ll. 20-21. Kisch suggests the "Unvereinbarkeit dieser mit seinen späteren Schriften" and points to the fact that Reuchlin had to defend himself in 1513 on account of this "Unvereinbarkeit" (p. 21 and p. 73, n. 11). However, Reuchlin managed to do this effortlessly in the *Defensio contra calumniatores suos Colonienses . . .* (Tübingen: Thomas Anshelm, 1513); Benzing, *Bibliographie,* p. 27, nr. 96; Böcking, part II, pp. 80-81. See Hermann von der Hardt, *Historia literaria Reformationis in honorem jubilaei anno 1717* (Frankfurt-Leipzig, 1717), part II, pp. 53-93; cf. in microfiche (n. 37 above), series 1981, fiche 744, nr. 1903. It was Pfefferkorn who tried to drive a wedge between the Reuchlin of the "Missive" and the "later" Reuchlin. Cf. Hans-Martin Kirn, *Das Bild vom Juden im Deutschland des frühen 16. Jahrhunderts, dargestellt an den Schriften Johannes Pfefferkorns,* Texts and Studies in Medieval and Early Modern Judaism 3 (Tübingen: J. C. B. Mohr — Paul Siebeck, 1989), p. 184.

39. *Tütsch Missive,* fol. a3r; Böcking, part I, p. 177, ll. 46.

40. *Liber Congestorum de arte praedicandi,* September 1502 (Pforzheim: Thomas Anshelm, 1504), fol. a2r; Benzing, *Bibliographie,* p. 23, nr. 86. Cf. Geiger, *Johann Reuchlin* (n. 4 above), p. 28. Whereas we find some basic data for Reuchlin's second wife, Anna Decker (born c. 1485 in Cannstatt or Stuttgart), we do not know more about his first and probably older wife than that her surname was Müller. See Decker-Hauff, "Bausteine zur Reuchlin-Biographie" (n. 4 above), pp. 86-93; 92-93. The *divortium* mentioned in Cardinal Peraudi's letter of 27 June 1502 stipulated the condition that Reuchlin's first wife would have to give her consent (Geiger, *BW,* nr.

gratitude for its hospitality, Reuchlin presented the recent discoveries in classical rhetoric. Ciceronian rhetoric in the service of innovative preaching[41] formed the heart of his brief instruction.[42] As Reuchlin pointed out, a successful sermon style is dependent upon a vivid use of illustrations *(demonstratio)*. In one of these illustrations, the Jews appear quite surprisingly in an unexpected allusion not demanded by text or content: if you want to have an impact on the congregation, the Brethren are told, you must display Christ's crown of thorns as a striking example of crimes perpetrated by the Jews in order to stir up passion against the Jews, *contra Judaeos*.[43]

This lecture to the Denkendorf cloister is not by any means Reuchlin's only publication in this middle and most creative period. For completeness' sake, one would have to consider the *Hebrew Grammar* with its programmatic preface and the *De Arte cabalistica* (1517), announced in the *Grammar*[44] eleven years earlier. But none of these adds

---

82, p. 77). Reuchlin describes himself as remarried *(digamus)*; letter to the Theological Faculty of Cologne, 27 January 1512; Geiger, *BW*, nr. 137, p. 153; cf. the letter dated the same day to Konrad Kolin, O.P., of Ulm; Geiger, *BW*, nr. 138, p. 158. *Digamus* does not necessarily imply *divorcium*; the Cologne Dominicans would not have failed to exploit such a divorce.

41. ". . . adolescentibus tuis viva voce declamavi, ut crescerent tandem in viros evangelicos, quorum sermonibus plebs ad meliores mores converteretur." *Liber Congestorum*, fol. a2r / v; cf. Geiger, *Johann Reuchlin* (n. 3 above), pp. 158-60. On Reuchlin's host, Prior Peter Wolff (1477-1508), and on the monastery of Denkendorf, see Otto Schuster, *Kirchengeschichte von Stadt und Bezirk Esslingen* (Stuttgart: Calwer Verlag, 1946); Heinrich Werner, "Kloster Denkendorf: Ein Gang durch seine Geschichte," *Blätter für württembergische Kirchengeschichte* 54 (1954): 3-74; Kaspar Elm, "St. Pelagius in Denkendorf: Die älteste deutsche Probstei des Kapitels vom Hlg. Grab in Geschichte und Geschichtsschreibung," in *Landesgeschichte und Geistesgeschichte: Festschrift für Otto Herding zum 65. Geburtstag*, ed. K. Elm, E. Gönner, and E. Hillenbrand, Veröffentlichungen der Kommission für geschichtliche Landeskunde in Baden-Württemberg, Reihe B, 92 (Stuttgart: W. Kohlhammer Verlag, 1977), pp. 80-130. For the secularization of Denkendorf under Württemberg rule, see the comprehensive study of Dieter Stievermann, *Landesherrschaft und Klosterwesen im spätmittelalterlichen Württemberg* (Sigmaringen: Jan Thorbecke Verlag, 1989).

42. Reuchlin formulates his main theme as *benedicere*, the art of "speaking well," evoking its traditional meaning "to bless": "Finis eius scilicet predicatoris est bene dixisse." *Liber Congestorum*, fol. a3r.

43. "Demonstratione rem ipsam oculis subiicere possumus, ut si contra Iudaeos ostendamus cruentum sudarium et spineam coronam Christi, et clavos et crucem . . ." *Liber Congestorum*, fol. b6r. A second "Jewish" reference can more easily be explained in terms of the context. Preachers should stick to the writings of the Old and the New Testaments and not only avoid love poems and Virgil, but all prattle, polemic, and "Iudaicae fabulae . . ." *Liber Congestorum*, fol. a4v.

44. "Inscriptio hujus libri est: de rudimentis hebraicis, eo quod non jam doctis, sed rudibus ac erudiendis ea volumina composuerim, deinceps altiora deo annuente

anything new to the overall picture: the Jews deserve our respect, even admiration, not as human beings of flesh and blood, but as carriers of ancient secrets. "Baruch," quite likely modelled after Reuchlin's beloved Jewish teacher Jakob ben Jehiel Loans, personifies the ancient and providential calling of the Jews — to hand down the secret teachings, only to be decoded with the name "Jesus." Contemporary Jews appear collectively as condemned under the curse of God, captives to the devil, and sorely in need of the waters of baptism.

One statement from 1506 appears to contradict our findings: "I am well aware of the miserable condition of the Jews in our time, expelled not only from Spain, but also from the German Empire so that they are forced to emigrate all the way to Turkey." Yet even here the Jews emerge once again merely as the bearers of precious wisdom: ". . . secret knowledge is disappearing with them completely, jeopardizing the study of Holy Scripture."[45] Exactly to make Jewish help redundant, Reuchlin wrote his Hebrew grammar, thus enabling Christians to learn the holy language without the need for Jewish masters. Such grammar instruction is essential, he adds in conclusion, because our German Jews ("nostrates Judaei") refuse to initiate Christians in their language, be it from envy or from ignorance ("vel invidia, vel imperitia").[46]

IV. Citizens in the Empire — Aliens in the Kingdom

1. From Servitude to Emancipation: The Beginning of the Reuchlin Dispute

On July 26, 1510, Emperor Maximilian I ordered four universities and three independent scholars, including Reuchlin, to write an expert opinion on the toleration of Jewish Books (Judenbücher), a task to be completed three weeks later.[47] Here begins the third phase of Reuchlin's

---

daturus, quae ad arcanae Pythagorae disciplinam et artem Cabalisticam deserviunt, a nemine prorsus intellecta, nisi Hebraice praedocto." Geiger, BW, nr. 95, p. 93.

45. "Sane recordatus miseros nostra aetate Judaeorum casus, qui non tam ex Hispaniae, quam etiam Germaniae nostrae finibus pulsi coguntur alias sibi sedes quaerere atque ad Agarenos divertere, quo futurum est, ut tandem hebraica lingua cum sacrarum literarum magna pernicie penes nos posset desinere atque evanescere . . ." Geiger, BW, nr. 95, p. 92.

46. Geiger, BW, nr. 95, p. 100.

47. Published by Reuchlin himself in his Augenspiegel (n. 22 above), which

life. Reuchlin research has traditionally regarded this period as the most significant,[48] and appropriately insofar as his *opinio* marks an important shift toward Jewish emancipation. Yet Reuchlin's stance vis-à-vis the Jews deserves another look since it has not been noticed that Reuchlin had to wage a two-front war in his attack against Johannes Pfefferkorn and in his conflict with the Cologne Dominicans.[49]

2. The Confrontation with Pfefferkorn

The campaign of Johannes Pfefferkorn — to confiscate and burn Jewish books in order to further the Christian mission among the Jews[50] — evoked a fierce response from Reuchlin against "that baptized Jew" *(Taufjuden)*, his preferred designation for Pfefferkorn. After all, this convert had dared to make two absurd charges: he claimed Reuchlin had only a superficial knowledge of Hebrew and had been bribed by the Jews to support their cause.

This assault on his good name by a converted Jew arouses Reuchlin to exploit the traditional arsenal of slander against the Jews in general and converted Jews in particular. Reuchlin now questions the motivation of all converted Jews by calling them *vagabundi* whose "treachery" *(perfidia)* draws them back to their own vomit.[51]

However, Reuchlin's harsh judgment of contemporary Jews does

---

appeared in time for the 1511 Autumn book fair. For the background see Winfried Trusen, "Johannes Reuchlin und die Fakultäten: Voraussetzungen und Hintergründe des Prozesses gegen den 'Augenspiegel'," in *Der Humanismus und die oberen Fakultäten*, ed. G. Keil, B. Moeller, and W. Trusen, Mitteilung XIV der Kommission für Humanismusforschung der Deutschen Forschungsgemeinschaft, Acta humaniora (Weinheim: VCH Verlagsgesellschaft, 1987), pp. 115-57; 120-23.

48. See G. Kisch, *Zasius und Reuchlin* (n. 5 above), pp. 23-36.

49. This also applies to the important work by James H. Overfield, *Humanism and Scholasticism in Late Medieval Germany* (Princeton: Princeton University Press, 1984). Overfield rightly points out that the Reuchlin affair has for too long been regarded in terms of the opposition between scholasticism and humanism, suggesting instead that we regard the subject of antisemitism as being central. However, this confuses the ignitor with the explosive. For a sober assessment of the conservative Cologne reaction ("conservatism in the face of humanist pressures") see Charles G. Nauert, Jr., "Humanist Infiltration into the Academic World: Some Studies of Northern Universities," *Renaissance Quarterly* 43 (1990): 799-812; p. 810. Cf., however, Erich Meuthen, *Kölner Universitätsgeschichte*, vol. 1, *Die alte Universität* (Köln: Böhlau Verlag, 1988), pp. 176-78.

50. For a detailed description of Pfefferkorn's intentions see H.-M. Kirn, *Das Bild vom Juden* (n. 38, above), p. 66.

51. See Geiger, *BW*, nr. 156, p. 183. For the charge of "reditus ad vomitum" see H.-M. Kirn, *Das Bild vom Juden*, pp. 169-70; 65-66.

not diminish his appreciation for the historical role of the Jews as bearers of divine wisdom. His collective condemnation of the Jews does not exclude the conviction that we owe our reliable medical knowledge not to the Greeks, but to the Jews: not to Hippocrates, but to Moses![52]

3. The Confrontation with the Cologne Establishment

While Reuchlin counters Pfefferkorn with withering force, he moves cautiously against the second front which unexpectedly opened. Against the Cologne Dominicans who sided with Pfefferkorn, Reuchlin comes close to a retraction, at least initially "soft-pedaling" his own position. In his initial defense, Reuchlin portrays himself as a simple layman unqualified to interpret Scripture, as one who never intended to approve of these Jewish books; it is as unjust to burn all Jewish books (except the Old Testament) as to retain them all intact *(illaesi)*.[53] But shortly after-

---

52. Letter to Johannes Stocker, who — as Spalatin reports — at times served during Imperial Diets as the private physician of Frederick the Wise. Geiger, *BW*, nr. 156, pp. 182-83. As concerns Reuchlin's respect for Hippocrates, see Stefan Rhein, "Johannes Reuchlin als Dichter: Vorläufige Anmerkungen zu unbekannten Texten," in *Pforzheim in der frühen Neuzeit: Beiträge zur Stadtgeschichte des 16. bis 18. Jahrhunderts,* ed. H.-P. Becht, Pforzheimer Geschichtsblätter 7 (Sigmaringen: Jan Thorbecke Verlag, 1989), pp. 51-80; 55-64.

53. Letter of 27 January 1512 to Konrad Kolin with the request to pass it on to Jacob Hochstraten and Arnold van Tongern (Arnoldus de Luyde); Geiger, *BW*, nr. 138, pp. 156 and 159. On van Tongern see Heinz Finger, *Gisbert Longolius: Ein niederrheinischer Humanist (1507-1543),* Studia humaniora, Reihe minor 3 (Düsseldorf: Droste Verlag, 1990), pp. 50-53. Almost continuously, Arnold van Tongern was an influential *regens* of the Albertian Bursa Laurentiana in Cologne. Referring to Arnold's commentary on Juvenal, Finger suggests that Arnold was "dem Humanismus nicht eigentlich feindlich gesinnt" (pp. 50-51). This elastic formulation contrasts with the otherwise precise style of this solid study; this uncharacteristic unclarity is due to a formal-abstract definition of the concept of humanism, which cannot but lead to a warped portrayal of Reuchlin's Cologne opponents. It should be obvious that Reuchlin's characterization of his Cologne opponents as anti-intellectuals is a caricature; it suffices to point to Arnold's commentary on Juvenal or to the *Orationes* of Ortwin Gratius. See James V. Mehl, "Ortwin Gratius' *Orationes Quodlibeticae:* humanist apology in scholastic form," *Journal of Medieval and Renaissance Studies* 11 (1981): 57-69, and his forthcoming article on Gratius in *The Rhetorics of Lifewriting in the Later Renaissance,* ed. T. Mayer and D. Wolf (Ann Arbor: University of Michigan Press, in press). The pertinent criterion is, however, whether philological findings are allowed to be significant in religious matters. To use the terminology of Erasmus, decisive is whether the *grammaticus* may simultaneously speak as *theologicus,* or whether only the *magister noster* may speak with authority. Not their publication of classical editions, but rather their claim to exclusive authority characterizes the "Obscure Men." For Reuchlin — as for Erasmus and Hutten — the obscure men of Cologne are not even theologians, but rather "Theologists" *(theologistae,* with

ward Reuchlin dares to speak more forcefully through an intermediary, warning his Dominican critics not to proceed against him.[54] Even so, Reuchlin remains humbly deferential in his public statements, probably because of the fearsome and far-reaching influence of the Cologne inquisitors throughout Europe. It was on their recommendation that an imperial mandate was issued before the Frankfurt fair of 1512, ordering the confiscation of all copies of Reuchlin's self-defense, the *Augenspiegel.* Tragically, Reuchlin, who so successfully saved Jewish books, could not safeguard his own: in 1514, his *Augenspiegel* was publicly burned in Cologne on demand of the Dominican Hochstraten, and reportedly in Nuremberg and Mainz as well.

Modern scholarship no longer regards the Reuchlin affair as the head-on confrontation between humanism and scholasticism. This is certainly an advance. Even the widely marketed and quickly reprinted *Letters of Obscure Men (Dünkelmännerbriefe),*[55] written in Reuchlin's defense, were certainly not backed by all German humanists. More recently it has been argued that the "attack of both the Cologne Dominicans and other Reuchlin opponents, from Pfefferkorn to Hoogstraten . . . was motivated by anti-Jewish and not anti-humanist sentiment."[56] This interpretation, however, does not distinguish between the two fronts, confusing Hochstraten with Pfefferkorn and thus the cause with the catalyst. Reuchlin himself saw matters differently. As reported to him from Louvain (1514), the central issue was a sinister strategy which sought first to eliminate Reuchlin, then Erasmus, and finally all the other "poets" one after the other.[57]

---

a play on *sophistae*), who place more trust in their syllogisms than in the wisdom of the Fathers. See the *Defensio* (completed 1 March 1513), fol. b4v; H. von der Hardt, *Historia* (n. 38 above), p. 60b. Cf. W. Trusen, "Johannes Reuchlin und die Fakultäten" (n. 47 above), pp. 145-46.

54. For the first indication of Reuchlin's willingness to resist, see his warning of 11 March 1512: "Crede mihi, non sum destitutus potentissimorum auxiliis. . . . Facile rixa oritur, sed difficiles habet exitus; hoc non tantum ego, sed etiam vos cogitare debetis." Letter to Konrad Kolin; Geiger, *BW,* nr. 144, p. 166.

55. Early printing history for the *Dünkelmännerbriefe;* Part I: 1515, 3rd edition, 1516; Part II: 1517, second edition 1517 / 18.

56. Thus Johannes Helmrath in his detailed and — except for this point — convincing review-article of J. H. Overfield's basic work, *Humanism and Scholasticism* (n. 49 above). J. Helmrath, " 'Humanismus und Scholastik' und die deutschen Universitäten um 1500: Bemerkungen zu einigen Forschungsproblemen," *Zeitschrift für Historische Forschung* 15 (1988): 187-203; 200.

57. "Lovanii fertur, hoc adversariis esse constitutum, ut si me oppresserint, Erasmum Roterodamum sint aggressuri, et ita singillatim omnes se velle poetas (sic enim bonarum literarum studiosos appellant) eradicare. . . ." Letter to Jakob

Under quite different circumstances Reuchlin, Erasmus, and Luther all came into conflict with the same theological claim; the church and the church alone interprets Scripture, a church personified not by the biblical scholar Reuchlin but by the Inquisitor, Hochstraten. This learned Dominican was so influential because he could rely on a close-meshed network reaching from Cologne via Louvain and Paris to Rome, a network in place well before Erasmus and Luther raised their voices. It is therefore misleading to attribute Reuchlin's condemnation (1520) to the emergence of Luther.[58] The catalysts varied, but the cause was the same. While in Erasmus's case his Latin commentary *(Annotationes)* on the Greek New Testament (1516) provided the spark,[59] and in Luther's case his critique of indulgences proved incendiary, in Reuchlin's case his defense of the Jews provided the fuse. At stake, however, were not the Jews or antisemitism, but the authority of the *Magistri nostri,* the authoritative Doctors of Cologne.

V. Characteristics of Late-Medieval Antisemitism

Johannes Reuchlin was deeply immersed in the antisemitism of the cultured elite.[60] *The Letters of Obscure Men* themselves abundantly document the mentality of this elite; as in a revealing mirror, they ridicule the "foolish" Dominicans of Cologne for being so friendly with a Jew. As far as Reuchlin himself is concerned, the evidence from his third and last

---

Questenberg, 21 November 1514; *Beiträge zur Reformationsgeschichte: Sammlung ungedruckter Briefe des Reuchlin, Beza und Bullinger nebst einem Anhange zur Geschichte der Jesuiten,* ed. G. Friedlaender (Berlin: Ferdinand Müller, 1837), p. 47; summarized in Geiger, *BW,* nr. 198, pp. 231-32.

58. ". . . die Wittenberger Unruhen spielten schon hinein." Wanda Kampmann, "Reuchlin und die Judenfrage," *Geschichte in Wissenschaft und Unterricht* 16 (1965): 634-36; 636. We may be well advised to trust instead Pirckheimer, who suggests exactly the opposite reaction when he writes to Reuchlin that Rome will treat him more leniently because of Luther: "mitius tecum agent," letter to Reuchlin, November 1518, Pirckheimer's *Briefwechsel* (n. 1 above), vol. 3, p. 432, l. 8.

59. For the Louvain campaign against Erasmus see Erika Rummel, *Erasmus and his Catholic Critics,* vol. 1, *1515-1522,* Bibliotheca Humanistica & Reformatorica 45 (Nieuwkoop: De Graaf, 1989), pp. 15-33 and 180.

60. As Conradin Bonorand has formulated so concisely: "Die meisten Humanisten empfanden, genau wie so viele andere Zeitgenossen, gegen die Juden zweifellos Haß, Abneigung und Verachtung." "Bücher und Bibliotheken in der Beurteilung Vadians und einer St. Galler Freunde," *Zwingliana* 14 (1974-78): 89-108; 93.

writing period shows that the paradoxical tension between tolerance and hostility in his earlier phases is retained unchanged. Tolerance denotes the defense of civil rights for the Jewish minority pertaining to the protection of property and life — but not unconditionally to religious freedom. While imperial censorship must establish which Jewish books are to be burned, those books passing inspection should be retained as a resource for the conversion of the Jews. The bottom line continues to be that for Reuchlin there is no place for the Jews as Jews ("so lang sie iuden sind"), but only insofar as these "fellow citizens" are en route to the baptismal font.[61]

By now it is clear that Reuchlin's view of the Jews is more complex than earlier scholarship has led us to believe. But in order to discern his place in the history of antisemitism, we have to realize that this phenomenon has no fixed coordinates and appears in variable modes and disguises. It is more like a snake which sheds its skins only to reappear in an ever new "Gestalt," recognizable in its continuity and skillfully adjusting to the new environment provided by cultural change. The full implications of Reuchlin's increasingly articulated position vis-à-vis the Jews can only be assessed properly within the context of escalating antisemitism in the later Middle Ages.[62] This frame of reference offers the historically reliable gauge for the measurement of the extent of antisemitism. As far as I see, there are four central categories for a proper diagnosis of late-medieval and early-modern antisemitism: (1) the criminalization of the Jews; (2) the polemic against usury; (3) the suspicion of baptized Jews; and (4) the charge of falsifying Holy Scripture.

1. The Criminalization of the Jews

The myth of Jewish well poisoning emerged in the wake of the plague which had scourged Europe since 1348. This superstition was by no means confined to the common man or to the naive piety of the uneducated. The influential Swiss humanist and admirer of Reuchlin, Joachim von Watt (Vadianus) (†1551) inserted horrifying stories into his chronicles, presenting them as factual reports: Many Jews in Zurich, Schaffhausen, Winterthur, Wil, and St. Gallen "were burned as punishment for their terrible deeds — the poisoning of wells."[63]

61. See n. 39 above.
62. See "The Stubborn Jews: Timing the Escalation of Antisemitism in Late Medieval Europe" (above, pp. 122-40).
63. Joachim von Watt (Vadian), *Deutsche Historische Schriften*, ed.

Equally widespread were reports of Jews desecrating the host. This libel, punishable by burning, was given renewed credibility by the avant-garde publisher of humanist works, Hieronymus Höltzel of Nuremberg. In 1510, the year Reuchlin submitted his expert opinion concerning Jewish books, Höltzel's Nuremberg press reported a shocking account in gruesome detail under the headline "Ein wunderbarlich geschichte": thirty-eight Jews have desecrated the host and were therefore burned at the stake.[64]

Belief in Jewish ritual murder extended to all social circles in Reuchlin's day — including leading scholars such as Johannes Eck, Reuchlin's host in Ingolstadt.[65] In 1267, residents of Reuchlin's birthplace, Pforzheim, had accused the Jews of the outrageous crime of kidnapping a young girl named Margaretha, draining her blood, and discarding her body in the river. In Reuchlin's own lifetime (1507), Dominican sisters opened Margaretha's grave and, with Cardinal Bernadino Carvajal as witness, reported discovering that Margaretha's corpse had not yet decomposed — full proof of her saintly martyrdom at the hands of the Jews.[66] This "miracle" encouraged ever new accusations of ritual murder — even until 1932![67]

2. The Polemic against Usury

Recent research has shown how the sermons of the mendicant friars, in particular the Franciscans of the fourteenth and fifteenth centuries, spread

E. Götzinger, vol. 1 (St. Gallen: Zollikofer'sche Buchdruckerei, 1875), pp. 389-90 and 447; cf. C. Bonorand (n. 60 above), p. 94.

64. *Roots of Anti-Semitism* (n. 34 above), pp. 97-99, 147-49.

65. *Roots of Anti-Semitism*, pp. 36-37.

66. Siegmund Friedrich Gehres, *Pforzheim's kleine Chronik: Ein Beytrag zur Kunde deutscher Städte und Sitten* (Memmingen, 1792), pp. 19-23; cf. Geiger, *Johann Reuchlin* (n. 4 above), p. 5. Cardinal Carvajal was papal legate to the court of Emperor Maximilian from 1507 to 1508.

67. In *Handwörterbuch des deutschen Aberglaubens*, under "Ritualmord," Will-Erich Peuckert cites more than one hundred "documented" cases of Jewish ritual murder for the time *after* Simon of Trent (1475) until 1932 (Paderborn). The author ends his enumeration with the revealing, in fact, horrendous sentence: "In connection with this shocking summary one question must yet be pursued: to what end did the Jews use this blood?" The following garbled words of "scholarly caution" are all the more devastating: "Erst eine wissenschaftlich einwandfreie und quellenkritische Forschung würde es gestatten, von mehreren exakt bewiesenen Fällen auf weitere in diesem Register verzeichnete und ihre Tatsächlichkeit zu schliessen." *Handwörterbuch des deutschen Aberglaubens*, vol. 7 (Berlin: Walter de Gruyter, 1935, 1936; repr. — unrevised! — 1987), cols. 727-39; 734.

anti-Jewish propaganda to a European-wide audience.[68] Poisoned wells, desecrated sacraments, and ritual murders became living legends which grew ever deeper in the soil of popular piety. It is thus tempting to assume that these legends rose from "below" to the "top" of society. This model, however, does not do justice to the evidence. For the educated elite not only disseminated such "evidence" uncritically, but also embraced it as part of their own basic convictions; in unison the civic elite and the common man charged the Jews with extortive money-lending practices — the vicious crime of usury.[69] The leading humanists were proud to be laymen no longer living under monastic vows. But a great many of them, especially humanists north of the Alps, retained the basic conceptions of their mendicant predecessors, perpetuating their animosity toward the Jews. The expulsion of the Jews was supported by all classes of society, including the educated.

3. The Marranos: Suspicion of the Baptized Jew

Two new developments emerge at the beginning of the sixteenth century. After the expulsion of unconverted Jews from Spain (1492), those "prepared" to be baptized, the Marranos, fell increasingly under suspicion. Baptized Jews were accused of the hypocrisy of concealing their opportunistic and diabolical motives. They secretly reverted to their previous faith, returning to their own "vomit" because they had "swallowed" the Christian faith unwillingly. This ugly caricature can be found among Reuchlin's opponents and allies; Reuchlin himself subscribed to this view. Erasmus of Rotterdam offered a variant of the same malicious charge

68. Jeremy Cohen, *The Friars and the Jews: The Evolution of Medieval Anti-Judaism* (Ithaca: Cornell University Press, 1982). Cf. František Graus, "Randgruppen der städtischen Gesellschaft im Spätmittelalter," *Zeitschrift für Historische Forschung* 8 (1981): 385-437; F. Graus, *Pest-Geissler-Judenmorde: Das 14. Jahrhundert als Krisenzeit*, Veröffentlichungen des Max Planck-Instituts für Geschichte 86, 2nd rev. ed. (1987; Göttingen: Vandenhoeck & Ruprecht, 1988), pp. 155-389; cf. F. Graus, "The Church and its Critics in Time of Crisis," in *Anticlericalism in Late Medieval and Early Modern Europe,* eds. P. A. Dykema and H. A. Oberman, Studies in Medieval and Reformation Thought 51 (Leiden: E. J. Brill, 1993), pp. 65-81.

69. "Die Predigten gegen Wucher und Hehlerprivileg waren bei der Ausbildung der Judenfeindschaft von dauernderer und entscheidenderer Bedeutung." Peter Herde, "Gestaltung und Krisis des christlich-jüdischen Verhältnisses in Regensburg am Ende des Mittelalters," *Zeitschrift für bayerische Landesgeschichte* 22 (1959): 359-95; 384. This propaganda did not reflect the skillful redefinition of "usury," which allowed the emergence of Christian "banking." For the concomitant decline of Jewish money-lending see Robert Bonfil, *Jewish Life in Renaissance Italy* (Berkeley: University of California Press, 1992), pp. 97-98.

when he suggested that countless unbaptized Jews would spring forth if Pfefferkorn were to be split open.[70]

Here we encounter not just anti-Judaism, as Erasmus scholars insist, but we touch on one of the roots of antisemitism. Gavin I. Langmuir proposes an intriguing definition of "antisemitism" to be handled with caution in view of his application of psychological criteria. Yet Langmuir rightly disagrees with the position of Hannah Arendt that antisemitism replaced anti-Judaism only in the modern era.[71] The fatal shift from anti-Jewish sentiment to racial antisemitism can already clearly be discerned when, in the later Middle Ages, the cleansing waters of baptism are no longer believed to purify the sinful Jew.[72] Hence holy baptism is no longer "color blind." This view applies to Reuchlin as well.

4. The Veritas Hebraica: Vilifying the Rabbis

A fourth factor behind the escalation in antisemitism during the later Middle Ages has not yet been identified as such and deserves closer consideration. When speaking about his own place in history, Reuchlin points to his discovery of the *veritas hebraica* as his greatest service to posterity. And indeed, Reuchlin's grammar had made the self-study of Hebrew possible.[73]

Yet, Reuchlin's achievement unleashed two kinds of polemic, one defending Christian "orthodoxy," the other attacking Jewish religion. The first assault Reuchlin expected. He had anticipated the reaction of the theological establishment to his insistence on the literal meaning of the Hebrew text: "They will cry, 'What a disgusting disgrace'!" ("proh scelus exclamabunt!"). His predecessor on this deviant path had already displayed the challenge of Hebrew by confronting the basic principle of

70. *Opus Epistolarum* (n. 12 above), vol. 3, p. 127, l. 24.

71. See Hannah Arendt, *The Origins of Totalitarianism*, 1st ed. (New York: Harcourt, Brace and Company, 1951), pp. 8-10; cf. Gavin I. Langmuir, *Toward a Definition of Antisemitism* (Berkeley: University of California Press, 1990), esp. p. 314.

72. Langmuir suggests that anti-Judaism cannot be traced back to Jesus and the original Christian community: "We cannot then describe Jesus and his immediate followers as anti-Jewish or their attitude to Judaic religions as anti-Judaism. . . . In its origin, Christianity, like Pharisaism, was neither anti-Jewish nor anti-Judaic." G. I. Langmuir, *History, Religion, and Antisemitism* (Berkeley: University of California Press, 1990), p. 279. This assessment must be modified insofar as anti-Judaism can be traced to more than one early Christian community.

73. In the preface to *De Rudimentis*, Reuchlin formulates a resounding Renaissance manifesto: "Awake, oh youth. . . !" ("Expergiscimini igitur, adulescentes. . . !") Geiger, *BW*, nr. 95, p. 96.

scholastic ontology and metaphysics.[74] Wessel Gansfort, on the basis of the Hebrew text, had changed the meaning of God's self-disclosure to Moses, "Ego sum qui sum" (Exod. 3:14), from God as being to God as person, from a statement about God's being to the revelation of his reliability: instead of "I am that I am," "I shall be who I shall be." With Reuchlin continuing on the innovative Hebrew way opened by Gansfort, the new philology started to shake the established foundations.[75]

In his dedication of *De Arte cabalistica* (1517), Reuchlin is still confident about his uncontested place in history. Here he could summarize his life's mission as a lasting contribution to the European Renaissance: "Marsilius [Ficino] has given Italy the genuine Plato, Faber Stapulensis has restored the original Aristotle to the French, and I, Capnio, will complete this trinity, by presenting to the German people Pythagoras born anew."[76]

Just over one year later his proud claim had given way to the saddening awareness of conflict. In a letter to Elector Frederick the Wise of Saxony (7 May 1518), he bluntly states his complete agreement with the *Letters of Obscure Men*: ". . . the sophists have hitherto led us by the nose [*Narrenseil*] with their useless prattle, and not without great harm to the church. And we, as long as we did not know Latin, Greek, and Hebrew tongues, have not been able to arrive at a true understanding of the wise men of old."[77]

The stage was set, and the battle lines drawn between the new biblical exegesis and the traditions of the old church. This daring advance into the virgin territory of God's original revelation is the basic thrust of Reuchlin's

---

74. See n. 26 above. Reuchlin not only bypassed Gansfort in silence, but also his other predecessor, Konrad Pellikan, who had published his own Hebrew grammar three years earlier (printed in Strasbourg in 1504), and then had assisted Reuchlin in the preparation of the latter's Hebrew grammar. See *Das Chronikon des Konrad Pellikan: Zur vierten Säkularfeier der Universität Tübingen*, ed. B. Riggenbach (Basel: Bahnmaier's Verlag, 1877), pp. 19-22. Reuchlin's omission of Pellikan's name might explain Pfefferkorn's accusation that Reuchlin had claimed all the glory for himself. Reuchlin's silence as to Gansfort can perhaps be explained by the fact that toward the end of Gansfort's life, this Dutchman became entangled with the Inquisition. Gansfort's role can, if at all, be read into the vague addition to Reuchlin's expression of gratitude to Jakob ben Jehiel Loans: "alias a singulis singula expiscatus sum." Geiger, *BW*, nr. 95, p. 97.

75. See "Wessel Gansfort: Magister contradictionis," pp. 113-16 and "Discovery of Hebrew . . . ," pp. 25-30 (both in n. 26 above).

76. Geiger, *BW*, nr. 238, p. 270.

77. ". . . die sophisten [haben uns] bisher mit ihrem unnützen geschwätz nicht ohne schaden der kirche am narrenseil geführt, durch das wir zu rechter verständniss der alten weisen aus mangel der lateinischen, griechischen und hebräischen zungen nie haben mögen kommen." Geiger, *BW*, nr. 256, p. 295.

work. It is the dominant theme, ultimately transforming the "Reuchlin dispute" into the "Reuchlin case," resulting in his condemnation (1520).

But this very advance in biblical studies, the discovery of the *veritas hebraica,* had unexpected implications for the development of antisemitism. The enthusiastic recovery of the most ancient biblical language produced a growing suspicion. Apparently the Rabbis had been untrustworthy guardians of the treasures entrusted to them; they had been intentionally withholding from Christendom the holy writings and mysteries entrusted to them. Luther expressed this view in particularly harsh fashion in "The Jews and their Lies" (1543).[78] For Luther, the corrupt, obscure men are this time not the scholastics, but rather the Rabbis who have knowingly distorted the text of the Old Testament. Thus, Luther advocated a severe restriction of tolerance for the Jews. He supported both the burning of synagogues and, though not the burning, the confiscation of rabbinic books in order to eliminate the centers from which the Jewish lies were spread.[79] Luther justifiably considered himself Reuchlin's pupil by insisting on the original meaning of the Hebrew text.[80] However, Luther's antisemitic recommendations separate him from Reuchlin. Although Luther never shared Pfefferkorn's hope for Jewish mass-conversion, like Pfefferkorn at the end of his life he did propose a pogrom-like policy for the Jews and called for a silencing of the Rabbis.[81] It was this Christian discovery of the *veritas hebraica* which thus led to this vilification of the Rabbis.

VI. Reuchlin and the Jews

1. The Reuchlin Test: Four Tough Questions

Reuchlin's view of the Jews can now be examined in light of the four crucial factors we discussed above.

(a) Traditional accusations against the Jews — the poisoning of

---

78. WA 53.417-552.

79. Cf. Heiko A. Oberman, *Luther: Man Between God and the Devil* (London: Fontana Books, 1992; New Haven, Conn.: Yale University Press, 1989), pp. 292-97.

80. See Luther's letter to Reuchlin, 14 December 1518; WA Br 1.269.39; Geiger, *BW,* nr. 227, p. 311.

81. Oberman, *The Roots of Anti-Semitism* (n. 34 above), pp. 113-22; 121-22. Such a sign of the "turning tide" some in the Jewish community associated with Luther; see Haim Hillel Ben-Sasson, "Jewish-Christian Disputation in the Setting of Humanism and Reformation in the German Empire," *Harvard Theological Review* 59 (1966): 369-90.

wells, desecration of the host, and ritual murder — were rife among the educated elite of Upper Germany. Of these charges no trace appears in Reuchlin's work.[82]

(b) The dread of the Jews, propagated by the preaching mendicants, spread like wildfire. This is not echoed by Reuchlin. But widespread approval of Jewish expulsion touches on a sensitive point, which until now has not been properly acknowledged. Contrary to the views of Ludwig Geiger and Guido Kisch, Reuchlin did indeed support a policy of forced expulsion. In his *Augenspiegel* (1511), he discussed the usual charge that Jewish usury damages the common good. Reuchlin does not question this charge at all and makes it the basis for an awesome alternative; the Jews must desist from their usury or face expulsion ("essent . . . reformandi seu expellendi").[83]

In determining the grounds for expulsion, Reuchlin advocates a principle radical for its time: in each case, individual guilt should be established since Jews are legally *concives;* just as the Christians, they are subject to imperial law and to the penalties based upon it.[84] It should

82. We encounter Reuchlin's "allies" — probably the same circle around Hutten and Rubeanus that planned the *Dünkelmännerbriefe* — in the revealing pamphlet *Die geschicht unnd bekantnuss des getaufften Juden / genannt Johannes Pfefferkorn* (1514-1515), Württembergische Landesbibliothek Stuttgart, HBK 142. A single quotation from Pfefferkorn's fictional "confession" extorted under torture suffices to document its antisemitic assumptions: "Item er hat auch bekant: er habe zwey kinder gestolen / dz ein den verkaufft und selber helffen martern / unnd gestochen das sy das blut von im überkommen haben / zu gebrauchen zu irer notturfft. Das annder kindt hat rot har gehabt / das selbig hat er wider hienweg geschickt on schaden." Fol. a2v. For this "red hair" as an indication of Jewish blood and for the legend of the "red Jews" (reported to be on the move in great numbers in the Ottoman Empire in order to reestablish the Davidic Empire in Israel) see Andrew Colin Gow, *The Red Jews: Antisemitism in the Apocalyptic Age, 1200-1600* (in press).

83. *Augenspiegel* (n. 22 above), fol. 30v.

84. This principle can be interpreted as the legal rule *in dubio pro reo*, a formulation not used by Reuchlin. In his letter to Konrad Kolin, he makes this same point by quoting Christ's words to the adulteress: "Has no one condemned you? . . . Neither do I condemn you" (John 8:10-11); Geiger, *BW*, nr. 131, p. 142. Cf. Andreas Osiander's reasoning on the occasion of the Pösing blood libel in the year 1540: "Ists aber das götlich, natürlich und Keyserlich recht, das man allein die ubeltheter und nicht die unschuldigen sol tödten. . . . Ob es war und glaublich sey, dass die Juden der Christen kinder heymlich erwürgen," anonymous text (n.p., n.d [Nuremberg, 1540]); repr. as *Andreas Osianders Schrift über die Blutbeschuldigung*, ed. M. Stern (Kiel: H. Fiencke, 1893; Berlin: Verlag Hausfreund, 1903; repr. Tel Aviv, n.d. [1980]), p. 39. On the date (before 1540?), see the introduction by Klaus Keyser in Andreas Osiander d. Ä., *Gesamtausgabe*, vol. 7, *Schriften und Briefe 1539 bis März 1543*, ed. G. Müller and G. Seebass (Gütersloh: Gerd Mohn, 1988), pp. 216-22; text on pp. 223-48, quotation on p. 245, ll. 19-21.

be noted that Reuchlin designates the legal status of Jews not as *cives*, but as *concives*, as subjects of the emperor, but with the status of "resident aliens." In Florence, for example, three quarters of century earlier, the Jews were already designated as *cives*.[85]

This "equality before the law" is a marked advance; but Reuchlin is also exceptional as the only Christian author of his time to grasp the tragedy of the Spanish expulsion (1492) for the history of European Judaism. Indeed, Reuchlin's perspective points to the wider significance of the year 1492: under the reign of Ferdinand and Isabella not only was America "discovered," but also the Jews were expelled. Those Jews who reported about their experiences in the Ottoman Empire held up a dark mirror of European "Civilization," when they reported their own "discovery" in finding more religious tolerance under Koran and Crescent than under Bible and Cross.[86]

Despite his opposition to the burning of Jewish books, Reuchlin did not take the critical step of opposing this fundamental flaw of Christianity. His horizon was limited to the world of scholarship. Expulsion of the Jews meant for him the loss of that expertise and knowledge absolutely necessary for decoding the sacred sources.

(c) Insofar as the "Pfefferkorn dispute" brought home to Reuchlin the threat posed by "baptized Jews," he shared the suspicion of the Marranos who had fled Spain, a view likewise held by Reuchlin's humanist allies. At the same time, it should be granted that his personal bitterness toward the *Taufjuden* Pfefferkorn is quite understandable. It must be borne in mind that Pfefferkorn's attack had ravaged the last ten years of Reuchlin's life. It

85. A Florentine law of 1437 required that Jews be treated and regarded as citizens "tractentur et reputentur . . . tanquam cives civitatis flor[entie]," "Capitoli tra il Comune e gli Ebrei (17 Ottobre 1437)," Firenze, Archivio di Stato, Capitoli, vol. 100, cc. 29, in Marino Ciardini, *I Banchieri Ebrei in Firenze nel secolo XV et il Monte de Pieta* (Borgo S. Lorenzo: Tipografia Mazzocchi, 1907), Document 1, pp. I-X; VII; quoted by Andrew C. Gow and Gordon Griffiths, "Pope Eugenius IV and Jewish Money-Lending in Florence: The case of Salomone di Bonaventura during the chancellorship of Leonardo Bruni," *Renaissance Quarterly*, in press. By 1399, a similar degree of toleration was already established in Pistoia, where Jewish civic rights, referred to as *immunitas* and *exemptio*, were extended by statute for a period of ten years. See Lodovico Zdekauer, "L'interno d'un banco di pegno nel 1417: on documenti inediti," *Archivio Storico Italiano*, 5th series, 17 (1896): 63-105; 91-92.

Guido Kisch translates the term *concives* in Reuchlin's brief as "citizens" and the accompanying rights as full civil rights. See Kisch, *Zasius und Reuchlin* (n. 5 above), pp. 26-28. I am not convinced that "citizens" is the precise equivalent in English. Compared with the Florentine *cives*, Reuchlin's *concives* has a nuance which can best be rendered by the term "resident aliens." The element of equality between Christians and Jews lies in the fact that both Christians and Jews are "subjects" of the emperor.

86. *Jewish Existence after the Expulsion from Spain*, ed. S. N. Eisenstadt (Jerusalem: in press).

even lamed his interest in his precious library, one of the great private holdings in Europe, a rich collection, which contained at its peak 250 volumes in Latin alone; after 1512 he would not add a single volume.[87]

(d) We find no evidence whatsoever that Reuchlin ever suspected the Rabbis of consciously distorting the biblical text. Yet he is in full agreement with the view that the discovery of cabalistic truth not only confirms the superiority of the Christian faith, but also "crushes the stubbornness of the Jews of our time, convicting them of their perfidy."[88]

2. Conclusion

At the end we return to the beginning, in keeping with the genius of the method Reuchlin had learned to admire in the Cabala. Accordingly, he opposed confiscation and burning. The sections of Jewish books which are not polluted by blasphemy should be protected as precious messages encoded by God. With this in hand, contemporary Jews are to be drawn to the faith, not forced to convert.[89] Reuchlin's own claim to enduring fame did not prove to be lasting. His *Hebrew Grammar* was soon superseded and his daring cabalistic speculations never entered the mainstream of scholarship. Rather, Reuchlin's significance lies in his insistence that the policy of toleration must not only be *in* the books, but also *on* the books, by codification of human rights guaranteeing the existence of the Jews in a Christian Europe; the protection of the Jews should not be dependent on Christian charity but on secular law.[90] Indeed, the lasting

87. Letter to Melanchthon, 12 September 1519; Geiger, *BW,* nr. 280a, p. 357.

88. Letter to Willibald Pirckheimer, 18 February 1519; Geiger, *BW,* nr. 280, p. 313.

89. Geiger, *BW,* nr. 125a, p. 132; cf. nr. 215, p. 246.

90. This legal dimension is to be highlighted since the importance of preserving the Talmudic books as such is not Reuchlin's lonely conviction. Mutianus Rufus (†1526), an admirer of Reuchlin, who sharply criticized the Cologne inquisition for burning the *Augenspiegel,* provides a precious foil to highlight Reuchlin's legal achievement. When Mutianus learned about the Imperial Mandate of 26 July 1510, he does not hesitate to call the Jews "damned" *(perditissimi)* and their theology "blabbering" *(cavillationes).* Yet he defends their toleration as necessary for the church. However, this toleration is not expressed in legal terms: "Actum est de scholis Germaniae. Quid enim scitur praeter nugas et mera taedia? Caesar mandavit quatuor academiis, ut quid de volumine Talmud sentiant, sitne perditissimis Judaeis reddendum, suis disputationibus explanent. Tendent sua retia sophistae, nunquam veritatem Talmudici codicis deprehensuri. Non enim dialecticae laqueis Cabalae abditum capi potest, utpote convelatum mysteriis, intricatum tropis et allegoria, demersum in altum Democriti puteum, simul ut judaica religio sit tutior, simul ut efficacius nostrae credulitati struantur insidiae. Imperiti cum ista umbratili disciplina Judaeos universos comburerent, propterea quod nos filii lucis non egemus lucerna Punica. Sed Bessarion et omnis eruditorum

part of Reuchlin's high views of Renaissance humanism is the insistence that "humanism" is to be transferred from the realm of ideas to the rule of law.

There is no better way to conclude this assessment of Reuchlin than by citing the prayer he composed at the end of his life, when he had already come to doubt the success of his appeal to Pope Leo X. Here he succinctly formulated his desire for reform in head and members: "I beseech God, that he grant us the grace to become better subjects in order that we in turn may deserve better leaders."[91] This ardent plea was a call for justice in Reuchlin's own case. But from the very beginning, this same view had formed the basis of his defense of the Jews as "resident aliens" (concives). For this reason Reuchlin has long been honored as a friend of the Jews and as a "Philo-semite." The results of our antisemitism test call for a revision of this traditional interpretation. However, Reuchlin's involvement in Christian antisemitism does not diminish, but rather increases his stature. The scholar from Pforzheim, the first true German humanist (homo trilinguis!), served the cause of "humanity," benefiting Menschlichkeit, to use Reuchlin's own term, in word and deed: notwithstanding his own theological reservations, social prejudices, and personal antipathy toward the Jews of his time. No doubt Reuchlin stood contra Iudaeos — holding up Christ's crown of thorns to unbaptized Jews. At the same time, he stood contra Christianos, against every form of coercion distorting Christianity into tyranny. In sum, Reuchlin was indeed a "forerunner," but of a Reformation and Enlightenment still to be achieved.[92]

---

coetus censet ex re esse christiana tolerare recutitae gentis cavillationes; quibus accedo. Nam si aliter facias, relinquere prophetas necesse habes, quorum lectio quam sit in aede sacra frequens, nemo est qui nesciat." Der Briefwechsel des Mutianus Rufus, ed. Carl Krause (Kassel: Freyschmidt Hof, 1885), nr. 146, p. 194. On Mutianus, see Spitz, The Religious Renaissance (n. 1 above), pp. 130-54.

91. "Ich bitte Gott, dass er uns gnade verleihe, dass wir unterthanen uns selbst bessern, damit wir besserer häupter würdig werden." Letter to Frederick of Saxony, 7 May 1518; Geiger, BW, nr. 256, p. 298.

92. Dr. Ursula Stock kindly drew my attention to an early, almost forgotten "disciple" of Reuchlin who deserves to be remembered here, namely, Johannes Tarnowski of Cracow. In his published opinion (Gutachten) of 1540, Tarnowski defends the human rights of the Jews: "Nam etsi ex Christianorum coetu eiecti sunt, tamen ius suum illis reddi debet, nec oportet eos praeter aequum violare: sunt enim perinde ac nos homines, fert eos res publica, deinde sunt commodo Camerae M[aiesta]tis Suae." E. Zivier, "Jüdische Bekehrungsversuche im 16. Jahrhundert," in Beiträge zur Geschichte der deutschen Juden: Festschrift zum siebzigsten Geburtstag Martin Philippsons, ed. Vorstand der Gesellschaft zur Förderung der Wissenschaft des Judentums (Leipzig: Gustav Fock, 1916), pp. 96-113; Appendix 6, p. 111.

IV. PROBLEMS AND PERSPECTIVES

IV. PROBLEMS AND PERSPECTIVES

The Impact of the Reformation:
Problems and Perspectives

I. The Event between Act and Impact

The earliest and still unsurpassed history of the ancient Near East may seem a surprising point of departure, but its opening lines alert us to the ambiguity of our term "event." They will only do so, however, if we avoid the translation errors, typical of all modern German and English versions and perpetuated even by the properly influential R. G. Collingwood, who sees in the Preface to his history of the ancient Near East a simple declaration of Herodotus's purpose "to describe the deeds of men."[1] As I read it, Herodotus distinguishes quite carefully between two dimensions of his awesome task, namely the outcome or impact of events, and the events themselves. He says:

> Herodotus of Halicarnassus publishes herewith the results of his [historical] investigation in order that future generations will be reminded both of what was achieved [= unleashed] by man and of the great and amazing deeds [themselves], whether performed by Greeks or by barbarians.

1. R. G. Collingwood, *The Idea of History* (Oxford, 1946), p. 19.

"The Impact of the Reformation: Problems and Perspectives," published in *Politics and Society in Reformation Europe: Essays for Geoffrey Elton on his Sixty-fifth Birthday*, ed. E. I. Kouri and T. Scott (London, 1987), pp. 3-31.

Whereas classical research has emphasized appropriately enough the capacious worldview of Herodotus and his moral courage in spanning the gap of cultural disdain between Greeks and barbarians, a second distinction has been overlooked: that between the *genomena (ex anthropōn)* and the *erga (megala te kai thomasta)* — the outcome or impact of an event, and the nuclear event itself. Important to note is that Herodotus acknowledges in "the deeds of man" not only the great but indeed the "amazing" dimensions, manifesting that mental attitude of the historian to which Geoffrey Elton summons our return.[2] Herodotus can do this precisely because he distinguishes between the processes unleashed by human beings and the amazing events: he does not allow events to be robbed of their contingency, does not force them into those chains of causation and structural developments which modern social historians often tend to associate with that dangerous word "process." Unfortunately, Collingwood is not far off with his conclusion: "Herodotus had no successors."[3]

In the preface to the earliest history of the Reformation, in Heinrich Bullinger's description of *enderung der religion* and *anrichten Christlicher reformation,* covering the years 1519-1532, the sentiment of amazement is retained but the distinction of Herodotus is absorbed in the expression *Händel und Louff,* which should be translated "act and impact," but has come to mean "the course of events":

> Dann diser iar Händel und Löüff, sind nitt nu wunderbar, vast frölich und ouch träffenlich trurig, sunder zu läsen lustig, und zu wissen nitt wenig nutzlich, darzu ouch nodtwendig.[4]

The *Louff* concerns less the deeds of human beings than the acts of God, or as Cotton Mather would later put it, the *magnalia Christi*. In keeping with the Renaissance vision of the function of history as *magistra vitae,* the vocabulary of Herodotus is pushed into the background by that raised finger of the headmaster who points to the *Bildung* and erudition that can be drawn — and must be drawn — for the present age from the events of the past.[5]

Although I quote Herodotus and Bullinger at the outset, I am not interested in abstract speculations about past views of history, but rather

2. G. R. Elton, *The Practice of History* (Sydney, 1967). See n. 55, below.
3. Collingwood, *The Idea of History,* p. 28.
4. J. Hottinger and H. Vögeli (eds.), *Reformationsgeschichte: Heinrich Bullinger* (Frauenfeld, 1838; Zurich, 1984[2]), p. 1.
5. Herodotus, too, sees the yield of history in keeping the past alive, but rather in the tradition of apportioning praise and blame he wishes later generations to know who was responsible for the outbreak and the course of war.

in drawing attention to the present dangers implied in the impact of structuralism on contemporary Reformation historiography. When one looks at Rainer Wohlfeil's *Einführung in die Geschichte der Deutschen Reformation,*[6] or Hans-Christoph Rublack's sketch of the social history of the Reformation,[7] it is obvious that Bullinger's *Louff* has become *Ablauf,* an historical process which allows the reader to master readily his sense of amazement about past events, once they "receive" their inevitable place in the chain of historical necessity.

Since this structuralist tendency is an overreaction in the service of a *necessary* crusade against the long-extended hegemony of free-floating ideas, we would be ill-advised to insist on a return to the primacy of the history of ideas based on literary sources alone. Yet it must be possible to find a common path — between the sole analysis of structures and a singular belief in so-called "leading ideas" — toward "total history." Such a history can be "total" only to the extent to which it makes room for that kind of intellectual history, which is so well encapsulated in the words of Felix Gilbert:

> Whatever one thinks of the forces that underlie the historical process, they are filtered through the human mind and this determines the tempo and the manner in which they work. It is the human consciousness which connects the long-range factors and forces and the individual event, and it is at this crucial point of the historical process that the intellectual historian does his work.[8]

Social history makes its special contribution to "total history" only to the extent that Gilbert's "human consciousness" is not bypassed.

II. The Failure of the Reformation: *"Die gescheiterte Reformation"*

The thesis that the Reformation is a failure is admittedly of longer standing, and reaches as far back as Luther's earliest opponents. But the

6. Rainer Wohlfeil, *Einführung in die Geschichte der deutschen Reformation* (Munich, 1982).

7. Hans-Christoph Rublack, "Gesellschaft/Gesellschaft und Christentum, VI: Reformationszeit," *Theologische Realenzyklopädie,* 13 (Berlin, 1984), 1-13.

8. Felix Gilbert, "Intellectual History. Its Aims and Methods," *Daedalus* 100 (1971): 80-97, 94.

conclusion of Gerald Strauss is not based on a confessional stance. In *Luther's House of Learning: Indoctrination of the Young in the German Reformation,* he observes that

> The Protestant message was pitched to the solid burgher. . . . As for the great multitude of men and women, they could have found little survival value in doctrines whose framers made no attempt to integrate their precepts with the practical needs and aspirations of plain people.

Strauss is willing to grant that a meaningful and lasting response to the Protestant message may well have been evoked before 1530: "Later in the century, one finds mostly apathy."[9]

A whole avalanche of articles and monographs has sought to document the same thesis with respect to other areas in and outside of Germany. Thus, Manfred E. Welti's *Kleine Geschichte der italienischen Reformation* ascribes the failure of the Reformation in Italy primarily to its lack of roots in the people.[10] Henry Heller, in *The Conquest of Poverty: The Calvinist Revolt in 16th Century France,* explains the loss of France to Calvinism by pointing to the fact that "the base of the Calvinist movement lay in the skilled craftsmen, merchants and notables of the towns." Calvin himself, however, encouraged

> the subordination of the Protestant movement to the aristocracy. . . . The fact is that on the eve of the civil wars the Calvinist bourgeoisie was eager to subordinate themselves to the nobility. In contrast, in 1789 the bourgeoisie was not prepared to do so.[11]

Although later generations may well note with suspicion that in our day stocks and bonds in failure issues are rising with such spectacular speed that we tend to uncover them everywhere from "the mission of Europe" to "the rise of Christianity," this is no proof that our *Zeitgeist* may not have an edge, at times, on an historical truth beyond the vision of former, more triumphant times. But at this point, surrounded by so many recent reports of failure in the sixteenth century, we might be well advised to look first at what hitherto has been claimed as the period of

9. Gerald Strauss, *Luther's House of Learning: Indoctrination of the Young in the German Reformation* (Baltimore, 1978), pp. 307-8.

10. M. E. Welti, *Kleine Geschichte der italienischen Reformation,* Schriften des Vereins für Reformationsgeschichte 193 (Gütersloh, 1985), p. 139.

11. Henry Heller, *The Conquest of Poverty: The Calvinist Revolt in 16th Century France,* Studies in Medieval and Reformation Thought 35 (Leiden, 1985), pp. 240, 243, 247.

success, the years 1521-1525. I should like to start with a study, at once admirable and challenging, by Thomas A. Brady, Jr., *Turning Swiss: Cities and Empire, 1450-1550:*

> The Evangelical leaders were well-educated clergymen from urban backgrounds — sons of patricians, merchants, and artisans. They gained hearings largely because they offered answers to long-posed questions, and they sowed seed on long-prepared soil. Even where such answers and such seed were not, from the preachers" perspective, central to their gospel, they hoped that by addressing such questions — usury, tithes, clerical immunities, clerical indiscipline — they would win a hearing for pure doctrine. Luther showed the way by trying to touch every sensitive nerve of his day, at the price of sowing unclarity about his message, though not about his person. Some of his partisans came to see the world through his central message; others did not. But in these years their cause was a common one. The urban preachers sensed this and tried skillfully to adapt Luther's message to the hegemonic corporate-communal values of their fellow citizens.[12]

Brady's latest book is again an admirable achievement, insofar as it is both well written and well documented, and so solidly argued that a serious review would claim many pages in a learned journal. His book is admirable above all because it is an eloquent and, in my opinion, convincing argument against the thesis that the Reformation was a "national tragedy" in slowing down the process of the German nation becoming a Bismarckian empire. The main title, *Turning Swiss,* reveals, and the footnotes document, a very different direction in which the Reformation could have had its impact both on Germany and, far beyond the German borders, on European history.

For our particular purposes, *Turning Swiss* is a challenge because it seems to offer the key to the question why the Reformation could be seemingly so successful in the early years when, as so many studies today assume, it was to lose its impact and power soon afterward. The answer is this. The earlier success was only a superficial one. The city reformers, after all, sowed seed in long-prepared soil, but for their own ulterior purpose of opening the ears for their "pure doctrine." Luther did not hesitate to touch every sensitive nerve, whereas the urban preachers tried "skillfully" to adapt Luther's message to urban values.

Though Brady does not himself draw this conclusion, which is not

12. T. A. Brady, Jr., *Turning Swiss: Cities and Empire, 1450-1550,* Cambridge Studies in Early Modern History (Cambridge, 1985), pp. 153-54.

central to his own impressive line of argumentation, the consequence for our quest is obvious: the impact of the Reformation must have been only of a temporary nature, since Luther and the urban preachers in the so-called victorious years of the Reformation harnessed social and political aspirations with an alien message of "pure doctrine." Their rejection of the peasant revolt as their own revolution is, then, not so much the cause as the proof that the cohesion between doctrine and communal life was an artificial one, a mere instrument of communication and ultimately of agitation. The apathy which Strauss finds later in the century becomes understandable, particularly in view of the divorce between doctrine and life, documented and bewailed in the visitation records. The same applies to the findings of Heller and Welti: Calvinism in France had to look for a coalition with the nobility, because the broader base of the countryside folk had been cut off in the 1520s; and the Italian Reformation never had a chance to grow outside limited urban areas: the Reformation had become an intellectual movement, obviously and explicitly separated from social and political concerns.

To summarize the prevailing failure thesis: after suffocating its own grassroots movement, the Reformation became a willing prey to the greedy princes; henceforth, the Protestant ruling elite could only survive in limited areas with state support and social control, or — as Erwin Iserloh put it in his history of the Reformation epoch — the movement which started as a genuine popular campaign for spiritual renewal aborted in the *Fürstenreformation,* a Reformation enforced "from above":

> Immer mehr nahm die Obrigkeit die Reformation in die Hand und nutzte sie aus, um die Untertanen in den modernen Staat einzugliedern. Wir können seitdem von der Epoche der Fürstenreformation sprechen. Statt eines Gemeindechristentums mit freier Pfarrerwahl kam die Landeskirche.[13]

So much for the *genomena ex anthrōpon* of Herodotus. Act and impact thus became irreparably divorced — or so it must seem.

---

13. Erwin Iserloh (ed.), *Handbuch der Kirchengeschichte,* vol. 4 (Freiburg im Breisgau, 1967), 145.

III. The Loaded Language of Social Analysis

In the foregoing summary I believe I have fairly presented the growing consensus of some of the major spokesmen in the field of sixteenth-century studies. Though the social study of the Reformation owes its present strength to emancipation from the hegemony of theology and the history of ideas, the ease with which the confessional view of Erwin Iserloh could be incorporated shows that there is an often hidden continuity between the old scholarship and the new. Yet the very terminology used calls for closer investigation of each clause. However self-evident the concatenation of clauses may seem in the rhetoric of historical evaluation, they lose their authority and credibility when looked at singly. Consider the five key expressions employed in the previous "convincing" summary.

1. "The Peasants' War is claimed to be the Reformation's 'own grassroots movement'." Karl Marx has pointed out that the peasants' uprising "an der Theologie gescheitert ist."[14] This may well be more true than originally intended: the revolutionary peasants were from the outset on a collision course with the Reformation. After all, it was Christoph Schappeler, the coauthor of the Memmingen articles, which were to be copied throughout Germany in later peasant manifestos, who reported to his mentor Ulrich Zwingli, after the bloody disaster of May 1525, that the original impetus had been thwarted and that in the escalation of the uprisings the initial leaders had been overtaken from the left (sinistre).[15]

Peter Blickle's restrictive interpretation of the crucial concept gemeiner Mann, and extensive definition of "communalism," obscure the distance between countryside, village, and city, and ignore — as Hermann Rebel has so convincingly shown[16] — the social stratification within the peasantry itself. Blickle's new definition of these two concepts seems to confirm the old thesis of the peasant uprising as the Reformation's own grassroots movement — a view which in turn may have a similar influence in the English-speaking world through the

---

14. Karl Marx, "Zur Kritik der Hegelschen Rechtsphilosophie," Deutsch-Französische Jahrbücher (Paris, 1844) (Reclam edition, no. 542, Leipzig, 1981), p. 159.

15. Cf. Heiko A. Oberman, "The Gospel of Social Unrest," in Bob Scribner and Gerhard Benecke (eds.), The German Peasant War. New Viewpoints (London, 1979), pp. 39-51, 48.

16. Hermann Rebel, Peasant Classes: The Bureaucratization of Property and Family Relations in Early Habsburg Absolutism 1511-1636 (Princeton, N.J., 1983), p. 13.

excellent and attractive translation by Thomas Brady and Erik Midel-fort.[17]

From Zurich's perspective, there did indeed exist an initial hope of channeling the uprisings in and outside the cities by "turning them Swiss," at least as far as the *Rotten* in Upper Swabia and Lower Alsace were concerned. Wittenberg, however, never enjoyed such short-lived hope with its subsequent sobering outcome. Already in 1518 and 1519, Luther had rejected the concept of revolt in the service of reformation. One of the most precious aspects of the rich works of Thomas Müntzer is exactly that he had both the training and the vision which enabled him to grasp and to formulate the difference in goals between the movement with which he became associated after 1524, and Luther's Reformation.

2. The next sentence in the above summary contains not one but two misleading terms: "The Reformation became a willing victim to the greedy princes." The first noun, "*the* Reformation" is a misleading, unclear collective cover-name for a whole series of movements. Under this broad umbrella hide at least two triads. First, the traditional triad: the Protestant Reformation, the Catholic Reformation, and the Radical Reformation. But then there is also that other triple-grouping *within* the Protestant Reformation which deserves our special attention if we are concerned with the question of impact: Luther's Reformation, the City Reformation, and the Reformation of the Refugees. This division thus highlights first the unique magnetism of Luther's program, and second the short-lived Reformation in the cities, during that quarter century between the Edict of Worms and the Schmalkaldic War (1521-1548); and third, the diaspora of the Reformation from Geneva to Italy, France, and through the Low Countries, Poland and Hungary, Great Britain and the New World. The City Reformation never became a "willing victim" of the princes but rather, initially at least, a most unwilling victim of the emperor. This turn of events marked the beginning of the third Reformation.[18]

3. As to the "greedy princes," three warnings are in order: one senses here a democratic and perhaps even populist assumption that "greed" is particularly partial to high places at the summit of the social hierarchy. More misleading, however, is the suggestion that the role of the *Fürsten* in the whole drama of the Reformation can be exhaustively described in terms of territorial expansionism under the mere *pretext* of

---

17. Peter Blickle, *Die Revolution von 1525* (Munich, 1977; 1983³); English translation, *The Revolution of 1525: The German Peasants' War from a New Perspective* (Baltimore, 1981).

18. For this distinction between the first, second, and third Reformations see Heiko A. Oberman, *The Reformation: Roots and Ramifications* (Edinburgh, 1994).

piety and thirst for justice. This self-serving quest for gain is just what Schappeler and Müntzer chastised in the peasants *que sua sunt quererunt — iustitiae praetextu!* It may be safely assumed that self-interest belongs to the constant forces in history on all levels of society. The crucial question is how self-interest is channelled, controlled, and legitimized: undisguised, naked greed has no impact.

But more importantly, it is not just ideological blindness but historical error to situate the role of the princes only at the end of the Reformation movement, as an unfortunate finale, as Iserloh has put it. Reformation scholars around the turn of the century still knew that territorial reform *in sacris* stands at the beginning of the Reformation — indeed, is part and parcel of the fifteenth-century reform movement, and forms in electoral Saxony the very cradle of Luther's Reformation in the early and sustained protection of Observant monasticism.

The third warning concerns the unreflected assumption that the *Fürstenreformation* is the typically Protestant outcome of the Reformation epoch. When we look at the Habsburg empire as the most immediate political context, there is no way to avoid the conclusion that the turn toward "absolutism" did not respect confessional boundaries. As Robert A. Kann has put it with respect to the Habsburg territories: "the ascendency of the Church over forces of the Reformation was largely state-sponsored and state-controlled"[19] — applying the same tools as the Protestant princes through property control and visitations of churches and monasteries — in the whole period reaching from Ferdinand II to Charles VI. We may conclude that the expression *Fürstenreformation* to designate the outcome of the Reformation is misunderstood if not extended to include the *Fürsten-Gegenreformation*.

Two more ambivalent expressions must be addressed, which seemingly are too often used in our historical analyses as if they are crystal clear expressions, but loaded with egalitarian sentiment: "ruling elite" and "social control."

4. I have no quarrel with the use of "ruling elite" for Pericles's Athens or Cato's Republican Rome, or for the sixteenth-century imperial city Strasbourg. If, however, with that term political suppression is implied, from the arrogantly high perspective of modern democratic achievements, it may be important to note that even in modern countries that understand themselves as democratically governed — whether the German Democratic Republic or the United States — the centers of

19. R. A. Kann, *A History of the Habsburg Empire 1526-1618* (Berkeley, Calif., 1974), pp. 133, 125, 134-35.

power are in the hands of a ruling elite, albeit under widely differing circumstances; in the one case because of the concentration of power in the party, in the other due to the low percentage of electoral participation. The real character test for any given ruling elite is the potential for upward social mobility; and it is exactly that which I am inclined to concede to those sixteenth-century imperial cities which moved from central government by the *Kleiner Rat* of the aristocrats and large entre-preneurs to the increasing involvement of the *Grosser Rat,* which repre-sented artisans, craftsmen, and small businessmen. "Ruling elite," there-fore, is an acceptable term, provided it is used in a descriptive fashion, cleansed of anti-elitist sentiment.

5. The last terminological pitfall lies in the expression "social con-trol." In vain one searches the works of Max Weber for this term. Though part of this historian's greatness was his discovery of the potential of sociological insights for historical investigation, he may well have sensed that "social control" is a misleading expression for describing relationships in late medieval society. On first sight, the expression is appealing: when Thomas N. Tentler presented his views on "The Summa for Confessors as an Instrument for Social Control,"[20] it seemed exactly the right term to describe the hold of the Confessors on pre-Reformation society. The religious and social protest, however, which we find in such varying forms reaching from the Waldensians in the High Alps to the Hussites in Bohemia, is not directed against the too *heavy burden* of a moral codex enforced by the Confessors, but rather against its *leniency* and unequal application. They turn against the lack of a thoroughgoing requirement for full contri-tion as a precondition for receiving absolution, and generally insist on a higher quality of life. This trend, which I have described as "the upsurge of Donatism," can also be described as "semi-monastic," as Steven Ozment put it in his pertinent conclusion: "Until the Protestant Reformation, lay religious practice remained an imitation of clerical religious practice."[21] In this very "imitation" lurks the spark of fiery protest.

Such a critique is not confined to the heretical fringes. It comes from within, as is eloquently documented by the impressive Dominican, Robert Holcot (†1349), who in his widely disseminated commentary on the Book of Wisdom exposes the *Klassenjustiz* of the Confessors: "prelati

20. T. N. Tentler. "The Summa for Confessors as an Instrument for Social Control," in Charles Trinkaus and Heiko A. Oberman (eds.), *The Pursuit of Holiness in Late Medieval and Renaissance Religion* (Leiden, 1974), pp. 103-25; cf. Tentler's monograph *Sin and Confession on the Eve of the Reformation* (Princeton, N.J., 1977).

21. S. E. Ozment, *The Age of Reform, 1250-1550: An Intellectual and Religious History of Late Medieval and Reformation Europe* (New Haven/London, 1980), p. 86.

moderni non divites et nobiles peccatores, sed pauperes ecclesiastica censura castigant."[22] The confessional — seemingly so private and secret; in effect, very public — functions as long as it corresponds with the communal, "semi-monastic," moral consensus. I am inclined to regard the very vehemence of popular critique as an index of the success of this institution for a long period of time, in extended areas, as a sensitive and sensible tool for the support of social cohesion.

However, the term "social control," in its *restrictive* sense, is fully appropriate for the analysis of the three conditions under which the Reformation and the Counter-Reformation managed to survive into the Confessional Age. For Lutheranism and Habsburg Catholicism, it means *Landesfürst* as Lord Protector by means of government support through legislation and visitation; for Calvinism it is the creation of independent congregations "under the cross" by means of the consistory and its *censura morum;* and for the Italian Counter-Reformation, the reintroduction of the Inquisition.

To this institution we must now turn, since the effect of the Inquisition is directly related to our search for the impact of the Reformation.

IV. How to Combat Protestant Heresy: A Vatican Instruction to All Inquisitors

Having exposed the hidden ideological assumptions on the contemporary historical battlefront, we are in a better position to return to the real fights of the sixteenth century. And battle is exactly the theme and center of a revealing treatise by Sylvester Mazzolini, named after his birthplace Prierias. On closer scrutiny, the treatise proves to be a pseudepigraphic satire in two distinct parts.[23] The first is dated Rome 1553 and assigned

---

22. *Super Libros Sapientie* (Haguenau, 1494), Lectio 77D.

23. *Modus solennis et autenticus ad inquirendum et inveniendum et convincendum Luteranos valde necessarius, ad salutem sanctae Apostolicae sedis et omnium Ecclesiasticorum anno 1519 compositus in Martini Luteri perditionem et eius sequacium per venerabilem Monachum magistrum Sylvestrum Prieratem* [sic] *ex sacrosancto ordine Praedicatorum, Magistrum sacri Palatii et generalem haereticae pravitatis inquisitorem. Anno 1553 revisus et satis bene emendatus ab erroribus per Reverendissimos Cardinales ad officium sanctissimae inquisitionis depuratos* [sic] *per S. D. N. Papam Iulium III. Romae, Per Iordanum typographum Pontificium* [sic]. *Anno 1553* (40 folios). Cf. WA 1.605. I owe the exceptional gift of this rare copy to my colleague James Tanis, the librarian of Bryn Mawr College.

to Prierias, professor of Thomistic philosophy in Rome from 1514 until his death in 1523; from December 1515, Prierias was *Magister sacri Palatii,* chief inquisitor, and responsible for preparing the Roman process against Reuchlin and Luther.

The satirical tone itself must make the reader dubious about one further point of information on the title page, namely that the 1553 edition is a revision of an earlier instruction which Prierias had sent out to all inquisitors in 1519, a manual to detect and convict Lutherans: *in Martini Luteri perditionem et eius sequacium.* But indeed, the satire was published in 1519, in Augsburg, Basel, Cologne, and perhaps in Wittenberg itself.[24] Whereas the Augsburg version is dedicated to Sylvester Prierias by an imaginary younger Dominican under the name of Logumenus (= *loquax* or verbose?), a later edition, printed by Eduard Böcking in the first supplementary volume of his Hutten edition,[25] is assigned not to Prierias but to an unnamed canonist, and directed not against Lutherans but against heresy in general — this time dedicated to both Prierias and the German chief inquisitor Hochstraten. Böcking believes the satire to have been written by Rubianus Crotus (†1545), in view of its obvious proximity to the style and tone of the *Letters of Obscure Men.*[26]

The second treatise — added, as its author says, merely in order not to leave precious pages blank (folios 26-40!) — is dedicated to Esprit Rotier (Spiritus Roterus), the French Dominican who functioned from 1523 until 1547 as the vicar-general of his congregation in France, and from 1547 until his death in 1564 (or 1569) as chief inquisitor in Toulouse. This treatise is to be found on the index of Benedict XIV (1758) and assigned to Pietro Paolo Vergerio. Meeting Luther as papal nuncio on 7 November 1535 in Wittenberg, Vergerio had regarded the reformer as the devil incarnate. But afterward increasingly open to the Reformation and despairing of the sincerity of papal reform efforts he converted, ending his life as a Protestant professor at Tübingen in 1565.[27]

---

24. I am indebted to Professor C. Augustijn and to the librarian of the Free University, Amsterdam, B. Lau, for access to the version most probably published in Augsburg in 1519.

25. E. Böcking (ed.). *Epistolae obscurorum virorum (Ulrichi Hutteni . . . opera . . . omnia,* supplementary vol. 1) (Leipzig, 1864; repr. Osnabruck, 1966), pp. 489-99. This version probably printed in Cologne in 1519.

26. Cf. Otto Clemen in *WA Br* 1, nr. 236, pp. 604-6. I doubt whether Clemen saw the 1553 treatise himself. Note his incorrect rendering of the title.

27. The author of the excellent monograph on Vergerio, Anne Jacobson Schutte, informed me in a letter of 17 February 1981 that she doubts Vergerio's authorship:

Vergerio referred to the work only six years after its publication in Basel. In

What we have here before us in the edition of 1553 is a double plot to ridicule the Inquisition, of which the earlier 1519 treatise presents a more light-footed sample, completely in keeping with the *Letters of Obscure Men*.[28] The second treatise is a much more embittered defense against Rotier's attack on the Genevan Reformation, which Rotier four years earlier in a book published in Toulouse in 1549 had identified as "the new Babylon." The first satire — divided into twelve so-called "rules," perhaps a takeoff on the four *Fundamenta* which Prierias had attached to his 1518 *Conclusiones* against Luther[29] — shows such precise information about theological terminology of the day that one may be inclined to assign it to one of Luther's students or younger colleagues, such as Johann Lang (1487-1548). The Inquisition is ridiculed by having Prierias send out from the Vatican an urgent warning "to all Dominicans and inquisitors in Italy, France, Spain, and elsewhere":

> They should stop interrogating these heretics in public, because of their infectious good faith and convincing knowledge of the Scriptures. They should be killed before it comes to a hearing — on the basis of the "old saw" that the one who sets the fire is always wiser than the one who is burned [*quia semper combustores sum doctiores combustis*]. If only the princes had allowed Reuchlin to receive his due, this thesis could have been wonderfully documented: the German heretic would have been burned; and to be wiser than Reuchlin really means something [*duodecima Regula*] . . . a beautiful feather in the cap of the Inquisition.

The final question raised is why the Holy Church did not burn any heretics in the first 1300 years, until the Council of Constance (1414-1418), yet cannot rule today without burning heretics galore? Answer:

Agli inquisitori che sono per l'Italia: Del catalogo di libri eretici stampato in Roma nell'anno presente 1559 (Tübingen [?], 1559), folio 42v, he said that he thought he owned a copy of this rare work and planned to have it reprinted. Since his references to books written and published by others and to books he himself issued are generally very accurate, my tentative conclusion would be that he was *not* responsible for the 1553 edition.

28. After a deficient bibliographical description, Friedrich Lauchert associates both parts with the *Epistolae obscurorum virorum*. In the first treatise Lauchert finds "mehr Gehässigkeit als Witz," citing particularly the irreverent treatment of papal infallibility: satire "durch törichte Verdrehung." Lauchert, *Die italienischen literarischen Gegner Luthers* (Freiburg im Breisgau, 1912), pp. 29-30; 30, n. 1.

29. Heiko A. Oberman, "Wittenberg's War on Two Fronts: What Happened in 1518 and Why," *The Reformation: Roots and Ramifications* (Edinburgh, 1994), 117-48.

I wonder that people can be so stupid that they ask such a question! It is obvious that they have not yet studied their Thomas. I say, therefore, that the solution is short, and, well, thus: at that time, there were not yet inquisitors. If they had been around in the early church, surely the heretics would have been exterminated by fire. Just as the truth grows over the course of time, so does also the purgation of the church increase. In the early church, there were not yet so many gifted students of Scripture as there are today thanks to the tutelage of Aristotle. I sincerely believe that if St. Jerome and St. Augustine were alive today — or even the apostle Paul himself — they would not so easily escape the fires of the Inquisition, because the inquisitors have become real experts today: *bene tibi, Paule, quod vixisti illo tempore, quando non erant subtilia ista ingenia.*

The second satire, edited and added in 1553, follows another procedure: a young respectful trainee of the great French inquisitor Rotier reports a long series of formidable problems he has encountered in defending the opinions of his master. Finding himself gutted time and again by the sharpness of the arguments of the opposition, he is unable — indeed, helpless — to defend Rotier without immediate advice and support. This time, it is not the infallibility of the pope which is carried *ad absurdum,* but Rotier's insistence on the Vulgate and directives against Bible translations. The inquisitor had published a book in Toulouse in 1548[30] to prove that Holy Scripture should not be translated into the vernacular, with the argument that then "the living spirit is converted into the killing letter":

How then to deal with the feast of Pentecost when the gospel was proclaimed in all languages? Do not think, great master, that in the debate about your thesis I succumbed. Thereby you would underestimate my long breath. However many convincing passages they showed me, they never silenced me. If you think that, you have forgotten my brashness. But it was difficult to argue against their solid proofs of structural weakness in your books, both in grammar and dialectics — especially the difficulty you have in grasping an argument of the

---

30. The following treatises of Rotier are alluded to:

De non vertenda Scriptura Sacra in Fulgarem linguam, deque occidente littera et vivicante spiritu dissertatio (Toulouse, 1548); *Parergi sive tabellae tres similitudinum, quibus suis coloribus haeretici, vera Ecclesia vulgaresque S. Scripturae traductiones describuntur* (Toulouse, 1548 quarto; 1549 octavo); *Responsio ad epistolam civium novae Babylonis Gebennae a Mornero insigni apostata editam* (Toulouse, 1549).

opposition and reporting it fairly: how fortunate it is that you have a terrifying, powerful institution behind you which scares readers of heretical books from touching them and from comparing them with yours. When they turned to such basic issues as sin and forgiveness, I found it hard to discover a passage in Thomas which could help me. But I hit on the right kind of solution to escape the force of their arguments: I could slither away under the pretext that one is not allowed to debate matters that have already been decided.

At this point, I break off my report on the second treatise. It is just as much a satire as the first one, though different in strategy. Here the young inquisitor reports his embarrassment and thus reveals the weakness of the arguments of his master, instead of the master himself prescribing antidotes for an "obviously" formidable challenge. The power of the Inquisition is ridiculed as a mirror of the disintegration of that Roman Church which sets itself up as infallible and hence as unassailable, and yet can only defend itself with external force.

Amid all similarities, a crucial new element should not be overlooked in the second treatise. The Inquisition is not merely a ridiculous Roman affair — that faraway, unpredictable court before which the great Reuchlin trembled, and where even Paul and Jesus would have had no chance: the Inquisition is now the direct and very present threat to the Genevan Reformation. Thirty-five years later, the struggle dramatically escalates: whereas Geneva is accursed as the New Babylon, the inquisitors are now unmasked as the soldiers of the antichrist. There is not just a difference in time — some thirty-five years — and a difference in locality — from German Lutherans to French Calvinists — but also a difference in a heightened sense of the diabolic power of the opponent: battle has grown out of banter. Behind the shift from irony to sarcasm we discern the growing awareness of the formidable obstacles on the path to reformation: its very impact is threatened.

V. The Nicodemites: Courageous Alternative to the Refugee

From haughty banter to harsh battle — this escalation reflected indeed the course of events. From its staging area in Geneva, the third Reformation had sought to close ranks with endemic evangelism and to infiltrate the main bastions of Roman Catholicism in Italy and France. But just as it seemed that the evangelical dreams of such disciples of Valdés

(†1541) as Bernardino Ochino and Peter Martyr Vermigli under the patronage of Reginald Pole — in touch with Giberti, Contarini, and Cortese — could be translated into structural reform, and just at the time when Viterbo, Modena, and Lucca had become centers of what the Council of Trent would later define and condemn as heresy, the Roman Inquisition was established in July 1542.

Cardinal Caraffa — the later Counter-Reformation Pope Paul IV (1555-1559) — gained control of what he fashioned into a powerful and feared institution.[31] Shortly afterward, in August 1542, Ochino and Vermigli, symbolically just at the time when Contarini was lying on his deathbed, decided to burn their Roman bridges behind them. They were the first in a long line of refugees going the arduous road of emigration over the Alps to Switzerland, and in the case of Vergerio, ultimately all the way to Swabia.

Were these refugees fainthearted or clear-sighted? Less than a decade later, by papal order of 12 August 1553, the Talmud and other rabbinical books were condemned to burning; in the next few months across Italy possibly hundreds of thousands of Hebrew books went up in flames.[32] The *spirituali,* in full accord with the rising tide of antisemitism, did not read the signs of the times, ignoring the medieval sequence "first the Jew, then the heretic".[33]

The index of forbidden books of 1549 was enhanced in 1554 to include works by Dante, Valla, Boccaccio, Machiavelli, and Erasmus.[34] Three years later, Caraffa — now Pope Paul IV — started to round up the *spirituali* in high places. Sanfelice and Soranzo were arrested, Morone sent to the dungeons of St. Angelo, and Pole was recalled from his mission as Papal Legate in England in order to allow the Curia to start proceedings against him. Erwin Iserloh called this crucial period from 1551 to 1559 the "Durchbruch der katholischen Reform."[35] Actually, it was a

31. Dermot Fenlon, *Heresy and Obedience in Tridentine Italy: Cardinal Pole and the Counter-Reformation* (Cambridge, 1972), p. 51.

32. Paul F. Grendler, *The Roman Inquisition and the Venetian Press, 1540-1605* (Princeton, N.J., 1977), p. 92. The Index of Paul IV is reprinted by F. H. Reusch, *Die Indices Librorum Prohibitorum des 16. Jahrhunderts* (Tübingen, 1886), pp. 176-288.

33. Cf. Heiko A. Oberman, *Roots of Anti-Semitism in the Age of Renaissance and Reformation* (Philadelphia, Pa., 1984).

34. Grendler, *Roman Inquisition,* pp. 95-96.

35. Iserloh, *Handbuch der Kirchengeschichte,* vol. 4, pp. 501-10. Cf., however, Hubert Jedin, "Die Regierung des Caraffa-Papstes war für alle Anhänger der Reform eine grausame Enttäuschung," *Geschichte des Konzils von Trient,* vol. 4 (Freiburg im Breisgau, 1975), 15. Jedin placed the breakthrough after 1559: "Der Pontifikat Pius IV. brachte den endgültigen Sieg der katholischen Reform und den Abschluß des Konzils von Trient." *Geschichte des Konzils von Trient,* vol. 4, p. 18. Cf. Donald Nugent's

time of failure for *Catholic* reform and the beginning of the *Roman* Catholic Counter-Reformation.

The refugees could not but feel confirmed in their decision. Those who had stayed behind and clung to the hope for reform from within — peculiarly dubbed, for lack of a proper designation, the *spirituali* — drew the wrath of the refugees, who regarded them as "timorous Nicodemists,"[36] as Vergerio designated Cardinal Reginald Pole.

But if Pole had acceded to the papal throne when, on St. Martin's Eve, the Holy See fell vacant through the death of Pope Paul III (10 November 1549) — on that fateful morning of 5 December Pole needed only one more vote in the conclave! — the *spirituali* would have been in charge of reform from above, and allowed to act so publicly that the charge of Nicodemism would never have arisen. Vergerio's charge is nothing but a red herring: understandable though his "name-calling" may be, it is deceptive, and has indeed deceived scholarship in its search for the roots of Nicodemism. The learned Tübingen professor, by applying a current pejorative term to Italian evangelism, suggests a connection between Nicodemism, cowardice, and spiritualism which most certainly does not apply to Nicodemism as it had emerged ten years earlier in France.

The enigma of Nicodemism is not due to the dissimulation of its adherents, but to the confusing reaction it has evoked among its interpreters, all the way from John Calvin to Carlo Ginzburg.[37] It has been generally recognized that a crucial, but unknown, phase in the history of Nicodemism precedes the intervention of John Calvin.[38] What has not yet been highlighted is the positive connotations associated with Nicodemus, as propagated in late medieval theology,[39] piety,[40] and

---

evaluation: "Paul's pontificate was a reign of terror rather than a reformation. . . . Given all this, one can hardly insist that Paul IV launched the Counter-Reformation without allowing at the same time that he was destroying the Catholic Church." *Ecumenism in the Age of the Reformation. The Colloquy of Poissy* (Cambridge, 1974), p. 29.

36. Anne Jacobson Schutte, *Pier Paolo Vergerio: The Making of an Italian Reformer,* Travaux d'Humanisme et Renaissance 160 (Geneva, 1977), p. 267.

37. A significant advance is made by C. M. N. Eire. "Calvin and Nicodemism: A Reappraisal," *Sixteenth Century Journal* 10 (1979): 45-69.

38. Albert Autin, *La Crise du Nicodémisme, 1535-1545* (Toulon, 1917); cf. Francis Higman (ed.), *John Calvin: Three French Treatises* (London, 1970).

39. Cf. Gabriel Biel, *Canonis Misse Expositio,* Lectio 18G; 1.157.4; Lectio 34L; 2.10.22.

40. Jacobus de Voragine, O.P. (†1298), elaborates on the significance of Nicodemus in his influential *Legenda Aurea* (1293). On the wide dissemination of the *Legenda,* see Sherry L. Reames, *The Legenda Aurea: A Reexamination of Its Paradoxical History* (Madison, Wisc., 1985), pp. 197-209.

art.[41] The positive connotation of the term clearly puzzled Calvin: after all, according to the Fourth Gospel, Nicodemus proved to be at the end one of the very few dedicated and steadfast disciples (cf. John 3 and John 19:39). Originally, "Nicodemite" may well have been an apologetic in-group designation to express the claim that though one cannot openly profess the gospel, one comes like Nicodemus to the Lord, albeit by night. In this charitable sense, it is used by the reformer of Schwäbisch-Hall Johannes Brenz in a letter of 1 June 1529 to the lord chancellor of Brandenburg-Ansbach, Georg Vogler. Brenz expects the secret confession to become a public one.[42] But when Calvin, twice within one year (1543 and 1544), and in no uncertain terms, attacks the French Nicodemites as traitors and apostates, the leader of the third Reformation discredits a movement which would thus be encouraged to subvert, rival, and in certain respects eclipse his own impact on later history.

Thanks to a precious find by that eminent Strasbourg scholar, Jean Rott, we have recovered a missing link in the correspondence of Antoine Fumée (1511-1568?), one of the leaders of French Protestantism in Paris. Long hidden in the library of Corpus Christi College, Cambridge, this letter sheds light on both the creed and the situation of the so-called Nicodemites in France. Writing to Martin Bucer and his colleagues in Strasbourg, Fumée reminds them of the fact that he is not in a position to teach the gospel publicly: "Scitote, fratres, non tam clare et diserte nobis licere, aut per infirmitatem, quam magnam in nobis agnoscimus, aut per assiduas improborum calumnias, docere justificationem hominis solius Dei gratiae esse, non operum."[43] Fumée proceeds to describe his

41. The account of the deposition in the *Gospel of Nicodemus* and in (Pseudo) Bonaventura's *Meditationes* — visibly represented and propagated in sculptures and paintings throughout Europe — usually presents both Joseph of Arimathea and Nicodemus as the *faithful* disciples who remove the nails from the crucified Christ. Cf. Wolfgang Stechow, "Joseph of Arimathea or Nicodemus?", in W. Lotz and L. L. Möller (eds.), *Studien zur Toskanischen Kunst* (Munich, 1964), pp. 289-302; 290, 292-96.

I am indebted to Dr. Jane Kristof for calling my attention to Stechow's article. In a paper not yet published Dr. Kristof makes a good case for interpreting Michelangelo's Pietà in Florence Cathedral as representing himself as a Nicodemite. Via Vittoria Colonna Michelangelo belonged to the Viterbo circle of the *spirituali*. The Pietà, begun about 1547, was mutilated and abandoned by him before December 1555; by that time the *positive* self-identification with Nicodemus might well have become self-incriminatory.

42. T. H. Pressel (ed.), *Anecdota Brentiana: Ungedruckte Briefe und Bedenken* (Tübingen, 1868), pp. 31-33; 32. Cf. Martin Brecht, *Die frühe Theologie des Johannes Brenz* (Tübingen, 1966), p. 55, n. 1.

43. Jean Rott and Olivier Millet, "Miettes Historiques Strasbourgeoises," in P. Barthel, R. Scheurer, and R. Stauffer (eds.), *Actes du Collôque Guillaume Farel*

theology in detail. Except for the invocation of the saints — legitimate, he argues, provided it is done in the name of God, and though not attested to in Scripture, not counter to it — it is completely "orthodox." This new letter should be read in conjunction with Fumée's earlier correspondence with Calvin.

Two points should be underscored. In the first place, "Nicodemians" have been erroneously confused with libertinists and epicureans.[44] Yet it was Antoine Fumée himself who alerted Calvin to these very dangers. Even more importantly, Fumée alerts us to the fact that the refugee is not the only true Christian, or the only Protestant prepared to suffer for his faith (after all, Calvin decided to flee); he takes no risks in criticizing those who dared to stick to their social and political responsibility: "hec te illic facile et predicare et monere posse, qui si hic sis aliter forte sentires."[45] Almost exactly a year before, toward the end of 1542, under an alias ("Capnius") Fumée had reported to Calvin the tremendous pressure under which the young French evangelical movement suffered through confusion in its own ranks and police pressure from outside. This had taken on such extreme forms that he expected shortly its *ruina*, and did not doubt "nos diu hoc statu non consistere posse."[46] And indeed, as the records show, the persecutions had intensified since the late summer of 1542, with public burnings in Bordeaux, Toulouse, Rouen, and of course in Paris itself.[47]

It is at this point that the newly found letter of Antoine Fumée is of such importance. A friend of Calvin's since the common study years in Orléans and Paris, he was born into the ruling elite. His grandfather, Paul Fumée, had been the personal physician of Charles VII and Louis XI, ambassador to Rome, and governor of Nantes; his father, Adam Fumée, served as member of Parliament, as did Antoine himself from 1536, at twenty-five years of age.[48] In complete agreement with Calvin as far as the rejection of libertinism is concerned, he takes grave exception to Calvin's attack on those in France who have to assume the posture of Nicodemites, and who do not give in to the temptation to flee — as

(Neuchâtel, 29 septembre–1er octobre 1980), 1, Cahiers de la Revue de Théologie et de Philosophie 9/1 (Geneva/Lausanne/Neuchâtel, 1983), 261-62, 264.

44. See Marc Lienhard (ed.), *Croyants et sceptiques au XVIe siècle. Le dossier des "Epicuriens,"* Publications de la Société Savante d'Alsace et des Régions de l'Est, Collection "Recherches et Documents" 30 (Strasbourg, 1981).

45. A. L. Herminjard (ed.), *Correspondance des Réformateurs,* 9 (Nieuwkoop, 1966), 126.

46. Herminjard, *Correspondance,* 8 (Nieuwkoop, 1966), 231-32.

47. Herminjard, *Correspondance,* 8, pp. 107, n. 18; 108, n. 20.

48. Herminjard, *Correspondance,* 8, p. 228, n. 1.

Calvin had done! — and therefore to make room for people who will subvert the course of the gospel in France.

At this early stage, it is certainly wrong to identify, as Carlo Ginzburg has done, Nicodemism with spiritualism: spiritualism emphasizes an interior religion which is indifferent to externals. Fumée, however, makes it quite clear that he is critical of the spiritualizing interpretation of the eucharist, as it has been reported to him about Strasbourg. The confusion of the two movements, which finds support in George Williams's characterisation of Nicodemism as "prudential spiritualism,"[49] is understandable insofar as Calvin attacks often in one breath a whole series of opponents, from libertines to spiritualists and Nicodemites lurking about in all parts of Europe. In his report of 21 January 1545 to Martin Luther, Calvin makes quite clear that the Nicodemites who "continue to defile themselves with the sacrilegious worship of the papists" are his own fellow countrymen in France. But these compatriots continue not only "to defile themselves" but also to hold out and persevere — they have to give account of their faith under extreme duress.

Nicodemism is not some kind of abstract ideology which a posteriori applies what it first, a priori, culled out of the pages of a book, as Carlo Ginzburg has argued, when finding the bible of Nicodemism in Otto Brunfels's Pandectae (1527)[50] and constructing a school of Brunfels through Wolfgang Capito, Sebastian Franck, Johannes Brenz, Camillo Renato, and Lefèvre d'Étaples. Carlos Eire has convincingly pointed to Ginzburg's overinterpretation of the Pandectae; Pierre Fraenkel established that one of Ginzburg's so-called Nicodemite documents actually is a letter of Bucer,[51] and Olivier Millet recently uncovered that the Margarita, whom Ginzburg identified with Margaret de Navarre, is Margreth von Lodieuse, a French refugee in Strasbourg since December 1534. Strasbourg, with its influential preachers around Brunfels, particularly Bucer and Capito, is not a staging area for the export of Nicodemism to France, but rather its court of appeal. The Paris Evangelicals, under the high pressure of royal persecution, and simultaneously harshly assailed by Calvin, appeal to Strasbourg to intercede with Calvin and, if need be, to get in touch with Luther and Melanchthon to silence Geneva.

49. G. H. Williams, The Radical Reformation (Philadelphia, Pa., 1962), p. 598.

50. Carlo Ginzburg, Il Nicodemismo: Simulazione e dissimulazione religiosa nell'Europa del '500 (Turin, 1970), pp. xiv, xvi, 154. Cf. Welti, Kleine Geschichte, pp. 50, 98.

51. Pierre Fraenkel, "Bucer's Memorandum of 1541 and a 'Lettra nicodemitica' of Capito's," Bibliothèque d'Humanisme et Renaissance 36 (1974): 575-87; Rott/Millet, "Miettes Historiques Strasbourgeoises," p. 271.

Calvin's sharp reaction is quite understandable in light of the fact that the sensitive point of his absence from the front line as a refugee is called into question. Yet at the same time, as commander-in-chief behind the front, he must keep the troops on the offensive. The impression he creates that the Nicodemists are uninterested in so-called "organized" religion is sheer propaganda. Later, but only after Fumée's forecast had become all too true, and the evangelical movement had met *ruina* under the pressures of the rising tide of the Counter-Reformation, the shift toward spiritualism occurs which Williams and Ginzburg see as its roots. When Calvin, some twenty years later, writes his *Response à un certain holandois* (1546) — successfully identified by George Williams as that enthusiastic follower of Sebastian Franck, Dick Volckertszoon Coornhert — Nicodemism has become that kind of ecumenism which pleads for a "Christianity above confessional diversity" and which relativizes or even dispenses with the visible church, its orders and sacraments.[52] In his creed, Fumée was explicitly a Protestant, and in his sense of priority of charity before faith he stands with Bucer and his colleagues. Yet in his rejection of vituperative and inflammatory attacks in confessional debate and in his insistence on the global Church of Love — which underlies his defense of the invocation of the saints — there are clear lines pointing to that development within the third Reformation which we may best designate as "irenicism."[53] As anti-institutional ecumenism, this is still a force today.

Turning back once more to the situation in the 1540s, Calvin had to respond sharply for personal and programmatic reasons. Eire misinterprets Calvin's silence on the exact identity of his Nicodemite adversaries. Refuting Ginzburg, he holds that Calvin is so given to attacking persons by name that, if there had been an "organized group" with a definite theology, Calvin would have made that explicit.[54] Whereas Eire justly criticizes Ginzburg for assuming a theory which precedes practice, here he himself has lost sight of the historical realities. The Fumée case shows why Calvin could not possibly attack such a person by name. Under daily threat of exposure, Fumée had to write under the pseudonym of Capnius. The one occasion on which Calvin broke the seal of silence was in the horrible case of Michael Servetus; but then, Calvin no longer counted him as a member of the true church. In short, the demarcation

52. Williams, *Radical Reformation*, p. 775.

53. See G. H. M. Posthumus Meyjes, "Jean Hotman's *Syllabus* of Eirenical Literature," in Derek Baker (ed.), *Reform and Reformation: England and the Continent, c. 1500–c. 1700* (Oxford, 1979), pp. 175-93; 179-80.

54. Eire, "Calvin and Nicodemism," p. 67.

line does not run, as Calvin had put it, between the courageous confessor and the dissimulating coward; rather, the alternatives were the *courage to flee,* and become a refugee for the cause of faith, or the *courage to be,* to stay and endure the daily threat of prison and fire.[55]

Fumée's solution, as he so clearly saw, could only remain viable for a limited period of time — an interim, provided relief came soon. The success of the Counter-Reformation in France forced the steadfast soldiers of faith who, like the Nicodemus of the gospel, fought night battles under the cloak of darkness, to embrace a creed of humanity and its divine rights independent of structures, whether of a church state or a state church.

In this new form, the third Reformation was to have a profound impact, even though it would deviate from the vision of its main architect, John Calvin.

VI. Luther: The Power of Prophecy

Luther is not the father, but neither is he the son, of a single movement. He can — and should — be described as Augustinian, nominalist, humanist and biblical scholar. But all of this would be to no avail if the core of his being is overlooked: he is Luther the Apocalyptic. From the year 1519 onward, he unquestionably understands himself as the forerunner of the coming great Reformation of God. As a Doctor of Holy

---

55. As an eminent example of the power of narrative history in the service of historical analysis, Geoffrey Elton wrote one of his finest vignettes "Persecution and Toleration in the English Reformation," *Studies in Church History* 21 (1984): 163-87. Though the issue of Nicodemism as such is not treated, the case of John Fox against Thomas More serves to gainsay the assumption that toleration is the child of tired scepticism when, all passions spent, the sober shores of the eighteenth century have been reached. Elton disproves the contention that "only the gradual evaporation of such passions produced a weariness with religious strife which made the return of mutual sufferance to early humanism à la More possible." "Persecution and Toleration," p. 163.

This thesis is not only unfounded because of More's explicit approval of and active support for persecution; more importantly, it is not "weariness" and tired scepticism which lead to the ideal of toleration. Himself a victim of persecution, John Fox is shown to be an advocate of toleration on the basis of his personal experience. "In a very real sense, he knew what he was talking about. Thus one result of the history of religious strife was that people came to experience persecution in reality: it jumped off the page into their lives." "Persecution and Toleration," p. 179. Exactly the same transition from the experience of persecution to the defense of toleration marks the history of the "forgotten" Calvinists.

Scripture, he must instruct the faithful by reopening the treasures of the gospel; as a pastor, he is responsible for gathering the congregation of the faithful "in these last days."[56]

Though widely accepted, this recovery of the "eschatological reformer" has evoked two substantial critical reactions which seem to neutralize each other. The first argues that this apocalyptic reinterpretation of Luther is too comprehensive; the second, that this interpretation is too limited and should be extended beyond Luther to the early leaders of the City Reformation generally. The first critique has been raised by the Hamburg Luther scholar Bernhard Lohse; the second by the Göttingen church historian, Bernd Moeller. Lohse takes issue with the apocalyptic interpretation of the young Luther, for which he finds no evidence; where there is unmistakable evidence, he regards its interpretation as overstretched. Lohse is prepared to admit that Luther regards the Reformation "ultimately" as the work of God, but as he sees it this is from beginning to end for Luther *an historical, not an eschatological event.*[57]

This is not the place to debate the interpretation of single texts. As I see it, Lohse misunderstands the significance of crucial terms, such as the "interim" before the "Day of the Lord'; he renders Christ's *Zukunft* as "future" instead of *Ankunft,* which means the "advent" of Christ.[58] The basic issue is that Lohse feels that he has to opt for an historical *or* for an eschatological interpretation of Luther's understanding of Reformation. It is precisely Luther's point, however, that these last days have already started, and that therefore the "last things" have commenced *in* our historical time, so that the eschatological clock has started to tick:

56. Heiko A. Oberman, "Martin Luther — Forerunner of the Reformation," in *The Reformation: Roots and Ramifications* (Edinburgh, 1994), pp. 21-52. The extent to which this shaped Luther's development and thoughts from beginning to end is spelled out in H. A. Oberman, *Luther: Mensch zwischen Gott und Teufel* (Berlin, 1982; 1985[3]); Engl. *Luther: Man Between God and the Devil* (New Haven, 1989).

57. "Vielmehr muß es u.E. dabei bleiben, daß Luther zwar die Reformation stets letztlich als Gottes Werk ansieht, daß sie für ihn jedoch auch in der Frühzeit ein innergeschichtlicher, nicht ein endzeitlicher Vorgang ist." Bernhard Lohse, "Luthers Selbsteinschätzung," in Peter Manns (ed.), *Martin Luther: Reformator und Vater im Glauben: Referate aus der Vortragsreihe des Instituts für Europäische Geschichte Mainz* (Stuttgart, 1985), pp. 118-33; 122; with pp. 131-32, esp. p. 132, n. 22.

58. Lohse, "Luthers Selbsteinschätzung," p. 130, nn. 6, 13, 16. The parallel between the use of "interim" at pp. 130, n. 13 and 131, n. 22 is overlooked. To translate "interim" by "vorläufig" in the sentence "una interim Consolatio tua erit futuri dies" ("Betont wird viel mehr der zunächst vorläufige Trost," "Luthers Selbststeinschäzung," p. 133, n. 3]) is to negate Luther's confident faith and *only* hope during the interim before the imminent end; as Luther's Reformation, the interim itself is *"vor-läufig"!* See further WA 40 I.367.13-15; 372.18-32; 581.23-25.

"demoliri coepimus Antichristi regnum."[59] Among a number of other things, this means that Luther, in contrast with the Nicodemite Fumée, does not regard the persecutions as a horrid sign of impending *ruina*, but as the hopeful sign of the recovery of the gospel, since the devil is bound to assail the true gospel and in these last days cannot but persecute its adherents: "Sentit enim Satan potentiam et fructus. . . ."[60] Luther's sense of time is in keeping with Revelation 20:3, and with St. Augustine's interpretation of the last phase of the Thousand Years of history, when — before the coming of the great Reformation — the devil will be loosed for a short time. When the first two martyrs of the Reformation are burned in Brussels in 1523, Luther is not surprised; instead, he is sad-dened that it is not granted him to sacrifice his own life in order to meet the onslaught of Satan.

From the opposite perspective, Bernd Moeller's criticism appears in an interesting article on the content of preaching in the cities in the early Reformation. He draws on some thirty-two so-called *Predigtsum-marien* between 1522 and 1529 to show that in the towns throughout Germany a unified interpretation of the gospel was proclaimed. Moeller documents his findings with references but without quotations, and pro-tects himself with the cautious provisos that these *Predigtsummarien* "leave the impression" that across Germany "more or less the same was preached." One foremost characteristic, Moeller notes, is eschatological urgency: the Kingdom of God has drawn near, and the present is threat-ened by the antichrist. There is no doubt that Luther's eschatological message was "received" in a wide variety of ways, and well beyond the year 1525.[61] Though I do not dare to go as far as Moeller by claiming

59. WA 40 I.583.29. Commentary on Gal. 4:6; 1531/35.
60. Commentary on Gal. 3:13; 1531/35; WA 40 I.444.28-29.
61. Bernd Moeller, "Was wurde in der Frühzeit der Reformation in den deut-schen Städten gepredigt?" *Archiv für Reformationsgeschichte* 75 (1984): 176-93; 184, 193. Before we lose ourselves in "apocalyptic" vagaries, however, the different types of eschatological expectation in early modern times should first be established. One of the best-known forms was the widespread expectation of cosmic upheaval. From the Tübingen astronomer Johannes Stöffler to the Nuremberg painter Albrecht Dürer the end of the world was calculated to occur sometime between 1524 and 1526. Present research indicates that this upheaval was frequently associated with the inter-vention of the antichrist. Gustav Hellmann, *Aus der Blütezeit der Astrometeorologie: Johannes Stöfflers Prognose für das Jahr 1524* (Berlin, 1914), pp. 5-67; Lynn Thorn-dike, *A History of Magic and Experimental Science*, 5 (New York, 1941), 178-233; Dietrich Kurze, *Johannes Lichtenberger: Eine Studie zur Geschichte der Prophetie und Astrologie* (Lübeck, 1960); Paola Zambelli, "Fine del Mondo o inizio della Propa-ganda?" in *Scienze Credenze occulte Livelli di Cultura* (Florence, 1980), pp. 291-368; 300. This "astrological" eschatology can be used just as well as a weapon *against* the

that Luther — on the basis of *this* evidence — can be claimed to be a "figure of world history," whatever that may mean, the implications of his apocalyptic view are far-reaching.[62]

Once it is clear, however, that Luther is to be regarded as the apocalyptic prophet, a number of conclusions can be drawn: in the first place, the understandable scepticism of the social historian that under the prophet's cloak the politician is hidden, and that by means of the gospel social control is exercised, is groundless. Luther does not exploit sensitivities concerning usury, tithes, clerical immunities, and clerical indiscipline: all these are rather signs of the end of time and the gruesome extent of the power of the antichrist.

Furthermore, far from being one of the calculating *politiques*, the apocalyptic prophet is so much convinced that only the elect will hear his voice that he can concentrate on the content of his gospel, without ulterior motives. The battle cry of *sola Scriptura*, which in the City Reformation came to mean the replacement of Canon Law by Biblical Law, meant for Luther the preaching of the gospel irrespective of political opportunism. As he put it, "This is the time when we have to be prepared to live dangerously."[63] The true Christian should not only be willing to

---

Reformation, and is structurally independent of Reformation theology. Cf. Max Steinmetz, "Johann Virdung von Haßfurt: Sein Leben und seine astrologischen Flugschriften," in H.-J. Koehler (ed.), *Flugschriften als Massenmedium der Reformationszeit*, Spätmittelalter und Frühe Neuzeit: Tübinger Beiträge zur Geschichtsforschung 13 (Stuttgart, 1981), pp. 353-72. Equally, it has been used *against* Luther to "unmask" him as the expected antichrist. Though not convinced that the "forecasts" can properly be divided into "consolation literature" and "apocalyptic warnings" since I regard their ultimate purpose precisely as consolation by placing the evils of the time on the divine timetable, Paola Zambelli has noted the need to develop typologies in order to distinguish varieties of apocalyptic expectation:

> È grosso modo possibile indicare una prevalenza di pronostici consolatori fra gli scrittori che restano fedeli al papato, e al contrario una inclinazione apocalittica fra quelli filo-luterani. "Fine del Mondo," p. 300.

62. Moeller finds in the *Summarien* such a far-reaching consensus with Luther that he speaks of a "lutherische Engführung" which in turn made "den Theologen Martin Luther zu einer Figur der Weltgeschichte." "Was wurde . . . gepredigt?", p. 193.

63. Oberman, "Forerunner of the Reformation," pp. 48-51. At this point Moeller inserts a surprising aside: "Heiko Obermans These, die eschatologische Orientierung unterscheide Luther von der übrigen Reformation, läßt sich anhand unserer Texte und also für die Frühzeit nicht verifizieren." This statement is all the more surprising when we learn that Moeller wishes to see his interpretation of the "unified Reformation message" confined to the period up to 1525; in his documentation no reason for reducing the span from 1522-1529 to 1522-1525 is adduced. I have been

endure persecution, but regard it as the sign of the extent to which we irritate Satan. For this reason, Luther criticized Melanchthon when the latter, during the Augsburg Diet in 1530, was prepared to enter into negotiations to gain political concessions in exchange for a less offensive formulation of the Protestant creed.

It is again the apocalyptic dimension which allows Luther to interpret the doctrine of justification by faith alone in a highly risky fashion, sacrificing the important impetus of reward for moral rearmament. And finally, once this apocalyptic stance is clearly seen, we can measure the distance which separates Martin Luther from a Nicodemite like Antoine Fumée. Though Luther's answer to Calvin has not been preserved, it is quite clear what he could and must have responded to Calvin's earnest question. After all, Fumée the Nicodemite[64] had become the most authentic *politique* of the century in protesting against all forms of sharp controversy, in the hope to avoid *ruina,* by courageously persevering with reform from within.

VII. Conclusion

In trying to fathom the complex question of the impact of the Reformation, we must distinguish between the first, the second, and the third "Reformation," to ensure that our conclusions have the necessary precision.

First, as the history of Christianity shows, apocalyptic moods are not continuous but come in waves — at the time of St. Paul, St. John on Patmos, the churches under Roman persecution, or during the crisis of the Western schism. Thus also the apocalyptic climate which allowed Luther to speak and be heard passed away, re-emerging during the Thirty

---

concerned to show that Luther, in the name of a whole series of city preachers, insisted on the introduction of visitations, in complete agreement with Melanchthon. But whereas the latter expected the visitations to establish peace and good order, and ultimately to lead to reconciliation with the papacy, Luther never left any doubt that the Reformation could not be introduced by visitations but only through an act of God announcing the end of the throes of this world. Melanchthon was supported in his view by such leaders of the urban Reformation as Bucer, Zwingli, and to a certain extent also Calvin. By his valuable discovery of the genre of *Predigtsummarien,* Moeller has been able to convey the impact of Luther's eschatological theology, which was not to become characteristic of the urban Reformation; the apocalyptic vision should be seen as one of the hallmarks of the first Reformation.

64. *Corpus Reformatorum* 12 (Halle a.d. Saale, 1844), 7.

Years' War and reappearing during successive crises ever since. In such times, the word of Luther is and will be heard afresh, and in this sense we can speak of the lasting impact of Luther. But also, Luther's single-minded, noncalculating investigation of the Scriptures would allow his voice to break through the cultural accretions to the gospel, even when modern findings differ from his.

Insofar as Luther was an active agent in the introduction of visitations, we can indeed speak of "failure," albeit not on the basis of the moral deficiencies reported by the visitation records — proof of moral amelioration is not to be expected there, since the sources are intent on looking for deviation and depravity. But we may speak of failure in so far as Luther expected from the visitations *Besserung,* a limitation of the greed of the ruling elite, which reached out to seize church goods. For Luther, the purpose of the visitations was not only to secure the teaching of Christian basics, but also to make sure that the secularization of the church possessions would furnish ministers' salaries and the founding of good schools.

Luther had counted on another failure: namely, that the gospel would not be victorious in Germany and hence would move elsewhere, like a *Platzregen* — a rainstorm. And finally, regarding the *Fürstenreformation,* whatever our critique may be concerning the development of the *Landesfürst* into the *Notbischof,* and of the prince into the leader of the territorial church in his own territory, the Inquisition and the Index were unable to silence the voice of the apocalyptic prophet. Marjorie Reeves once observed that "men's dreams are as much a part of history as their deeds."[65] With Luther, the prophetic dreams themselves made history.

Second, as far as the significance of the second Reformation — the City Reformation — is concerned, we can be brief. It is a crucial *intermezzo* — an *intermezzo* insofar as it is limited to some twenty-five years until the free cities, which had already lost their economic power on the eve of the Reformation, lost also the last chance for spiritual revitalization, when imperial troops marched in and enforced the Interim, in 1548 and 1549.

At the same time, it is *crucial,* for the *intermezzo* provided the Reformation with more than printing presses and Latin schools, the pulpits, and the learning to understand, interpret, and multiply Luther's voice; it also allowed the political space to experiment with what Bullinger called *enderung,* which encompasses the horizontal dimensions of the Reformation message. Within the city walls, the "semi-monastic" tenets in late

---

65. Marjorie Reeves, *The Influence of Prophecy in the Later Middle Ages: A Study in Joachimism* (Oxford, 1969), p. 504.

medieval lay piety could be translated into laws and a lifestyle which would be its — ambiguous — legacy to the third Reformation.

Third, the impact of the third Reformation — the Reformation of the Refugees — is to be traced along two lines of development. The first is the victorious path of the Revolution of the Saints, who erected and extended the Kingdom of Christ wherever they could seize power and, where such seizure proved impossible, at least survived independently of town council and *Landesfürst,* as congregations under the cross. This Reformation failed to flower in the key territories of France and Italy, but was able to establish itself in many other areas north of the Alps, in Great Britain, and beyond.

The second line of impact has its inauspicious beginnings with the Nicodemites of the 1540s in Paris. Wherever the victory of the Revolution of the Saints collapsed, whether in the Netherlands, Scotland, England, or the New World, the former Nicodemites could provide a new platform of unchurched ethics and voluntary societies — perhaps the stepchild of the Puritan ethic, but pervasive and adaptable to a new civic religion, which would make it a natural ally for socialism and ecumenism.

The subtitle of this paper is "Problems and Perspectives". The formidable task of measuring the impact of an ideology — in this case of a Christian reform movement — is a problem of perspective. John A. Tedeschi has characterized the impact of the Index and the "devastating effects" of Roman censorship in these words: "With the outlawing of Boccaccio and Machiavelli, the Renaissance had ended in Italy."[66] A combination of Index, Inquisition, and infantry spelled the end of the Reformation in Italy, France, and the Habsburg territories. However, we would not dedicate our professional lives to the study of the Middle Ages, the Renaissance, and the Reformation if we held that in the case of Renaissance humanism, of Catholic reform, or of the Reformation, the "end" is to be identified with ultimate failure. It may have been the end of the *erga,* the amazing events of the fifteenth and sixteenth centuries, but that does not spell the end of the *genomena ex anthrōpon* — of what was unleashed by these events, their outcome, and that heritage which Herodotus saw as being shaped by Greeks and barbarians alike.

66. John A. Tedeschi, "Florentine Documents for a History of the 'Index of Prohibited Books'," in Anthony Molho and John A. Tedeschi (eds.), *Renaissance Studies in Honor of Hans Baron* (Dekalb, Ill., 1971), pp. 579-86.

Die Gelehrten die Verkehrten: Popular Response to Learned Culture in the Renaissance and Reformation

Isti sunt subversores pietatis, derisores simplicium, decep-
tores vulgi.

From a letter by Geert Groote
to William of Salvarvilla, early 1379

. . . du soltt inen nit glauben, so sie sprechen:
ja, die bawrenn verstehen die sach nit.
Meint ich doch, weil die verkerrten gelerrten die Schrifft
verstünden, sie würden am ersten Selig.

Eynn Dialogus oder gesprech . . .
(Erfurt, 1523), fol. a ii b; b ii a

"The Reformation was made not just by many individuals holding a common belief, but by collective forms of behavior."[1] I regard this statement by Bob Scribner as a fine formulation of the advance made

1. Robert Scribner, "Is There a Social History of the Reformation?" *Social History* 4 (1976): 483-505; 501.

"*Die Gelehrten die Verkehrten*: Popular Response to Learned Culture in the Renaissance and Reformation," in *Religion and Culture in the Renaissance and Reformation*, ed. Steven Ozment, Sixteenth Century Essays and Studies 11 (Kirksville, Mo., 1989), 43-62.

in Reformation scholarship over the last twenty years. The formulation would be cleaner and less subject to misinterpretation if it had said explicitly that the Reformation was made not just by many individuals holding a common belief, but *also* by collective forms of behavior. The finely honed balance and true duality in this vision is a high ideal,[2] behind which actual scholarship in the field of sixteenth-century studies has fallen consistently.

I. *Die Gelehrten die Verkehrten*

Admittedly, the theory of economic causation is no longer held up as the sole factor determining communal behavior, except in Western — especially West German — caricatures of the Marxist contribution to the history of the transition from a late feudal to an early capitalist society. But the primacy of social history over intellectual history is the seldom voiced, yet virulent presupposition of much of the best work done in our field today. Insofar as the emphasis on communal groups still tolerates the study of individual agents, their intellectual or, as the case may be, religious motivation is all too often privatized. The widespread but equally anachronistic use of the loaded French word *politiques* tends to suggest that such private convictions did not allow these agents to escape from the "scientific law" that history is the story of the struggle for gain: for prowess, power, and prosperity.

Against this stubborn tendency to slight the evidence that we are dealing with an epoch when reform always comprised individual *and* communal, religious *and* social renewal, the dialectic between social and

---

2. A significant theoretical clarification is provided by the Chicago School of Sociology (Interactionism) as interpreted by Ronald F. E. Weissman: "The primary unit of analysis is the social relation linking individuals, for it is individual interaction that mediates or underlies what is perceived as group interaction or group identity." Here quoted from "Reconstructing Renaissance Sociology: The 'Chicago School' and the Study of Renaissance Society," in *Persons in Groups: Social Behavior as Identity Formation in Medieval and Renaissance Europe,* ed. R. Trexler (Binghamton, N.Y.: Medieval & Renaissance Texts and Studies, 1985), pp. 39-46; 41. Weissman's point of departure applies obviously to the Middle Ages and the Reformation as well: "What Renaissance sociology requires is a more pragmatic, Nominalist approach to the study of society." "Reconstructing Renaissance Sociology," 40. The same balance can be noted in the work of the Sorbonne medievalist Bernard Guenée, "directeur d'Études" at the E.P.H.E. For him, the analysis of structures is "irremplaçable": "Elle éclairat le passé d'une merveilleuse cohérence. Mais elle le rendait trop simple. . . . L'étude des structures me semblait aussi donner une place trop large à la nécessité." *Entre l'Église et l'État* (Paris: Galimard, 1987), pp. 13-14.

intellectual history offers the integrating analytical principle which enables us to rise above both determinism and elitism — to use the two terms which the opposing parties prefer in describing each other.

The most concise expression of both the division of labor and the common goal is, it seems to me, as follows: *conditions of life* (I take this to comprise *Strukturgeschichte* and *Ereignisgeschichte*, i.e., economic, demographic, geographic, dietary data in the narrowest sense of the word, as well as crises, such as famine, war, and social disorder) *only become historical factors shaping a communal mentality when recorded, evaluated, and advanced by intellectual leaders.* This formulation has a double critical edge: first, it insists, against traditional intellectual history, that ideas are never sufficiently grasped when the study of treatises and documents is not extended to the analysis of their social matrix and their societal impact. The edge against traditional social history is that the study of matrix and impact cannot be short-circuited, but must bow to the iron rule of the sequence of conditions–program–impact.[3] This sequence requires that central attention be given to intellectual history in order to understand both spokesmen and leaders.

Thomas A. Brady, Jr., concluded his fine essay on the state and task of social history in Steven Ozment's *Reformation Europe: A Guide to Research* with a programmatic thesis: "Neither confessional nor racial/cultural explanations of the place of the Reformation in European history have survived the fire of historical criticism. Perhaps the social-historical explanation will."[4] I do not see how this can or should come about unless social history is prepared to respect and pursue this three-stage procedure: conditions–program–impact.

If the foregoing might still seem to be an exercise in abstractions, we now turn to an area closer to our daily battleground. The popular broadsides against so-called "Whig history" tend to slay both the deserving and the undeserving. They tend to separate — indeed, divorce — literate, elite culture from an illiterate, popular culture. Thus, I understand Rodney Hilton's disdain for the earlier interpreters of "the English peasantry in the later Middle Ages":[5] their fatal error appears to be that

3. Robert M. Kingdon, *Geneva and the Coming of the Wars of Religion in France: 1555-1563* (Geneva: Droz, 1956), p. 128, illuminated this interaction with the felicitous phrase "social smoldering" when he expressed his interest "in the process by which ideological leadership may assist social smoldering toward explosion."
4. Steven Ozment (ed.), *Reformation Europe: A Guide to Research* (St. Louis: Center for Reformation Research, 1982), pp. 161-81; 176.
5. R. H. Hilton, *The English Peasantry in the Later Middle Ages* (Oxford: Clarendon, 1975), pp. 9ff.

they relied on the witness of spokesmen for the upper levels of society. And thus I understand the hesitation of Bob Scribner to accept my analysis of the German Peasants' War as "basically a religious movement" because it drew on the evidence of eyewitnesses belonging to the cultured elite.[6] This also, I surmise, is a basic factor in the warm reception which Carlo Ginzburg received for *The Cheese and the Worms*. After all, he presents the not-so-simple miller, Menocchio (1532–c. 1600), as the nonelite representative of a silent majority and recipient of an "ancient oral tradition," yet sufficiently literate to allow Ginzburg to explore an otherwise unknown "substratum of peasant beliefs."[7]

By insisting on the crucial role of the so-called "cultured elite," we do not underrate the "common man"[8] or reduce him to mere passivity in the communication process. A trend in this direction is not to be ignored. A case in point is the important and stimulating monograph of Bob Scribner, *For the Sake of Simple Folk*. His point of departure is sound and convincing: "Printing was, in fact, an addition to, not a replacement for, oral communication."[9] But in concentrating on the pamphlet literature as "propaganda," Scribner is increasingly more fascinated by the pamphlet as the means to *shape* popular culture — and thus create a new "symbolic world" — than by the extent to which it *reflects* popular culture. Bernd Moeller's insistence on the primacy of the sermon over the pamphlet as decisive medium is, however justified, in this respect no real advance.[10]

I share Ginzburg's hypothesis of the two-way permeation of high and low culture, but regard his timetable for its termination (1525/35) and his assumption of an ensuing one-sided "indoctrination from above"

6. Heiko A. Oberman, *The Dawn of the Reformation* (Edinburgh: T. & T. Clark, 1986), pp. 155-78; 172. Cf. Robert Scribner, "Is There a Social History of the Reformation?" p. 494 n. 29.

7. Carlo Ginzburg, *The Cheese and the Worms: The Cosmos of a Sixteenth-Century Miller*, trans. John and Anne Tedeschi (Baltimore: Johns Hopkins University Press, 1980), pp. xxii, 20-21, 51, 59, 71.

8. See n. 15, below; cf. n. 26, below.

9. Robert Scribner, *For the Sake of Simple Folk: Popular Propaganda for the German Reformation* (Cambridge: Cambridge University Press, 1981), p. 2.

10. See Bernd Moeller's review in *Historische Zeitschrift* 237 (1983): 707-10. For the preceding stage in this discussion, see Robert Scribner, "How Many Could Read? Comments on Bernd Moeller's 'Stadt und Buch'," in *Stadtbürgertum und Adel in der Reformation: Studien zur Sozial-geschichte der Reformation in England und Deutschland*, ed. W. J. Mommsen et al. Veröffentlichungen des Deutschen Historischen Instituts London 5 (Stuttgart: Klett-Cotta, 1979), pp. 44-45.

as untenable.[11] Divested of modern sentiments, indoctrination has always been the goal of the pursuit of knowledge. Throughout the Middle Ages, "pure" research was just as far removed from the mind of the most abstract scholastic master as from the soul of the mystic most devoted to the *vita contemplativa*.

In the following, I will be concerned with how "learned culture," if considered as a separate universe of communication and in this sense as an elitist "textual community," could have such a popular impact that (as we all seem to agree) literacy developed and grew by leaps and bounds. In concentrating on one revealing and hitherto unexplored source, it is my intent to show that in the later Middle Ages, notwithstanding deep-rooted suspicion of scholars, scholarship, and scholarly institutions, an equally deep-rooted and socially broad-based confidence can be discerned — a confidence in true learning and in its crucial contribution to church and society.[12]

The title chosen for this section is one of the best-known slogans of sixteenth-century pamphlet literature. The phrase *Die Gelehrten die Verkehrten*[13] has the attraction of rhyme, just as easily memorable as *Affen* and *Pfaffen*. Both proved to be powerful weapons in the heyday of the spread of pamphlet literature in the service of the Reformation —

---

11. Cf. Ginzburg, *The Cheese and the Worms*, 126. "Thus there is a symptomatic value in a limited case such as Menocchio's. It forcefully poses a problem the significance of which is only now beginning to be recognized: that of the popular roots of a considerable part of high European culture, both medieval and post-medieval. Such figures as Rabelais and Breughel probably were not unusual exceptions. All the same, they closed an era characterized by hidden but fruitful exchanges, moving in both directions between high and popular cultures. The subsequent period was marked, instead, by an increasingly rigid distinction between the culture of the dominant classes and the artisan and peasant cultures, as well as by the indoctrination of the masses from above. We can place the break between these two periods in the second half of the sixteenth century, basically coinciding with the intensification of social differentiation under the impulse of the price revolution. But the decisive crisis had occurred a few decades earlier, with the Peasants' War and the reign of the Anabaptists in Münster."

12. This corresponds with the confidence of a reformer like Luther to collect "popular" aphorisms as nuggets of wisdom. See my article "Stadtreformation und Fürstenreformation," in *Humanismus und Reformation als kulturelle Kräfte in der deutschen Geschichte*, ed. Lewis W. Spitz (Berlin: de Gruyter, 1981), pp. 80-103; 81-82.

13. See Ernst Thiele (ed.), *Luthers Sprichwörtersammlung* (Weimar: H. Böhlaus Nachfolger, 1900), pp. 33-34. *Johann Kesslers Sabbata*, ed. Historischer Verein des Kantons St. Gallen (St. Gallen: Fehr'sche Buchhandlung, 1902), p. 537. E. Hampel, "Fischarts Anteil an dem Gedicht: 'Die Gelehrten — die Verkehrten'," in *Programm des Realgymnasiums zu Naumburg* (1903). Quoted by Otto Clemen, *Flugschriften aus den ersten Jahren der Reformation*, 4 vols. (Nieuwkoop: De Graaf, 1967; repr. of ed. Halle, 1907-1911), 1.48, n. 20.

broadly speaking, in the decade from 1515 through 1525. Afterward, this form of indoctrination tapered off noticeably, probably under the impact of the criminalization of what the authorities called the *schlechten Prediger,* who lost their livelihoods or lives in the aftermath of the peasants' revolt.[14]

This slogan, invented to discredit the proud claims of the "ivory tower," was put in the mouth of peasant and burgher in order to eradicate by ridicule the authority of the medieval doctors in general, but its sarcasm reached a notably shrill tone when pitched against the monks. They should have been responsible for the education of the masses, but, as Eberlin of Günzburg (†1533) put it: ". . . itel schul thandt halten sie dem schleckten volck für. . . . Es ist ein arm ding, das so grosse eslische unwissenheit regiert in den klösteren."[15] If one wishes to retain something of the original alliteration and sentiment, one should translate *Die Gelehrten die Verkehrten* as "those dangerous deviant doctors — they stray and 'stroy."[16]

Though we know far less than hitherto assumed about the social distribution of the readers of pamphlet literature and the number of re-editions, a conservative estimate of numbers sold — between 1501 and 1530 approximately ten million copies, or just under one copy per capita for the empire[17] — suffices to confirm the traditional German identification of the broadsheets as *Sturmtruppen der Reformation,* the avant-garde indoctrination of the populace with a new "symbolic world." And yet, there is another dimension: the pamphlets allow us glimpses at widely spread reform aspirations. By carefully listing the concatenation of arguments and

14. See the revealing record of the prosecution of "Peasant Preachers" drawn up by Justus Maurer, *Prediger im Bauernkrieg* (Stuttgart: Calwer Verlag, 1979), esp. pp. 247ff.

15. Johann Eberlin von Gunzburg, *XV. Bundsgenossen* s. l, s. a. (Basel, 1521), ed. Ludwig Enders (Halle a.S., 1896), *VI. Bundsgenoß,* 58; 60. It should be noted that Eberlin — just as Luther — used "common man," here and throughout, not for "poor people" (or "peasants"!), but for the *simplices,* the "uninformed" or, more often, the "ill-informed laity"! I am following his usage.

16. This critique is here not directed against the monastery as an institution, but against its deformation and devaluation: what "jetz kleine kind wissen, können alte männer in klösteren nit, so doch etwan [!] grosse kunst in der kutten was." *VI. Bundsgenoß,* 58; 60.

17. See the timeline suggested by Hans Joachim Köhler, "Erste Schritte zu einem Meinungsprofil der frühen Reformationszeit," in *Martin Luther: Probleme seiner Zeit,* ed. Volker Press and Dieter Stievermann (Stuttgart: Klett-Cotta, 1986), pp. 244-81; 270. Cf. Köhler, "Die Flugschriften: Versuch der Präzisierung eines geläufigen Begriffs," in *Festgabe für Ernst Walter Zeeden,* ed. Horst Rabe, Hansgeorg Molitor, and Hans-Christoph Rublack (Münster: Aschendorff, 1976), pp. 36-61; 43.

clusters of biblical quotations, one can observe that by the end of 1523 the pamphlets had succeeded in establishing a common market of *gravamina* through "swap and exchange" between locally and territorially active literary circles which apparently formed social networks as *sodalitates* in the cities and *confraternitates* around the monasteries. At the same time, the early pamphlets had an impact reaching far beyond these "textual communities"[18] because they not only conveyed but also confirmed what was alive and fermenting in a much broader illiterate social layer. Just like the sermons, the pamphlets created their own audience; but far more than the sermons, the pamphlets played to an already existing gallery. By focusing on the Modern Devotion as one vocal section in this gallery, it is possible to shed new light both on the movement itself and on popular aspirations on the eve of the Reformation.

II. The Program of the *Devotio Moderna*

When we now turn our attention to the Modern Devotion, we discover that its chief tenet is the pursuit of the true monastic vision of St. Bernard, St. Francis, and St. Bonaventura. Yet in a new "secular" key, its most revealing slogan is the loaded phrase "purus Christianus, verus monachus," reflected — I am convinced — in the telling adage of the early Erasmus, written at the time of his *Enchiridion* (1501): "monachatus non est pietas."[19] Its cutting programmatic edge is immediately evident when

18. Cf. the important extension of this term advocated by Brian Stock, *The Implications of Literacy: Written Language and Models of Interpretation in the Eleventh and Twelfth Centuries* (Princeton: Princeton University Press, 1983), pp. 9ff., 90-91, 405-6. A constitutive factor for each "textual community" is the search for legitimation of change (reform). With reference to the movements associated with the so-called "Peasants' War," this is highlighted in the theoretically significant article of Wilfried Schulze, "Soziale Bewegungen als Phänomen des 16. Jahrhunderts," in *Säkulare Aspekte der Reformationszeit,* ed. Heinz Angermeier (Munich: Oldenbourg, 1983), pp. 113-30; 129-30.

19. Desiderius Erasmus, *Opus Epistolarum*, ed. P. S. Allen, 12 vols. (Oxford: Clarendon, 1906-1958), 1.374.28 (nr. 164), quoted by Eugene F. Rice, Jr., *Saint Jerome in the Renaissance* (Baltimore: Johns Hopkins University Press, 1985), p. 133. The most revealing "Brethren statement" is the preceding clause: ". . . perinde quasi extra cucullum Christianismus non sit" (ll. 24-25). On this point I differ from the excellent biography of Erasmus by Cornelis Augustijn, *Erasmus von Rotterdam: Leben, Werk, Wirkung* (Munich: Beck, 1986) (Dutch original, Baarn, 1986), pp. 51-52: "Im Kreise der Devotio moderna . . . konnte man mir diesen Worten nichts anfangen."

By pursuing the "trail of St. Jerome," Eugene Rice noticed that Erasmus was

placed against the background of the claim that only the monastic vows are the sure road to the *vita perfecta,* or, when contrasted with the official teaching that the vows provide, "the monopoly on the perfect life."[20]

Even six hundred years after the founding of the Windesheim Congregation in 1387, one serious weakness in the presentation of the Modern Devotion still prevails: that the establishment of the Windesheim Congregation was an unfortunate deviation from the original vision of Geert Groote. But also in this clerical branch the view has never been questioned that the whole movement issuing from Geert Groote represents the *status medius* between the monastery and the world. Even in Gabriel Biel's *De Communi Vita* (c. 1480), Groote's insistence on the common life as the crucial alternative to the cloistered life is clearly articulated: "religion" should not be understood as "the monastic life," but as Christian faith![21] For all three branches — the Sisters, the Brethren, and the Canons Regular of the Windesheim congregation — the true Christian is the true monk: *purus Christianus, verus monachus.*

The most recent literature[22] shows that a major advance has been

---

"especially irritated by religious who claimed that Jerome had founded their order." *Saint Jerome,* p. 133. In Gabriel Biel's defense of the *Devotio Moderna* (c. 1470), we find the general critique of the proud appeal to founding father in his terse retort: we seek perfection "sub uno abbate Christo Jhesu. . . ." See my *Masters of the Reformation* (Cambridge: Cambridge University Press, 1981), p. 54. Some fifty years earlier, Dirk of Herxen (near Zwolle) explicitly rejected the claim of the Dominican Grabow that St. Jerome set the standard of the true monastic life. See Willem Lourdaux, "Dirk of Herxen's tract 'De Utilitate Monachorum': A Defence of the Lifestyle of the Brethren and Sisters of the Common Life," *Bijdragen: Tijdschrift voor filosofie en theologie* 33 (1972): 412-36. Yet, just as Erasmus held Jerome in the highest regard as biblical exegete, the Brethren were eager to associate their name with his: the House in Delft was called St. Hieronymusdal, and the Latin School in Utrecht was named after him.

20. See Kaspar Elm in the best available orientation about the present state of research, "Die Bruderschaft von Gemeinsamen Leben," *Ons Geestelijk Erf* 59 (1985): 470ff. In a more general sense, see W. Lourdaux, "De Broeders van het Gemene Leven," *Bijdragen: Tijdschrift voor filosofie en theologie* 33 (1972): 372-416; 397.

21. Cf. my discussion in *The Harvest of Medieval Theology: Gabriel Biel and Late Medieval Nominalism,* (Cambridge, Mass.: Harvard University Press, 1981³; 1963), pp. 14ff.; and in *Werden und Wertung der Reformation: Vom Wegestreit zum Glaubenskampf* (Tübingen: Mohr, 1980³; 1977¹), pp. 8-9; (English version, *Masters of the Reformation*).

22. Reaching from the congress volumes, *Moderne Devotie: Figuren en Facetten* (Nijmegen, 1984) and *Geert Grote en Moderne Devotie* (Nijmegen Congress, 1984), ed. J. Andriessen, P. Bange, and A. G. Weiler, *Ons Geestelijk Erf* 59 (1985): 113-505 (Nijmegen, 1985), to G. H. Gerrits's study of Gerard Zerbolt of Zutphen, *Inter Timorem et Spem: A Study of the Theological Thought of Gerard Zerbolt of Zutphen (1367-1398),* SMRT 37 (Leiden: Brill, 1986), and to the rich English anthology edited by John Van Engen, *Devotio Moderna. Basic Writings* (New York: Paulist Press,

made through the clarification of the legal status of the movement as *medius status* between the *saeculares saeculariter viventes* and the *status religiosorum*. This advance, however, has not yet been recognized as the breakthrough it really is. The Modern Devotion was apparently not just a local Dutch movement, but the tip of the iceberg of late medieval organized lay piety, reaching from communities of virgins and widows, and from *Hospitalbrüdern* and *Bußbrüdern* to the members of fraternities and confraternities. This *medius status* of lay religiosity was, in the words of Kaspar Elm, "für die Zeitgenossen (jedoch) mindestens so wichtig, wie das seit Jahrhunderten mir größerem Nachdruck erforschte Ordenswesen."[23]

For the first time, we start to get in our historical sights an initially loosely tied association of lay organizations which managed first to survive and then to gain in social status, notwithstanding the constant climate of suspicion and restraining tactics promoted by the established orders, particularly the Dominicans. The sharp accusation of heresy by Matthew Grabow, O.P., during the final days of the Council of Constance had the opposite effect when his defamation of *Devotio Moderna* was countered (3 April 1418) by no one less than the "Church Father of the later Middle Ages," Jean Gerson.[24] The charge that the Sisters and Brethren were really a cover organization for Beghards and Beguines helped instead to raise the latter's status.

Bernd Moeller, in his sketch of late medieval piety, concluded from the decrease in heresy cases during the fifteenth century that heresy itself apparently *(offenbar!)* disappeared "weil der Ausbruch aus dem kirchlichen System seine frühere Attraktion verloren hatte."[25] This conclusion is an optical illusion due to a too narrow theological understanding of both church and heresy. Suspicion of heresy is not directed at "Ausbruch" but at "Umbruch" — in the fourteenth as much as in the fifteenth century. The *Devotio Moderna*, speaking for a much broader movement of vol-

---

1988). For earlier literature, see W. Jappe Alberts, "Zur Historiographie der Devotio Moderna und ihrer Erforschung," *Westfälische Forschungen* 2 (1958): 51-67. For the history and impact of the Windesheim Congregation, see the preciously precise and encompassing three-volume work of J. G. R. Acquoy, *Het Klooster Windesheim en zijn Invloed* (Utrecht: Gebr. Van der Post, 1875-1880).

23. Kaspar Elm, "Die Bruderschaft von Gemeinsamen Leben," p. 476.

24. For Grabow's "conclusiones," see Jean Gerson, *Opera Omnia*, 5 vols., ed. Lud. Ellies Du Pin (Antwerp, 1706), cols. 470-74. Gerson's defense in Gerson, *Oeuvres*, ed. Palémon Glorieux, 10.70-72.

25. "Deutschland im Zeitalter der Reformation," in *Deutsche Geschichte*, ed. B. Moeller, M. Heckel, R. Vierhaus, and K. O. von Aretin, vol. 2: *Frühe Neuzeit* (Göttingen: Vandenhoeck & Ruprecht, 1985), p. 26.

untary lay associations, never intended to "break out of the church," but piously enlarged its boundaries by irreverently redefining its nucleus, the monastic life. Particularly the records of the Dutch Sisterhouses are replete with references to investigations and accusations by inquisitors who succeeded in forcing several communities to join the Franciscan Tertiaries; obviously their "irreverence" was interpreted as trespassing the critical borderline to heresy.

On the eve of the Reformation, the carriers of the New Devotion not only had achieved far more than a foothold in late medieval society, but also had learned to endure and counter the attacks of the monastic elite. To be fair, particularly the mendicants — often contrasted with the "good monks," the Carthusians — had been assiduously assailed. At the beginning stood the charge of Geert Groote, early in 1379, ranking them with the Pharisees and the lawyers: "Ubi pietas, ubi religio?" Groote had not hesitated to throw a threefold curse on the mendicants' preaching as the source of all heresy and as the poison killing piety in all of Europe: "terrena, animalis, diabolica." And again, it had been Groote who had not minced words, speaking for the sake of common man: "Isti sunt subversores pietatis, derisores simplicium, deceptores vulgi."[26] Here we find nothing less than the Latin version of the accusation that "they stray and 'stroy." The slogan *Die Gelehrten die Verkehrten* is not a novel weapon in the arsenal of Reformation propaganda, but is the exact formulation of a conviction hardened by a century of repression and cow(l)towing. Once again, we are alerted to the fact that the pamphlets of the sixteenth century not only shaped but also reflected what might be called public opinion.[27]

---

26. Letter to his Parisian friend and mentor William of Salvarvilla, dated early 1379. *Gerardi Magni Epistolae,* ed. Willelmus Mulder (Antwerp: Sumptibus Societatis Editricis Neerlandiae, 1933), p. 27. "Hic pharizei, iuriste et religiosi . . . ; hic sunt qui suas iusticias faciunt, Dei iustitiam ignorantes" (p. 28). "Deus, Deus, quale mixtum ex cortice et nuce scripturarum et ex cantu Syrenarum suboritur! Hinc perfidie contra Deum et veritatem, omnem Europeam capientes, hinc hereses, hinc philosophia, nam philosophia, secundum Jeronimum [PL 22.667] mater et nutrix heresium" (pp. 29-30). Here we touch on the heart of Groote's "anti-intellectualism": the simple folk cannot understand you — in the ẽnd, you preach only to the clergy; "Quid restat ut solis clericis predicetis . . ." and few among them! (p. 32).

27. See my article "Zwischen Agitation und Reformation: Die Flugschriften als 'Judenspiegel'," in *Flugschriften als Massenmedium der Reformationszeit,* ed. Hans-Joachim Köhler (Stuttgart: Klett-Cotta, 1981), pp. 269-89; 287-88. Cf. "Stadtreformation und Fürstenreformation," in *Humanismus und Reformation als kulturelle Kräfte in der deutschen Geschichte,* ed. Lewis W. Spitz (Berlin: de Gruyter, 1981), pp. 80-103; 81-82.

III. The Pursuit of Holiness

It is still widely assumed that the Modern Devotion was not only an anti-scholastic but also an anti-intellectual movement.[28] Upon closer scrutiny, this traditional evaluation strongly relies on trends in fourteenth-century sources; that is, on the seminal works of the founding fathers Geert Groote (†1384), Gerard Zerbolt of Zutphen (†1398), and Florens Radewijns (†1400). And, admittedly, there is some justification for the characterization of any movement in terms of its *initia*. Yet, by the time the *Devotio Moderna* is confronted with Renaissance and Reformation, it is some 130 to 150 years after the founding period.

Hence we have to ask a new question: What characteristics survived or surfaced in the latter part of the fifteenth century? By that time, the third — clerical — branch of the movement had reached not only Paris in the West, but also Württemberg in the South, where Gabriel Biel (†1495) and Wendelin Steinbach (†1519) were outspoken representatives of the movement, both of them university professors, both of them without a trace of anti-intellectualism. Insofar as it can be argued that the truly popular impact of the movement can be seen in the lay branches of the Brethren and Sisters of the Common Life, we must turn to the widely dispersed writings of later generations to perceive the shift in self-understanding visible in the anecdotes *(exempla)* they used to memorialize the founding fathers in chronicles best subsumed under the general title *De viris illustribus*.

After the middle of the fifteenth century, we notice a true eruption of such pious portrayals,[29] which as a genre continued the original *rapiaria* for meditation.[30] They are inspiring recollections from "our

28. An exception has to be made for the corrections to R. R. Post, *Modern Devotion,* offered by G. Codina Mir, *Aux sources de la pédagogie des Jésuites: Le "modus Parisiensis"* (Rome: Institutum Historicum Societatis Iesu, 1968), esp. pp. 160ff.; and W. Lourdaux, "De Broeders van het Gemene Leven," p. 397.

29. See, e.g., the Chronicle of Mount St. Agnes, written by Thomas à Kempis (†1471) but continued through 1477. Available in English: *The Chronicle of the Canons Regular of Mount St. Agnes Written by Thomas à Kempis,* trans. J. P. Arthur (London: Kegan Paul, Trench, Trübner, 1906). Cf. Hubert Jedin's perceptive article "Thomas von Kempen als Biograph und Chronist," in his volume of collected essays, *Kirche des Glaubens, Kirche der Geschichte,* 2 vols. (Freiburg: Herder, 1966), 1.49-58. In the combination of three characteristic elements — *conversio, humilitas,* and *apostolatus* — Jedin finds the justification "die Devotio Moderna als Vorstufe der Katholischen Reform anzugliedern . . ." (p. 58).

30. Petronella Bange, *Spiegels der Christenen: Zelfreflectie en ideaaldbeeld in laatmiddeleeuwse moralistisch-didactische traktaten* (Nijmegen, 1986), has delineated an important second devout didactic genre, also feeding into the *Collationes.* For her cautious analysis of the readership of these *Specula,* see pp. 229-32 in her book.

own" religious tradition, something like a *Legenda Aurea* of the Modern Devotion. One such excerpt from a devotional *vitae fratrum*, to be dated about 1480 and compiled by an anonymous author, clearly belongs to the orbit of Deventer and Zwolle. It deserves our particular attention because of the peculiar way in which it touches upon our quest for the popular impact of learning. The title is really a brief table of contents: "Here follow some excerpts from the lives of our Founding Fathers, offering proper material for our *collationes* at noon and at eventide."[31]

The text is unique in that it combines the typical theme of the *devoti*, namely, the pursuit of holiness — or in their own terminology, the *reformacio virium*[32] — with virtuous scenes from the lives of the founding

---

31. *Hic aliqua sequuntur ex vitis fratrum nostrorum prout materie convenit collationum nostrarum meridianarum et serotinarum,* Museum Wasserburg, Anholt (Cleve). In the following pages, references in my text point to the running line numbers of the critical edition prepared by John Van Engen in *Revue Bénédictine* 98 (1988): 178-217. A Dutch version, including many of the same portrayals, is to be found in the Frensweger manuscript of 1494 (UB Utrecht, Hs. 8 L. 16), edited by W. J. Alberts and A. L. Hulshoff (Groningen, 1958). I shall refer to it as *FH*. *Hic aliqua sequuntur* was drawn up on the basis of two earlier writings: Rudolph Dier of Muiden, *Scriptum de Magistro Gerardo Grote, Domino Florencia et aliis devotis Fratribus,* published by G. Dumbar in *Reipublicae Daventriensis ab Actis Analecta, seu vetera aliquot scripta inedita,* 3 vols. Deventer, 1719-1725, 2.1-87) and the *Continuatio Scripti Rudolphi Dier de Muiden* by Petrus Hoorn (in Dumbar, *Analecta* 1.88ff.).

32. In the context of this present investigation, we cannot develop the complex theme of the characteristics of the "devotion" typical to this pursuit of holiness. Striking is the major role of *timor Dei,* in the Dutch chronicles usually rendered not as "vrees" but as "anxt" or "angstlichheyt," a mood probably best captured as "pious anxiety." According to both biographers of Geert Groote — Thomas à Kempis (†1471) and Petrus Hoorn (†1479) — this was already so dominant with the founder, Groote, that he often abstained from communion: ". . . sumeret corpus Salvatoris, quatenus saepe eum spiritualiter manducaret quem sacramentaliter sumere frequentius formidabat." Petrus Hoorn, *De vita magistri Gerardi Magni,* ed. W. J. Kühler, *Nederlands Archief voor Kerkgeschiedenis* 6 (1909): 325-70; 359. See Thomas à Kempis, *Vita Gerardi Magni,* ed. M. I. Pohl, in *Opera Omnia* 7 (Freiburg i.B., 1922), 31-115; 63-64. Cf. *Scripture,* ed. G. Dumbar, *Analecta* 1 (Deventer, 1719), 4. Stephanus Axters, *Geschiedenis van de Vroomheid in de Nederlanden, 3: De Moderne Devotie,* 4 vols. (Antwerp: De Sikkel, 1950-1960), p. 55, has noted this anxiety (rendered by him more innocently as "schroom") and finds here the explanation for the hesitation among many of Geert's disciples to seek ordination. The text quoted is far more revealing, however, than expressing anxiety as such. Whereas the distinction between partaking *(sumere corpus) sacramentaliter* and *spiritualiter* is traditional church doctrine (see my *Dawn of the Reformation,* pp. 243-44), the suggested sufficiency of the spiritual eating is the missing link with the famous "Letter of Hoen" (1524). Derived from the library of Wessel Gansfort, who was closely associated with the Brethren in Groningen, Hoen's letter was spurned by Luther, but praised by Zwingli as the key for the interpretation of *est* as "significat" in the words of institution, "Hoc est Corpus meum." See Cornelis Hoen, "Epistola Christiana," in *Huldreich Zwinglis sämtliche Werke,* ed.

fathers of the Modern Devotion. This "proper" material was intended for the so-called *collationes*, a typical institution of the Modern Devotion,[33] a kind of revival meeting, organized twice a day for the members, open to the townspeople but particularly directed at the young students of the city schools placed under the pastoral care of the Brethren and Sisters.

The "historical" or — as the case may be — hagiographical scenes are organized under the headings of major virtues. Without structuring the evidence, I am now first going to report the entries that pertain to our theme:

1. De Studio

Under the heading "De studio," Geert Groote, explicitly introduced with his academic title *Magister*, liked to make a quick pizza *(pisa)* — contrary to Italian lore, apparently a typical Dutch dish![34] — so that he had more time for his studies: "Liberius vacaret studio" (32-34; see n. 31 above).

2. De Oracione

Under the heading "De oracione" it was recalled that Rudolph — Rudolph Dier of Muiden (1384-1459) — could always, except when he sat at his desk to write, be found on his knees, since in accordance with

---

Emil Egli et al., 14 vols. (Berlin: C. A. Schwetschke und Sohn, 1905-1959), 4.512. 21-22. (The letter was carried by two Dutchmen, Johan Rodius and Georg Saganus, who met with Zwingli probably in the late summer of 1524. See Walther Köhler, *Zwingli und Luther*, 2 vols. [Leipzig: Heinsius Nachfolger, 1923-1954], 1.61-62.) All this is by now well known, as well as that there are some significant differences between the interpretations of Hoen and Zwingli, as there are also between those of Gansfort and Geert Groote. A new line of investigation is opened up, however, by "the missing link" of the psychological factor in the development of a scholastic distinction to an alternative in the *praxis pietaris:* the religious experience of "anxiety."

For a discussion of recent literature on the theme of anxiety in the later Middle Ages, see Dennis D. Martin, "Popular and Monastic Pastoral Issues in the Later Middle Ages," *Church History* 56 (1987): 320-32; 321-22. Vis-à-vis the trend to see the Reformation as the answer to the anxiety spawned by the teaching and sacraments of the "official" late medieval church, it is to be noted that church-critical reform movements did not oppose but intensified this state of mind.

33. The *collatio,* usually after the evening meal and for members of the house only, was a general monastic institution. It can be traced back to the *Regula Benedicti,* chap. 42, which refers to the *collationes* of the "Father of all monks," John Cassian. See *PL* 49-50.

34. Far less appetizing, but unfortunately more convincing, is the assumption that the Dutch concoction might have been pea soup. See Theodore van Zijl, *Gerard Groote: Ascetic and Reformer (1340-1384)* (Washington, D.C.: Catholic University of America Press, 1963), p. 130.

the advice of St. Francis he prayed more than he read. Rudolph liked to quote the word of some Father: "primo devoti, secundo scientifici, tertio dissoluti" (people are first devout, then become scholars, and hence go to pot) (43-44). It is to be noted, however, that "scholars" are here referred to as *scientifici*, perhaps best rendered as "knowledge freaks" or "eggheads." But the meaning is clear: we have here in Latin the psycho/historical explanation for the satire of the pamphlets, *Die Gelehrten, die Verkehrten.*

3. De Labore

Under the heading "De labore," a Dutch colleague of the Italian Menocchio is introduced, namely the miller Matthias, who is highly praised for the fact that whenever his manifold tasks allowed, he loved to be studying on holy days "dans se lecioni et meditacioni . . ." (116-17).[35] Brother Petrus Hoorn (†1479) is presented as a man who was so dedicated to the high duty of writing, in this case transcription *(opus scripture)*, that even in the winter he would continue to pen his lines till the freezing cold made him drop the quill from his stiff fingers — never allowing food or sleep to interfere with his duties as *scriptor,* a task which he executed till his death (134-40). Petrus rather sat behind his desk to write under the worst of circumstances. He never desired a higher office in the liturgy or rule of the house ("nunquam ad alia se officio facienda ordinari postulat"), but wanted to remain a scriptor till his death. He was willing to make only one exception: for delivering regular homilies to the school boys *(scolares,* 205) in public and private sessions. If Brother Petrus would have died a hundred years later as a Protestant, he would undoubtedly serve as proof of the "new" work ethic.

4. De Vana Gloria

Now we come to an entry "De vana gloria," on boasting, intended to document the virtue of humility, an entry which we could have easily overlooked in the pursuit of our quest. This section starts with the story of Henricus of Gouda, the Father Confessor of the Sisters of the Common Life in Zwolle, who sometimes walked in *clompen* (347), the wooden shoes of the common man — as far as I can see, here referred to for the

---

35. If this is the same lay brother as described in FH (n. 31 above), then his interest in learning is not surprising since he "magschien een meister in den vruen Kunsten was," which means "perhaps he had earned his MA." *FH,* 183.

first time in Dutch (though identified by the chronicler as a German word)· and implicitly identified as the typical footwear of the lowly. Henricus displayed the humility of the Brethren by coming into the *Grote Kerk* in Zwolle with his wooden shoes, and before ascending the high pulpit to preach his sermon he shed his *clompen* at the foot of the stairs (cf. *FH*, 43-44; see n. 31 above).

But in the same section we get an intriguing while rewarding report on the humility of the founder of the movement, Geert Groote himself. Again introduced with his academic title *magister*, it is soberly pointed out that Geert is called The Great for no other reason than that was the name of his family. His father, after all *(nam!)*, belonged as mayor to the ruling elite of the city of Deventer, and was already known as Werner Groote. But as a young man, magister Geert had, according to reliable testimony, gone to study in Paris and become such an outstanding student that he was second to none in the whole world, be it in the liberal arts, philosophy, ethics, secular and canon law, as well as theology: "Nulli secundus esset in orbe" (332; cf. *FH*, 2). Such high praise of the academic achievements of the founding father would have been completely out of place if the entry had not continued with the conversion of Geert Groote, who, "even though he was such a great man of learning" *(talis ac tantus,* 333), was henceforth dressed in humble clothing, displaying his state of utter penance and poverty even as an academic in Paris.

Yet, and now the point of the story comes, "there it was that he bought all those books with which he has endowed our library, paying for them so much gold as can be placed in a large wine glass." The interest of the author of the manuscript was obviously directed toward the voluntary character of Groote's poverty, but in the meantime — as it were, unintentionally — he highlighted the fact that Geert, after his conversion, invested a large sum of gold in buying books from which the Brethren profited: "emens ibidem libros de quibus nostra libraria est ditata . . ." (336-37; cf. *FH*, 5).[36]

---

36. The actual course of events is considerably telescoped. Three years after his conversion (1374), Geert trekked for the third time to Paris, where he had received his B.A. (1357) and M.A. (1358), and returned to study law (1362-1366). This third time, "perhaps before the end of 1377," he journeyed to Paris to buy the books which, at the end of his life, he donated to the Brethren. See Van Zijl, *Gerard Groote,* pp. 121-22. His splendid original library he had abandoned before his conversion; its "black magic," i.e., astrological books, he publicly burned in the market in Deventer (p. 53). His early delight in learning is, however, as well documented as his later warnings against it.

Again, while the author continues to be interested in the record of humility, we are about to learn something else. There was a far more intimate relationship between the Latin school and the Houses of the Brethren than recent scholarship has led us to expect. Post's insistence on the institutional difference between school and Brethren house is amply confirmed, and yet the task of the Brethren and their presence in the schools clearly exceeds the mere supervision of their pupils' school work at night.

The fourth rector of the house in Deventer, Godfried, the third successor of Groote after Radewijns and Amilius, was himself, as is explicitly noted, a former teacher ("fuerat lector in scolis," 374). Whenever the relation between School and House is touched upon, the intended — or should one say conscious — thrust is that the Brother concerned is not exempt from the embarrassing dress code, shortened gowns, and patched surplices because of his former status as a teacher (FH, 56; cf. 67, 202). But indirectly and by contrast, we learn that to be a teacher at a Latin school was regarded as a high station. Accordingly, it is not surprising that, for instance, the rector of the Brother house in Nijmegen, to which in 1475 a school building was added, accepted the obligation to feed *and* teach each year "six poor boys" for a yearly stipend. The contract clearly suggests more than pastoral care.[37]

Another glance at the state of learning gives the entry "De superbia" with the information that magister Geert Groote always insisted on speaking Latin with the Brethren. The fine to be paid for a Dutch slip of the tongue was to kneel down and kiss the earth. This story would of course not have been complete if it did not also refer to the one time that magister Gerardus himself unwittingly made such a slip. As soon as he realized that the Brethren around him had started to giggle — after all, they did not dare to correct him — he immediately threw himself on his knees and kissed the floor (384-89).

---

37. The endowment, dated 1 July 1523, describes the duties as "bedwangck ende leringe" — discipline *and* instruction. See Schoengen, *Monasticon Batavum* 2 (as in n. 41, below), 142-43, nr. 14. R. R. Post, *The Modern Devotion*, p. 609, is inclined to interpret this provision as stipulating "a little supplementary tuition at home from the *repetitor*." His arguments are convincing insofar as even in Nijmegen most of the *scolares* living with the Brethren would have attended the much better endowed city school. But at least one of the Brethren is referred to as "onss schoelmeister" — our school teacher — which goes to show that not only *former* school teachers lived as Brethren.

5. De Zelo Animarum

Three recollections under the heading "De zelo animarum" complete our picture. In the case of Geert Groote, the zeal for pastoral care went so far that he did not hesitate to take to sea in order to preach the gospel. One time, when he wanted to take his message all the way to Holland, the devil tried to block his route by evoking such a storm over the Zuider Zee (now Ijsselmeer) that Geert was hardly able to save his hand library, which had been carefully packed in a crate to protect the books from water damage (526-30; cf. *FH, 6*).[38]

The most revered Rudolph of Muiden, whom we met before, was known to hate verbosity. He liked to quote from St. Bernard, "Nuge in secularibus nuge quidem sint, in sacerdotibus autem blasphemie: ferende fortasse nonnunquam, sed nunquam proferende" (*De cons.* 2.22; 543-45). Rudolph here continued the medieval crusade *contra nugas,* which in the sixteenth century became the open war against "papist preachers" who replaced the solid food of God's word with idle talk of their own invention.

Petrus Hoorn shared this attitude of extreme reticence, but this did not prevent him from talking at length about Holy Scripture and the life of the saints, particularly of "our own fathers" (557). His word had great authority because it was in keeping with the Fathers and with Holy Scripture: "conforme fuit [consilium suum] sentenciis patrum et sacre scripture testimonio approbatum" (571-72); but even more so because his learning was authentic: all of "us" knew him as a sincere and upright man who gave his counsel in fear of God and in keeping with his conscience ("ex timore Dei et conscientia sua," 575).

6. De Perseverantia

I conclude with one entry under the heading "De perseverantia," which draws together the several themes touched upon hitherto. The event was written down some eighty years after it occurred in the year 1400. A young man by the name of Stephan came to study in Deventer from the area of Louvain — or rather Leuven, as the Flemish must insist in view of the inroads made by the Francophones. Stephan sought to live the devout life, and was therefore placed by the rector Amilius in a dormitory *(bursa)* with other students under his spiritual direction. However, when Stephan's father came to visit him in Deventer and there discovered that

---

38. Cf. van Zijl, *Gerard Groote,* pp. 158-59.

his son had fallen in with the Brethren of the Modern Devotion ("incidere more devotorum"), he became furious.

Unable to change the mind of his son, the father withdrew the money that he had given Stephan for his studies. Absolutely beside himself, the father ran into the main square of Deventer, publicly cursing the Brethren. But God moderated his tongue so [wonderfully] that he started to speak French, even though he knew Dutch very well. Hence, the people did not understand a word of what he was saying. When the son, who had been put into hiding four miles away in Diepenveen — probably in its Sisterhouse — returned to Deventer after his father had left, rector Amilius asked him whether, now that he was penniless, Stephan would be prepared to beg for his food. When the boy said yes, Amilius took pity upon him. He took the boy into the house of the Brethren and made him an associate member of the community ("cum esset ipse Stephanus litterature," 674-75).

Even this last story yields only indirectly the information we seek. The intended point is clearly the perseverance of Stephan and, accordingly, the end of the tale is an expected devout version of living happily ever after: "Stephan, even though young in body, was strong in spirit and zeal for 'our' devout tradition, an example of humility and obedience, exceedingly beloved with almost all the *fratres*." For us, however, the point lies rather in the motivation of the rector. He did not admit Stephan because of his striking humility, but because of his impressive *litterature* — a new, as yet unrecorded word or a fumbled version of *litteratus*. This may mean that Stephan was lettered and well read, or merely that he could read and write. In either case, the story of Stephan supports our findings, and it documents the deep respect and the high ranking of literacy and erudition; for rector Amilius, it made all the difference!

IV. *Pietas Quaerens Intellectum*

Such chronicles are storehouses of stories used in the time-honored tradition of *exempla* intended to bridge the gap between the *eruditi* and the *simplices*. They are the perfect literary form for the *medius status* between doctrine and life.

Typical of the *medius status,* the movement existed legally under civic jurisdiction but spiritually in a world between the walls of the monastery and the walls of the city. With its ascetic/practical bent, it had little affinity with the philological expertise of the leading city humanists, but it was explicitly antagonistic to the theology of the monks, with its despised arrogance and verbosity. Hence, the *Devotio Moderna* stands also intellectually "between the walls," which helps one to understand why the campaign *contra vanam curiositatem*[39] did not yield the anti-intellectualism so long associated with it.

The source we have turned to is precious not only because it allows for glances at daily life in the Brethren community. It also shows us the spectacles with which the earliest Golden Age was viewed one century later, and thus provides us with that ideology of the movement which it wanted to convey, in order to guide the present and gain the next generation. We are only one step removed from the sentiment expressed in a Reformation pamphlet of the year 1523: "When God says 'this is my beloved son, listen to him' (Matt. 17:5), he did not say 'Listen to the monks and the humanists.' No. . . !"[40]

I am inclined to regard the movement of the Brethren and Sisters of the Common Life as a remarkable success. Within the borders of today's Netherlands alone, there were between 1380 and 1480, in the heyday of the movement, two hundred foundations. Of these, thirty-five monasteries and thirty nunneries belonged to the network of the Windesheim Congregation. The extent to which the *Devotio Moderna* was a women's movement has not been noticed because it was not noted that more than half (105) were communities of the Sisters and only 15 percent (30) establishments of the always much more discussed Brethren of the Common Life.[41] Yet, the mere tabulation of houses cannot do full justice to

39. Cf. my reconstruction of the history of the medieval crusade "against vain curiosity," *Contra vanam curiositatem: Ein Kapitel der Theologie zwischen Seelenwinkel und Weltall* (Zurich: Theologischer Verlag, 1974), esp. pp. 23-32. In a richly documented book-length article, Klaus Schreiner has traced the manifold forms of resistance against the increasing access of the laity to knowledge and erudition in the later Middle Ages. Describing the widely felt sense of *Ungleichheit der Bildung* as *Ausprägung sozialer Ungleichheit*, Schreiner points to the concomitant view of society as divided into two estates: "In 'litterati' und 'illiterati' oder in die 'gelerten' und den 'gemeinen man'." "Laienbildung als Herausforderung für Kirche und Gesellschaft: Religiöse Vorbehalte und soziale Widerstände gegen die Verbreitung von Wissen im späten Mittelalter und in der Reformation," *Zeitschrift für Historische Forschung* 2 (1984): 257-354; 329.

40. "Do sagt got nit: höret den munchen oder den humanisten. Nein, höret meinen sun, der ewre sunde am stam des heylgen Creutzs uberwunden hat. . . ." *Eynn Dialogus ader gesprech . . .* (Erfurt, 1523), fol. a iii b.

41. This calculation is based on my computation of the data provided by Michael Schoengen, *Monasticon Batavum 2: De Augustijnse orden benevens de Broeders en Zusters van het Gemeene Leven*, Verhandelingen der Nederlandsche Akademie van Wetenschappen, Afd. Letterkunde, N.S. 45 (Amsterdam, 1941). The numbers indicated do not include the considerable number of houses that joined the

the remarkably high percentage of women. For none of the Brethren houses is a head count available which comes close to the Orthenconvent in 's Hertegenbosch where, c. 1450, seven hundred Sisters are reported as each operating her own loom: the first recorded factory in the Netherlands.[42] Though this example highlights the material dimension of voluntary poverty, and generally suggests that *conversio* may not have meant for most *devoti* a radical change in poverty level, there is no reason to doubt the spiritual motivation. The rapid spread of the movement along the fertile crescent to the Rhine and upper Germany can best be explained in terms of its consonance with that pan-European religious revival mobilizing the lay world in the form of fraternities and confraternities, hospital associations, and third orders of well-established monastic organizations.

It has been argued that, around the turn of the century, the *devoti* reached the end of their economic rope since the *scriptorium* could no longer compete with the successful printing presses. But a quick adjustment to the new technique is amply documented by the disproportionately high number of incunabula produced by the Houses.[43] More

---

Sion congregation, even though often initiated by the *devoti*. For Germany, Gerhard Rehm, *Die Schwestern vom gemeinsamen Leben im nordwestlichen Deutschland: Untersuchungen zur Geschichte der Devotio moderna und des weiblichen Religiosentums*, Berliner Historische Studien 11: Ordensstudien 5 (Berlin: Duncker & Humblot, 1985), has noted sixty-seven Sister houses founded between 1400 and 1500, with an average of fifty members in each. In contrast with my emphasis on the impressive popularity and growth of the Sisters in the Netherlands, Rehm is more restrained in his estimate of their significance as "wenig bedeutsam": "Spektakulär war die Geschichte der Schwestern vom gemeinsamen Leben auch im 15. Jahrhundert nicht" (p. 331). He bases his judgment on the fact that they did not produce "einprägenden Heiligen, Mystikerinnen oder Schriftstellerinnen." I cannot contest this last conclusion, but for two reasons do not regard the argument as convincing. First, for the initiation of the process of canonization, not "die Nachwelt" in general, but a "remembering community" is essential: after the emergence of the Reformation, their "community" faded away. And second, the combination of humble social background and nonostentatious spirituality — programmatically averse to high mysticism — goes far in explaining both the scarcity of exceptional figures and their wide appeal.

42. As the time of capitulation of Den Bosch to Prince Frederik Hendrik in 1629, the community still comprised 104 Sisters. See Schoengen, *Monasticon*, p. 97, nr. 23.

43. See the conclusion of R. H. Rouse, "Backgrounds to Print: Aspects of the Manuscript Book in Northern Europe of the Fifteenth Century," in *Proceedings of the Patristic, Mediaeval and Renaissance Conference*, 6 (Villanova, Pa.: Augustinian Historical Institute, Villanova University, 1981), 37-50; 48: "It is due to the Windesheimers and the Brethren, most of all, that the 'new book' achieved a dissemination far beyond the walls of ecclesiastical houses." Rouse points to the Fraterhouses not only as the "market," but also as the "investors" who "hired printers to publish for them" (p. 49). Rouse goes in this judgment far beyond Post, *The Modern Devotion,*

importantly, the economic motivation for the tradition of transcription has been overrated. The office of the *scriptor (Broeder van den penne)* was, within each house, in such high standing because he or she was in this way involved in the "apostolate of writing" and could thus provide for the daily devotional readings *(rapiaria)* and for the *exempla* used by the speakers at the *collationes* for schoolboys and members alike. Being to such a large extent a community of craftsmen, they could provide for their own needs.

But the lowness of their economic status is reflected in the shocked reaction of the Flemish father of Stephan, who was driven to French curses when he learned with what kind of people his son had come to associate. However, the income of the *devoti* was not primarily based on the writing and selling of books, but on their own artifacts and, when necessary, on the mendicant life. At times the Brethren went door to door to beg for bread. One of them, John Kessel, liked to shout, "Give a poor pilgrim something for his trek to Jerusalem." Afraid of being misunderstood by his readers, the chronicler was quick to add that Kessel meant his pilgrimage to the eternal Jerusalem (719-21; cf. *FH,* 47). Indeed, the *devoti* were not interested in any other career than their progress *in via* to the eternal Jerusalem — an arduous path on which, to use the simile of St. Augustine, a load of knowledge is only a burden, slowing down the pilgrim.

Yet, since about the middle of the fifteenth century a new dimension emerged when the young generation started to give account of the history of its own movement and to emphasize along with Scripture and the Fathers that glorious part of the tradition of their own fathers which was available to them in the *Gesta* of the founding fathers. The *rapiaria* are no longer a loose collection of biblical sayings, and the chronicles are no longer just a list of entries enumerating the offices held, with the death dates for the Brethren and Sisters. They start to become that kind of historical source which in all cultures provides for the matrix of new learning.

Through the establishment of the canons regular in Windesheim (1387) — the third, in some ways perhaps even most important branch[44]

---

p. 553, who regards the contribution of the *devoti* as "modest," and in comparison with a number of city presses, "quite insignificant." J. P. Gumpert, *Die Utrechter Kartäuser und ihre Bücher im frühen funfzehnten Jahrhundert* (Leiden: Brill, 1974), p. 311, however, compares the *devoti* with the Carthusians and comes to the conclusion that ". . . in ihrer Auffassung des praedicare manibus, sind die Devoten wirklich 'modern' " — books are made for the market and not only an ascetic exercise.

44. Thus argued by C. van der Wansem, *Het ontstaan en de geschiedenis der Broederschap van het Gemene Leven tot 1400* (Leuven: Universiteitsbibliotheek, 1958), pp. 96-97.

— the movement provided the impetus for reform of long-established monastic orders, by supporting what was called at that time "the Observance."[45] In all the Observant wings of the orders, which developed after the Council of Constance (1414-18), the new emphasis on the original *regula* went hand in hand with a renewed interest in the origins of the order and its original intentions. The concomitant study of the Scriptures and of the Fathers, with all the available "modern" tools, did not usually lead to a return to scholasticism as we find it in the coalition of the *Devotio Moderna* and the *Via Moderna* in Tübingen. More often, it led to some form of what can best be called monastic humanism.[46] It developed a new sensitivity to erudition as the knowledge of the sources of wisdom *(sapientia)*, if not of secular inquiry *(scientia)*.[47]

One story — inconceivable a hundred years before — may serve at the same time as illustration and summary. It is tucked away in an overlooked entry in the Frensweger manuscript, a chronicle which breaks off at the death of Reyner of Texel (†1483), the third rector of Albergen (near Ootmarsum, Twente). Like most of the Brethren, Reyner is presented as originally a simple man; he was unschooled before his conversion. But after he came to the Brethren, he started to study all the books in the library so assiduously "that he became a formidable authority in

45. The impact of the Windesheim Congregation went well beyond the Observants. See, e.g., Kaspar Elm, *Beiträge zur Geschichte der Wilhelmitenordens* (Cologne: Böhlau, 1962), pp. 144-45. At times, the impact was mutual, as in the case of Henri Herp, who joined, in 1450, the Observant Franciscans after having served as rector of the Brethren house in Delft. His sermons do not mark him as a deviant. See the critical edition of Georgette Epiney-Burgard (ed.), *Henri Herp: De Processu humani profectus: Sermones de diversis materiis vitae contemplativae* (Wiesbaden: F. Steiner, 1982). For the cooperation and exchange between the Windesheim Congregation and the Benedictine Bursfeld Congregation, see Nicolaus C. Heutger, *Bursfelde und seine Reformklöster in Niedersachsen* (Hildesheim: A. Lax, 1969), pp. 25ff.

46. Cf. Noel L. Brann, *The Abbott Trithemius (1462-1516): The Renaissance of Monastic Humanism* (Leiden: Brill, 1981), esp. pp. 218-21.

47. William Bouwsma, "The Renaissance and the Broadening of Communication," in *Propaganda and Communication in World History,* ed. Harold D. Lasswell (Honolulu: University of Hawaii Press, 1980), 2.3-40; 22, goes even a step further in closing the gap: "But the differences even between earlier Italy and the rest of Europe were not absolute. The movement known as the *Devotio Moderna,* which spread from the Low Countries into much of northern Europe in the fifteenth century, suggests that everywhere townsmen were discontent with the specialized and inaccessible subtleties of scholastic discourse and craved a spiritual and moral guidance that spoke directly to their condition in a language they could understand; this need found prominent expression in the *Imitation of Christ* by Thomas à Kempis. The schoolmasters of this movement, the Brethren of the Common Life, showed an interest in classical texts that paralleled that of the humanists in Italy."

all the arts and sciences."[48] This story is the exact inversion of the earliest legend about the Founding Father Geert Groote, who was as learned before conversion as the devout Reyner afterward.

We stumble here over a law perhaps characteristic of the piety of all "book" religions. The history of the Modern Devotion, together with its indirect continuation in the Observant movement, reflects that same curve which one can observe in the development of medieval monasticism after the days of St. Bernard (†1153). Bernard's vociferous campaign *contra nugas* in the twelfth century did not prevent the next generation of disciples from becoming fully involved in the scientific investigation of nature; and the warning of St. Francis (†1226), *scientia inflat*, in the thirteenth century, did not prevent the next generation of Franciscan friars from becoming eminent university professors.

Similarly, the Modern Devotion started out in the fourteenth century by taking over the battle cry of St. Bernard and St. Francis against secular scholarship as a real threat to true devotion. But once again, the defense of true devotion led to such an involvement in learning that the very effort to ward off its concomitant dangers required an intellectual concentration which became the bedrock of a new erudition. It may not give way to our modern notion of secular scholarship, but it most certainly fostered a *pietas quaerens intellectum*.

We started our quest for the popular impact of learned culture with the assumption of a social hierarchy in which learning was the privilege of the elite, reaching the lower echelons of society only at the time of the Renaissance and the Reformation. The evidence presented rather points to a dialectical movement in which, by reaction to high culture and its claims to scholarship, the unschooled common man — in this case primarily the artisan and craftsman — in his search for holiness first rejected the rational rule of the "establishment" and then in response developed an impatient thirst for information which, by the beginning of the sixteenth century, came to yield its own kind of broad-based intellectual sense and sensibility.

The common man was by no means just a plebeian reduced to abject poverty — even though Groote saw this dimension quite

---

48. "Hie was weynich gheleert doe hie yn der scholen was ende ter bekieringe quam, meer hie hadde wonderlick groet natuerlick verstant, ende toe hie toe Alberghen totter armer vergadderinghe ghecomen was soe was hie soe seer vlitich te lesen ende doer te siene alle boeke ende schriften, dat hie soe wijs ende wittich wart dat hie by nae van allen scriften, wijshheiten ende konsten, zeer vele wiste." *FH*, 259.

clearly.[49] When our sources refer to the common man — or as the Frenswegen manuscript put it in Dutch, the *ghemeyne volck* (*FH, 8*) — that kind of simple, underprivileged, and uninformed folk is intended from which the *devoti* recruited, and with which they associated themselves. Along the road of voluntary poverty, a new self-esteem grew which did not lay claim to academic titles, but succeeded in forming its own "intelligentsia." Reformation propaganda found a ready and alert audience, as is succinctly formulated in one of the most impressive Reformation pamphlets: "Don't believe them when they say, 'ja, die bawrenn verstehen die sach nicht.' "[50]

49. Against the "much-heralded" missions of the mendicants to the pagan world outside of "Christian" Europe, Geert Groote, *Epistolae,* pitched his "much more needed" mission to the poor in Christian territories: ". . . unde michi visum est simplices pauperes et abiectos et ignaros magno fervore et labore amplecti debere, qui et quanto nudiores ab altis fastigiis tanto verbi Dei receptibiliores sunt. . . ." See van Zijl, *Gerard Groote.* As later with Thomas Müntzer (†1525), poverty in body and poverty in spirit are not (yet) split up. Cf. Schreiner, "Laienbildung als Herausforderung für Kirche und Gesellschaft," p. 320.

50. *Eynn Dialogus ader gesprech* . . . (Erfurt, 1523), fol. a ii b.

The Virgin Mary
in Evangelical Perspective

There are a number of presuppositions which cannot be argued here in detail — at least not within the narrow confines of a single essay. However, we shall try in what follows to make these presuppositions as explicit as possible.

1. The first and most basic one is the assumption that an evangelical theology properly so called is executed in obedience to Holy Scripture, in communion with the Fathers, and in responsibility to the "Brethren."

2. Through the sacrament of baptism one is placed in this *communio sanctorum*, the *kaine ktisis* or new reality[1] which exists and radiates in three concentric circles: *kerygma, didache* and *leitourgia*. Through baptism the Christian participates in the three corresponding offices of prophet, doctor, and priest.

---

1. "The tangible reality of the Sacraments became the vehicle by which it could be said that the Kingdom had come, and yet was still to come." Krister Stendahl, "Theology and Liturgy," in *The Living Liturgy*, ed. ULCA, Department of Worship (Fort Wayne, 1960), p. 12. Ernst Käsemann does not futurize eschatology and warns us explicitly to interpret the "gewandelte Existenz" as merely a new "sittliche Gesinnung." "Denn das eschatologische Geschehen besteht gerade darin, dass Gott angefangen hat, die ihm gehörende Welt für sich zurückzugewinnen." Ernst Käsemann, "Gottesdienst im Alltag der Welt (zu Rm 12)," in *Judentum, Urchristentum, Kirche* (*Festschrift* for Joachim Jeremias), ed. Walther Eltester (Berlin, 1960), p. 167.

"The Virgin Mary in Evangelical Perspective," *Journal of Ecumenical Studies* 1 (1964): 271-98.

3. The *kerygma* is constitutive of the church. It is preserved and handed down through *didache*. It is celebrated or activated — the original sense of its probable root *celer* means "full of movement" — in formal worship, in the public service of the *communio* to the old reality, and in the Christian life.

4. *Formgeschichte,* and *Traditionsgeschichte,* indicates that the virgin birth does not belong to the *kerygma* but to the form in which the *kerygma* is preserved and transmitted, that is, to *didache*. The creed received at baptism is anchored in the *leitourgia* of the church as the community of memory and hope.

5. The formula *lex orandi lex credendi* tends to be misleading insofar as it presents *leitourgia* as an authority for faith instead of as its activation — as a normative rule instead of as the church's very breath of life.[2] "The formula *lex orandi est lex credendi* means nothing else than that theology is *possible* only within the church, i.e., as a fruit of this new life in Christ, granted in the sacramental *leitourgia*. . . ."[3]

6. The history of Mariology shows that the proper order of the concentric circles, *kerygma, didache, leitourgia,* has been reversed. Popular Marian devotion was able to influence first *didache* and then *kerygma* — the latter understood as *depositum fidei* — and ultimately to be defined in 1854 and 1950. The way to these developments was paved by the Latin interpretation of *lex orandi lex credendi*.

7. Our last preliminary observation is concerned with the final part of the above description of a truly evangelical theology: to be executed "in responsibility to the 'Brethren.'" It has been observed that Mariology is a Roman Catholic problem which has no bearing on the Reformation tradition. Three considerations would seem to expose this attitude as indefensible and — as the conclusion of this essay shall suggest — even dangerous.

First, while we respect the basic differences between West and East,[4]

---

2. Yves M.-J. Congar points to this assumption when he says: "Que la liturgie soit un 'lieu théologique' privilegié, le fait est trop bien connu et aujourd'hui trop generalement reconnu pour qu'il soit utile de l'établir." *La tradition et les traditions,* 2, *Essai theologique* (Paris, 1963), p. 117. We should note here the Orthodox critique on this typically Latin approach to *leitourgia* by Dean Alexander Schmemann: "Liturgical tradition is not an 'authority' or a *locus theologicus;* it is the ontological condition of theology, of the proper understanding of kerygma." "Theology and Tradition," in *Worship in Scripture and Tradition,* ed. Massey H. Shepherd (New York, 1963), p. 175.

3. Schmemann, "Theology and Tradition," p. 175.

4. Reading, e.g., the *Eastern-Rite Prayers to the Mother of God,* one is struck by the theocentric character of Eastern Mariology, where the Virgin Mary is consistently made transparent, never detaching her from the glory of God. Translated and edited by John H. Ryder (New York, 1955).

it cannot be ignored that Mariology in the Orthodox and Roman Catholic traditions, constituting two-thirds of Christendom, is a challenge which has to be answered by every new generation of children of the Reformation.

Granted that this may still be no more than a quantitative argument, never convincing for those who know that at times God upheld his church as a "remnant,"[5] the relevance of this first consideration may yet appear in the light of a second one.

The "Brethren" to whom the theologian is committed in responsibility cannot possibly be limited to members of one's own denomination; this title should be extended to all baptized Christians and baptizing communities, the Christian churches.[6] Exposed to the various traditions within the World Council of Churches and the forces of renewal within modern Roman Catholicism, we are granted the great privilege, not given in the same degree to the preceding generations, of being transposed into the situation of the first generation of reformers, who were not primarily founders of new denominations but *doctores* of the catholic church[7] calling for reformation exactly on the basis of their responsibility to all catholic Christians.[8] Both in his doctoral and in his prophetic office Martin Luther understood his own responsibility as extending to the whole church.[9]

This does not mean that one should not criticize or even reject. But as Karl Barth formulated it in a substantial chapter of his *Church Dog-*

5. Cf. Martin Luther: "Si enim solus essem in toto orbe terrarum, qui retinerem verbum, solus essem ecclesia et recte iudicarem de reliquo toto mundo, quod non esset ecclesias." *WA* 42.334. Cf. Calvin in his "Prefatory Address to King Francis": ". . . interdum etiam ecclesiae suae exteriorum notitiam ab hominum aspectu auferat." *Opera Calvini*, 2 (Brunswick, 1869), p. 23.

6. This is not meant to deny that in *leitourgia* Christian action is included which bridges church and world and that there is a place for apologetic theology which assumes responsibility for the "Brethren" in a universal sense.

7. Martin Chemnitz finds the very basis for the continuity of God's vocation of true *doctores* in the catholicity of the church: "Quia enim Ecclesia est Catholica, Deus semper excitavit in diversis locis aliquos. . . ." *Loci Theologici* (1591), Hypomnemata VI.

8. In a letter dated 25 January 1521, Luther states: "quidquid scripsi et docui secundum meam conscientiam, juramentum et obligationem, ut indignum doctorem sanctae Scripturae, ad laudem et gloriam Dei, ad salutem et felicitatem Ecclesiae catholicae . . . et ad liberationem totius christianae reipublicae . . . proposuisse et fecisse." *WA* 2.254.

9. Cf., e.g., also the excellent article, "Luthers Autorität," by Karl G. Steck, in *Ecclesia Semper Reformanda*, "Sonderheft" to *Evangelische Theologie* (Munich, 1952), pp. 104-20.

matics on "Authority in the Church," there will be ample opportunity for that. The first attitude is not one of critique but of honor and love, not only for the Fathers but also for the "Brethren."[10]

The third observation is then that the word "challenge" is far too secular, or rather a-theological, to express the meaning of the witness of a part of the church, be it heretical or catholic in the true sense of the word. To quote Karl Barth again, this challenge is to be considered as "authority" insofar as it is the point of departure for my own confession.[11] The reformed tradition has never lost sight of the fact that the bidden communion of the faithful, and therefore the church of Jesus Christ, may well extend itself to post-Tridentine Catholicism as much as to Orthodoxy and Neo-Protestantism. A confession can only hope to be catholic when it exposes itself to the whole church, including its heretical aberrations.[12] It is in this light that it seems appropriate to deal with the theme proposed.

I. Problems in Biblical Interpretation

It cannot be our task to present an exhaustive exegesis of all passages in Holy Scripture in which the Mother of Jesus Christ is referred to. There are, however, some basic issues which one cannot avoid if one wants to take the principle of "obedience to Holy Scripture" seriously.

1. The problem of the relation of Scripture and tradition underlies the hermeneutical task of every exegete. Within the Roman Catholic communion, however, it has not only become determinative for the development of Mariology, but it can also be shown that *vice versa* the history of Mariology has determined the authority of extrabiblical tradition.[13]

---

10. One should respect the witness of those "die vor mir in der Kirche waren und mit mir in der Kirche sind . . . als das Zeugnis meiner Väter und Brüder ehren und lieben. . . ." *Kirchliche Dogmatik*, I/2 (Zollikon, 1939), p. 658.

11. Continuation of last quotation: "und so, in seiner damit gesetzten Überlegenheit, werde ich es hören. Indem ich das tue, indem ich der Kirche vor mir und neben mir diese Vorordnung zuerkenne, wird sie mir zur Autorität."

12. We believe it possible that there is a "wenn auch verborgene Gemeinschaft der Heiligen und also Kirche Jesu Christi auch im nachtridentinischen Katholizismus und auch in der neuprotestantischen Abirrung. . . . Wir haben also keinen Anlass, uns bei unserer Frage nach den Vätern der Kirche die Ohren nach irgendeiner Richtung zum vornherein zu verstopfen." Barth, *Kirchliche Dogmatik*, I/2, p. 686. Cf. *Confessio Belgica*, art. XXVII.

13. Cf., e.g., Heiko Oberman, *Harvest of Medieval Theology* (Cambridge, Mass., 1963), p. 390.

(1) Without closing one's eyes to the variety of Mariological schools and currents within contemporary Roman Catholicism one can find an interpretation of Holy Scripture on the basis of later doctrinal developments and dogmatic decisions which gives Roman Catholic hermeneutics its own character. Whether one turns to Carolus Balic, the President of the Mariological Academy in Rome,[14] or to the progressive theologian Hans Küng,[15] one observes that Holy Scripture is not source but resource, not authoritative evidence but elucidating example. Though Küng calls for an "understanding of Protestant difficulties over the new Marian dogmas," the characteristic Roman Catholic conception of the relation of Scripture and dogma finds expression when he goes on to conclude: "There is still much work to be done on deepening and rounding out the theological and especially the scriptural basis of these dogmas."[16]

This formulation points to the erosion of the doctoral office and documents which we have elsewhere described as the transformation of the vital teaching office of the medieval doctor of Scripture, standing together with the bishop as custodian of the deposit of faith, into the apologete of the teaching office of the church.[17]

(2) The basic difference between the tradition of the Reformation and Roman Catholicism on this point can perhaps best be designated as the difference between an analytic and a synthetic hermeneutic. It can be said that between analytic and synthetic interpretation of biblical and ecclesiastical sources runs the demarcation line dividing Protestant and Roman Catholic scholarship. The Reformation acknowledges the *communio sanctorum* as the *con*text and tradition as the *re*source. At the same time the Reformation builds into its hermeneutics — as did Thomas Aquinas and Nicholas of Lyra to a certain extent earlier — the two chief principles of the "secular" code of historical inquiry designated by the terms *e mente auctoris* (historical purpose) and the nature of *anachronism* (historical time).[18]

---

14. Cf. his "Die sekundäre Mittlerschaft der Gottesmutter: Hat Maria die Verdienste Christi für uns de condigno mitverdient?" *Wissenschaft und Weisheit* 4 (1937): 1-22; and "La corédemption de Marie: Le problème central de la mariologie contemporaine," in *Pour le centenaire de Lourdes* (Montreal, 1958), pp. 105-9.

15. Cf. his *Rechtfertigung: Die Lehre Karl Barths und eine katholische Besinnung* (Einsiedeln, 1957), p. 287.

16. *The Council: Reform and Reunion* (New York, 1961), p. 127.

17. "Quo Vadis, Petre? Tradition from Irenaeus to *Humani Generis*," *Scottish Journal of Theology* 16 (1963): 252-53.

18. "One of the most characteristic preoccupations of the humanists was their interest in history. Their sense of historical time was largely based upon their researches in philology and their discovery that words could have different meanings in different

(3) Synthetic interpretation, on the other hand, implies an exegesis of texts in Scripture or tradition which has its point of departure in the present understanding of the deposit of faith by the church, usually based on the immutable identity of truth and the promise of abiding assistance of the Holy Spirit.[19] Though it is the task, then, of the Roman Catholic theologian to find in Scripture and/or tradition a more or less clear expression of the faith as defined by the Magisterium, it would be contrary to the facts to state that now *ipso facto* all Roman Catholic exegetes are apologists rather than biblical scholars. There is a group which is as much committed to the "secular" codes of scholarship as its Protestant counterpart. Even though this group is officially unable to draw from its archaeological, philological, and historical research conclusions which do not find their *norma normans* in the Magisterium, their findings contribute in this fashion to a better understanding of the sources.

The biblical exegesis, however, that in the past promoted and underlay Mariological developments has to be classified as apologetic rather than as biblical theology.[20] Typical examples of its procedures are the use of biblical passages as illustrative material, allegorical interpretation

---

epochs. Hence was born the notion of anachronism. . . ." Myron P. Gilmore, *Humanists and Jurists* (Cambridge, Mass., 1963), p. 63. For late medieval parallels see Oberman, *Harvest*, p. 378-79.

19. One of the condemned "Errores Modernistarum" reads: "Ecclesiae interpretatio sacrorum Librorum non est quidem spernenda, subiacet tamen accuratiori exegetarum iudicio et correctioni." Denzinger, nr. 3402. (According to the numeration of Denzinger, *Enchiridion Symbolorum*, by Adolfus Schönmetzer, S.J. [Freiburg, 1963]). *Humani Generis* (1950) describes the task of the theologian in the following words: "Verum quoque est, theologis semper redeundum esse ad divinae revelationis fontes: eorum enim est iudicare qua ratione ea quae a vivo Magisterio docentur, in Sacris Litteris et in divina 'traditione,' sive explicite sive implicite inveniantur." Denzinger, nr. 3886. The intimate connection between Mariology and the relation of Scripture to tradition has been the impetus for the publication of *Schrift und Tradition* as the first volume in the series Mariologische Studien (Essen, 1963); see there especially H. M. Koester, "Der Stand der Frage über das Verhältnis von Schrift und Tradition unter Berücksichtigung der Mariologie," pp. 11-36. When one adds to this the collection of articles published by the "Pontifica Academia Mariana Internationalis," *De Scriptura et Traditione*, ed. C. Balic (Rome, 1963), there is no reason to believe that Father G. Tavard is right in claiming that almost all Catholic theologians have rejected the traditional interpretation of the decree by the Council of Trent. Cf. his statements in *Commonweal* (August 1963). For the contrary view see the conclusion reached by the Roman Catholic historian and widely acknowledged specialist on the history of the Council of Trent, Hubert Jedin, *Geschichte des Konzils von Trient, II: Die erste Trienter Sitzungsperiode 1545/47* (Freiburg, 1957), p. 61.

20. Cf., however, René Laurentin, *Structure et Théologie de Luc 1–2* (Paris, 1957).

without a literal basis elsewhere in Holy Scripture, and the use of the so-called Anselmian rule, according to which one should ascribe to the Virgin Mary "so much purity that more than that one cannot possibly imagine except for God."[21] Closely related to this instance of reliance on natural theology is the application of logic as the connection between biblical passages and interpretation. For example: The church is the living Christ (Eph. 1:22), the Virgin Mary is the Mother of Christ (Luke 1:36). Ergo: the Virgin Mary is the mother of the church. It should perhaps be noted that this way of dealing with Holy Scripture as if it were a collection of propositions transcends confessional boundaries.

2. Next to the problem of Roman Catholic hermeneutics as the basis for biblical interpretation we have to concern ourselves with the results of *Traditionsgeschichte* and *Formgeschichte*. We can no longer be satisfied with merely collecting all the biblical statements about the Virgin Mary. A few observations are in order, drawn from recent investigations:

(1) Although the virgin birth is the basis of all the later doctrinal developments, it can no longer be overlooked that only at two places is the virgin birth attested, that is, in the infancy narrative of Matthew 1–2 and Luke 1. These should not be looked upon as two forms of the same story in view of the characteristic differences between them.[22]

(2) It has been suggested that the heading "virgin birth" would be a misleading one for Matthew's presentation. Krister Stendahl comes to the conclusion that we face here "an account which knows of a 'virgin birth,' but the supernatural element is neither stressed nor glorified. It rather has the form of a divine overcoming of a stumbling block and counteracting of misunderstanding and slander."[23] As regards the Lucan account it should be noted that the point of the story is the conception through "overshadowing" by the Holy Spirit. The birth, virginal or not, is not at all mentioned.[24]

21. "Decens erat, ut ea puritate, qua maior sub Deo nequit intelligi, virgo illa niteret." Anselm, *De conceptu virginali*, cap. 18, in *PL* 158. 451A. Cf. Scotus, *Opus Oxoniense*, 3, d. 3, q. 1, contra 2. A variation of this rule is applied in the 1950 definition of the Assumption of the Virgin Mary: "cum eam posset [Redemptor] tam magno honore exornare, ut eam a sepulcri corruptione servaret incolumen, id reapse fecisse credendum est." Denzinger, nr. 3900.

22. Krister Stendahl, "Quis et Unde? An Analysis of Mt. 1–3," in Eltester, *Judentum* (n. 1 above), p. 96.

23. "Matthew," new and revised edition of *Peake's Commentary* (Edinburgh, 1962), col. 674i, p. 771.

24. "Das Wunder liegt in der Erzeugung; nicht in der Geburt, die überhaupt nicht erwähnt wird." Martin Dibelius, "Jungfrauensohn und Krippenkind: Untersuchungen zur Geburtsgeschichte Jesu im Lukas Evangelium," *Botschaft und Geschichte, Gesammelte Aufsätze von Martin Dibelius*, ed. Günther Bornkamm, 1 (Tübingen,

(3) While the Gospel of Mark does not mention the virgin birth, we find in the Prologue of John the "concept of virgin birth" applied to all the children of God who, notwithstanding their birth from natural parents, have been given "the right to become children of God, not born of any human stock, or by the fleshly desire of a human father, but the offspring of God himself."[25] Though Hans von Campenhausen grants that the issue cannot be decided with absolute certainty, he points out that this passage might well be a polemical allusion to an early virgin birth tradition.[26] We choose to omit here a discussion of the six other "children" of Mary (Mark 6:3), among whom Jesus was the "firstborn" (Luke 2:7).

(4) The Pauline corpus does not show any interest in the virgin birth either. The one much-discussed text, Gal. 4:4: "God sent his own Son, born of a woman, born under the law," does not so much contradict the virgin birth tradition because of the use of the word "woman." But the very point Paul wants to make — the depth of the *kenosis* of Christ in order to identify himself with all humans under the law — would be lost if he intended to say "born of a virgin."[27]

(5) In the Gospels two attitudes toward the figure of Mary can be discerned. First of all there is the emphasis on the distance between Christ and his Mother, not bridgeable by ties of blood but only by ties of faith.

While Jesus is described as a cause of irritation to his environment which knows so well that he is the son of Joseph rather than the expected Messiah (Mark 6:3; cf. John 6:42), Mary herself comes to share this irritation (Mark 3:21; 6:4). The identification of the birth of Christ and the birth of all the faithful as children of God — which we noted in our discussion of John 1:12-13 — finds clear expression in Jesus' answer to the woman who said: "Blessed is the womb that carried you and the breast that suckled you": "No, blessed are those who hear the word of God and keep it" (Luke 11:27-28). And again, according to Mark 3:32: "Your mother and your brothers are outside asking for you"; to which

---

1953), p. 16. Cf. p. 78: ". . . hier (Luk 1) steht im Vordergrunde die Botschaft von dem Messias auf Davids Thron, den Gott selber auf wunderbare Weise aus heiligem Geist erschaffen wird."

25. *The New English Bible* (Oxford, 1961), John 1:12, 13.

26. ". . . denn einer jungfräuliche Geburt im wörtlichen Sinne, wie sie von andern für Jesus behauptet worden war, wird durch die Ausdehnung der Vorstellung auf die Christen insgesamt vielmehr um ihren Sinn gebracht und zurückgewiesen." *Die Jungfrauengeburt in der Theologie der alten Kirche.* Sitzungsberichte der Heidelberger Akademie der Wissenschaften, Philosophische-historische Klasse, Abh. 3, 1962, p. 12.

27. Dibelius, "Jungfrauensohn und Krippenkind," p. 29, n. 47; von Campenhausen, *Jungfrauengeburt,* p. 13.

Jesus answers: "Whoever does the will of God is my brother, my sister, my mother."

The blood relationship is not the basis but — initially — rather an obstacle to a faith relationship of Mary to Jesus. The tendency to assign the Virgin Mary a supernatural place transcending the level of the faithful argued on physical-metaphysical grounds must have been an ancient and a natural inclination. The remarkable unanimity of the Gospels — including John's account of the wedding at Cana (2:3-5) — points to the fact that Jesus has consistently answered that faith alone provides a proximity to him in time and space, a relation formulated by Paul as "being in Christ" (Gal. 3:28).

(6) It has been said that the *Magnificat* displays exactly the opposite attitude to the figure of Mary: the Lucan birth narrative puts first on the lips of the angel and then on those of Mary herself a benediction of the Mother of Jesus which Jesus so clearly rejected.[28]

Though the *Magnificat* has indeed its own texture and intention, it does not, however, seem to stand opposite to what we described above as a biblical image of Mary nor to continue the "womb theology" rejected by Jesus. The Lucan emphasis falls on the humility of Mary, not on her person but on her office as representative of the remnant of Israel. It is the New Testament reformulation of the Song of Hannah: "the feeble gird on strength . . . the hungry have ceased to hunger . . . the barren has borne seven . . . the Lord brings low, he also exalts . . ." (1 Sam. 2:4-7). The tension between the promise of the angel that Mary shall conceive in her womb and bear a son (Luke 1:31; cf. 2:21) with her virginity is one of these signs of God's eschatological initiative,[29] a variation on the theme of Sarah who bears a child in her old age: "And God said to Abraham, 'As for Sarah your wife . . . I will bless her, and she shall be a mother of nations; kings of peoples shall come to her' " (Gen.

28. "Die späten mythischen Stücke über Jesu Herkunft, welche vorliegen, besonders in den lukanischen Vorgeschichten, lassen den Engel und dann im Loblied indirekt sogar Maria selber (Luk 1:48) gerade jene Seligpreisung der Mutter Jesu aussprechen, welche Jesus ganz deutlich abgelehnt hatte." Jakob Amstutz, "Die Verehrung Mariae vom freien Protestantismus gesehen," *Evangelische Marienverehrung: Eine Heilige Kirche,* ed. Friedrich Heiler and Fr. Siegmund-Schultze, 1 (1955-1956), 39.

29. Frère Max Thurian has described this very concisely and beautifully in his *Marie mère du seigneur-figure de l'église* (Taizé, 1962), p. 27. There is, however, a shift of emphasis when he proceeds to meditate on the significance of the virginity of Mary as such: "La Vierge Marie introduit donc en le monde, où le mariage est devenu loi universelle, selon l'ordre de la création, la nouveauté du Royaume de Dieu qui fait irreption avec le Christ. Ainsi la virginité de Marie est un triple signe. . . , " p. 51.

17:15, 16). These are the covenantal words to Abraham (Luke 1:55 and 73!) which are echoed in the "Blessed are you among women!" (Luke 1:28, 42).

For an understanding of later developments it is important to observe that Luke and Matthew in their birth narratives look in different directions — the first more "dogmatically" interested in how a human being can be the Son of God, the latter more "apologetically" inclined in pointing out that Jesus was the expected Messiah.[30] At the same time Luke is so interested in showing the continuation and fulfillment of the history of salvation in the line Sarah–Hannah–Elisabeth–Mary that one cannot understand this distinction as mutually exclusive. On the contrary, it should be seen as a more dogmatic presentation of the same apologetic motive vis-à-vis the unbelieving Jews, a motive which so clearly underlies Matthew's account.[31] This difference between "apologetic" and "dogmatic" is perhaps best clarified by the observation that "in Matthew Joseph is the main person. It is he who receives the revelations and through him the action progresses. . . . In Luke Mary is the recipient of revelation and Joseph is described as he who stands by."[32] One is inclined to observe that whereas within the Protestant tradition there is a tendency to apply the Matthean Joseph image to the Virgin Mary, within Roman Catholicism there is and has been the inclination to extend the Lucan Mary image to Joseph.[33]

3. Next to the issues of Roman Catholic hermeneutics and *Formgeschichte* there is in the third place the question of Protestant hermeneutics. Concerned to avoid the docetism of the Spirit which the reformers found to the right in Counter-Reformation theology and to the left in sections of the Radical Reformation, the Protestant tradition has emphasized that the Spirit speaks *in* the word and that understanding originates

---

30. "Lukas und Matthäus blicken also in verschiedene Richtungen. . . . Wir können sie kurz als die 'dogmatische' und die 'apologetische' Tendenz bezeichnen." Von Campenhausen, *Jungfrauengeburt*, p. 20.

31. Only if one underlines the word *ausschliesslich* can one agree with von Campenhausen: "Die Darstellung bei Matthäus ist von vornherein anders gestaltet . . . es geht Matthäus ausschliesslich um den Weissagungsbeweis. . . , " p. 19.

32. Stendahl, "Quis et Unde?" p. 95.

33. This is not a recent development but accompanied and followed both the first declaration of the dogma of the Immaculate Conception promulgated by the Council of Basel in 1439, and the second declaration by Pope Pius IX in 1854. Cf. Geiler of Keisersberg: "Joseph is geheiliget worden in muoterlieb wie Maria," *Evangelibuch*, fol. 157[r 1-2]; cf. Gerson, *Opera Omnia*, 3, cols. 848ff. Quoted and discussed by E. Jane Dempsey, *The Doctrine of Justification in the Preaching of Doctor John Geiler of Keisersberg* (Ph.D. diss., Harvard University, 1962), pp. 317-18.

from exposure to Scripture rather than from direct illumination, be it individually or collectively received.

Obedience to Holy Scripture as the testimony to and receptacle of what God "in these last days" has spoken by his Son (Heb. 1:2) implies the use of all means to come to an exegesis which is "sachgemass" or appropriate to its subject matter. The use, for example, of *Form-* and *Traditionsgeschichte* is a basic part of this sober listening to Scripture itself.

At the same time Scripture is understood only in the church. The church approaches Scripture not without preconceived ideas, as a *tabula rasa,* but on the basis of a whole history of understanding. One may well call this history "tradition" if one first makes clear that this tradition is not the *authoritative vehicle of divine truth,* but the *instrumental vehicle of Scripture* which comes alive in a constant dialogue with the faithful.

Protestant hermeneutics has led to certain emphases as regards the interpretation of the place and function of the Virgin Mary, which can be indicated in a few words: the *Magnificat* as a poetic confession of justification *sola gratia* and *sola fide.*[34] She believes the word of the angel and trusts God's promises; she knows that it is God's mercy which made him turn to her. The humility of Mary, then, is not seen as a disposition which provided the basis and reason for God's choice, but is regarded rather as the result of God's election and prevenient grace.

It is clear that not only the view of the relation of Scripture and tradition but also the understanding of justification determines the presentation of the role of the Virgin Mary in the history of salvation. It is on these grounds that, on the one hand, the Roman Catholic Eduard Stakemeier can claim that the catholic elements in the Mariology of the reformers had to disintegrate,[35] while, on the other hand, the Protestant Roger Mehl can state that Mariology is the focus and locus where all

---

34. Cf. Luther, *WA* 15.476; 17 II.399; 52.692; Calvin, *Inst.* II, 3, 13; Zwingli, *ZW* 1.396ff. See Eduard Stakemeier, "De Beata Maria Virgine eiusque cultu iuxta Reformatores," *De Mariologia et Oecumenismo,* ed. C. Balic (Rome, 1962), pp. 424-77; *Das Marienlob der Reformatoren,* ed. Walter Tappolet (Tübingen, 1962), esp. the useful index on pp. 357ff.; Walter Delius, *Geschichte der Marienverehrung* (Basel, 1963), pp. 195-234; Gottfried W. Locher, "Inhalt und Absicht von Zwinglis Marienlehre," *Kirchenblatt für die reformierte Schweiz* 107 (1951): 34-37.

35. "Profunda reformatorum diversitas a mariologia catholica provenit ex principiis reformatoriis et specialiter ex sex dictis 'sola particulis.'" Stakemeier, "De Beata Maria Virgine," p. 474. On Luther: "Inductus principiis 'solius Scripturae' necnon 'solius Dei operantis,' paulatim tam meritum quam intercessionem Matris Dei negavit eiusque invocationem dissuasit vel exclusit," p. 450. Calvin interprets Scripture and the Fathers "secundum suas praeiudicatas opiniones," p. 460.

the heresies of Roman Catholicism are welded together.[36] Though in both traditions the Virgin Mary can be regarded as *typus ecclesiae,* the function of *ecclesia* is conceived of in fundamentally different ways.

To summarize the Protestant position on this point, one might well conclude this section by recalling the words of Karl Barth at the end of his discussion of Roman Catholic Mariology: "Revelation and reconciliation are irreversibly, indivisibly and exclusively the work of God."[37]

II. Problems in the History of Mariology

It is not our intention to sketch the whole history of Mariology. Instead a selection is made of aspects of this history that seem to have a bearing on a contemporary evangelical approach to Mariology. Accordingly we should like to make some comments on Mariological developments in the early church, in the Middle Ages, and in the Reformation period in the light of recent investigations.

1. Early Church

(1) In an important article Bishop Paulus Rusch of Innsbruck argues that there are two historical roots of Mariology.[38] The first is a pretheological affection for the Virgin Mary as a Mother figure displayed, for example, by the Philomarianites.[39] This group overemphasized the orthodox epithet "Theotokos" to the point that the Virgin came to be looked upon as a deity. Epiphanius Salamis (†403), reporting on this sect with horror, concludes his description by saying: "They should not say: 'We honor the queen of heaven.' "[40] Asceticism is designated by Bishop Rusch as the second root, the cradle of true Marian devotion, where the praise of

36. "C'est pourquoi nous ne pouvons opposer à la mariologie prise dans son ensemble qu'un non résolu. Nous sommes persuadés qu'elle constitue une sorte d'engrenage mortel pour la foi évangelique. En elle se rejoignent toutes les héresies du catholicisme. . . ." *Du Catholicisme Romain. Approche et Interpretation* (Neuchâtel-Paris, 1957), p. 91.

37. Barth, *Kirchliche Dogmatik,* I/2, p. 160.

38. "Mariologische Wertungen," *Zeitschrift für katholische Theologie* 85 (1963): 129-61.

39. More often called "Kollyridians." See *Lexikon für Theologie und Kirche* VI (1961): 382-83; Delius, *Geschichte der Marienverehrung,* p. 100.

40. *Haereses,* 79.8, ed. K. Holl, in *Die griechischen christlichen Schriftsteller der ersten drei Jahrhunderte* 37.483; quoted by Delius, *Geschichte der Marienverehrung,* p. 331.

the Virgin is directed toward her as the prototype of virginity. This emphasis was retained by the monastic movement. Bishop Rusch goes on to observe that in the fifth century heretics are the first to defend Mariological theses, which later came to be generally accepted; for example, the representatives of Docetism defend the virginity of Mary *post-partum*, while the Pelagians maintain the doctrine of her complete sinlessness. Moreover, the first to uphold the Immaculate Conception was again a Pelagian, Julian of Eclanum (†454).[41]

For our purposes it is important to observe that in the light of the foregoing, the rejection by Nestorius († c. 451) of the title "Theotokos" for the Virgin Mary appears in a new light. Traditionally Nestorius is presented as a heretic who with christological motivations accidentally seized on the title of the Virgin Mary with the purpose of declaring that there are two separate Persons in the incarnate Christ.[42] It may well be closer to the truth, however, to say that Nestorius, setting out on a purposeful crusade against a heretical Mariology, accidentally compromised himself as regards Christology. Bishop Rusch, indeed, suggests that Nestorius turned against a tendency to interpret the "Theotokos" title so that Mary would be the Mother of God not only according to the humanity of Christ *(secundum humanitatem)*, as Chalcedon had stated, but also according to the divinity of Christ *(secundum divinitatem)*, in the same way as there are mothers of gods in pagan religions.[43] The "Theotokos" title, therefore, as upheld by the Council of Ephesus (431) and interpreted by the Council of Chalcedon (451), should not be isolated from its historical context, but regarded as the *via media* between a paganizing Mariological heresy and a Nestorianizing Christological heresy. Where the first aspect is ignored, as is usually the case, the ambivalence of the title "theotokos" is overlooked, and the term itself then necessarily leads to new Mariological heresies.

---

41. Rusch, "Mariologische Wertungen," p. 138; cf. p. 158: "Ja, es trat das Überraschende zu Tage dass Irrlehrer im Altertum nicht selten eine später anerkannte mariologische These, etwa die Pelagianer die unbefleckte Empfängnis, vorwegnahmen." Rusch refers to R. Laurentin, *La vierge marie: Initiation théologique*, 4 (Paris, 1956), 261ff. P. Pourat points out that in the East Marian devotion was at times an indication of heresy: *La spiritualité chrétienne*, 1 (Paris, 1947), 477; quoted by Rusch, "Mariologische Wertungen," p. 130, n. 6.

42. Berthold Altaner, *Patrologie* (Freiburg, 1958), p. 302; J. N. D. Kelly, *Early Christian Doctrines* (New York, 1958), pp. 310ff.

43. "Es gab eine Bestrebung, Maria zur Gottesmutter im heidnischen Sinn zu erklären, also *secundum deitatem*, wie es denn in den heidnischen Religionen eigentliche Mütter von Göttern gab. Dagegen hatte sich Nestorius gewandt und war dabei in das Gegenteil geraten." Rusch, "Mariologische Wertungen," p. 139.

(2) A second recent study dealing with the pre-Chalcedonian period alerts us to the fact that the virginity of Mary, as in the creedal clause "natus ex Maria Virgine," is genetically seen not to be regarded as the safeguard of an orthodox approach to the mystery of the Incarnation. This is a matter of later interpretation.

The belief in the virginity of the Mother of Jesus, of which we traced the beginnings in the birth narratives of Matthew and Luke, could not possibly determine the course the second-century church should take, surrounded as it was by Jews, Jewish Christians, and Adoptionists on the one side and various schools of Gnostics on the other side. Over against the Gnostics the catholic theologians were concerned to "defend," as Hans von Campenhausen points out, the reality of a "truly and in the full sense of the word human birth, not really a virginal birth." And over against the Judaizing wing the catholic apologetes are "above all interested in emphasizing the pretemporal birth of the Son, i.e., in his preexistence, and again therefore not in the birth from a virgin."[44]

The virgin birth could not be the necessary means, therefore, for preserving the true meaning or the full reality of the self-identification of God with the world,[45] for which it has later so often been held by Roman Catholic and Protestant orthodoxy. It has rather to be seen, as we noted above, as a sign of God's eschatological action, to be grasped in faith, at once more hidden *and* the culmination point of the same line running from Sarah and Hannah to Elisabeth and Mary. The absence of an inherent, systematic necessity of the virgin birth is well expressed by Martin Luther, who, while personally holding not only the virgin birth but also the perpetual virginity of Mary, could say: "It is not that important whether she is a virgin or a woman. . . ."[46]

(3) We have noted the theological ambivalence of the "Theotokos" title and the pretheological token character of the virginity of Mary. It is

---

44. Von Campenhausen, *Jungfrauengeburt*, p. 18.

45. "Die Jungfrauengeburt ist eben nicht einer theologischen Tendenz zuliebe formuliert worden. Sie ist einfach ein überkommenes vermeintlich 'apostolisches' Stück biblischer Überlieferung." *Jungfrauengeburt*, p. 18.

46. "Nihil dictum de matre, quia, sicut supra dixi, leyt nit vil dran, an sit virgo vel femina, quamquam deus voluit virginem esse." *WA* 15.411. Gerhard Ebeling regards this statement as "die extremste Aussage" of Luther on this point and as an "okkamistische Rekurs auf die potentia dei ordinata." *Evangelische Evangelienauslegung: Eine Untersuchung zu Luthers Hermeneutik* (Darmstadt, 1962), p. 247. However, Luther writes this as a comment on Matt. 2:6, which deals with the fulfillment of the OT and of Israel. In *this* context the distinction between woman and virgin is not crucial. The last five words of the above Luther quotation should be "lightly read," as an appended afterthought.

important to note in a last comment on the beginnings of Mariology in the early church that with the progress of time the "dogmatic" element in the Lucan account becomes more prominent at the expense of the "apologetic" tendency which we found to underlie both Matthew 1 and Luke 1. Ignatius of Antioch († c. 115), the only "Apostolic Father" to teach the virgin birth,[47] can be looked upon as a representative of the "dogmatic" school of thought. Justin Martyr († c. 165), on the other hand, can be regarded as perhaps the last representative of the purely "apologetic" approach.[48] At the end of the second century these two currents meet in Irenaeus († c. 200). His contrast between the obedient Mary and the disobedient Eve,[49] placed within the context of his recapitulation theory, can serve to show both the fulfillment of the Old Testament and the inner connection between Adam's formation out of virginal earth with Christ's birth from a virginal woman. There is no sign yet of the later identification of the Virgin Mary with the church or with the heavenly Jerusalem, which seems to stem from Manichean sources.

At the end of the second century a new element is introduced into the discussion. Whereas we saw that Matthew dealt with the questions *Quis* and *Unde,* "Who is Christ?" and "Whence did he come?"[50] and that Luke added the question *Qua,* "In what manner"[51] could Mary be the Mother of the Christ? increasingly the interest now turns to the question *Quo,* "By what means?" and "To what purpose?"[52] The attention begins to focus on the person of Mary herself, her eminent purity and sanctity as prerequisite for the Incarnation and ascetic example for the Christian community. In view of the programmatic asceticism of Gnosticism this new development could not take place till after the threat of Gnosticism had subsided.[53] We do not here follow this development from the *Protoevangelium Iacobi* (before A.D. 200) into Alexandrian theology in the East and the pre-Augustinian theology of Ambrose and

---

47. Robert M. Grant has a more than usually high regard for the witness of Ignatius since he "preserved apostolic tradition as it had been interpreted at Antioch in the generation before him." "Hermeneutics and Tradition in Ignatius of Antioch: A Methodological Investigation," *Archivo di Filosofia* 1-2 (1963): 200.

48. For this and the following see von Campenhausen, *Jungfrauengeburt,* pp. 22ff., and Delius, *Geschichte der Marienverehrung,* pp. 34-103.

49. ". . . Maria virgo oboediens . . . Eva vero inobaudiens. . . ." *Contra Haereses* 3.22.4.

50. Cf. Stendahl, "Quis et Unde?" (n. 22 above).

51. As in the school example: "illuc qua veniam?"

52. As in: "quo mihi prodest?"

53. On sexual asceticism in the early church see Hans von Campenhausen, "Die Askese im Urchristentum," *Tradition und Leben: Kräfte der Kirchengeschichte* (Tübingen, 1960), pp. 133-53. In Corinth St. Paul was confronted with "Gnostische Ideale eines asketischen Übermenschentums." "Askese im Urchristentum," p. 139.

Jerome. The spread of the monastic movement and the anthropological presuppositions leading to the identification of sexuality with sin made for a moralizing elevation of the Virgin Mary which finds its clearest expression in the *semper virgo* doctrine, Mary's virginity *ante-partum*, *post-partum*, and even *in partu*.

While the questions *Quis, Unde,* and *Qua* had been concerned with Jesus Christ, the question *Quo* is geared toward his mother and thus forms the basis for what we have come to know as Mariology. While the references by Matthew and Luke to the virgin birth had been Christological devices, part of the *didache* meant to preserve and transmit the *kerygma*, there are clear indications that by the end of the second century Mariology started to become part of the *kerygma* itself: the sign becomes the thing signified. Time and again we get a glimpse of the impact of *leitourgia* on this development. A virtue-centered interpretation of the *Magnificat*, perhaps part of "the" early Christian hymnbook, and the spread of private Marian devotions led in the fifth century to the incorporation of Marian feasts into the liturgical calendar, which in turn could later serve as a point of departure for further Mariological developments.

2. Middle Ages and Reformation

(1) It is not unknown that Mariology was able to develop so strikingly in the Middle Ages — in other respects not dogmatically productive — because of Christ's receding into heaven, sitting at the right hand of the Father, and preparing for his return to judge the quick and the death. In the confrontation with Arianism in the East the divinity of Christ had to be strongly emphasized, and thus the figure of the cosmic Christ, the *Pantocrator,* had become prominent. In the West the Crucifixion rather than the Incarnation became the living center of Christology. But even so, according to the influential Anselmian interpretation, the atonement took place in the realm between Christ and God. The atonement is more the basis for the efficaciousness of the sacraments than the event through which those who are in Christ have "free access" to God. In other words, Christ's mediation is largely restricted to the cross.

Due to theological difficulties so eloquently formulated by Bernard of Clairvaux and Thomas Aquinas, the Immaculate Conception was not promulgated till 1439 (by the Council of Basel in a session which remained unconfirmed) and the relation of Mary's death to her Corporeal Assumption was not yet sufficiently or convincingly clarified.[54] But both doctrines were strongly supported on the eve of the Reformation.[55] Two themes in particular seem to contribute to the centrality of the place and function of the Virgin Mary. There is first the theme of Mary's assumption, her reception into heaven, and her reunion with her Son. In his welcoming speech Christ announces that he will share the Kingdom of his Father with her; Mary will rule the Kingdom of Mercy and thus become *Mater misericordiae;* Christ shall reign in the Kingdom of Truth and Justice and therefore function as the *iudex vivorum et mortuorum.*[56] A fifteenth-century miniature presents, under the title "Mary mediator between God and man," the Queen of Heaven as protecting the faithful under her skirts from a God who tries to find a target for the arrow, ready on his bow, among those faithful who dare to venture out from under Mary's protection.[57] Most prominent are the breasts of the Virgin, which suggest that the angry God figure is the Son, since according to popular tradition Mary shows her breasts to her Son, who in turn intercedes with the Father.

(2) The second theme is of a more strictly theological nature. The argument is that the Virgin Mary is *pura creatura* or *homo purus,* here not in the sense that she is pure as regards original sin but pure in the sense of "real": she is a real creature or truly human. This now is contrasted with Christ who is not *homo purus* but *homo Deus:* Christ is not pure nature because his humanity is united in hypostatic union with the Godhead. In contrast to Mary, Christ did not, therefore, really and fully belong to humankind. The term "pure nature" serves here as a basis for establishing a gulf between Christ and humankind which can be bridged only by the Virgin Mary: the foundation for human *fiducia,* the confident hope of eternal life, is therefore the resurrection of the Virgin Mary rather than the resurrection of Christ.

Because of her "breasts" related to God, and because of her "pure nature" related to humanity, the Virgin Mary can occupy that place of mediation which in classical orthodox theology had been held by Jesus Christ.

(3) For the reformers, Mariology could not possibly be a side issue

54. Cf. Carolus Balic, *Testimonia de Assumptione B.V.M. ex omnibus saeculis* 1 (Rome, 1948).

55. For the following, cf. the chapter on "Mariology" in Oberman, *Harvest,* pp. 281-321.

56. Cf. Oberman, *Harvest,* p. 311.

57. *Speculum humanae salvationis* (Munich, 1585). The following statement by Jaroslav Pelikan therefore requires clarification: "The cult of the Blessed Virgin Mary has likewise helped to soften the harsh picture of God which prophetic religion so frequently produces." *The Riddle of Roman Catholicism: Its History, Its Beliefs, Its Future* (New York, 1959), p. 139.

since it touched so directly on their common main theme, the redemption by God in Jesus Christ. All three major reformers, Martin Luther, Ulrich Zwingli, and John Calvin, retained important elements of the early church tradition but rejected unanimously the medieval developments as sketched above in the two themes of "Mother of Mercy" and "pure nature."

Luther's translation of the hymn by Venantius Fortunatus, *Agnoscat omne saeculum:* "Der aller Weltkreis nie beschloss der liegt nun in Mariae Schoss,"[58] could perhaps best serve as the heading for his interpretation of the role of the Virgin Mary. The Virgin Mary is the sign of the exinanition of God. For Luther she is the Virginal Mother, the "Theotokos," and even the perpetual Virgin,[59] but all these titles are conferred upon her against the background of a reinterpretation of the *Magnificat.*[60] There is indeed little chance that Mary can become the thing signified rather than the sign when one can let her say as Luther did: "I am only the workshop in which God operates."[61]

The warm praise which Luther has for the Mother of God throughout his life, his last sermon on 17 January 1546 included,[62] is not based upon the great qualities of Mary herself but upon the grace granted to her. As a person, Luther can say, the Virgin Mary is not greater than Mary Magdalene, the sinner, since through faith all Christians are equal.[63]

When Luther in 1535 attacks the theme of Mary the Mother of Mercy, as contrasted with Christ the Judge,[64] this is not an *ad hoc* reference but the outgrowth and application of his discovery of the meaning of *iustitia.* In his *Commentary on the Psalms,* 1513-1515, Luther insists that in Christ mercy and righteousness are united.[65] When one destroys this unity, Christ is no longer "*veritas*" but has become "*severitas*"!

Luther also rejects the implications of the second medieval theme

58. ". . . quem totus orbit non capit, portant puellae viscera": He whom the whole world could not contain [and: grasp!] is now in Mary's womb. WA 35.435.

59. WA 11.320.

60. Cf. H. D. Preuss, *Maria bei Luther* (Gütersloh, 1954), and Tappolet, *Marienlob* (n. 34 above), esp. pp. 58ff.

61. "Ego nihil sum quam fabrica, in qua Deus operatur. . . ." WA 7.573.

62. WA 51.128.

63. 1525: WA 10 I.2.432.

64. WA 41.199.

65. "'Iustitia et pax osculatae sunt' quia idem Christus est utrumque." Ps. 84(85):11; WA 4.16. Cf. Heinrich Bornkamm, "Zur Frage der Iustitia Dei beim Jungen Luther," *Archiv für Reformationsgeschichte* 52 (1961): 28. This reference functions in Bornkamm's presentation as one of his effective arguments against Ernst Bizer's thesis, according to which Luther's "breakthrough" should not be dated before 1518. *Fides ex Auditu* (Neukirchen, 1958), esp. p. 101.

noted above. The very point of his doctrine of the Incarnation is that God emptied himself to become human, truly human. The contrast between Mary as *purus homo* and Christ as *homo Deus* could not be more alien to his thought. It is impossible that *fiducia* should be placed in Mary — and, of course, even more impossible that a greater *fiducia* should be invested in Mary than in Christ — since *fiducia* can be used synonymously with what traditionally is known as *latreia*: "For *fiducia* is the highest honor, due only to God, who alone is truth."[66]

(4) As is usually the danger in describing the position of the Reformation, one is tempted to highlight and therefore to overemphasize those points on which the preceding tradition is rejected. Rather than showing how far Zwingli and Calvin shared Luther's critique, we prefer to call attention in a final comment on the positive elements in the attitude of these Reformers to the Virgin Mary.

In 1529 Zwingli defends the use of the "Ave Maria," not as a prayer but as praise "in order to salute and laud Mary."[67] He feels that the best way to honor the Mother of God is to imitate her virtues.[68] Instead of

---

66. 1522: "Nam fiducia est summus honor Deo soli debitus, qui solus est veritas." *WA* 10 II.166. One should compare a hymn in the *Crailsheimer Schulordnung* of 1480 with Luther's interpretation.

> Sancta Maria steh uns bey
> so wir sullen sterben.
> Mach uns aller sunden frey
> und lass uns nicht verderben.
> Vor dem teufel uns bewar
> rayne magt Maria,
> hilff uns an der engelschar
> so singen wir alleluia.

Friedrich Spitta, *Ein fester Burcht ist unser Gott* (Göttingen, 1905), p. 268. See Luther's interpretation in his *Trinitatislieder:*

> Gott der Vater wohn uns bei
> und lass uns nicht verderben
> mach uns aller sünden frei
> und helf uns selig sterben.
> Für dem Teufel uns bewahr
> halt uns bei festem Glauben
> und auf dich lass uns bauen
> aus Herzensgrund vertrauen. . . .
> Jesus Christus wohn uns bei . . . etc.
> Heilig Geist wohn uns bei . . . etc.
> *WA* 35.450. Cf. Spitta, *Ein fester Burcht*, p. 266.

67. *ZW* 1.408.23.

resorting to the usual medieval tendency he *associates* Mary and Christ to the point where he can say: "The more honor and love for Christ, the more also the esteem and honor for Mary, since she has borne us such a great and at the same time merciful Lord and Redeemer."[69]

While Calvin points to the danger of honoring the Virgin Mary as person rather than as elected instrument, he insists on the close connection between Mary and Christ: "Today we cannot celebrate the blessing given us in Christ without commemorating at the same time how high an honor God has granted to Mary when he chose to make her the mother of his only Son."[70] In a comment on Luke 1:43[71] Calvin gives us the opportunity to see his standards for a proper esteem for the Virgin Mary more clearly than anywhere else. He finds in Elisabeth's praise for Mary the true *via media* between shying away from "honor where honor is due" and superstitious adoration. "There are few who do not fall into one of these two sins, since at the one side there are those who are so extremely pleased with themselves that they cannot stand the gifts of God to their Brethren; at the other side there are those who adore human beings so superstitiously that they make deities out of them." And again: "Elisabeth takes the *via media* which we should follow: i.e., she honors the Virgin, in as much as Mary was honored by God. . . . But at the same time she does not stop at this point . . . she shows that the Virgin Mary has no dignity of herself but that rather everything hinges on God's wish to accept her."[72]

Indeed, the reformers wanted to safeguard the true measure of honor due to Mary because of its close connection with a true understanding of the person and work of Jesus Christ.[73] True worship is true knowledge and *vice versa*.

In their pastoral concern for all the "Brethren" the reformers made

---

68. Cf. Stakemeier, "Beata Maria Virgine" (n. 34 above), p. 457. His discussion of Zwingli needs correction on several points. Most important is that his observation that "Zwinglius sibi conscius est Scripturam solam non sufficere ad stricte probandam perpetuam Beatae Mariae virginitatem" is argued on the basis of an incomplete citation which omits the contrary proof (p. 453). See *Huldreich Zwingli's Werke*, ed. Melchior Schuler and Johannes Schulthes (Zurich, 1828ff.), 5.617 and 6.205-6. See further Locher, "Inhalt und Absicht von Zwinglis Marien lehre" (n. 34 above), p. 36: "Zwingli hat den Einwand gekannt. . . . Er ist ihm mit Entschiedenheit entgegengetreten. . . ."

69. ZW 1.427-28.

70. *Harmonia Evangelica*, comment on Luke 1:42; CR 45.35.

71. *Harmonia Evangelica*; CR 45.35.

72. CR 46.107.

73. "Atque hic cardo fidei Christianae versatur, ut credamus Christum filium dei in utero Virginis vere conceptum esse, absque tamen virili semine, virtute spiritus sancti." Zwingli (n. 68 above), 6.204. Cf. Calvin, CR 45.35.

themselves responsible for the true understanding of the Christian faith even on the most popular level, no longer willing to allow for the gulf between a thinking person's faith and "vulgar" Catholicism. When this is threatened, Luther can exclaim as he did in 1523: "I could wish that the cult of Mary would be completely abrogated, solely because of abuse."[74] It is this latter attitude which has largely determined post-Reformation developments within Protestantism. At the same time the reformers' search for the right middle way "chosen by Elisabeth" implies that a third way was granted between a Mary-less Christianity and a superstitious Marian cult. Luther's angry call for abrogation of the Marian cult and the sharp criticism flowing out of the pen of Zwingli and Calvin should not be isolated but regarded as part of their quest for the right *via media*.

In a final section we should like to indicate some of the landmarks on this road that will have to be plotted on the ecclesiastical map of our time if we as *doctores* wish to discharge our responsibility for the "Brethren," in the more restricted *and* in the larger sense of the word.

III. *Natus ex Maria Virgine*

1. The dangers on the right side of the *via media* are perhaps more conspicuous than those on the left: the Marian *leitourgia* has left marks on the *didache* which have become ineradicable in 1854, through the dogmatization of the Immaculate Conception, confirmed in 1950, by the promulgation of the dogma of the Corporeal Assumption of the Virgin Mary. Both dogmas show how far the tendency of drawing attention to the person rather than to the office of Mary has progressed. The dogma of 1854, however, is the far more serious threat to a truly catholic Christology, because it isolates the Mother of Christ from the rest of humankind by conferring upon her "such a fullness of innocence and sanctity, greater than which cannot be conceived under God."[75] Thus the radical depth of God's descent in the Incarnation is curtailed.

---

74. "Ego velim, quod Mariae cultus penitus tollatur solum propter abusem." *WA* 11.61.

75. ". . . eam innocentiae et sanctitatis plenitudinem prae se ferret, qua maior sub Deo nullatenus intelligitur . . . ," in *Ineffabilis Deus,* 8 December 1854; Denzinger (n. 19 above), nr. 2800. The observation by Jaroslav Pelikan is quite appropriate: "Not only must she be a warrant for the true humanity of Christ, her own true humanity must be recaptured" (n. 57 above), p. 142. René Laurentin points out that in the (medieval) debate about the Immaculate Conception, the Virgin Mary became for the first time "signe de contradiction." *La question mariale* (Paris, 1963), p. 60.

One can make the important positive observation that in the dogma of 1950 a unity of body and soul is taught[76] which might give new, much-needed life to the last words of the Apostles' Creed: "resurrection of the flesh." This applies, of course, only when Mary is seen as one of the faithful rather than as the Mother of the church who transcends the church. Though proleptic, this presentation of the Virgin Mary can serve to show what God has in store for all the faithful, once his kingdom is fully established.

The lack of catholicity of this dogma is not so much due to its christological implications as to its significance for the relation of Scripture to tradition and of these two to the Magisterium. Never before has a doctrine been elevated to the status of dogma with so little support from either Scripture or the early Christian tradition. It has been carried and supported by strong waves of a Mariocentric piety which was in turn inspired by it. The great popularity of the *peregrinatio* of the Madonna of Fatima may lead to incidental criticisms on the part of progressive Roman Catholic theologians.[77] One may hope that evidence of the strength of the undercurrents of Marian piety will force theologians to go beyond an Erasmian call for moderation.[78]

The intriguing interplay between Marian congresses and Mary-apparitions has led to the claim that this age should be regarded as the *epocha Mariana,* that the kingdom of Mary is the condition for the coming of the Kingdom of Christ,[79] and finally that Mary should be regarded as *co-redemptrix,* argued on the basis of her fiat to cooperate in the Incarnation and her offer of Christ on the cross.[80]

---

76. ". . . corpore et anima ad supernam caeli gloriam eveheretur. . . . ," in *Munificentissimus Deus,* 1 November 1950; Denzinger, nr. 3902.

77. See the honest appraisal by Oskar Schroeder, "Die Diskussion über die wahre Marienverehrung in der römisch-katholischen Kirche von heute." *Eine heilige Kirche* (n. 28 above), pp. 42-60. One reads with new interest his reference to two letters from the former vice–Secretary of State Montini, later Pope Paul VI, warning against sentimental Marian piety, on p. 45. See also Pope John XXIII in *Osservatore Romano,* 25 November 1960.

78. A most encouraging stance is taken by Bishop Paulus Rusch, who dares to go beyond any criticism known to me when he says, for instance: "Unsere Gläubigen haben kein Christusgebet." In "Mariologische Wertungen" (n. 38 above), p. 134.

79. "Adveniat regnum Mariae, ut adveniat regnum Christi." Schroeder, "Diskussion über die wahre Marienverehrung," p. 44.

80. An extremely clear and helpful survey of the present status of the theological discussion is *De natura co-redemptionis Marianae in theologia hodierna (1921-1958),* by Guilelmus Barauña (Rome, 1960), esp. pp. 105ff. The Protestant theologian C. A. de Ridder stated in 1960 that though the number of those who reject the title "co-redemptrix" was decreasing, the time did not seem ripe for any official proclamation. *Maria*

Though one should acknowledge that the so-called maximalists form by no means a clear majority, the Protestant observer cannot help but be greatly concerned by the fact that the shift from the sources of Revelation to the Magisterium frustrates any effort to bring the biblical witness to bear on Mariological developments within contemporary Roman Catholicism.[81]

The principle of development and growth has not yet been matched by a principle of reduction and trimming. Nevertheless, one should not conclude this section without pointing out that since the pontificate of Pope John XXIII we have witnessed a series of unpredicted signs of renewal. For this reason it is more than ever appropriate to follow the example of Dr. G. C. Berkouwer, who in 1948 kept open the avenue of hope and expectation by terminating his discussion of Roman Catholic Mariology with the quotation from Luke 18:27: "What is impossible with men is possible with God."[82]

(2) Malformations in Western Mariology are so much in evidence that one may well be inclined to echo the words of Luther: "I could wish that the cult of Mary would be completely abrogated because of abuse." It might be a sign of a true ecumenical interpretation of the word "Brethren" if one would argue that the name of Mary has to be stricken out of Protestant thought and piety as an act of witness within the world church, stemming not from a reactionary antipapalism but rather from a new emphasis on the positive original significance of the verb *protestari*.

One would, however, be unfaithful to the heritage of the Reformation if one were to interpret Protestantism solely as a "prophetic" critique accompanying and alongside the "priestly" church. The Reformation

---

Medeverlosseres? (Utrecht, 1960), p. 123. This impression is confirmed by the discussion during the second session of Vatican II. See further Giovanni Miegge, *The Virgin Mary: The Roman Catholic Marian Doctrine* (London, 1955), esp. pp. 155ff.

81. Cf. the statement by H. Volk, presently one of the leading progressive theologians: "Unser Glaube an die leibliche Aufnahme Mariens in den Himmel ist für uns völlig darin begrundet und rundum gesichert, dass die Kirche uns dies zu glauben lehrt." *Das neue Mariendogma* (Cologne, 1951), p. 25. See also my "Quo Vadis Petre?" *Scottish Journal of Theology* 16 (1963): 253.

82. *Conflict met Rome* (Kampen, 1948), p. 238. At the same time we should stress the relevance of Luther's rejection of the *fiducia*-in-Mary theme with which he was confronted. The last words of Pope John XXIII suggest to the Protestant observer that the attitude toward the Virgin Mary, described above in its late medieval context, is not a closed chapter in the history of Roman Catholic piety. At the solemn commemoration of the election of Pope John five years before on 28 October 1958, Cardinal L. Suenens of Brussels-Mechelen declared that the last barely audible words had been dedicated to the Virgin Mary when Pope John said: "My Mother, my confidence." *Katholiek Archief* 18 (December 1963): 50, col. 1286.

tradition understands itself as the true manifestation and therefore continuation of the one, holy, catholic church of the Apostles' Creed. Ecumenical theology does not presuppose and does not originate from a "seesaw" understanding of the church, in the sense of the cold war "balance of power," but rather from the deeply felt need to grow in fullness of truth, through "Lend-Lease" and through exposure to other traditions.

It is for this reason that Protestantism, not satisfied to function as the equalizer, searches to find the *via media,* to avoid not only Marian excesses at the right but also Marian minimalism at the left. The landmarks to the left of the *via media* are perhaps less prominent and eye catching, but for that reason no less significant. Exactly in those traditions which one can characterize as minimalistic or even Mary-less, deep inroads have been made by the two main christological heresies: Docetism and Adoptionism. These heresies deny either that Jesus Christ is truly human or that he is truly God, and can therefore not accept the doctrine of the Incarnation as interpreted by the Council of Chalcedon (451) and signified by the Marian title "Theotokos." In turn there is least interest in participating in the quest for the middle way in circles where the historical Jesus has been transformed into the Christ-idea or where Christ has become the teacher of great ethical truths.

(3) As we saw in our discussion of the biblical image of the Virgin Mary, the virgin birth is located at the margin of the canon and cannot be regarded as part of the *kerygma.* It is a sign that this *kerygma* constitutes not only a message (Christ-idea) but also the beginning of a historical reality, *kaine ktisis,* the new creation. As a sign it requires interpretation and is open to misinterpretation, as the succeeding history has shown us. Acceptance of this sign cannot constitute a safeguard, guarantee, or doctrinal test for the true understanding of the mystery of the Incarnation.

At the same time, the biblical and classical Protestant appreciation of the functional significance of Mary is concisely expressed by Hans Asmussen, when he says: "One does not have Jesus Christ without Mary."[83] In this confession the true humanity of Christ is expressed. It would indeed be disregarding the biblical account of the *kerygma* and the historical evidence of the role the virginal birth played in the second-century doctrinal struggles if one were to make it a condition for orthodoxy to extend this statement to the *Virgin* Mary. However, insofar as "Virgin Mary" is a contraction and shorthand for the Chalcedonian

83. *Maria, die Mutter Gottes* (Stuttgart, 1950), p. 137.

"truly man and truly God," one will have to take the *natus ex maria virgine* seriously as the *didache*-form in which the full meaning of the *kerygma* is preserved.

Though the very fact that Father Gustave Weigel could find traces of Nestorianism in Paul Tillich[84] while Father George Tavard noted "an unavowed Docetism"[85] could suggest the proximity of this great theologian to Chalcedonian orthodoxy, one cannot help but be disconcerted by his observation that just as "Apollo has no revelatory significance for Christians: the Virgin Mother Mary reveals nothing to Protestants."[86]

The same observations we have made with reference to the virginal birth could be applied to the "Theotokos" title. When it is interpreted to mean that the child of Mary is the eternal Son of God, its rejection implies the denial of the biblical understanding of the Incarnation. At the same time we have seen that Nestorius's objection to the use of this title might well have stemmed from his concern about Mariological aberrations connected with it. History provided ample proof that this title could become the justification for a further entrenchment of a physical-metaphysical "womb" theology clearly rejected by Jesus. It is the task of the Protestant theologian to be the sentry protecting the right understanding of the "Theotokos" title, alerted whenever this title is rejected, aware that its use is no guarantee for orthodoxy,[87] acknowledging it as a *didachean* form in which the *kerygma* is preserved and transmitted.[88]

(4) Our discussion of the virgin birth and the "Theotokos" title does not contain a hidden plea for the development of a Mariology on Protestant soil. It rather suggests that an independent Mariology cannot do justice to the biblical presentation of the figure of Mary, the Mother of Jesus Christ. What we have called "womb" theology proved to be the reliable indication that the Virgin Mary was being hypostatized and granted a place in her own right alongside or even opposite Christ. Our

---

84. "Contemporaneous Protestantism and Paul Tillich," *Theological Studies* 8 (1950): 194.

85. *Paul Tillich and the Christian Message* (New York, 1961), p. 131.

86. Tillich, *Systematic Theology,* 1 (Chicago, 1951), 128.

87. Michael Servetus does not hesitate to use "Theotokos" or "Dei Genetrix" to designate the Virgin Mary; see George H. Williams, *The Radical Reformation* (Philadelphia, 1962), pp. 326, 337. Caspar Schwenckfeld can reconcile his "celestial flesh" concept of Christ's human nature with the "Theotokos" title. See Paul L. Maier, *Caspar Schwenckfeld on the Person and Work of Christ* (Assen, 1959), pp. 55ff.; 61.

88. Cf. Karl Barth: "Die Abwehr des Missbrauchs, der mit der in dieser Bezeichnung ausgesprochenen Erkenntnis getrieben worden ist, wird nicht fehlen dürfen. Aber jene Erkenntnis und darum auch diese Bezeichnung selbst darf deswegen doch nicht unterdrückt werden." *Kirchliche Dogmatik,* I/2, p. 152.

conclusion has to be that a truly catholic and evangelical Mariology is Christology.

This is not an arithmetical equation and therefore not arithmetically reversible, since Jesus Christ is not only *natus ex maria virgine* but also and first *conceptus a spiritu sancto*. There is more to be said about Jesus Christ than we can glean from the figure of Mary, and because of this "more" it is important and worthwhile to say anything at all. But this kerygmatic "more" cannot be expressed, preserved, and transmitted when one bypasses the figure of Mary; her office is that of a beacon which one cannot ignore without peril. She is chosen into this office, *mutatis mutandis,* just as "the First Lady" is chosen into office as the President's wife. "Virgin" and "Theotokos" can then be looked upon as degrees conferred upon her, *honoris causa,* to express respect for the Presidential office rather than for her personal qualities. This is what Luther had in mind when he hailed the Virgin Mary as *fabrica,* the workshop of God, and what Calvin formulated when he called her blessed as the elect instrument of God's work of redemption.

Thus we may be enabled to find the *via media* in the church of our time, aware of the dangers for Christology in a Mary-less Christianity on the one side, and a Marian personality cult on the other side. When speaking in responsibility to the "Brethren" in a wider sense of the word, that is, to the *fratres separati,* we shall have to emphasize this latter danger as strongly as at the time of the Reformation; when speaking in responsibility to our more closely related Brethren, we might today have to emphasize the first even more than in the sixteenth century.

IV. *Lex Credendi Est Lex Orandi*

In a few words we now indicate some of the subsidiary offices which are not to the same extent unique to the Virgin Mary, but exactly for that reason possibly beacons for the church of our time in areas where vision seen as jeopardized.

With the expression "subsidiary offices" we wish to indicate that the proper understanding of the place and role of the Virgin Mary in the life of the church is not restricted to Christology but has of necessity its impact on other areas as well, not the least of which is the worship of the church. This is indeed the appropriate direction, but formulated by inversion of the traditional adage: *lex credendi est lex orandi.*

1. Together with Simeon, Anna, Zechariah, Elisabeth, and John the

Baptist, Mary belongs to the expecting church on the threshold of fulfillment between the Old and the New Covenant. Confronted with the phenomenon of a culturalized American Protestantism, which tends to become a New Testament Christianity, it may be not without significance to be alerted to the historical continuity of the church as the people of God. In order to see the full dimensions of the kingship of Christ, it is important to retrace this history beyond Pentecost to Abraham, the father of all believers.

2. From an unexpected side — the great liberal historian of Christian thought, Adolf von Harnack — we are reminded that there are truly evangelical elements in the medieval understanding of the place of the Virgin Mary vis-à-vis God.[89] Indeed, provided she is seen as the *typus ecclesiae*, that is, as the prototype of the faithful, there is great soteriological relevance in her bold dealings with God, in which one can find a proper understanding of Hebrews 4:16: "Let us then with confidence draw near to the throne of grace, that we may receive mercy and find grace to help in time of need."

3. From an evangelical perspective it is clear that the role of the Virgin Mary within the context of the Christian *leitourgia* cannot be to receive our prayers in order that she may intercede for us with God. She is not to be looked upon as the "Mother of Mercy," *mater misericordiae,* over against the Son or the Father as the severe judge.

But when the church is taken seriously as a fellowship of memory and hope, the *koinonia* is extended through space *and* time. The dimensions of Christian worship are enlarged when the militant church does not isolate itself as an ever-repeated new beginning, but exercises the fellowship spanning the times by not praying *to* but *with* those who have gone before.

On 11 October 1963, Pope Paul VI said in a prayer concluding his speech in S. Maria Maggiore that with the Western separated Brethren "the remembrance and the veneration for you, O Mary, begins to dawn like morning. Call with us all these your sons to the same unity under your maternal and celestial protection."[90]

---

89. "Das einzig Versöhnende an der Mariologie is die Wahrnehmung, dass der fromme Glaube sich über das Verhältnis der Maria zu Gott und Christus Aussagen erlaubt, die er über sein eigenes Verhältnis nicht zu machen wagt. In diesem Sinn ist in der Marienlehre — es scheint freilich paradox — manches Evangelische." *Lehrbuch der Dogmengeschichte* 3 (Tübingen, 1932), p. 655, n. 1.

90. Published by Ufficio Stampa, Concilio Ecumenico Vaticano II, Handreichungen in Deutscher Sprache Nr. 27, 16 October 1963. Cf. Pope Leo XIII: ". . . permagnum unitatis christianae praesidium divinitus oblatum est in Maria." Litt. enc.

At the end of our investigation we have reason to wonder whether it is either appropriate or realistic to invoke the protection of the Virgin Mary for the rapprochement to which an ever-increasing number of Christians of both confessions are dedicating themselves today.[91] When, however, we are allowed to interpret her call to unity as the light of the beacon pointing away from herself to Jesus Christ, Protestants and Roman Catholics can join in hailing her as "the Mother of God."

Adiutricem Populi, in *Leonis XIII Acta* 15.308. Quoted by Carolus Balic, "De motu mariologico-mariano et motione oecumenica XIX et XX," *De mariologia et oecumenismo*, p. 528.

91. René Laurentin, among Mariologists the most aware of Protestant life and thought, rightly warns against the tendency to find in contemporary Protestantism "symptomes de redécouverte de la Vierge." *La question mariale*, p. 132. The rule which he indicates as the guideline for his own task can be accepted also by a Protestant as a realistic and promising ecumenical program for the years ahead: "Redécourvrir la Vierge *dans* la Bible, tandis que les Protestants la decouvriraient *par* la Bible." *La question mariale*, p. 141.

From Confrontation to Encounter: The Ugly German and the Ugly American

America is hard to see
Less partial witnesses than he
In book on book have testified
They could not see it from outside
— or inside either for that matter
We know the literary chatter.

Robert Frost

Amerika, du hast es besser
Als unser Continent, der alte,
Hast keine verfallenen Schlösser
und keine Basalte.
Dich stört nicht im Innern
zu lebendiger Zeit,
Unnützes Erinnern
Und vergeblicher Streit.

Goethe

Some years ago, *The New Yorker* published a cartoon showing two Puritans nodding their heads to one another in greeting: "Have a pious, thrifty, and industrious day." Today, an American is more likely to wish his fellow citizen the very best by saying, "Take it easy!" I am inclined to believe that Americans no longer notice what this salutation really calls for, and that only a foreigner hears what is actually said. Yet, this same foreigner may well be tempted to give this "revealing" greeting a content that is at once false and not at all in keeping with its cultural

"From Confrontation to Encounter: The Ugly German and the Ugly American," in *German-American Interrelations: Heritage and Challenge*, ed. James F. Harris (Tübingen, 1985), pp. 1-5.

environment. In meeting each other as foreigners, we are threatened by
the same trap that caught the medieval scholastics who philosophically
developed *universalia:* They came to trust their abstractions so much that
they lost the critical capacity to check the extent to which these reflected
reality.

As we dedicate ourselves to the theme of this conference, which has
been so impressively — and opaquely — formulated as "German-
American Interrelations," we do well to realize that we have arrived in each
other's company with very clear but abstract images of who the other is, of
what is strange and what is peculiar in the other's tradition. To smooth the
shock of losing long-held and therefore beloved assumptions, we have given
this conference a cover theme, with a cover-up title: "German-American
Interrelations" is much too kind a description for what we are expected to
accomplish, for here we must confront the "Ugly American" and the "Ugly
German." In fact, the only thing that recommends the term "interrelation"
is that the word has lost its meaning to such an extent that we can give it
our own. "Inter" should give an extra substance to "relation," because that
substance is no longer there. This becomes apparent when we ponder the
Latin background: The absurd duplication contained in the Latin *inter-
referre* makes it perfectly clear that this word had to be embellished because
the original root had dried out.

In order to cope with the task and theme of the "Ugly American"
and the "Ugly German," we have planned this conference in a way that
facilitates true confrontation. Both national delegations contain three
groups: scholars, journalists, and politicians. Each of these groups enter-
tains a caricature of the others, as appears from the way in which scholars
tend to think about journalists or talk about politicians, the way in which
journalists refer to people in academia and in politics, not to mention
what politicians think, when they do — all of which makes it very hard
for us to listen and cooperate in a productive fashion. For purposes of
this conference, it seemed to me that we should try not just to *protest*
against caricatures but to *test* them, to check their validity and to hunt
for the grain of salt that may prove to be a mountain range. If we succeed
in this venture, we can prepare the way for a more lasting cooperation,
and we will be able to perform a service that goes beyond just the
relationship between the United States and Germany.

When ideology creeps in, caricatures are no longer a laughing
matter; indeed, caricature has become a powerful factor in journalism,
election campaigns, politics, and cultural competition. This kind of
competition is the natural breeding ground for alienation and even animosity. It cannot be denied that in Europe we hear the loud voice of

anti-Americanism; at the same time, the Moral Majority in the United States is no longer as internationally sensitive and self-critical as it used to be. We shall therefore ask each other questions that are not academically remote or refined; we want to have constantly before our eyes the daily and harsh reality in the encounter of our two nations.

The Ugly American, published in 1958, presents the portrait of a very nice American; I must emphasize that point at the outset. But this nice person is utterly ignorant, and for that very reason extremely dangerous. Furthermore, in this case, he is officially what all of us are privately: The ignorant American is "in foreign service." I quote a concluding sentence of that best-seller because it is still so very true: "We do not need that horde of one and a half million Americans, mostly amateurs, who are now working for the U.S. overseas. What we need is a small force of well-trained, well-chosen, hard-working and dedicated professionals. They must speak the language of the land of their assignment, and they must be more expert in the problems than are the natives."

I believe that this picture is grossly incomplete: Today we have, in addition to the ignorant American, the ignorant European. The latter is no longer able to reach beyond the Atlantic, to "read" the signs of development stretching from coast to coast in the continental United State. He is increasingly impatient with what he does not understand, impatient with the end of his dream: America as Europe's spatial extension.

In contrast with this recent and still unpredictable "Ugly European," it seems quite easy to sketch the profile of the "Ugly German." He has a pedigree of longer standing insofar as he is identified with a period of political fermentation in the sixteenth century, when he is said to have become submissive in politics and intolerant in scholarly matters. In the post-Nazi era, he is placed either in Prussia or in Bavaria (Americans do not always know where they have to stand on this matter). But whatever components are used to construct the Ugly German, he is the one who looks down upon the American as naively interested only in know-how; the American, on the other hand, looks at the German as the man who is interested only in know-why. They need each other to find a way to that old English word which has almost died, "whither," *wozu.*

Over the last two decades, I have tried to get a reading on the generations that matured in the educational systems of Germany between 1920 and 1960, with two particular questions in mind: What did they know about the United States? How were they informed? They read Karl May, *Uncle Tom's Cabin,* James Fenimore Cooper, Mark Twain, Jack London, Upton Sinclair, Sinclair Lewis, Tennessee Williams, and Eugene

O'Neill. Europe still had a wholesome picture of the United States — not unlike the one suggested in the quotation from Goethe — because there was a limited canon of some ten authors who provided a unified vision. Since that time, for the younger generation, American culture has become so diversified that there is no longer clarity about what America is.

This information gap is unfortunate; its American counterpart, however, is just as grotesque, and even more unfortunate because it is fostered by the "elite." For example, William F. Buckley, a self-confessed conservative and highly intelligent politician, once used his television program to point out that in Germany natural law had been negated by Martin Luther and that *therefore* Hitler could set up his concentration camps. He discussed his thesis with much-respected professors at Notre Dame, not one of whom dissented. A second example comes from an important article in *Time* by Henry Kissinger on the reform of NATO. Strikingly, the commentaries in all the U.S. newspapers that reported on this essay underscored Kissinger's interpretation of the peace movement in Germany as neutralist, and *therefore* as anti-American. A third example: The new Roman Catholic archbishop of New York took occupancy of his see with the words, "Ich bin ein New Yorker." He may have been aware that he was using the German language; obviously he was imitating John Kennedy's maiden speech in the former *Reichshauptstadt*. But what makes this identification of New York with Berlin so intriguing is that this same man claimed that the legalization of abortion is a greater threat to life "than Hitler's Holocaust."

Three uses of German history! It is essential that we start our program with the most sensitive historical events that are constantly cited by scholars, journalists, and politicians. One example of the German use of American history may suffice to show that the confusion of history and agitation is by no means an American prerogative. A colleague in Tübingen recently stated that two capital crimes against humankind have been committed in our century: Auschwitz and Hiroshima. Apart from the question whether a German is the most objective spokesman in this matter, the very confusion of systematic genocide with the horrendous termination of war is a crime against all standards of historical judgment.

I hope that these introductory observations have conveyed to you the strong commitment of the organizers, who have been preparing this conference for over two years. I have participated in the organization of many a conference where scholars were called upon to deal with important historical issues. Here we are gathered not simply to analyze a scholarly theme; I am sincerely convinced that we are working on one of the most sensitive issues in Western culture. There is an American vitality and a European wisdom — this very distinction may document my own need to overcome caricatures! — which must be "interrelated" and bound together in order to sustain a civilization that can be protected, but not prolonged, by NATO.

In 1630, at the departure of the Winthrop fleet from England for Massachusetts Bay, the Puritan George Herbert interpreted the Great Move West in light of the biblical vision of the Promised Land:

> Religion stands on Tiptoe in our land,
> ready to pass through to the American strand. . . .
> Then shall religion to America flee:
> they have their Times of Gospel ev'n as we.

It seems to me that in this Puritan vision of the United States lies at once the problem and the promise of the Atlantic community. The *problem* is that the American Moral Majority regards this dream as already fulfilled in American society, whereas Europe is inclined to believe that the secular gospel of political wisdom and social justice stands merely "on tiptoe" in the Promised Land. The *promise* is realization of the *same* vision of a world freed from fear of poverty, oppression, and illness.

Abbreviations

AWA	Archiv zur Weimarer Ausgabe der Werke Martin Luthers
CO	Corpus Reformatorum: Ioannis Calvini Opera quae supersunt omnia
CR	Corpus Reformatorum
LThK	Lexikon für Theologie und Kirche
LW	Luther's Works: American Edition
PL	Patrologiae cursus completus: Series Latina
SMRT	Studies in Medieval and Reformation Thought
WA	D. Martin Luthers Werke: Kritische Gesamtausgabe, Schriften
WA Br	D. Martin Luthers Werke: Kritische Gesamtausgabe, Briefwechsel
WA Tr	D. Martin Luthers Werke: Kritische Gesamtausgabe, Tischreden
ZW	Corpus Reformatorum: Huldreich Zwinglis sämtliche Werke

Index of Names, Places, and Modern Authors

Index of Subjects

antichrist, 41-42, 61-62, 107-9, 134-40, 196

anti-Judaism: 86; of Eck, 100-102; of Erasmus, 102-6, 124-27; and Hebrew, 164-66; of Luther, 110-13, 116; of Lutherans, 113-16; of mendicants, 133-34; papal strategy, 127-31; of Pfefferkorn, 94-98; of Reuchlin, 87-94, 152-56, 166-70

antisemitism: 161-66; and apocalyptic fervor, 107-10, 134-40; and historians, 81-83; myths of ritual murder, 98-102, 107, 133-34, 161-62

apocalypticism, 56-63, 68, 107-10, 134-40, 194-98

biblical exegesis, 228-36

Cabala, 88-91, 113, 152

culture: learned, 205-6, 223-24; popular, 203-5, 223-24

devil, 31, 33, 43-47, 57-63, 66, 196

Devotio moderna, x, 23-25, 207-24

ecclesiology, 29-34, 36, 41-42, 43-47

ecumenism, 65

eschatology, 56-63, 68, 97, 108-9, 134-40, 194-98

eucharist, 14-21

God: and the devil, 57, 63; mercy of, 43-47; omnipotence of, 6-21

history: church, 52-53, 64-66; intellectual, ix-x, 22, 66-67, 173-75, 202-4; social, ix-x, 22, 52, 66-68, 173-75, 201-4; social history of ideas, ix-x, 22, 202-3

humanism, 145-50

humility, 214-16

immaculate conception, 240-41, 245-46

inquisition, 85, 159-60, 183-87

Jews: 81-82, 90; baptized, 163-64; as citizens, 92-93, 167-68; conversion, 95-98, 127-34, 137; emancipation, 122-23, 126-27; expulsion/integration, 109-11, 127-34, 139-40; ghettos, 127-30; stubbornness of, 139-40; and Third Reformation, 117-21

Mariology, 225-52

Modern devotion, x, 23-25, 207-24

monasticism, 24-25, 207-10, 218-19

nationalism, 69-78

Nazism, 70-71, 74-76

Nicodemites, 187-94, 198